THE HART-FULLER DEBATE IN THE TWENTY-FIRST CENTURY

This book presents the papers and comments on those papers delivered at a colloquium held at the Australian National University in December 2008 to celebrate 50 years since the publication in the *Harvard Law Review* of the famous and wide-ranging debate between HLA Hart and Lon L Fuller. These essays do not to re-run that debate and they are not confined to discussion of the jurisprudential issues canvassed by Hart and Fuller. Rather they pick up on strands in the debate and re-think them in the light of social, political and intellectual developments in the past 50 years and changed ways of understanding law and other normative systems. This collection looks forward rather than backward using the debate as a point of departure and inspiration.

The Hart-Fuller Debate in the Twenty-First Century

Edited by Peter Cane

·HART·
PUBLISHING

OXFORD AND PORTLAND, OREGON
2010

Published in the United Kingdom by Hart Publishing Ltd
16C Worcester Place, Oxford, OX1 2JW
Telephone: +44 (0)1865 517530
Fax: +44 (0)1865 510710
E-mail: mail@hartpub.co.uk
Website: http://www.hartpub.co.uk

Published in North America (US and Canada) by
Hart Publishing
c/o International Specialized Book Services
920 NE 58th Avenue, Suite 300
Portland, OR 97213–3786
USA
Tel: +1 503 287 3093 or toll-free: (1) 800 944 6190
Fax: +1 503 280 8832
E-mail: orders@isbs.com
Website: http://www.isbs.com

British Library Cataloguing in Publication Data
Data Available

ISBN: 978-1-84113-894-7

Typeset by Columns Design Ltd, Reading
Printed and bound in Great Britain by
TJ International Ltd, Padstow, Cornwall

Preface

The essays in this volume were written for presentation at a colloquium held at the Australian National University, 17–19 December 2008. The conference was funded and organised by the John Fleming Centre for Advancement of Legal Research in the Australian National University College of Law.

The aim of the colloquium was not to rerun the famous debate (contained in HLA Hart's classic article 'Positivism and the Separation of Law and Morals' (1958) 71 *Harvard Law Review* 607, and LL Fuller's equally famous 'Positivism and Fidelity to Law: A Reply to Professor Hart' (1958) 71 *Harvard Law Review* 630). Nor was the intention to confine discussion to the jurisprudential issues canvassed by Hart and Fuller. Rather the plan was to identify themes that lay on or below the surface of the debate and to rethink them in the light of social, political and intellectual developments in the past 50 years, and of changed ways of understanding law and other normative systems. The aim was to look forward rather than backward, using the debate as a point of departure and inspiration.

The format of most of the sessions of the meeting was that one scholar spoke to a precirculated paper and a second scholar spoke to a precirculated commentary. Both the paper and the commentary were then discussed by the 50-or-so participants. The topics of the eight sessions are represented by the essays in this volume. Nicola Lacey's meticulously researched paper set the colloquium off to an inspiring start by addressing 'The Context and Significance of the Debate'. Over the following two days, the topics discussed were 'Human Rights' (Hilary Charlesworth and Karen Knop); 'International Criminal Law' (Larry May and Christopher Kutz); 'Pluralism' (Jeremy Waldron and Margaret Davies); 'Instrumentalism' (Leslie Green and Anthony Sebok); 'Law, Language and Discourse' (Desmond Manderson and Ngaire Naffine); 'The Evolution of Normative Social Behaviour' (Philip Pettit and Richard McAdams) and 'Legal Reasoning and Law-Making' (Gerald J Postema and Brian Bix). The topic of the remaining session was 'Law in Transitional Societies'. Unfortunately, the scholar invited to present the lead paper in this session was, in the event, unable to attend the meeting and the commentator, Martin Krygier, valiantly performed the dual role of protagonist and commentator.

It is fair to say, I think, that amongst the speakers there was some scepticism about the value of treating the Hart–Fuller debate as a springboard rather than simply taking it on its own terms. At least one wondered whether the debate was of any but historical interest, while at least one other questioned the wisdom of using it as a lens through which to view issues that were not explicitly addressed by the antagonists and may not even have been in their minds. However, the colloquium was counted a great success by those who attended. The tangible result, presented here, is a collection of papers of the very highest quality that generated, at the meeting, a set of wide-ranging discussions and engaged the lively interest of all involved. In my opinion, they demonstrate that this debate between two of the twentieth century's greatest legal theorists continues to present a rich, and by no means exhausted, seam of jurisprudential ideas waiting to be mined in the years to come.

I wish to thank all those who participated in the colloquium as speakers, commentators and audience. Thanks to funding generously provided by the Vice-Chancellor of the ANU, Professor Ian Chubb, and the Dean and Convenor of the ANU College of Law, Professor Michael Coper, the John Fleming Centre was able to organise what must rank as the most significant and exciting meeting of legal theorists to have been held in Australia in many years. Thanks are also due to Richard Hart and Hart Publishing for agreeing to publish the essays, and to all those involved in its production.

Peter Cane

Contents

Contributors

Brian H Bix is the Frederick W Thomas Professor of Law and Philosophy at the University of Minnesota.

Hilary Charlesworth is Australian Research Council Federation Fellow and Professor in the Regulatory Institutions Network at the Australian National University.

Margaret Davies is Professor of Law at Flinders University, South Australia.

Leslie Green is Professor of the Philosophy of Law at the University of Oxford and a Fellow of Balliol College.

Karen Knop is Professor of Law at the University of Toronto.

Martin Krygier is Gordon Samuels Professor of Law and Social Theory at the University of New South Wales.

Christopher Kutz is Professor of Law at the University of California, Berkeley.

Nicola Lacey is Professor of Criminal Law and Legal Theory at the London School of Economics.

Desmond Manderson is Canada Research Chair in Law and Discourse at McGill University.

Larry May is Professor of Philosophy at Washington University in St Louis and Strategic Research Professor of Social Justice in the Centre for Applied Philosophy and Public Ethics at Charles Sturt University, Australia.

Richard H McAdams is Bernard D Meltzer Professor of Law at the University of Chicago.

Ngaire Naffine is Professor of Law at the University of Adelaide.

Philip Pettit is LS Rockefeller University Professor of Politics and Human Values at Princeton University.

Gerald J Postema is Cary C Boshamer Professor of Philosophy and Professor of Law at the University of North Carolina at Chapel Hill.

Anthony J Sebok is Professor of Law at Benjamin Cardozo School of Law, Yeshiva University.

Jeremy Waldron is University Professor at New York University School of Law.

1

Out of the 'Witches' Cauldron'?

Reinterpreting the Context and Reassessing the Significance of the Hart–Fuller Debate

NICOLA LACEY*

Just over half a century ago, perhaps the premier law school in the English-speaking world[1] provided the setting for a debate between its two most influential legal theorists. HLA Hart, Professor of Jurisprudence at Oxford since 1953, and visiting Harvard for the academic year 1956–57, was invited to give the Law School's annual Holmes Lecture. Hart took this opportunity to enunciate, in economical and trenchant form, the kernel of his emerging theory of legal positivism, staking out his claim to be the twentieth-century successor to Jeremy Bentham and John Austin. Lon L Fuller, Carter Professor of General Jurisprudence at Harvard, a man who had long ploughed a rather lonely jurisprudential furrow as a scholar and teacher committed to exploring the morality of law, and hence not infrequently accused of stirring the 'witches' cauldron'[2] of irrationalist natural law theory, paced up and down at the back of the room 'like a hungry

* I owe a particular debt of gratitude to Neil Duxbury, Kristen Rundle, John Schlegel, David Warrington and Kenneth Winston, who not only commented on drafts of this chapter but were also exceptionally generous in providing relevant materials. I am also grateful to Jo Braithwaite, Jan Kleinheisterkamp, Martin Krygier, Stanley Paulson, Anna Silver, Robert Summers, William Twining and Jeremy Waldron for helpful comments on an earlier draft; to David Soskice, and to participants in the LSE Law Department's research seminar for discussion of the argument; to the Fellows of Harvard College for permission to quote from The Papers of Lon Fuller held in the Special Collections Room of the Law School Library; and to Marshall Cohen for permission to quote from his letter to Fuller. I have made every effort to trace the authors of other letters from which I have quoted, and apologise to anyone whom I was unable to contact. This chapter was written during my tenure of a Leverhulme Trust Major Research Fellowship; it gives me pleasure to record my gratitude to the Trust for its support.

[1] I should immediately add that this estimation would have been resoundingly challenged by Yale! See text following n 80 below.

[2] The phrase was used by Fuller himself: see Robert S Summers, *Lon L. Fuller*, Jurists: Profiles in Legal Theory (Palo Alto, CA, Stanford University Press, 2004) 63, 162.

lion', and later demanded a right to reply.[3] As the sponsor of Hart's visit, and as a man of keen sensitivities and no little degree of *amour propre*, Fuller might reasonably have felt a whiff of personal hurt as well as intellectual frustration in the face of Hart's insouciant dismissal of the natural law tradition. Whatever the origins of his feelings, there is plenty of evidence that Fuller did feel very strongly about Hart's lecture; and it stimulated him to produce a correspondingly trenchant formulation of the distinctive natural law position for which he was to become famous. The rest, as they say, is history.[4]

In this chapter, I revisit that history, and give it a somewhat different interpretation from the one which it has generally received. As a preliminary approach to this reinterpretation, let us take a moment to reflect on the quite astounding impact and status of the debate—but also on the rather different reception of its two components. We live in the world of the internet, and so (crude indicator of reception though it is) it is interesting to look at the number of references to the debate on widely used search engines trained on academic work. A clear pattern emerges from a search of Google Scholar on 9 September 2008. This generated the following results from, respectively, a general and an advanced search of the exact title of the relevant books and articles: 'Hart The Concept of Law', 91,000 and 4,880 references respectively; 'Fuller The Morality of Law', 49,000 and 1,840; 'Hart Positivism and the Separation of Law and Morals', 5,240 and 1,420; 'Fuller Positivism and Fidelity to Law', 1,260 and 911.

This rough indicator of reception confirms the relative reputations of Hart and Fuller as legal philosophers at the start of the twenty-first century. The published evidence of the stature of both men as legal theorists is impressive, and almost certainly provides a more accurate benchmark. Fuller's work is commemorated in four dedicated volumes, one of which is an annotated edition of a selection of his essays, some of them previously unpublished, with a substantial introduction.[5] Each of these books devotes considerable attention to his jurisprudential scholarship. But the contrast with Hart is marked. For Hart's work has generated two festschrift volumes, a biography, a collection of essays assessing his legacy, and three single-author monographs devoted exclusively to his contributions to legal theory; one of these books has run to a second, revised edition; and that book, the essays on his legacy and the biography have appeared in the last five

[3] According to the recollection of Joel Feinberg: see N Lacey, *A Life of H.L.A. Hart: The Nightmare and the Noble Dream* (Oxford, Oxford University Press, 2004) 197.

[4] See HLA Hart, 'Positivism and the Separation of Law and Morals' (1957–58) 71 *Harvard Law Review* 593; Lon Fuller, 'Positivism and Fidelity to Law: A Reply to Professor Hart' (1957–58) 71 *Harvard Law Review* 630.

[5] Kenneth L Winston (ed), *The Principles of Social Order: Selected Essays of Lon L. Fuller* (Durham, Duke University Press, 1981; revised edn, Oxford, Hart Publishing, 2001); Thomas W Bechtler, *Law in a Social Context: Liber Amicorum Honouring Professor Lon L. Fuller* (Deventer, Kluwer, 1978); Willem J Witteveen and Wibrem van der Burg, *Rediscovering Fuller: Essays on Implicit Law and Institutional Design* (Amsterdam University Press, 1999); Summers, n 2 above. I leave aside here a further literature which builds on Fuller's 'The Case of the Speluncean Explorers' (1949) 62 *Harvard Law Review* 616 in examining styles of legal reasoning: see further n 10 below.

years.[6] In addition, the posthumously published postscript to *The Concept of Law* (itself barely 40 pages in length) generated an edited collection over four times that length, and one whose contributors included some of the leading scholars in contemporary jurisprudence.[7] Even scholars who are entirely unsympathetic to his approach have devoted huge attention to Hart's work: as well as the books already mentioned, I am aware of two further books devoted exclusively to a critical assault on his theory of law.[8] For obvious reasons, it is difficult to assess the large secondary literature in journals and edited collections discussing each man's work. But it would be fair to say that although this literature in relation to Fuller's work is substantial,[9] it is markedly smaller than that in relation to Hart's. While it is difficult to find contributions to the burgeoning field of analytical jurisprudence, particularly in Britain and North America, which do not use Hart's work as a primary point of reference, Fuller's presence in the field tends to be defined by his role as Hart's debating opponent.[10] As even his sympathetic editor, Kenneth Winston, puts it, 'because of his passionate defence … of a modest "secular natural law" theory, Fuller has received a largely unsympathetic

[6] In chronological order, they are PMS Hacker and J Raz, *Law, Morality and Society: Essays in Honour of HLA Hart* (Oxford, Oxford University Press, 1977); Neil MacCormick, *H.L.A. Hart* (London, Edward Arnold, 1981; revised edn, Palo Alto, CA, Stanford University Press, 2008); Michael Martin, *The Legal Philosophy of HLA Hart: A Critical Appraisal* (Philadelphia, PA, Temple University Press, 1987); Ruth Gavison (ed), *Issues in Contemporary Legal Philosophy: Essays for H.L.A. Hart* (New York, Oxford University Press, 1987); Michael D Bayles, *Hart's Legal Philosophy* (Dordrecht, Kluwer Academic Publisher, 1992); Lacey, n 3 above; Matthew Kramer, Claire Grant, Ben Colburn and Antony Hatzistavrou (eds), *The Legacy of H.L.A. Hart: Legal, Political and Moral Philosophy* (Oxford, Oxford University Press, 2008).

[7] Jules Coleman (ed,), *Hart's Postscript* (Oxford, Oxford University Press, 2001).

[8] P Leith and P Ingram (eds), *The Jurisprudence of Orthodoxy: Queen's University Essays on H.L.A. Hart* (London, Routledge, 1988); Robert N Moles, *Definition and Rule in Legal Theory: A Reassessment of H.L.A. Hart and the Postivist Tradition* (Oxford, Basil Blackwell, 1987).

[9] For key examples, see Ronald Dworkin, 'The Elusive Morality of Law' (1965) 10 *Villanova Law Review* 631; Marshall Cohen, 'Law, Morality and Purpose' (1965) 10 *Villanova Law Review* 640 (these two papers formed part of a symposium on Fuller's *The Morality of Law*, discussed below: see text at nn 65–7 and 128 below); David Lyons, 'The Internal Morality of Law' (1970–71) *Proceedings of the Aristotelian Society* 71; Frederick Schauer, 'Fuller's Internal Point of View' (1994) 13 *Law and Philosophy* 294; Peter Nicholson, 'The Internal Morality of Law: Fuller and his Critics' (1974) 84 *Ethics* 307; Stanley L Paulson, 'Lon L. Fuller, Gustav Radbruch and the "Positivist" Theses' (1994) 13 *Law and Philosophy* 313; Jeremy Waldron, 'Why Law: Efficacy, Freedom or Fidelity?' (1994) 13 *Law and Philosophy* 259; Kenneth Einar Himma, 'Functionalism and Legal Theory: The Hart-Fuller Debate Revisited?' (1998) 14 *De Philosophia* 213; Jeremy Webber, 'The Grammar of Customary Law' (2009) 54 *McGill Law Journal* (forthcoming).

[10] For a recent example, see Jules Coleman, *The Practice of Principle* (Oxford, Oxford University Press, 2001). To students of jurisprudence, Fuller is of course equally well known for his memorable 'The Case of the Speluncean Explorers' (1949) 62 *Harvard Law Review* 616, a paper which cleverly invites the reader to examine the different conceptions of law disclosed by varying styles of judicial reasoning. This article has itself generated a substantial literature: see, eg Peter Suber, *The Case of the Speluncean Explorers: Nine New Opinions* (London, Routledge, 1998, reprinted 2002); William N Eskridge, Jr, 'The Case of the Speluncean Explorers: Twentieth Century Statutory Interpretation in a Nutshell' and Naomi R Cahn, John O Calmore, Mary I Coombs, Dwight L Greene, Geoffrey C Miller, Jeremy Paul and Laura W Stein, 'The Case of the Speluncean Explorers: Contemporary Proceedings' (1993) 61 *George Washington Law Review* 1731 and 1754 respectively. The 'Speluncean Explorers', along with his general taste for allegorical exploration of theoretical arguments, arguably qualify

hearing from the scholarly community for his jurisprudential writings'.[11] Though argument continues about who 'won' the debate—with influential legal philosophers, including David Dyzenhaus, Leslie Green and Jeremy Waldron,[12] all recently affirming crucial aspects of Fuller's position—a fair-minded observer of the jurisprudential scene would have to conclude that Hart, as it were, won the war.[13]

In this chapter, I will reflect on why this is the case; and in particular on why the points on which Fuller undoubtedly prevailed over Hart in the debate did relatively little to enhance his reputation, or that of his brand of natural law theory, in the dominant discourse of English-speaking legal philosophy in the second half of the twentieth century. The straightforward answer to these questions would be that Hart simply had better arguments than Fuller, and moreover articulated those arguments more effectively. I disagree with this view: or, to put it more precisely, I think that this view is only defensible if we judge the issue in terms of rather narrow criteria. In essence, my argument will be that Fuller was at an inevitable disadvantage, not only because he was merely responding, and hence drawn into a battle whose terms of engagement were set by Hart, but also because of the very different worldviews with which the two men approached questions of legal theory. Because of Hart's agenda-setting position, the terms of the debate are those of analytic legal philosophy; and the reception of the debate has, understandably, both interpreted and evaluated Fuller's argument largely in terms of criteria internal to that discipline. But while

Fuller as a progenitor of the law and literature movement: see John Jay Osborn, Jr, 'UFOs in the Law School Curriculum: The Popularity and Value of Law and Literature Courses' (1990) 14 *Legal Studies Forum* 53; see further, text at nn 38–9 below.

[11] Winston, n 5 above, at 11: like Winston, I regard this as in part due to the failure of later scholars to 'place the [jurisprudential] arguments in the context of the general theory which informs the body of Fuller's work' (*ibid* 11–12). Fuller himself appears to have been sensitive to the possibility that his debate with Hart would obscure other scholars' and students' vision of his broader contribution: in the revised edition of *The Morality of Law* (1969) he advises those interested in the sociology and anthropology of law to skip the chapter on the debate: see Willem J Witteveen, 'Rediscovering Fuller: An Introduction' in Witteveen and van der Burg, n 5 above, at 30: see also *ibid* 21–2 on the way in which the debate dominates Fuller's reputation; and Karol Soltan's comment ('A Social Science that Does Not Exist', in the same collection, *ibid* 387 at 408) that the social science Lon Fuller worked on is a 'barely visible intellectual sideshow' which deserves to be transformed into 'a serious and large-scale enterprise' in legal scholarship. On the 'partial eclipse' of Fuller in contemporary jurisprudence, see also David Luban, 'Rediscovering Fuller's Legal Ethics' in Witteveen and van der Burg, n 5 above, 193–225 at 194–9; and Kristen Rundle, '"Forms liberate": Reclaiming the Legal Philosophy of Lon L. Fuller' (Doctoral Thesis (University of Toronto, 2009, Bora Haskin Library, University of Toronto)) ch 1.

[12] See the papers collected in (2008) 83 *New York University Law Review, Symposium: The Hart-Fuller Debate at Fifty*: David Dyzenhaus, 'The Grudge Informer Case Revisited' at 1000–34; Leslie Green, 'Positivism and the Inseparability of Law and Morals' at 1035–58; Jeremy Waldron, 'Positivism and Legality: Hart's Equivocal Response to Fuller' at 1135–69. On the impact and status of the debate, see also Nicola Lacey, 'Philosophy, Political Morality and History: Explaining the Enduring Resonance of the Hart-Fuller Debate' at 1059–87 of the same collection.

[13] For a trenchant example of this judgment, see Matthew H Kramer, *In Defence of Legal Positivism: Law Without Trimmings* (Oxford, Oxford University Press, 2003) ch 2.

Hart's Holmes lecture can justly be seen as exemplary of his broader contribution, Fuller's most original interventions in legal scholarship originated not so much in a philosophical view but rather in a broader cross-disciplinary interpretation of legal institutions and processes—a set of interests which justifies Summers' assessment of him as 'the greatest proceduralist in the history of legal theory'.[14] Though, as I shall argue, Fuller might have drawn on this broader work to raise questions about Hart's approach, his detailed interest in legal processes potentially giving him a certain advantage in the debate, he did not do so nearly as effectively as he might have done, an omission which itself proceeds from some interesting aspects of his scholarly approach and personality. Hence the salience to Fuller's reputation of his role as Hart's natural law opponent marginalises some important strengths of his scholarship.

I shall preface my argument with a historical and biographical sketch: introducing the protagonists and their intellectual and personal preoccupations; setting the scene for the debate in terms of contemporary legal scholarship and legal education, particularly at Oxford and Harvard; and providing both a necessary background for my own interpretation and, I hope, a richer context in which to assess the debate's overall significance for legal scholarship today.

In Quest of Hart and Fuller

Who, then, were these two men whose engagement in the pages of the *Harvard Law Review* casts such a long shadow over jurisprudential scholarship?

Herbert Hart was born into a Jewish tailoring family in Harrogate in 1907. He had a brilliant student career at Oxford, where he read 'Greats', ie philosophy, classics and ancient history. He went on to have a glittering career at the Chancery Bar in the 1930s, before becoming a highly placed counter-espionage officer in MI5 during the Second World War. In 1945, reluctant to return to a career which he had come to see as mainly involving saving rich people money, he returned to Oxford as Philosophy Fellow at New College. Here, despite suffering agonising feelings of insecurity about his capacity to take up academic work after such a long break, Hart quickly became a leading figure in the group of linguistic philosophers around JL Austin and Gilbert Ryle. In 1952, he was elected to the Chair of Jurisprudence, and over the next decade established himself as the world's leading legal philosopher in the analytic tradition.[15]

[14] Summers, n 2 above, at 151.

[15] I leave aside Hans Kelsen, who would clearly have a claim to the position of the twentieth century's most important legal philosopher, but whose work (notwithstanding striking structural similarities to Hart's) derives from a very different philosophical tradition.

It would be difficult to overestimate the importance of Hart's year at Harvard in making this extraordinary achievement possible.[16] His three years as a member of the Oxford Law Faculty had done nothing to unsettle his primary identification as a philosopher. This is hardly surprising when one bears in mind both the excitement then surrounding linguistic philosophy at Oxford, and the primarily 'black-letter' and atheoretical orientation of most of Oxford's law teaching and scholarship. Hart's dim view of the intellectual stature of law schools was challenged by what he found at Harvard; and his experience there provided an important stimulus to his writing. Though already the holder of England's most prestigious position in legal philosophy, he had at the time of his arrival at Harvard in the autumn of 1956 published only a handful of articles. Both *Causation in the Law*[17] and *The Concept of Law*[18] existed in draft form: but *Causation* was delayed by Hart's hesitations about some aspects of his co-author Tony Honoré's ideas for the book;[19] and he seems to have felt little urgency about publishing his own monograph, which he had been delivering as lectures since 1953. The year at Harvard changed all this. In the stimulating and (at least in comparison with Oxford)[20] publishing-oriented atmosphere of a top American law school, Hart began to see the importance of a more active record of publication; and out of the context of his normal family and professional obligations, he embarked on a period of intense intellectual creativity, pondering or drafting during the course of the year almost all the work for which he was to become famous.

This is not to say, however, that Hart's year at Harvard was an entirely comfortable one. The extensive diaries and letters home which survive from this period give us a clear view of his experience: wry observations of his colleagues and of the broader American environment are infused with a sense of intense intellectual excitement, but are also punctuated by characteristic moments of insecurity. Always a sensitive person, he was acutely aware not only of Harvard's

[16] Hart's year at Harvard, and its impact on his career, are explored in greater detail in ch 8 of my *A Life of H.L.A. Hart*, n 3 above.

[17] HLA Hart and AM Honoré, *Causation in the Law* (Oxford, Oxford University Press, 1959; 2nd edn 1986); *The Concept of Law* (Oxford, Clarendon Press, 1961).

[18] *The Concept of Law* (Oxford, Clarendon Press, 1961).

[19] See Lacey, n 3 above, at 209–11.

[20] The qualification is important: Hart and Sacks failed formally to publish their significant work, Henry M Hart, Jr and Albert M Sacks, *The Legal Process: Basic Problems in the Making and Application of Law* (Westbury, NY, The Foundation Press, 1994) for several decades, despite the fact that it was being used not only by them but, in mimeographed form, by other American law schools from at least 1958: and, as Summers' monograph (Summers, n 2 above) explains in detail, Fuller himself was slow to publish some of his most important research. For example, his important 'The Forms and Limits of Adjudication' (1978) 92 *Harvard Law Review* 353, originally drafted during the late 1950s, was published only after his death in 1978 (for details of its genesis, see nn 52–5 and 97 below). This example raises interesting questions about the culture and the incentive structures which characterised contemporary law schools. But the fact remains that by the time Hart visited Harvard, it was widely recognised that publication of one's ideas was an important part of being a successful legal academic.

failure to subscribe to the Oxford view of philosophy as 'queen of the disciplines', but moreover of the local tendency to equate positivism with the 'formalism' which, in the local reaction against the Langdell era, was so reviled: as he noted in an interview later in life, he once overheard a Harvard colleague remark, 'You know he's a positivist, but he's quite a nice man'![21] Neither the sociological jurisprudence of Roscoe Pound, represented at Harvard that year in both the substantial person of Pound himself and that of Hart's fellow visitor Julius Stone, nor the moralised vision of Fuller, appealed to him; and though he had some admiration for aspects of the 'process' school of Hart and Sacks and for the constitutional law scholarship of Freund, and a serious respect for the applied utilitarianism of Wechsler, it seems clear that their genre of work did not engage his deep intellectual interest.

In short, he felt somewhat isolated: and in this context, his already strong tendency to identify with philosophers in his own analytic mould was probably confirmed. It is clear in particular that he did not entirely 'click' with Fuller during the year. His diary gives the impression that this was a matter in part of intellectual incompatibility, Hart's rejection of natural law teaming up with a feeling that Fuller's exposition of it failed to meet the highest standards of clarity or economy of expression. Hart recalled that: 'He was rather testy. He couldn't keep his cool in arguments. But I liked him and he liked me. But he thought I was a radically mistaken positivist'.[22]

Yet one senses a lack of personal chemistry—an intuition which is confirmed by the following entry in Hart's Harvard diary:

> L. Fuller sweating opposite me [in the Faculty Club] announced he was going to comment [on the Holmes Lecture] in HLR. I felt I ought to show signs of appreciation and apprehensiveness but I didn't.[23]

Such warmth of relationship as the two men ever did achieve was generated, ironically, by the debate itself, and in particular by Fuller's prompt and effective intervention with the student editors of the *Harvard Law Review* when they butchered Hart's paper in a conscientious attempt to make it suitable for publication in an American law journal:

> Dear Lon
>
> I was delighted to receive your reply to my poor thing and I am about to get down to it.
>
> Meanwhile a spot of trouble! The L. Rev. boys had *mutilated* my article by making major excisions of what they think is irrelevant or fanciful. They have made a ghastly mess of it and of the references to Bentham and I have written to say that they must not publish it under my name with these cuts which often destroy the precise nuance. I took great care and much time over what they have coolly cut out.

[21] Lacey, n 3 above, at 181.

[22] Interview with David Sugarman, quoted in Lacey, *ibid* 181.

[23] See Lacey, *ibid* 198.

Could you induce them to be sensible? Such an interference with an author's draft is unthinkable here and I am astonished that that so gross and insensitive a thing should be possible at Harvard.

I have told them if they will undertake to restore the listed cuts I will get down to the unwelcome task of patching it up all over again. But meanwhile I will not return the proof.

So sorry but it is important to me to get precisely what I said printed. Best of wishes. I will write anyhow on your reply,

Yours ever

Herbert Hart[24]

Dear Herbert

After receiving your letter I went over to the Review and found the President busily engaged in restoring your article to its original form. I am sorry for what they did, though I have to confess that this sort of thing comes close to being standard practice with articles written by American authors. Being near at hand I could save my baby from mayhem. Had I dreamed they would take such liberties with your text, I would have stood over them.

... Give my best to your wife and accept my wishes for a very merry Christmas for both of you

Sincerely

Lon L. Fuller.[25]

One senses that Hart, exceptionally quick in argument and gifted in seminar or one-to-one debate, found Fuller's wide-ranging but less closely focused approach somewhat ponderous—an intuition which is confirmed by Hart's rather snooty comment to philosopher Morton White: 'Lon Fuller has replied at enormous length and (I think) obscurity to my Holmes Lecture. This piece of logomachy will appear in the Harvard Law Review shortly'.[26] There is no sense here that Hart felt much intellectual curiosity about what really underpinned Fuller's intellectual commitments: he was content simply to pigeonhole Fuller as a natural lawyer, and to use his position to illustrate what he saw as the absurdities of the natural law tradition.

Since I have written extensively elsewhere about Hart's life and personality, and about the significance for him of the debate with Fuller, I will here devote more space to introducing Fuller. There is no biography of Lon Fuller, but it is possible to make a sketch of the man on the basis of materials in the Harvard Law School archive, and of published work; notably Robert Summers' *Lon L. Fuller* and Kenneth Winston's introduction to *The Principles of Social Order*, which give

24 Hart to Fuller, 13 December 1957, The Papers of Lon Fuller, Harvard Law School Library, box 3, folder 14.

25 Fuller to Hart, 17 December 1957, The Papers of Lon Fuller, Harvard Law School Library, box 3, folder 14

26 Hart to Morton White, December 1957.

some personal details as well as a comprehensive assessment of Fuller's work.[27] Born in 1902 in Hereford, Texas, Fuller's parents moved to California in 1906. Initially of modest means, during his earliest childhood his father was engaged in ranching as well as his office job. He went on to have a successful career in banking, eventually rising to be president of the El Centro National Bank. We get a rare glimpse of Fuller's childhood environment, and of its contribution to his persisting interest in the bearing of distinctive decision-making or negotiating processes on the resolution of social problems, from the introduction to his 1965 paper, 'Irrigation and Tyranny':

> I spent most of my childhood and youth in a reclaimed desert area wholly dependent on water brought from the Colorado River across many intervening miles of arid sands. Though this area—the Imperial Valley in the southeast corner of California—is counted as one of the most productive in the United States, it has only about two inches of rainfall a year, most of which seemed to us to come down in one torrent. Many of the most vivid memories of my childhood are connected directly or indirectly with irrigation and flooding. For a while we lived, or thought we lived, under the threat that the Colorado might decide to turn back into the Valley, instead of emptying safely into the Gulf of California. The ugly scars of its past misbehavior were everywhere around us, interrupting the fertile fields with miniature bad lands ... I can remember being impressed at an early age by a foreign-sounding word that stood for a strange and important person, the zanjero [watermaster]. I never saw a zanjero but I pictured him as a kind of biblical figure, dividing the waters and quieting the alarms of farmers whose crops could be destroyed in a few days by a lack of moisture ... In all this there was nothing remotely suggesting tyranny or autocratic government. Instead there was a strong sense of community such as I have never experienced since. The political issues under most earnest discussion were those affecting the Irrigation District, and everyone had a sense of participating in the affairs of the District. We were all parts, of one another, and we knew it.[28]

Fuller's mother died when he was a small child, and he was brought up by his father and stepmother. We know little about the nature of his childhood, but the tone of the extract just quoted gives reason to think that it was a happy one. In 1926, he married Florence Gail Thompson (Gail), with whom he had two children: Francis Brock and Cornelia. Their marriage lasted until her death in 1960, following a long and crippling illness which necessitated her removal to the warm climate of Arizona for the last part of her life.[29] Towards the end of 1960, Fuller married Marjorie ('Marnie') D. Chappell, whom he had met at Thomas

[27] See nn 2 and 5 above: see also Robert S Summers, 'Professor Fuller's Jurisprudence and America's Dominant Philosophy of Law' (1979) 92 *Harvard Law Review* 433.

[28] 'Irrigation and Tyranny' (1965) 17 *Stanford Law Review* 1021, 1021–2; the article is an extended review of a book arguing that, historically, irrigation has been associated with tyranny, hence the remark towards the end of the quotation. I am grateful to Kristen Rundle for drawing this curious and fascinating paper to my attention.

[29] Surviving materials (for information on which I am indebted to Kenneth Winston) include a note from Fuller to a flower shop in Tucson in 1959, giving characteristically detailed instructions about the delivery of a bouquet to Gail, who suffered from an acute form of arthritis.

Reed Powell's 75th birthday party. Fuller's father seems to have encouraged him to have the education which one assumes he himself had lacked; in this, his early experience was strikingly similar to Hart's. Hart seamlessly discarded his Yorkshire origins in favour of the genteel Oxonian persona which led one of his Oxford students to remark in an interview, reporting his surprise at learning from Jenifer Hart's autobiography[30] that Herbert Hart was Jewish, that he had assumed that Hart was 'descended from generations of patrician public school boys'.[31] Similarly, Fuller cultivated an East coast persona which led Hart into the mistaken description of him as a 'nice New Englander with some quite original ideas'.[32]

But from here on Hart's and Fuller's experiences were very different. A social scientist rather than a philosopher by training, Lon Fuller majored in economics at Berkeley and then at Stanford, graduating in 1924, before moving into law and taking his JD in 1926. He headed straight for academic life, immediately securing a position at Oregon, moving on to Illinois in 1928, to Duke in 1931, and finally, in 1939, to Harvard. Here he spent the rest of his career, holding the Carter Chair (formerly held by Roscoe Pound) from 1948 to his retirement in 1972. Like Hart, Fuller had some experience in legal practice: during America's period of involvement in the Second World War he worked for a Boston law firm in the labour relations field, and continued to engage in labour arbitrations until 1959.[33] But the nature of his practice was very different from Hart's: it was far less trained on technical legal interpretation and more strongly oriented to skills of negotiation and dispute resolution. As Summers puts it in relation to legal theory, 'Fuller's was a "physiological" orientation to law, as opposed to the more "anatomical" concerns of most legal positivists'.[34]

A man of tremendous energy and imagination, Fuller was actively engaged in institution-building both at and beyond Harvard. His Harvard colleagues remembered him with respect and affection as a modest, friendly man who had made a key contribution to legal education.[35] Deeply involved in debates about

[30] Jenifer Hart, *Ask Me No More* (London, Peter Halban, 1998).

[31] Interview with Peter Campbell; see Lacey, n 3 above, at 131.

[32] In a letter to Jenifer Hart, autumn 1956. American colleagues whom I asked about this story when researching my biography of Hart confirmed that Fuller's persona was such that he might well have been read in this way even by an American contemporary.

[33] See Winston, n 5 above, at 125: as Winston notes, Fuller was 'almost alone among Anglo-American legal scholars' in his intellectual interest in arbitration and mediation; see also Marc Hertogh, 'The Conscientious Watermaster: Rediscovering the Interactional Concept of Law' in Witteveen and van der Berg, n 5 above, at 364–87.

[34] Summers, n 2 above, at 31.

[35] See Erwin N Griswold, 'Lon Luvois Fuller, 1902–1978' and Albert M Sacks, 'Lon Luvois Fuller' (1978) 92 *Harvard Law Review* 351 and 349 respectively. This issue of the review was a tribute to Fuller; alongside these obituaries, his own paper 'The Forms and Limits of Adjudication', n 20 above, edited by Kenneth Winston, appeared in print for the first time, as well as an article assessing 'Forms and Limits' by his co-author, Melvin Aron Eisenberg: 'Participation, Responsiveness and the Consultative Process: An Essay for Lon Fuller' at 410–32, and Robert Summers' 'Professor Fuller's Jurisprudence and America's Dominant Philosophy of Law', n 27 above.

curriculum development at Harvard, he chaired from 1944–47 the Law School's Committee on Legal Education, crafting reforms which, during the next decade, reshaped both the substance of the curriculum and teaching methods, and advocating in 1946 the establishment of an Institute in International Legal Studies focused on comparative law and on educating American lawyers in the law of other jurisdictions, and overseas scholars in American law.[36] He was actively concerned in ensuring that adequate materials for the study of jurisprudence and of contracts should be available in affordable form to students, and was a popular teacher: 'vigorous yet kindly', as Griswold put it: 'He set high standards, but terror was never an element in his method'.[37] That last phrase is significant. In an era in which the brutal teaching methods immortalised in John Jay Osborn's *The Paper Chase*[38] were much more than a distant memory, Fuller represented a more humane and open approach, as well as being a magnet for students who found the normal diet of legal education unappetising. This role, and the relish with which Fuller played it, are amusingly recalled by Osborn in the following vignette:

> What saved my law school experience was, I think, analogous to what law and literature courses are doing today for law students. I read Professor Lon Fuller's *Morality of Law.* Though that book is generally philosophical and sociological, it makes its argument by way of a narrative ... The book gave me hope that there were alternative ways of thinking about the law. At the end of my first year, I went into Fuller's office to ask if I could work as his research assistant. 'Mr. Osborn', he said, 'I had a research assistant several years ago, and it didn't work out'. I stumbled toward the door. Fuller called me back. 'By the way', he said, 'why was it that you wanted to work for me anyway?' 'Because you're a genius', I said, 'Because your book, *The Morality of Law*, is the only thing that makes sense in this law school'. Fuller looked at me. 'Mr. Osborn', he said, 'Come back. Sit down. Perhaps I've been too hasty'. So that summer, I worked for Fuller as his research assistant. My assignment was to read certain books Fuller said he needed to know about for his work. I was to abstract what I considered important in them ... Then we would discuss it. These books ranged from literature to studies of primitive

[36] There is a great deal of evidence of this involvement in the correspondence held among the papers of Lon Fuller at Harvard Law School Library. For a general assessment of Fuller's views on legal education, and his institutional involvement in curriculum reform, see Summers, n 2 above, ch 11; on the Institute of International Legal Studies, see Arthur E Sutherland, *The Law at Harvard: A History of Ideas and Men, 1817–1967* (Cambridge, MA, Belknap Press of Harvard University Press, 1967) 333; on the reform committee, see Sacks, n 35 above, at 350; Griswold, n 35 above, at 352.

[37] Griswold *ibid* 351. Fuller's popularity with students also surfaces in the archive: in a letter from the early 1950s, a student tells him that he has been declared, '*E pluribus Unus*', to be 'the tops' among first year instructors: Student to Fuller, 25 March 1951, The Papers of Lon Fuller, Harvard Law School Library, box 2, folder 9. Both Griswold and Sacks emphasise in their obituaries his gifts as a teacher, and his commitment to getting across the importance of theoretical issues and of legal processes broader than the appellate cases which tend to dominate the law student's literary diet.

[38] *The Paper Chase* (Boston, Houghton Mifflin Company, 1971): the book generated a film in 1973 and a TV series in 1978–79. For the less adventurous Harvard students, Fuller's contracts course tended to be more popular than his jurisprudence class. His fame as a contracts teacher led to some speculation that he might have been the model for Osborn's intimidating contracts professor, Kingsfield: in fact, as the vignette quoted next reveals, Fuller was the very antithesis of Kingsfield.

> culture. Toward the end of the summer, Fuller said, 'This abstract you've done on Malinowski's law in the Figi tribe, I really think you've ignored something on page eighty-nine'. Suddenly it hit me: Fuller had in fact read all the material he had assigned to me. I had not been helping him at all. He had been giving one of the first law and literature courses, an individual tutorial.[39]

Fuller was, in all senses (and in stark contrast to Hart) a political animal. In his professional life, he was, for example, an energetic promoter of initiatives at Harvard such as Hart's and Stone's visits, and a generous operator in the long struggle to find a suitable position for Hans Kelsen when he arrived in America as a political refugee.[40] On a broader canvas, he was an early and energetic advocate of America's entry into the Second World War, also writing to Charles Lindbergh remonstrating with him about his support for the German cause and urging him to abandon it.[41] But here as elsewhere the surviving materials give the sense of a somewhat volatile personality, as well as of someone whose temperamental as much as intellectual predisposition was to mark out and follow an approach which was distinctively his own. As Winston puts it in relation to Fuller's work, 'Characteristically, he followed the idiosyncratic path'.[42] A lifelong Democrat, he nonetheless became an active supporter of Richard Nixon's unsuccessful bid for the White House in 1960, even chairing the Scholars for Nixon Committee; an advocate of an expanded and more interdisciplinary and comparatively focused curriculum at Harvard, he nonetheless distanced himself (often in trenchant terms) from the more full-blooded socio-legal or sociological approaches of some of his colleagues; an enthusiast for democracy, he nonetheless studied with real attention the case for economic planning and indeed the general situation of the Soviet bloc countries; a contributor to the legal defence fund for Professor Wendell Furry, who was threatened with contempt proceedings for his refusal to disclose the names of his former associates in the Communist Party to the infamous McCarthy Committee, he nonetheless took the view that Furry should

[39] Osborn, n 10 above, at fn 3.

[40] In one of a number of letters to prospective university employers advocating Kelsen's merits, he amusingly described Kelsen's need for an institutional affiliation with token payment, which was a condition of his continuing to enjoy a stipend from a charitable foundation, as presenting 'the opportunity to get a scholar of world-wide reputation at truly bargain rates'. His instinct for promoting a good bargain is not, perhaps, followed up with the most consistent of cases: he continues; 'I have found Kelsen very stimulating as a colleague. He is conversationally very entertaining, and not at all the heavy Teutonic type of scholar. His lectures have been pretty abstract, and I'm afraid most of our men got little out of them. His English is quite good now, and, though there are slips in idiom, is easy to understand': letter from Fuller to Dean Paul William Brosman, Tulane University of Louisiana College of Law, 10 January 1942, The Papers of Lon Fuller, Harvard Law School Library, box 2, folder 1.

[41] Fuller to Lindbergh, 18 September 1940, The Papers of Lon Fuller, Harvard Law School Library, box 2, folder 1; see Summers, n 2 above, at 7.

[42] Winston, n 5 above, at 249: *cf* Sacks, n 35 above, at 349: 'Lon Fuller was not content simply to follow existing schools of philosophy, though his views fit most comfortably among natural law thinkers, nor did he establish a new school to which other philosophers flocked. He was most interested in working out his own ideas'.

have disclosed the information.[43] In this last instance, we see a clear reflection of his lifelong commitment to procedural forms, and a clue to the distinctive character of the natural law theory for which he was to become famous: though he disapproved of Furry's stance, he thought him entitled to the best possible defence. In private life, his interests were more practical, less cerebral, than Hart's: in contrast with the latter's deep preoccupation with literature, architecture, painting and music, Fuller enjoyed the crafts of cookery, carpentry, gardening and photography.[44]

Leaving aside the unforgettable 'Case of the Speluncean Explorers',[45] Fuller is best known to legal theorists today for his reply to Hart and for the more elaborate statement of his natural law position in *The Morality of Law* (which originated in the prestigious Storrs lectures, delivered at Yale in 1963).[46] But (again in contrast to Hart) Fuller's theoretical ideas did not proceed exclusively from philosophical commitments. Rather, they were deeply intertwined throughout his career with his work as a scholar of law and procedure.[47] His published work displays an impressive imaginative range and an unusual courage in engaging with extra-legal disciplines. He authored an innovative contracts casebook, which gave a primary role to remedies—a topic which only found a real place on the agenda of English teaching in this field some 30 years later.[48] The book was original in giving a central place to the concept of reliance loss, and it had a key influence on Patrick Atiyah's path-breaking work published in 1979.[49] Fuller also wrote a number of important papers on legal ethics[50] and on different

[43] Correspondence, 1955, The Papers of Lon Fuller, Harvard Law School Library, box 3, folder 6: Richard Nixon had been a student of Fuller's at Duke.

[44] Summers, n 2 above, at 9.

[45] See n 10 above.

[46] *The Morality of Law* (New Haven, CT, Yale University Press, 1964; revised edn, 1969). Fuller's legal philosophy is also expounded in two other shorter books which deserve mention: *The Law in Quest of Itself* (Evanston, IL, Northwestern University Press, 1940) and *The Anatomy of Law* (London, Pall Mall Press, 1968). Other Harvard scholars whose Storrs lectures retain a place in the canon of twentieth century legal scholarship include Roscoe Pound (*Introduction to the Philosophy of Law*) and Benjamin Cardozo (*Nature of the Judicial Process*); see Sutherland, n 36 above, at 305.

[47] As the surviving correspondence on the development of 'Forms and Limits of Adjudication' shows, the converse was also true: in his exchanges with colleagues, Fuller not infrequently made reference to what he saw as the philosophical underpinnings of the project: see, eg Fuller to Boris I Bittker, 4 April 4 1960; Fuller to HLA Hart, 19 October 1959; Fuller to Samuel Mermin, 30 November 1959, The Papers of Lon Fuller, Harvard Law School Library, box 14, folder 1.

[48] *Basic Contract Law* (St Paul, MN, West Publishing Company, 1947); this book went into three editions (written, respectively, with Robert Braucher in 1964 and with Melvin Aron Eisenberg in 1972) in Fuller's lifetime. In the 4th edition, published by Eisenberg in 1981, Fuller's innovative structure was abandoned: see Alfred S Konesfky, Elizabeth B Mensch and John Henry Schlegel, 'In Memoriam: The Intellectual Legacy of Lon Fuller' (1981) 30 *Buffalo Law Review* 263. The enduring legacy of Fuller's contracts scholarship is also discussed in Karl Klare, 'Contracts Jurisprudence and the First-Year Casebook' (1979) 54 *New York University Law Review* 876, 877 fn 3 and 881–6.

[49] *The Rise and Fall of Freedom of Contract* (Oxford, Oxford University Press, 1979). On Atiyah's acknowledgment of his debt to Fuller, see Summers, n 2 above, at 14, 63, 162: for a perceptive analysis of Fuller's contracts scholarship, see generally *ibid* ch 10. See also Winston, n 5 above, at 169–70.

[50] For a thoughtful analysis of this aspect of Fuller's work, see David Luban, 'Rediscovering Fuller's Legal Ethics' in Witteveen and van der Burg, n 5 above, at 193–225.

legal processes in which he began to develop what we might call a structural or functional theory of the suitability of particular forms of process (civil adjudication, legislation, arbitration, mediation, managerial direction, decision by lot, customary governance) to the resolution of particular forms of dispute or other social problem.[51] The earliest version of what later became his famous posthumously published article 'The Forms and Limits of Adjudication'[52] was written around the time of Hart's visit to Harvard: this version already drew on Polanyi's notion of 'polycentricity' in articulating the sorts of problems unsuitable for adjudicative resolution.[53]

It is important to see that Fuller's deep interest in the significance of institutions and processes was not a separate research agenda, but rather found

[51] See Summers, n 2 above, chs 6–9.

[52] See n 20 above. For readers interested in the co-evolution of Fuller's procedural and theoretical ideas, a further note on the genesis of 'The Forms and Limits of Adjudication' may be useful. Published not long after his death in 1978, the paper was first presented at the Harvard Law School legal philosophy discussion group in 1957; a revised version was prepared for use in Fuller's jurisprudence class, and presented to a roundtable on Jurisprudence at the 1959 meeting of the Association of American Law Schools; and a third version (the basis for the one which found its way into print 17 years later) was produced in 1961. The 1959 version expands substantially on the argument of the 1957 draft, adding in particular a section on the limits of adjudication envisaged by but not included in the earliest draft, which however opened with a discussion of definitional issues omitted from the later drafts. There are only very minor differences between the 1959 and 1961 drafts. Kenneth Winston's final edit for the 1978 publication mainly added references and a section on the significance of adversarial presentation drawn from Fuller's joint paper with John D Randall, 'Professional Responsibility: Report of the Joint Conference' of the American Bar Association and the Association of American Law Schools in 1952, published in (1958) 44 *American Bar Association Journal* 1159, which was referred to but not quoted in the 1959 and 1961 drafts. Though regarding the paper as insufficiently polished for publication, Fuller incorporated parts of its arguments in 'Adjudication and the Rule of Law' (1960) 54 *American Society for International Law Proceedings* 1, and in 'Collective Bargaining and the Arbitrator' (1963) *Wisconsin Law Review* 3: see Winston, n 5 above, at 86.

I am indebted to Kenneth Winston for sending me all three typescript versions of Fuller's paper, and to David Warrington for providing me with a substantial correspondence between Fuller and colleagues across the United States about the 1959 draft. The correspondence, parts of which are quoted elsewhere in this chapter, is of interest not least in identifying the main criticisms with which Fuller was contending. These were, first, that his conception of adjudication was under-inclusive (excluding genuinely adjudicative processes which nonetheless engaged with polycentric issues: see Boris I Bittker of Yale Law School to Fuller, 4 April 1960); secondly, that it was over-inclusive (in that it encompassed other non-legal and non-adjudicative practices such as those of university committees: see Boris I Bittker *ibid*; Walter Gellhorn of Columbia University to Fuller, 19 October 1959; Nathaniel L Nathanson of Northwestern University to Fuller, 29 October 1959; Frank C Newman of Boalt Hall Law School, University of California at Berkeley to Fuller, 19 October 1959); thirdly, that the paper's sideswipes at contemporary philosophy were wide of the mark (Samuel Mermin of the University of Wisconsin to Fuller, 24 November 1959) (all letters from The Papers of Lon Fuller, Harvard Law School Library, box 14, folder 1). The correspondence included a letter to then Vice-President Richard Nixon (9 October 1959) and an exchange with Louis J Hector, author of an influential report for the government on administrative agencies: the report appears to have provided an important context for the development of Fuller's ideas at this time.

[53] Winston, n 5 above, at 86: see n 20 above. Eisenberg, in his *Harvard Law Review* essay on 'Forms and Limits', places its origins yet earlier when he refers to Fuller's essay as being published 'thirty years after it was written', n 35 above, at 426. Fuller drew Polanyi's ideas from his *The Logic of Liberty: Reflections and Rejoinders* (London,Routledge and Kegan Paul, 1951).

consistent expression in his explicitly jurisprudential work. His own sense of the connections between these two branches of his work is explicit in a letter which he wrote to Hart about 'Forms and Limits of Adjudication', in which he drew an analogy between philosophical analysis of linguistic usage in the style of JL Austin and an analysis of institutions in what we might call a broadly Wittgensteinian tradition:

> On the problem of legal method implicit in *The Forms and Limits* it occurs to me that there may be some affinity for the study of ordinary linguistic usage. In effect, what is proposed by Austin ... is that the philosopher trace out the complex implications of ordinary language, the theory being that much wisdom will thus be uncovered. How about tracing out the implications of our institutions, such as adjudication? Michael Oakshott [*sic*] does indeed in his inaugural address suggest studying the 'intimations' of our traditions.[54]

Here as elsewhere, however, Fuller's intellectual stance is characterised by a degree of ambivalence. Much of his teaching was informed not just by philosophy but by other disciplines, notably by anthropology and economic theory,[55] and he was alive to the relevance of social science disciplines (sociology and psychology as well as economics and anthropology) to a proper understanding of legal processes. As Winston puts it, Fuller believed that 'the effort at governance must be informed by the cumulative learning of the social sciences'.[56] Yet he was a lifelong critic of the idea that legal argumentation could be reduced to, or equated with, scientific reasoning, and, as we shall see, an outspoken sceptic about the place of funded socio-legal research at Harvard.[57]

Notwithstanding these characteristically maverick oscillations, I want to argue that an understanding of Fuller's broad scholarly interests—far, far broader than those entertained by Hart—is crucial to an understanding of why the terms of the debate disadvantaged him in important respects. One the one hand, the

[54] Fuller to HLA Hart, 19 October 1959, The Papers of Lon Fuller, Harvard Law School Library, box 14, folder 1. The difference between an Austinian and a Wittgensteinian approach to legal theory is considered in Lacey, n 3 above, ch 9.

[55] For example, David N Smith recalls, in his Preface to Bechtler, n 5 above, at viii, that he and Fuller co-taught a course on 'Law and Social Change in Africa' which drew, inter alia, on the work of Max Gluckman: Fuller's sensitivity to cross-cultural differences in legal forms is amusingly reflected in his comment to FF Stone of the Institute of Comparative Law at Tulane University that one of the reasons why he was still not ready to publish 'Forms and Limits' was that it was 'horribly Anglo-American': Fuller to Stone, 22 January 1960, The Papers of Lon Fuller, Harvard Law School Library, box 14, folder 1. On Fuller's use of economics, see text at n 89 below.

[56] Winston, n 5 above, at 14. My interpretation of the relationship between Fuller's jurisprudential work and his process scholarship chimes with Kristen Rundle's claim that, far from 'represent[ing] two separate spheres of Fuller's thought', Fuller's 'eunomics' and his work on legality 'give expression to a common jurisprudential vision': the posthumous publication of papers like 'Means and Ends' (Winston, n 5 above, at 47–64) and 'The Forms and Limits of Adjudication' (n 20 above) obscures the fact that he was working on these related lines of thought throughout his career: K Rundle, '*Forms Liberate*': *Reclaiming the Legal Philosophy of Lon L* Fuller (Doctoral Thesis, University of Toronto, 2009) (Bora Laskin Library, University of Toronto), ch 1.

[57] See text at nn 82–3 below.

philosophical terms of the debate made it difficult to articulate some of the most original aspects of his thinking, and drew him into incautious generalisations which both flattened the subtlety of his vision of law as a social institution and generated some rather crude philosophical positions (and indeed empirical claims). On the other hand, his own ambivalence about the precise intellectual relationship between philosophical and social science resources, and his uncertainty about how to bring them into a satisfactory synthesis, further prompted him to retreat into abstractions which evoke, without ever really pinning down, the institutional insights drawn from his broader work. Next to Hart's more precise philosophical formulations, these looked vulnerable.

'Perhaps that word "Natural Law" is still sticking in your throat': Fuller in the Light of the Harvard Archive

Before returning to this substantive reading of the debate, however, it will be useful (and I trust not without entertainment value) to develop these insights into Fuller's intellectual stance. In the rest of this section, I accordingly examine a selection of archival resources in quest of some further sense of Fuller as a person, and in particular a sense of how he might have been expected to respond to the jurisprudential controversy which overshadowed Hart's year at Harvard and which finds clear expression in the published 'debate'.

Here again, I want to suggest that there are some interesting differences between the two men. Certainly, and particularly in his early career, Hart had occasional moments of defensiveness, infused with more than a tinge of Oxford philosophical arrogance.[58] But he was—remarkably, given his persistent and serious insecurities—not particularly thin-skinned about criticism of his work. Indeed, he appears to have enjoyed the debate which emerged from robust intellectual disagreement. This was, after all, the man who promoted the claim of his most vigorous critic to the Chair of Jurisprudence which he vacated in 1968.[59] And while he certainly became sadly obsessed with Dworkin's critique of his position in later life (as indeed, to a lesser extent, by other criticisms which bore on the positivist kernel of his theory of legal obligation, notably those of John Finnis and Gerald Postema),[60] one has the sense that this proceeded in large part from what he saw as a deep commitment to eliciting the truth of the matter at hand. Though a perfectly effective institutional operator when he put his mind to it (think notably of the important legacy of his publishing creation, the Clarendon Law Series), there was little of the entrepreneurial in his approach to his academic career. Notwithstanding what many observers regarded as his supreme intellectual confidence, one suspects that his own assessment of his contribution was that he had, in effect,

58 See, eg Lacey, n 3 above, at 146–7.
59 *Ibid* 291–3.
60 *Ibid* 345–52.

become famous by 'selling philosophy to the lawyers': an attitude which is aptly summed up by his off-hand remark that 'the philosophers thought I was a marvellous lawyer, and the lawyers thought I was a marvellous philosopher'.[61]

Conversely, a strong entrepreneurial side to Fuller emerges very clearly from the substantial archive of correspondence which survives at Harvard. The man who emerges from the letters is warm, impulsive, even a little volatile; given to forthright expressions often leavened by a sense of humour; a truth-seeker, certainly; but also an energetic promoter of his own work, a prodigious distributor of offprints, a passionate defender of his ideas—and a testy and thin-skinned adversary when feeling that he had been treated unjustly or with some lack of respect. Whether engaging with colleagues about their reaction to his work, or explaining himself to Harvard colleagues (as in an amusing two-page letter to Dean Erwin Griswold in 1951, listing and indeed elaborating no fewer than five reasons why he would be at least a month late in returning his grades),[62] Fuller was an energetic defender of his own cause, even where the precise nature of that cause was not entirely clear. Indeed the archival materials might be taken to suggest that Fuller's difficulty in bringing his wide-ranging interests into a clear intellectual synthesis may have fed his sensitivity to criticism, in particular prompting a hypersensitivity to any charge of irrationalism, and reinforcing his inclination to use the debate with Hart to bolster his credentials as an analytical legal philosopher.

Perhaps the sample of letters which survives is a skewed one, but Fuller does seem to have had a tendency to get into wrangles with colleagues over their public treatment of his ideas. Yet his outbursts of pique are rather endearing, punctuated as they are by attempts to defuse the very row he is in the midst of creating, and concluded as they often are by remarkable pourings of oil on troubled waters, even amounting to straightforward climbing down. Probably the most spectacular examples relate to two philosophers, each, as it happens, by the name of Cohen. Here is Fuller, writing to Morris Cohen in 1941 about his reaction to *The Law in Quest of Itself*.[63] It is a letter which both typifies the style of his engagement with his critics, and already reflects, many years before his debate with Hart, a distinct sensitivity to being cast as an 'irrationalist' natural lawyer:

[61] Interview with David Sugarman, quoted in Lacey, n 3 above, at 171.

[62] Fuller to Griswold, 21 March 1951 (six days after the grades had been due!) Unfortunately, Griswold's reply does not seem to have survived: The Papers of Lon Fuller, Harvard Law School Library; box 3, folder 9. Fuller's reasons span the medical excuse, the excuse of pressure of administrative work, the excuse of extra-curricular demands such as external talks, and the excuse of curricular demands such as having to bone up on economic theory for his new seminar. Judging by the warmth of his obituary, the incident doesn't seem to have affected Griswold's high opinion of Fuller (see n 35 above).

[63] 'Should Legal Thought Abandon Clear Distinctions?' reproduced in M Cohen, *Reason and Law* (New York, Free Press, 1950): see Winston, n 5 above, at 293–4. Winston reproduces in full the longest of Fuller's exchanges with other scholars about their reaction to *The Law in Quest of Itself*: a letter to his Harvard colleague Thomas Reed Powell which spans nine printed pages in Winston, n 5 above, at 294–303. Powell's original letter is even longer (*ibid* 293) and gives us some sense of the time which contemporary scholars thought it proper to devote to correspondence with colleagues. My extracts from Fuller's correspondence should, of course, be interpreted in this light.

> Dear Professor Cohen
>
> I am returning herewith the manuscript of your review of my book. I am genuinely disappointed that you found so little in the book to approve. My disappointment is all the more marked since I have been an open admirer of your philosophy for many years. I was, however, not unprepared for your adverse judgment. In the first place, rumors had reached me that you viewed the book quite critically. In the second place, a third reading this spring of your 'Reason and Nature' made me aware of a widening gulf between my own thought and yours. My divergence from your thought is in a direction you would call 'irrationalism'.
>
> The fact that a fundamental difference in philosophic viewpoint underlies nearly all our disputes about specific points makes it difficult for me to comment on your review. I must say in all frankness that it seems to me neither entirely fair nor entirely accurate in its treatment of my book. However, I suppose no one who had received as severe a criticism as this review contains would be likely to think otherwise.

After disclaiming any pretension to a thorough rebuttal, but nonetheless picking his way in some irritation, and some detail, through a number of specific objections, there is a classic Fullerian concession:

> Speaking more seriously, I am convinced that I was mistaken in assuming that my use of this quotation would not be interpreted as classifying you with the positivists. It was simply a piece of carelessness on my part for which there is little excuse. I am genuinely sorry for it.

Showing again a typical sensibility to what others are saying about him, he notes that:

> Some one reported to me that you had said of my book, 'Everyone knows that it is difficult to distinguish the is and the ought, but why anyone should revel in that fact is more than I can understand'.

And he ends in characteristically frank, conciliatory and generous style:

> I hope you will forgive any touches of bitterness which may have crept into this letter, for I genuinely do not feel any personal animosity. I cannot feel that because it is obvious to me that your adverse judgment of my book arises from convictions which are very deep with you. Nor shall I let your review obscure a fact that is plain in my own mind, which is that I have derived a great deal from your work; it has shaped my thought in more ways than I could myself enumerate.
>
> Sincerely yours,
>
> Lon L. Fuller[64]

Twenty-four years later, in a set-to with another Cohen and with Ronald Dworkin about their treatment of Fuller at a symposium and in arrangements for

[64] Letter from Fuller to Prof Morris R Cohen, 6 August 1941, The Papers of Lon Fuller, Harvard Law School Library, box 2, folder 9. Kenneth Winston has suggested to me that Fuller's strong reaction is partly to be explained by the fact that Cohen's published views were indeed closer to his own position than the review implied: hence Fuller would have felt that Cohen's acerbity was unjustified.

a subsequent publication discussing his work, the tone of exasperation at not being properly understood is remarkably similar, though here it is underpinned by a vein of deep indignation at what he sees as procedural injustice. Fuller's complaints were that he had not received the critical paper to which he was to reply in due time, for either the seminar or the final publication; that the critics had spoken for too long, hence cutting down the time available to him; that Cohen had failed to respond to his letters; and that the critics had been allowed to amend their papers after the seminar but that he had not been given adequate opportunity to amend his own rebuttal. The episode begins with a four-page, single-spaced salvo from Fuller to Dworkin, copied to Cohen. Opening (under cover of conciliation) with a rather *de haut en bas* remark that he feels, as the person with most experience in organising such events, some responsibility for the 'misunderstandings' which had arisen, Fuller details all his grievances, culminating in the following explosion:

> To my mind you have been somewhat thoughtless in this whole affair, but I do not mean to suggest any plot. All I want to say is that you are now insisting that I hold my copy fast, and introduce no changes of substance, while your close associate is improving his statement and I cannot change my rebuttal to meet his changes without at the same time making new answer to what you said at the meeting and in the U[niversity] of P[ennsylvania] Review. This you say would violate our agreement.[65]

He then moves on to specify, in some procedural detail, the terms on which he proposes that the issues be resolved. Of what must have been a longer correspondence, only a handwritten (emollient but firm) note from Dworkin survives; but meanwhile Cohen weighs in on his own behalf:

> Dear Professor Fuller
>
> In view of the false statements of fact, and the extraordinary inferences you draw from admitted ones I feel that I must tell you how the affair looks to me. (I shall not speak to your criticisms of Dworkin who, as you know, can take care of defending himself.)[66]

There follows a forensic self-defence against all charges. Fuller's response is a characteristic climb-down:

> Dear Professor Cohen
>
> I thought matters had reached the maximum temperature before your letter arrived, but I see I was mistaken.
>
> I'm sorry if I seemed to imply bad faith throughout, and that I made 'false statements of fact'. [Note the lawyerly inverted commas there.] Things were badly balled up, and the basic difficulty was that no one assumed the role of laying down ground rules.'

[65] Letter from Fuller to Ronald Dworkin, 17 June 1965, The Papers of Lon Fuller, Harvard Law School Library, box 2, folder 13.

[66] Letter from Marshall Cohen to Fuller, 24 June 1965, The Papers of Lon Fuller, Harvard Law School Library, box 2, folder 9.

After reiterating in radically toned-down form the sources of his original anger, and asserting his disagreement with Cohen's summary of his views, he concludes:

> I don't think I am quite so obsessive a character as you depicte [*sic*] me, and I see (perhaps through self-deception) some inklings of an intellectual development that you deny to me. Perhaps in some more leisurely context I shall have occasion to return to the points you make. Meanwhile I hope you bear no rancor, for I certainly do not.
>
> Sincerely[67]

In short, one has the impression that Fuller courted—even relished—the odd skirmish with colleagues. This judgment is confirmed by his remark to Robert Summers, in a casual encounter at Phillips Book Store in Harvard Square, where Summers was working to support himself during his student years. Recognising Summers from his jurisprudence class, Fuller said 'Well, I am tangling with an Englishman in the *Harvard Law Review* soon. I think he is wrong, and wrong clearly!'. He made similar remarks in the class itself. As Summers puts it, Fuller's combative disposition gave him 'a penchant for polemics'.[68]

Yet more interesting from the point of view of our retrospective interpretation of his debate with Hart is his correspondence with other scholars about the *Harvard Law Review* articles. Fifteen such letters appear in the archive, several of them consisting in warm exchanges with people who had written to express approval of Fuller's position,[69] and to opine that this was, as one admiring correspondent put it, 'incomparably the liveliest issue (up to p. 672) your publication has put out in donkey's years'.[70] Fuller's letters show a real sensitivity to Hart's attack, while being tempered by ostensible fair-mindedness with a tinge of the backhander about it. Here is a representative example:

> Dear Mr. Bayley
>
> Thank you very much for your letter. I was greatly cheered by it. As you recall, Professor Hart's favorite jibe at his opponents was that they were not clear, that they perceived things dimly, etc. At one time I had in my article a quip about 'those high standards of clarity which Professor Hart so rightly prizes and so often exemplifies'. Restraints of international courtesy led me to change 'often' to 'generally', thereby forfeiting the whole point of the remark.
>
> I must say I did enjoy Hart's visit here last year, and the running arguments we have all year long. I'm sure we have learned much from each other.[71]

[67] Letter from Fuller to Marshall Cohen, 28 June 1965; Cohen replied graciously on 29 June, and there the story ends, though see Fuller's comment to Hart about the symposium, quoted at n 129 below; The Papers of Lon Fuller, Harvard Law School Library, box 2, folder 9.

[68] Personal communication with Robert Summers, 8 August 2008.

[69] See, eg the exchange with Melbourne University's David Derham: Letter from Derham to Fuller, 28 April 1958; Fuller's prompt reply, 5 May 1958, The Papers of Lon Fuller, Harvard Law School Library, box 3, folder 15.

[70] Harry Jones to Fuller, 8 March 1958, The Papers of Lon Fuller, Harvard Law School Library, box 3, folder 15.

[71] Letter from Fuller to Frank S Bayley, 3 March 1958, The Papers of Lon Fuller, Harvard Law School Library, box 3, folder 15.

Fuller's interdisciplinary sensibility would have appreciated the following letter from a colleague at Smith College:

> When I was at Oxford this past year, I took the opportunity to go to Hart's class on legal theory. At the end of one of the sessions I summed up his position as that of 'natural law with minimum content'. This he thought rather amusing, but I am not so sure you can put your foot on the biological bottom rung of the ladder and stop there, as he seems to wish to do. My feeling was that greater acquaintance with psychological theory might make him willing to go up another step, but then one cannot be sure.[72]

Typical of Fuller's more combative engagements is his letter to Jerome Hall:

> Dear Jerome
>
> I have been asked by the Buffalo Law Review to write a 'comment on, or reply to, Professor Hall's criticism of your position'. Since I think you are entitled to know why I declined that invitation, I am enclosing a copy of my letter to the Editor-in-Chief.
>
> I know that every writer who is criticized is inclined to think his views have been distorted, and I cannot claim a sufficient introspective objectivity to be sure that I am free of this kind of bias. But frankly, and utterly without rancor, I do think you have given the reader a most distorted view of my writings. Let me give a few illustrations.

Two and a half pages of closely typed examples follow, rounded off with a reference to Cohen's comment about Fuller's revelling in the difficulty of distinguishing between 'is and ought': a jibe which was still rankling 17 years after it was delivered. And the whole is concluded by the typical Fullerian step back from the brink of all-out warfare:

> Please don't think I am angry. In the first place, I like and admire you and your work too much for that. In the second place, I have got so used to this sort of thing that I have lost the capacity for anger, even when it comes from an unexpected source … Anyway, as you and I both know, most readers are so far from comprehending the issues in a dispute like this that no one can predict their reactions. Probably many readers will shout, 'Hurrah! That's my man', when they learn (quite incorrectly) that I urge lawyers to argue rightness and to ignore rules of law.
>
> I hope we can get together soon again.
>
> Sincerely,
>
> Lon L. Fuller[73]

As in this exchange with Hall, Fuller repeatedly displays acute sensitivity about being understood as a 'witches' cauldron'-style metaphysical natural lawyer. Indeed, he sometimes expresses ambivalence about being labelled a natural

[72] Letter from John Chapman to Fuller, 18 September 1958, The Papers of Lon Fuller, Harvard Law School Library, box 2, folder 8.

[73] Letter from Fuller to Jerome Hall, 28 April 1958, The Papers of Lon Fuller, Harvard Law School Library, box 3, folder 3.

lawyer at all. In answer to Boris Bittker's letter criticising his attempt in the 1959 version of 'Forms and Limits' to identify the 'essence' of adjudication, Fuller for example retorts:

> Perhaps that word 'natural law' is still sticking in your throat. I notice you say that adherents of natural law very seldom present any conclusions without purporting (speciously) to derive them from natural law premises. Please count me out on that.[74]

He felt, in short, that the debate consolidated a tendency to cast him in the mould of a genre of natural law theory which he in fact rejected:

> in all candor, the task of responding to your comments is rendered very difficult for me because the views you attribute to me seem to my perhaps prejudiced eyes so remote from what I said as to interpose an almost insurmountable obstacle to communication. When I read, for example that it is my general position 'that law is not "law" unless it is related to that unchanging omnipresence in the sky', I can't help wondering whether you read the article that I wrote.[75]

Intellectually, one of the most intriguing items in the correspondence about the debate is a long letter from the natural lawyer Alexander d'Entrèves. I shall return to this letter in my substantive analysis of the debate. In the meantime, it is worth reflecting on how much Fuller must have enjoyed the following remark, made in the context of d'Entrèves' argument that the kernel of the Hart/Fuller engagement lay in the question of whether or not, and in what sense, values ground legal obligation:

> It is this point about the 'ground of obligation' of the law which I would seize upon also in discussing the burning issue of the German predicament. Let me say, by way of preface, how warmly I share your feelings about Hart's 'strokes of the oar'. I confess that in both hearing and reading his strictures on Radbruch and on German 'liberalism' I could not help feeling sorry for the incurable smugness of our English friends.[76]

[74] Fuller to Boris I Bittker, 4 April 1960, The Papers of Lon Fuller, Harvard Law School Library, box 14, folder 1.

[75] Fuller to Abram T Collier, 31 March 1958, The Papers of Lon Fuller, Harvard Law School Library, box 3, folder 15; the letter continues: 'Now, about the Nazi situation. I may be naïve, but I have spent a good deal of time in Germany and I think I know something of the German character. I did not counsel any foolish, self-destructive act after the Nazis were firmly in the seat. Indeed my comments were generally not directed to this problem at all, but cleaning up the situation after the war. Insofar as I made any comment about what might have been done while the Nazis were consolidating their power, I was, I believe, rather cautious. (See the last full paragraph on page 659.)'.

[76] Alexander d'Entrèves to Fuller, 8 April 1958, The Papers of Lon Fuller, Harvard Law School Library, box 2, folder 13.

Setting the Scene: Harvard Law School in the Mid-1950s and Fuller's and Hart's Place in that Context

I observed earlier that, in their different ways, both Fuller and Hart were ploughing a lonely furrow in the context of the prevailing jurisprudential climate of Harvard Law School.[77] In Hart's case, the reasons for this isolation are clear: he was advancing a conception of legal theory associated at Harvard with the bugbear of formalism. In Fuller's case, it may seem strange: Harvard had, after all, long been his intellectual home; he held its chair of Jurisprudence: and his position at Harvard was bolstered by (and doubtless premised on) a substantial national (as well as international) reputation which must itself have added to interest in the debate. However, as the correspondence which I have quoted also shows, he nonetheless felt that, as a legal philosopher, he was widely misinterpreted and misunderstood. And notwithstanding the differences, there are interesting analogies between the stances of the two men.

Both sought to tread a path between the vices of formalism and what they saw as the excesses of realism and of sociological jurisprudence; both rejected the idea that legal argumentation could be aligned to scientific reasoning; both, albeit in different ways, were committed to theorising the 'normativity' as much as the 'facticity' of law: Hart through his critique of the predictive nature of both Austin's positivism and American Realism and through his account of the 'internal aspect' of rules; Fuller through his account of the inner morality of law. Both, moreover, were firmly committed to applying philosophical techniques to law (both Hart and Fuller, for example, were present at the inaugural American conference on legal and political philosophy held in October 1952, and Fuller was the instigator, along with Paul Freund and Henry Hart, of a legal philosophy reading group at Harvard). The extent to which they shared such common causes helps to explain why Fuller reacted so sharply to what he suspected (rightly) to be a lack of intellectual respect on Hart's part: for Hart, but not for Fuller, jurisprudence was all about legal philosophy—and Fuller was not a philosopher. But equally important, I suggest, is the way in which the pressures of life as a highly placed academic in an elite environment can conduce to feelings of vulnerability even among relatively stable and securely placed people.

[77] This is confirmed in Fuller's case by the following comment in Sacks' obituary (n 35 above at 350): 'During most of the time that he and I were colleagues on this Faculty, his impact on me and others did not grow out of his convincing us that his answers were right. His success lay in convincing me that his questions were right'.

Space precludes me from giving anything more than a brief sketch of Harvard at the time.[78] Both socially and institutionally, Harvard was peculiar in all senses of the word. For a start, its status in American elite culture at the time far exceeded that of any comparable university in Britain. This is summed up by the well-known story of a late-nineteenth President of Harvard, who asked his secretary to place a telephone call to the then US President, Teddy Roosevelt. When the President picked up the phone, the secretary said, 'I have the President for you, Mr. Roosevelt'. As well as status, Harvard had wealth unimaginable even to the richest British universities. This wealth and status generated a mesmerising array of extra-curricular activities. In the pages of the *Law School Record*, reports of improving reading and discussion groups, of debates on important matters of the day such as capital punishment, and of visits from luminaries of the political, cultural and intellectual worlds, nestle up against news of social and sporting events and of fund-raising activities. On 21 February 1957, Thurgood Marshall lectured on the contribution of political inactivity on desegregation to racial bigotry, while just a week later, a debate about the dangers of radioactive fall-out and of nuclear weapons was seamlessly followed by one of the regular Faculty Wives' Fashion Shows. Beyond the important phenomenon of the fashion shows, it goes without saying that Harvard was at this time a steadfastly male-dominated institution. Women had been admitted to the Law School for the first time in 1950,[79] but Hart's and Fuller's casual references to 'the Law Review boys' in letters quoted elsewhere in this paper suggest that women still had some way to go to achieve full membership in the School, notably in the minds of its professors. The *Harvard Law Record* on 22 June 1956 reported the birth of a child to a first-year student and his wife in the following terms: 'A possible infanticide was averted Sunday night when a son was born to FH Condon'. This Delphic statement was illuminated by a cartoon, by none other than Mrs Condon herself, with the caption, 'If my wife has a *** daughter, I'll drown her'.[80] (Notwithstanding the report, it seems unclear whether it was the child or the mother who was at risk.)

In terms of the curriculum, the quality of the discussion at Harvard makes the complacent contemporary world of legal education at Oxford seem, frankly, to belong to the Dark Ages. Regular efforts were being made both to give students further writing experience and to broaden the syllabus, often with an eye on what was happening at Yale, where Dean Eugene Rostow was widely regarded as an exemplary innovator in legal education. In a report from the *Harvard Law Record* on 22 March 1956, the curriculum changes at Yale are cited as moving towards greater integration of law and social studies in the light of the need for lawyers, in

[78] My account is drawn from a reading of issues of the *Harvard Law Record* and *Bulletin* for the middle years of the 1950s. See also Sutherland, n 36 above, ch 10 of which deals with the Erwin Griswold's period as Dean from 1946 (at 313–59).

[79] See Sutherland, n 36 above, at 319–20: as Sutherland notes, Harvard Law School had by this time been home for many years to one of the country's leading women scholars, Eleanor Glueck, and invited Soia Mentschikoff as visiting professor a couple of years before admitting women as students.

[80] *Harvard Law Record*, 22 June 1956, 4.

a new world order, to think how to improve the administration of justice and methods of economic control. There was a need for 'creative originality in scholarship', and for comparative and international law to help in analysis of policy problems. Just a year later, on 14 March 1957, Yale's law teaching methods were again under consideration in the *Record*, and were described as aiming to give 'broad-gauged, policy-oriented exposure to law, not as a self-contained verbal system, but as a social phenomenon in its full perspective of history, philosophy and social science'. At Harvard, this engendered a general drift towards a more empirical and wide-ranging syllabus, a move which Fuller supported, while he worried about the reductive approach to legal reasoning invited by too ready an embrace of social science approaches, and about the amoral instrumentalism which seemed to be a side-effect of the continuing reaction against formalism.[81]

Indeed, although his own research agenda would surely have counted as one of the more innovative in the Law School, Fuller was very far from being an enthusiastic supporter of all efforts to broaden the scholarly base towards the social sciences. In the early 1950s, Erwin Griswold appointed Fuller's former Duke colleague, David Cavers, architect and editor-in-chief of the intellectually innovative *Law and Contemporary Problems*, as Associate Dean with a portfolio for 'fostering, encouraging and developing research'.[82] Cavers set to work with enthusiasm, and presented in 1955 a wide-ranging, 82-page *Report to the Faculty Concerning Research Activities in the Harvard Law School and Some of the Problems They Present.* The Report argued, inter alia, that the Law School should be prepared to give financial support to empirical research projects designed to appeal to both legal scholars and law reformers. This case for an institutional research programme was, to put it mildly, not to Fuller's taste. Focusing on this one aspect of what was in fact a rather balanced analysis, he responded to Cavers' Report with a 10-page counterblast, entitled 'An Analysis of the Effects of Programmatic Research on the Pursuit of Truth and Academic Freedom'. Objecting in the strongest terms to what he dubbed 'projectitis', as tending to a 'decline of the American academic mind', Fuller drew on all of his rhetorical gifts (and, one might add, indulged his taste for hyperbole) to undermine the Report, weaving amid a welter of arguments a parable in which Faraday is diverted from the invention of electricity by being recruited to a government-sponsored 'Fuel Project'. His memo culminated in the following sweeping denunciation:

[81] See Leslie Green's Chapter 9 for an analysis of the merits of Fuller's position on this point.

[82] On Cavers' involvement in the foundation of this journal, the first faculty-edited law review in the United States, see John Henry Schlegel, 'David Cavers, Legal Research and Legal Education', Introduction to David F Cavers, *'To Throw Light on Matters Which will be of Aid in Securing to Humanity a Greater Degree of Justice': A History of the Alter E. Meyer Research Institute of Law* (Amherst, NY, Walter E Meyer Research Institute of Law, 1997) 1–22 at 3–5.

> We hear of wide-scale 'bootlegging' of science in Russia. This is not a phenomenon confined to totalitarian regimes. In this country, under the shadow of huge governmental grants for research, we have developed an extensive grey market for pure science. It is not entirely wide of the mark to say that the scientific spirit is being kept alive today only by a systematic misappropriation of funds.
>
> To some the hypocrisies involved in this situation are of no moment. I cannot view the matter in that light, for I believe that academic freedom and the question for truth itself are at stake. The only justification that can be given for academic freedom is that it is the best means of finding the truth. When the quest for truth sails under false colors, it forfeits its own moral integrity and loses its capacity to defend itself. Even if it were free from outside attack, the pursuit of truth must inevitably die in an atmosphere tainted by falsehood.[83]

The memo speaks volumes about Fuller's individualistic—even libertarian—attitudes, and gives strong proof of his own preference for the 'lone scholar' model of research. Yet, as Willard Hurst observed in a letter to Griswold three years later, while 'Lon Fuller raises important and pertinent questions and puts them well ... I can't get for myself a fully persuasive statement out of what he says, as to its meaning and application'.[84] Meanwhile, one assumes that the episode did not improve his relationship with Cavers.[85]

In fact, many of Fuller's commitments as a teacher were ones which he and Cavers shared. For example, Fuller described his second year Jurisprudence course as introducing students to the 'ends of government: In examining the premises underlying the legal system, the student should gain an overview of the system's aims and its relation to the whole life of man in society'.[86] Fuller also referred to his commitment to relating the course to the work of practising attorneys, by tackling 'problems of human organization that run through all of a lawyer's work', and not confining student's attention to appellate decisions, which in his view represented failures of planning and negotiated problem solving rather than the epitome of the legal form.[87] But this, he acknowledged, was a difficult task given the varying backgrounds of the students: 'As I see it, the whole of legal philosophy should be animated by the desire to seek out those principles by which men's relations in society may be rightly and justly ordered'. He ruefully reported scepticism on the part of some of his students, who were inclined to the view that 'the mores can make anything right and anything wrong'. There is, of

[83] Lon Fuller's response, 24 October 1955, at 10. I am very grateful to John Schlegel for providing me with the Cavers Report, Fuller's response, and associated correspondence. Fuller's correspondence with Cavers, and with Dean Griswold, is held at Harvard: The Papers of Lon Fuller, Harvard Law School Library, box 2, folder 4, and box 3, folder 9, respectively.

[84] Professor J Willard Hurst of the University of Wisconsin to Dean Griswold, 6 January 1958.

[85] For an interesting discussion of the episode, see Schlegel, n 82 above, at 10–16. Cavers stood down as Associate Dean in 1958, and became President of the Meyer Research Institute.

[86] These and the following quotations are from the *Harvard Law Record*, 28 March 1957.

[87] See Griswold, n 35 above, at 352.

course, a large clue here to Fuller's hostility to positivism:[88] already isolated amid social science oriented teachers who saw their task as overcoming students' moral dogmatism, Fuller realised that his own course, which was explicitly concerned with justice, went against the grain.

But Fuller himself was a contributor to the broadening of the syllabus even beyond his Jurisprudence course. For example, in the year of Hart's visit, he was teaching a seminar on the relationship between freedom and planning which pondered, among other things, the question of whether markets could exist under socialism.[89] In his views on the law curriculum we see clear evidence of what were perhaps Fuller's most enduring and innovative intellectual preoccupations: his interest in the institutional form (or, to be more precise, forms) through which social governance realises itself; his perception of the links between distinctive procedural forms and substantive outcomes; and his view of the dependence of law upon informal social practices.[90] This interest went back to the very earliest part of his career, and it is strongly reflected in later commentators' assessment of Fuller's contribution: indeed the title of Winston's edited collection of Fuller's essays, *The Principles of Social Order*, is drawn from a work which Fuller was planning at precisely the time of his debate with Hart, and in which he hoped to develop his ideas about both the inextricable links between institutional means and substantive ends and the importance of law as a form of 'social architecture'.[91]

[88] The depth of this hostility is vividly apparent in the following comment in a somewhat testy letter in response to Samuel Mermin's comments on 'Forms and Limits of Adjudication': 'The deep division in men's thinking that has been introduced by domagatic [*sic*] positivism is, I think the most calamitous event of the past century. I do not see any cure for it, so long as the positivists simply put everything said in criticisms of their view through the sieve of their own preconceptions': Fuller to Mermin, 30 November 1959, The Papers of Lon Fuller, Harvard Law School Library, box 14, folder 1.

[89] Though Fuller's political association with Nixon might suggest him to have been something of a 'cold warrior', in characteristically idiosyncratic style, he was equally an advocate of broad cultural and trade contacts with the USSR. In a discussion of the conditions which need to exist for a meaningful rule of law, he argued that it is crucial 'not merely to promote "good understanding" and an atmosphere of good will but to create a community of interest from which adjudication can draw intellectual sustenance': 'Forms and Limits of Adjudication', n 20 above, at 378.

[90] See Gerald J Postema, 'Implicit Law' in Witteveen and van der Burg, n 5 above, at 255–75: see in particular at 256 and 268: '[L]aw cannot hope to facilitate self-directed social interaction unless it remains substantially congruent with and integrated into ordinary social practices and conventions in the community it serves. Fuller's conclusion, then, is that enacted, pedigree-validated, authoritative norms ("made law") represent only the surface phenomena of law. Law has a social depth which we must recognize if we are to understand adequately the nature and modes of functioning of these salient surface phenomena' (*cf* Jeremy Waldron's thought-provoking interpretation of Fuller's position vis-à-vis legal pluralism in Chapter 7). Fuller's view of law's dependence on its social environment also appears to have been a focus of his course with David Smith (see n 55 above). It is interesting to speculate about whether this insight inhibited his willingness to raise social science questions in the debate with Hart: the stability of law in the Nazi era raises questions about the fit between the sociological and the natural law dimensions of Fuller's views.

[91] The book was never completed, but parts of it appear in Winston,n 5 above, as Winston explains (*ibid* 15; see also his Introduction, *ibid* 26–33, for a discussion of the procedural and problem-solving orientation (at 31) of Fuller's scholarship). See also Summers, n 2 above, chs 6–10; Witteveen and van der Burg, n 5 above, Part IV.

The broad range of Fuller's interests is strongly reflected in the surviving correspondence. Whereas the bulk of Hart's intellectual correspondence was with philosophers, Fuller also had an extensive correspondence with sociologists, psychologists and economists. In 1965, a sociologist from MIT wrote to him about *The Morality of Law*:

> as a sociologist interested in the 'empirical import' of ideas and especially concerned with problems of procedural due process, I found your analysis of legality immensely enlightening. It would easily lay the groundwork for significant comparative and historical research.[92]

In a comment which illuminates the close relationship between Fuller's theory and the phenomenological approach in sociology, he continued:

> As you probably know, many sociologists are philosophically Janus-faced and I might even say schizophrenic: they claim that in theory and research they are positivists, eschewing normative and teleological propositions and seeking to discover uniformities and mechanisms about social life; however, as purposive human beings in a world bursting with social problems, they, too, are concerned about the prevention of war and the elimination of tyranny, poverty, and injustice. Notwithstanding their positivist stance, the problems they choose to work on often betray a variety of value judgments ... From an 'empirical' and 'behavioral' point of view—if you will pardon these well worn terms—a social scientist can study a legal system both as a 'purposeful enterprise' and as a 'manifested fact of social power'. Further more, from a sociological standpoint, the concept of law can be stretched to include the internal systems of rules regulating the behavior of members of non-governmental organizations—what I speak of as 'private legal systems' in my essay in *Law and Sociology.*

In the light of this sociological position, one might wonder at Fuller's apparent lack of attraction to some form of synthesis with Hart's position: while Hart's 'external aspect' might capture the reality of 'law as a manifested fact of social power', the 'internal aspect might capture the reality of law as a 'purposeful enterprise'. But of course Fuller was committed to the idea that such 'purposiveness' was morally driven in quite a robust sense: his reputation as a natural lawyer is, after all, not undeserved, and both moral and structural/functional concerns pervaded his work throughout his career.[93] This sort of linkage is nicely illustrated by his correspondence with Erving Goffman. Fuller wrote to Goffman

[92] William M Evan to Fuller, 15 July 1965, The Papers of Lon Fuller, Harvard Law School Library, box 2, folder 16.

[93] *cf* Frederick Schauer, 'Fuller on the Ontological Status of Law' in Witteveen and van der Burg, n 5 above, at 124, 125: 'Because Fuller is simultaneously understood both as a proponent of (a version of) natural law and also as someone very interested in the seemingly nonnatural and pragmatic topic of institutional design, one possibility is that Fuller's interest in law was multifaceted, encompassing questions of high abstract theory as well as questions of "low" institutional design. But Fuller's own statements belie such an interpretation. Rather, he seems to have believed that there was some important unity of this thought about institutional design and his thought about the essential nature of law'.

Like Schauer, while entertaining doubts about whether this unity can be established, I think it is

trying to 'inveigle' him into reading 'three pieces of mine' (including 'Irrigation and Tyranny' and his draft paper posthumously published as the influential 'The Forms and Limits of Adjudication').[94] His letter makes it clear that he was drawn to Goffman's work on social roles and their attendant responsibilities, but was puzzled about how to apply them to the role of arbitration, to which he had given so much practical and academic attention over the last quarter century:

> Taking the 'morality' out of this discussion [in 'Irrigation and Tyranny'], the idea remains that the doing of a given social task may be made impossible, or awkward, by the unavailability of an apt role for its discharge. There are suggestions of this idea in the literature, especially in anthropology, but I know of no full-blown, explicit discussion of it ... The problem I am concerned with is this: Sociological studies of role tend to assume that the responsibilities that go with a role are imposed on the performer from outside himself; 'social norms' tell him what he should do or not do. Now this conception fits very badly the role of the arbitrator as it appears to him. He does not consult social norms, for there really are none. He must take account of the expectations of those who submit their cases to him ... In short, he has to find his own way: he must analyze the implications of his job and carve the job out so that his performance of it will not cause injury and confusion. This idea, I must confess, I find nowhere even hinted at in the literature of sociology.

Unless Fuller is talking specifically about arbitration, this is a strange comment given the preoccupation of much sociology with the issue of how roles are infused with values. But Fuller wanted to reach beyond an acknowledgment of the normative orientation of much human interaction to a more objective position in ethics.[95] And further light is shed on his comment by the concluding part of his letter. Going on to register his bewilderment that the moral aspects of such roles do not register in the sociological debate, he wonders:

> Can this be because of a moral dread of talking or thinking about issues that may be called 'moral'? But there seems no taboo against a supposition that moral standards are imposed on the role-occupant by something called 'society' which forms those standards by procedures not only not examined, but not even hinted at. Would not a more realistic appraisal seek to understand the job, and its 'moral' demands, as it looks to the

impossible to assess Fuller's arguments without understanding his belief in it. This distinctive mixture of concern with morality and institutional design pervades the whole of Fuller's career; his focus on morality was not displaced by a growing concern with institutional design: rather, the two concerns went hand in hand. I should note here that I have deliberately chosen to avoid using the word with which Fuller indicated this aspect of his enterprise ('eunomics') on the basis that such currency as the term had at the time Fuller was writing has since evaporated, and that my interpretation can readily be cast in more generally used language. See also n 56 above.

[94] See n 20 above.

[95] For other, more fully synthesised attempts to bring natural law and sociology into closer relation, see Philip Selznick (with whom Fuller had a substantial correspondence: The Papers of Lon Fuller, Harvard Law School Library, box 7, folder 6) 'Sociology and Natural Law' (1961) 6 *Natural Law Forum* 84; and Webber, n 9 above. Selznick's paper makes brief but approving reference to Fuller's conception of law's inner morality (at 98).

man who has to perform it and who has to draw his guidance from his own insight, powers of analysis and sense of responsibility?[96]

While Fuller's interest in the role of extra-legal as well as legal norms on legal decision-making motivated the exchange with Goffman, his deep preoccupation with the structural distinctiveness of different decision-making processes brought with it an interest in the emerging field of public choice and game theory. This is evident from an interesting correspondence with the (later) Nobel Prize-winning economist James Buchanan and his colleague Gordon Tullock in 1964, a correspondence which gives a sense of the breadth of Fuller's interests. In this exchange, Fuller's bewilderment and even anger at the absence of what he saw as an appropriate moral dimension to the social sciences, so clearly echoed in the exchange with Goffman, drops entirely out of the picture, in favour of an agenda squarely within the four corners of what we might call positive social science:

Dear Professor Buchanan

I have been reading with great pleasure and profit *The Calculus of Consent.* I had previously read the works of Arrow, Downes and Black and was therefore generally familiar with the approach underlying your book. But you and Tullock have developed it greatly …

For some years now I have myself been working on a problem that is a close cousin to those which are discussed in *The Calculus.* I have an unpublished and rather unsatisfactory article entitled, *The Forms and Limits of Adjudication.* What I am trying to do in that article is to analyse the kinds of problems that are fit material for solution by adjudicative forms. Just as economists have examined what can and what cannot be done through free contract and open markets, and 'fence-row cultivators' have analysed what can and cannot be done through elections, as a lawyer I have raised the same sort of question about adjudication. This question goes beyond the ordinary limits of domestic law and extends to labor and commercial arbitration, to international tribunals and—above all—to administrative tribunals and agencies. So far as I know I am the only scholar who has attempted to tackle the problem in this broad form.

I am not clear whether matrices such as those used in game theory would be useful in dealing with this sort of problem. I hope soon to have a talk with Tom Schelling about it … Incidentally, I have a book coming out in the fall entitled *The Morality of Law* which, in its final chapter, deals at some length with problems of institutional design in the law.[97]

[96] Fuller to Erving Goffman, 26 October 26 1966, The Papers of Lon Fuller, Harvard Law School Library, box 3, folder 12.

[97] Fuller to James M Buchanan, 8 January 1964, The Papers of Lon Fuller, Harvard Law School Library, box 2, folder 2. Fuller's engagement with game theory represented by this correspondence with Buchanan and Tullock is expressed, in the successive drafts of 'Forms and Limits of Adjudication', n 20 above, by references to Kenneth Arrow's *Social Choice and Individual Values* (London, Chapman Hall, 1951) (in the 1957 draft) and then to RB Braithwaite's *Theory of Games as a Tool for the Moral Philosopher* (Cambridge, Cambridge University Press, 1955) (in the 1959 and 1961 drafts). These changing points of reference resulted, however, in no substantial development of his argument.

Buchanan replied promptly:

> Dear Professor Fuller …
>
> I enjoyed reading the noted parts of your paper on collective bargaining. And I can appreciate the relationship between your analysis and our own. Let me indicate my interpretation of this relationship. You are trying to examine, and ultimately, to array the various tasks that are suitable for processes of adjudication. We are trying examine and to array the tasks that might be suitable for either voluntary market adjustment or collective action, by which we really mean voting. Look first at the simple yes-no or either-or issue. Here adjudication can work, as you say, and so can ordinary majority rule. But no mutual adjustment, or interaction process can. Now let us change the model slightly so that we can include two, not one, either-or issue. [*sic*] Here some possible mutual interaction can enter into the analysis, to the extent that intensities differ. Adjudication can still work reasonably well, but some mutual adjustment may be more efficient. Then, as we increase the number of separate issues … we approach more and more to the clear conclusion that some form of mutual interaction, be this log-rolling through political process, or a form of market, is more efficient than adjudication by third parties who cannot 'read' intensities of preference.
>
> Tullock and I … want to work out, if possible, the formal conditions for 'optimality' or 'efficiency' that are possible when a group must simultaneously deal with n [multiple] issues, not a simple issue as most political analysis assumes. Note that this is really our version of what you, after Polanyi, call polycentric tasks.[98]

As the letter to Goffman shows (and for reasons which I have neither the biographical nor the historical information to unearth), Fuller's concern to find not merely a practical or functional but also a moral logic to decision-making processes was something which ran very, very deep with him: the analytic separation which Hart found so convincing had no appeal to him whatsoever. But how was this moral concern to be reconciled with his interest in institutional forms and their suitability to the resolution of problems of a particular structure which underpins his exchange with Buchanan? That this was a persistent concern for Fuller is reflected in Winston's judgement that his 'principal concern is … the discovery of natural laws of social order, that is, the compulsions and opportunities necessarily contained in particular domains of objective social reality, in certain ways of organising men's relations with one another'.[99] But when Fuller thought in terms of institutional design, his concern was not merely with optimality in Buchanan's and Tullock's sense: rather, like Ronald Dworkin, he thought of particular institutions and processes as having 'integrity' in the sense not only of a distinctive logic which lent itself to the efficient resolution of certain kinds of problems, but also of its serving certain kinds of values: reciprocity, fairness, 'avoiding injury and confusion', and so on. In the grip of a powerful impulse to synthesise his passionate moral concerns and his interest in and grasp

[98] Buchanan to Fuller, 13 January 1964, The Papers of Lon Fuller, Harvard Law School Library, box 2, folder 2.

[99] Winston, n 5 above, at 12.

of the dynamics of institutions, he was drawn to craft a natural law theory out of the unlikely material of certain formal precepts governing legal processes.

The Anatomy of the Debate: Physiology on the Dissecting Table?

Joel Feinberg described Fuller's demeanour at the Holmes lecture which opened 'the debate' as that of a 'hungry lion': a stance which is more than explained by the sense of incomprehension which Fuller felt from his anti-formalist, sociological colleagues and, perhaps yet more woundingly, from Hart: a man who asserted the genuine normativity of law, yet nonetheless derided the natural law position. Hungry lions, however, are perhaps not best placed to make wise strategic decisions about the timing and object of their hunt for food. And my suggestion in this section is that, in selecting Hart as his prey, by demanding a right to reply to the Holmes Lecture, and by using it as a platform from which to proclaim a natural law position, Fuller was risking an encounter in which his credentials as a legal philosopher were bound to be the primary focus, and in which he found little opportunity to draw on his broader expertise and interests. Indeed, even had he fully exploited such opportunity as the debate presented, the incompletely synthesised quality of his varied interests prompted him to take up a position in which his moralised conception of law was presented in terms of formal precepts rather than in a substantive analysis of the values implicit in the legal processes and institutions which he had begun rather effectively to explore in his papers on adjudication and arbitration.[100]

Let us first refresh our memory of the contours of the debate as it took place. Hart used the lecture to map out his distinctive vision of legal positivism. In particular, he defended analytical jurisprudence in the positivist tradition deriving from Bentham and Austin against the charges laid by the two groups of legal theorists whom he saw as its main antagonists at Harvard. He rejected the charge, current in much American Realist jurisprudence, that legal positivism provides a mechanistic and formalistic vision of legal reasoning, with judges simply grinding out deductive conclusions from closed sets of premises. And, as against the claim of modern natural lawyers—notably Fuller—he defended the positivist insistence on the lack of any necessary, conceptual connection between law and morality, and denied that this betrayed an indifference to the moral status of laws. Indeed, he claimed that there are moral advantages to making a clear separation between our understanding of how to determine what the law is and our criticisms or vision of what it ought to be.

[100] Notably 'The Forms and Limits of Adjudication', 'Adjudication and the Rule of Law', and 'Collective Bargaining and the Arbitrator', n 20 above.

This underlying disagreement with Fuller was thrown into relief, given poignancy and made immediately accessible by the fact that it took place in the shadow of widespread discussion of the legitimacy of the Nuremberg Trials, and centred on a vivid example. This was the case of the 'grudge informer': a woman who, during the Third Reich, had relied on prevailing legal regulations to denounce her husband as a political dissident. After the war, the woman was charged with a criminal offence against her husband. The question, as Hart presented it, was whether her legal position should be governed by the law prevailing during the Third Reich, a law now regarded as deeply unjust; or by the just law prevailing before and after the Nazi regime.[101] In short, the case raised in direct and striking form the question whether law's validity is dependent on its credentials as just or otherwise morally acceptable. Hart defended the view that since the woman had committed no crime under the positive law of the time, the only legally valid way of criminalising her would be by passing a piece of retrospective legislation. Although this was, on the face of it, an unjust solution, it might nonetheless be the morally preferable thing to do: the lesser of two evils. And this solution had the advantage that it avoided blurring the distinction between 'what the law is' and 'what the law ought to be'.[102]

Perhaps awkwardly for Fuller's argument that the positivist position sidelined crucially important moral issues, at the foundation of Hart's argument lay not so much an analytic as a substantive moral claim. It is, according to him, morally preferable, more honest, to look clearly at the variety of reasons bearing on an ethically problematic decision rather than to close off debate by dismissing certain considerations as irrelevant: arguing that something never was the law because it ought not to have been the law. There is a liberal aspect to this argument: it is up to citizens to evaluate the law, and not merely to take it that the state's announcing something as law implies that it ought to be obeyed. But there is equally a utilitarian strand to Hart's position: an implication that things will

[101] As HO Pappe argued in an early commentary on the debate ('On the Validity of the Judicial Decisions in the Nazi Era' (1960) 23 *Modern Law Review* 260) and as David Dyzenhaus has more recently confirmed ('The Grudge Informer Case Revisited', n 12 above), Hart's was in fact a simplistic reading of the legal issues in the case.

[102] It is worth noting that Fuller's position, as much as Hart's, necessitated in practical terms an (arguably retrospective) judicial decision: on this point, as well as in relation to the fact that Fuller's inner morality of law was presented as only one aspect of law's morality, as Kenneth Winston has suggested to me (personal correspondence, 28 October 2008), Hart and Fuller were not so far apart as the structure of the debate would imply. It is also worth noting in this context that Fuller's views about law's capacity to foster social order absent any deeper political, economic or cultural 'community of interest' were, like Hart's, modest: in a memorable passage in 'The Forms and Limits of Adjudication', attention to which might usefully have informed recent British and American foreign policy, he wrote: 'Uncritical proponents of extending the rule of law propose to build community on law. It cannot be done' (n 20 above, at 374); *cf* Martin Krygier, 'The Rule of Law: Legality, Teleology, Sociology' in Gianluigi Palombella and Neil Walker (eds), *Re-locating the Rule of Law* (Oxford, Hart Publishing, 2008). Several chapters in the present collection, notably those by Hilary Charlesworth, Chapter 2, Margaret Davies, Chapter 8, Desmond Manderson, Chapter 11 and Ngaire Naffine, Chapter 12, also note significant continuities between the approaches of Hart and Fuller.

turn out better, in terms of resistance to tyranny, if citizens understand that there are always two separate questions to be confronted: First, is this a valid rule of law? Secondly, should it be obeyed? Predictably, no evidence was adduced in support of the second, empirical aspect to his argument. But it had a piquancy. This was not only because it gave the lecture a moral dimension but because a famous German jurist, Gustav Radbruch, was characterised by both Hart and Fuller as having argued that the experience of the Third Reich should turn us all into natural lawyers.[103] And although this interpretation of Radbruch's 'conversion' has been persuasively questioned by at least one influential commentator,[104] there was certainly some warrant for Hart's and Fuller's view. For Radbruch had explicitly associated the positivist position with the unquestioningly compliant 'might is right' attitude widely believed to have assisted the Nazis in their rise to power:

> We must hope that the denial of the fundamentals of law and justice that occurred under Hitler will remain an isolated and not-to-be-repeated aberration of the German people in a state of temporary derangement. Yet to be prepared for every eventuality we must arm ourselves against the return of such a state of affairs. To do this we must thoroughly overcome the positivistic legal philosophy that rendered impotent every possible defense against the abuses of the National Socialist legislation.[105]

One can hardly imagine an intellectual morsel more tempting to a hungry natural law lion. Fuller, duly picking up Radbruch's claim, and coming out strongly in his defence, argued that the Nazi law under which the woman had acted was so evil that it could not even count as a valid law. In his view, law—the process of subjecting human conduct to the governance of rules—was informed by an 'inner morality'. Unlike the theological traditions, Fuller's was not a dogmatic, substantive natural law position: rather, it was a position which built out from certain valued procedural tenets widely associated with the rule of law. These included the requirements that laws be coherent, prospective rather than retrospective, public, possible to comply with, reasonably certain in their content

[103] Hart, 'Positivism and the Separation of Law and Morals',n 4 above, at 616; Lon L Fuller, 'American Legal Philosophy at Mid-Century' (1954) 6 *Journal of Legal Education* 457, 481–3 and 'Positivism and Fidelity to Law: A Reply to Professor Hart', n 4 above, at 632–3, 646, 648–61.

[104] See Stanley L Paulson, 'Radbruch on Unjust Laws: Competing Earlier and Later Views?' (1995) 15 *Oxford Journal of Legal Studies* 489. While acknowledging that 'in Germany and abroad, Radbruch became known as the leading force in what proved to be a short-lived renaissance of natural law thinking in post-War Germany' (at 489), Paulson argues that 'Radbruch's concept of law remained unchanged in his earlier and later views, and he imposed stringent restrictions on the scope of application of the post-War formulae' (at 493); 'Radbruch's later emphasis on justice over legal certainty in cases of truly extreme conflict between statute and justice is best seen as the correction of a mistake in his earlier work—the mistaken idea, stemming from the disproportionate weight assigned to legal certainty, that the judge had to apply the statute, come what may' (at 500). On the interpretation of Radbruch, see also Pappe, n 101 above; Paulson, n 9 above.

[105] Gustav Radbruch, *Gesetzliches Unrecht und Übergesetzliches Recht* (Berliner Wissenschafts-Verlag, 1946), reprinted in *Rechtsphilosophie* 4th edn (1950) 347, 352–5, quoted in Fuller, 'American Legal Philosophy at Mid-Century', n 103 above, at 485.

and general in their application. It was this universal 'inner morality of law' which provided the necessary connection between law and morality, and not the 'external' or substantive morality which infused the content of law in different ways in different systems. The 'inner morality' guaranteed a law worthy of 'fidelity', underpinned the existence of an obligation to obey the law, and marked the distinction between law, which addresses its subjects as responsible moral agents,[106] and arbitrary power, which does not. And, Fuller claimed, Hart's own position could not consistently deny some such connection between law and morality. For in his argument about the open texture of language, Hart claimed that judges deal with 'penumbral' cases by reference to a 'core' of settled meaning. This, Fuller argued, suggested that legal interpretation in clear cases amounted to little more than a cataloguing procedure. Yet even in a very simple case such as a rule providing that 'no vehicles shall be allowed in the park', the idea that judges can appeal to a 'core' meaning of the single word, 'vehicle', was problematic. In deciding whether a tricycle or an army tank put in the park as a war memorial breached the rule, the core meaning of 'vehicle' in ordinary language would be next to useless in judicial interpretation: rather, judges would look to the purpose of the statute as a whole. Anticipating in important respects the work of Ronald Dworkin, Fuller argued that these questions of purpose and structure would inevitably introduce contextual and evaluative criteria in the identification of the 'core'.[107] But Hart of course, in the debate and beyond it, took strong objection to Fuller's central assertion: namely that law, understood as the process of subjecting human conduct to the governance of rules, was invariably informed by moral purposes.[108]

On the specific point about adjudication, and about the illusory quality of the 'core meaning' of legal terms, on which he is widely viewed as having scored some significant points over Hart, Fuller was on Hart's weakest, and his own strongest, ground: the elaboration of theoretical conceptions of law which take seriously its distinctive institutional form and processes. The main preoccupation of positivist analysis is to provide an 'anatomy of law';[109] ie to explain, as Joseph Raz put it in his first book, how to identify the 'momentary legal system'[110]—all the norms valid in one system at any one point in time. By contrast, Fuller's own concern in his broader scholarship was with the living 'physiology of law'—with the institutional processes through which human conduct is subject to legal governance. Hart's lack of interest in law's institutional form (an interest which, significantly,

[106] I draw this aspect of Fuller's claim, which again reveals an important continuity between his and Hart's political visions, from Kenneth Winston's 'The Internal Morality of Chinese Legalism' (2005) *Singapore Journal of Legal Studies* 1, 9.

[107] On Dworkin's debt to Fuller, see Summers, n 2 above, at 14.

[108] Or indeed by any purposes beyond the very thin conception of social survival or order, sketched in his later elaboration of the 'minimum content of natural law': *The Concept of Law*, n 17 above, ch IX.

[109] As Summers puts it in *Lon L. Fuller*, n 2 above, at 31; see also text at n 34 above.

[110] Joseph Raz, *The Concept of a Legal System* (Oxford, Clarendon Press, 1970).

finds some expression in the working notebook for *The Concept of Law*, but which has more or less disappeared in the book itself)[111] made it extremely difficult to defend himself against Fuller's attack, or indeed against Ronald Dworkin's later account of adjudication.[112] In the absence of any sophisticated account of the judicial role, it was difficult for Hart to carve out a path between a formalist vision, on the one hand, and a vision of broad discretion implying, in effect, judicial legislation, on the other.

As we have seen, Fuller, by contrast, had a long-standing and deep-rooted interest in adjudication as an institutional form: adjudication lent itself readily to the resolution of certain kinds of issues, while those embedded in practices characterised by 'heavy and complex interdependence'[113] (marriage, corporations, public housing) lent themselves rather to resolution through mediation. The nature of this interest, best reflected in his posthumously published article 'The Forms and Limits of Adjudication',[114] is nicely illustrated by his correspondence with Buchanan and Tullock referred to in the last section. But a paper articulating a natural law critique of positivism was not a good vehicle for showcasing these broader aspects of Fuller's ideas: his subtle and differentiated vision of forms of legal institution, and his sense that institutional design, in law as elsewhere, made a difference to outcome; that certain forms of institutional process lent themselves to the effective resolution of particular sorts of issue. Moreover his 'procedural' version of natural law took the form not of an institutionally elaborated conception of law such as that which might have been drawn out of papers such as 'The Forms and Limits of Adjudication',[115] but rather of a number of formal precepts articulated at a level of abstraction similar to that of Hart's own mode of argument.[116]

Of course, Fuller was not alone among contemporaries in seeing law and legal interpretation as informed by substantive purposes: the 'process school' represented by his colleagues Henry Hart and Albert Sacks also accepted this proposition. But Fuller went one important step further than his process school colleagues in arguing that there was particular reason to think that, when certain procedural forms were respected, those purposes would be morally attractive ones—a claim whose status, like several of Hart's own claims, is ambiguous as between analytic truth and empirical generalisation. Fuller's position was therefore vulnerable to the philosophical objection that while the inevitably purposive aspect of law may imply a certain analytic link between means and ends, between

[111] See Lacey, n 3 above, ch 9.

[112] Ronald Dworkin, *Taking Rights Seriously* (London: Duckworth, 1977).

[113] See Winston, n 5 below, at 125.

[114] See n 20 above; nn 20, 52–3 and 97 above give details of the decades-long genesis of this article.

[115] See n 20 above.

[116] On the sense in which Fuller's natural law conception is formal rather than procedural, and on the significance of the difference, see Jeremy Waldron, 'All We Like Sheep' (1999) 12 *Canadian Journal of Law and Jurisprudence* 169, 181–5; and 'Positivism and Legality: Hart's Equivocal Response to Fuller', n 12 above, at 1145 and 1169 fn 35.

is and ought, this link is not necessarily a moral one; and to the empirical objection that he was making a gross and unsubstantiated generalisation about social and political realities. But as we have seen, Fuller was determined to bring his moral and his procedural concerns together: for him, the (absolutely persuasive) insights that form was inseparable from substance (in the sense that form helped to shape outcomes) and that procedural forms are often shaped by values, therefore became, in the context of the debate, the (logically dubious) proposition that, analytically, means and ends, is and ought, are inseparable. This further led him into doubtful empirical claims. For example, the persuasive insight that certain forms may conduce (under certain circumstances) to the realisation of certain values, or that failure to respect certain procedural forms entails distinctive moral wrongs, was overstated as a claim about the likelihood of certain procedures ensuring morally good outcomes at least over time: the claim that conformity with the procedural tenets of the 'inner morality of law' would tend to 'work the law pure' in a substantive sense. Fuller's interest in institutions, along with his interest in economic and social theory and in anthropology, gave him a keen sense of the way in which institutional forms enhanced certain kinds of governance; a sense which finds only crude expression in the debate, in the form of the contrast between law and managerial direction. But beyond that point, this textured account of distinctive legal procedures surfaces little in the debate. And while one can sympathise with Fuller's view of the importance of the evaluative commitments of actors within institutions, to reduce this to a conceptual proposition about the inextricability of is and ought was both to undersell his own arguments and to invite (as he had already discovered in 1941) philosophical contempt.

It is interesting to compare Fuller's formulation of the 'form/morality' nexus in the debate with Hart with his more institutionally elaborated statement of it in 'Irrigation and Tyranny'[117] seven years later. Addressing himself to 'certain fundamental problems of method and of theory that are shared by law, sociology, economics, political science, and social psychology',[118] and in the context of an argument which questions a supposed link between irrigation and tyranny, Fuller raises the question of whether the existence of certain procedural forms would make a difference to the chances of the power inherent in systems of irrigation being abused. For example, where governments levied an irrigation tax which took the form of a share of farmers' crops, this arrangement 'would seem to create an overlapping of interest between the government and the farmer that might put some brake on tyrannical abuses'.[119] Fuller further argued that values like reciprocity, embodied in established procedures, could act as constraints on power: '"informal" or "real" power is subject to intrinsic limitations even in its most direct and brutal manifestations ... the holder of power will find himself

[117] See n 28 above.
[118] *Ibid* 1021.
[119] *Ibid* 1025.

hedged in by a network of reciprocities that trace the limits of his control'.[120] So far, even an economist would find little to object to in the argument. But of course, Fuller wanted to push the argument further; and in a trenchant sideswipe at 'converging streams of ethical philosophy'[121] ranging from Kant through utilitarianism to emotivism and non-cognitivism in ethics, he proclaims the idea of an 'institutional or procedural morality' and enjoins philosophers to enrich their abstractions with the 'simple picture of human beings confronting one another in some social context, adjusting their relations reciprocally, negotiating, voting, arguing before some arbiter, and perhaps even reluctantly deciding to toss for it'. Yet this, it must be admitted, was an enrichment which was missing as much from his own as from Hart's contribution to the debate. His conclusion that:

> The development of moral insight through participation in institutional procedures is nowhere more clearly revealed than in the negotiation of complex agreements, such as those involved in treaties or collective bargaining contracts. The good negotiator in such a case must not only make a genuine effort to understand the declared aims of the opposing party, but must be capable of some sympathetic participation in those aims[122]

is more controversial, particularly if we understand it (as it is clear Fuller means us to do) as a conceptual as well as an empirical claim. But even this falls well short of the generalised propositions about the nature of law which underpin his reply to Hart.

Perhaps more puzzling is Fuller's failure to drive home the advantage that his sophisticated view of law's institutionalised forms might have been expected to give him on the jurisprudential question of what distinguishes law from other systems of social rules such as those of a club, a sport or an organised religion. While Hart attempted in *The Concept of Law* to delineate some basic differences between law and morality as systems of rules, his account of law's distinctiveness from other systems of social rules depends (leaving aside the distinction between primary and secondary rules, which applies just as readily to other such systems) on the distinctiveness of legal sources encapsulated in the 'rule of recognition'. Indeed it is hard to see how he could have gone much further than this, given his lack of interest in law's institutional form. As d'Entrèves put it, pondering the relationship between effectiveness, validity and existence, Hart's article was far from clear on 'What, in other words, is the ultimate distinguishing feature that makes a law a "law"'.[123] Fuller, surely, could have provided a far richer account of

[120] *Ibid* 1028.
[121] This and the following quotation, *ibid*1033.
[122] *Ibid* 1033–4.
[123] D'Entrèves continued (n 76 above): 'For my part, I must confess that, *pace* Kelsen, I have never been able to understand how a law can be "valid" unless it is effective, nor how it can be "effective" unless it is accepted'. This in d'Entrèves' view linked with another topic which might be seen as the core issue of natural law theory, and on which both Finnis and Dworkin were to cause Hart considerable unease in later years, yet which the debate skirted around: that of the grounds on which laws are accepted as valid, and become effective. In d'Entrèves' account, we see a genre of broad

law's distinctiveness. And even if the terms of engagement with Hart precluded such a positive elaboration, he might have made more of the weakness of Hart's own position and of the way in which it precluded him from developing a more satisfactory account. But in sticking closely to the terrain as Hart had delimited it in the Holmes lecture (and, perhaps, in the grip of his own uncertainties about how to synthesise his philosophical and his social-scientific interests), Fuller ensured that this important issue, which particularly lends itself to the techniques of sociological jurisprudence, more or less dropped out of view in the debate.

In short: whatever the merits of his argument, Fuller's attempt to build a natural law theory out of his long-standing interest in, and grasp of, the shaping power of processes (articulated, as it was, in terms of a set of formal precepts) was doomed, in the tradition of analytical jurisprudence, neither to satisfy more substantive natural lawyers nor to appease legal positivists. His own sense of the likely impact of the debate on his reputation is poignantly summed up in a letter to Boris Bittker of Yale in 1960:

> In my debate with H.L.A Hart I don't think I presented any conclusion as a deduction from natural law premises, yet nine readers out of ten seem to read that exchange as if I were apologizing for natural law throughout. The result is that I am widely credited by intelligent readers with espousing a doctrine I never proposed, namely, that a law that is evil enough in its intention is not really law at all …

historical speculation which neither Fuller nor Hart was prepared to hazard: 'It is this point about the "ground of obligation" of the law which I would seize upon also in discussing the burning issue of the German predicament … The real cause of the distortion of the "positivistic philosophy" in Germany seems to have escaped you. In my view it was not positivism as such and the slogan "law is law" that caused all the trouble. Positivism prevailed in Italy too, and yet it would be absurd to make it responsible for Fascism. I can remember more than one case when "fidelity to law" proved to be an efficient safeguard of "human freedom and dignity" in this country [i.e. Italy]. What the Germans did was to see a particular "value" expressed in that slogan, taking it as an adequate, a sufficient, and indeed a metaphysical ground of obligation of law itself: it was as the emanation of "the state" that positive law became to them something sacred. It may well be that behind such developments lay deep "ideological" predispositions: Hegelianism seems to be endemic in Germany as Machiavellism is in Italy. Yet such "theories of power" have worked in opposite directions in the two countries. Machiavelli has led the Italians to a pessimistic, indeed to a cynical attitude towards the State and politics. Hegel has taught the Germans to rever [*sic*] power as such and to see in the State the highest ethical value. The question, then, as it seems to me, is not one of one kind of "positivism" against another … It is a question, rather, of the choice between one ground of obligation and another, between the values that make law a "good" law thereby ensuring its "acceptance" … Perhaps, from a strictly legal point of view, you and Hart are right in feeling uneasy with the medicine adopted, the recourse to a "higher law" to declare Nazi laws null and void, and actually to assert (retrospectively) that they ought never to have been accepted as valid. Yet, as a historian, I think I can see some justification in this kind of solemn act of atonement. At any rate, you will forgive me for saying that this seems to me to have been a better course than the one which you and Hart would have preferred, the recourse to some form of retroactive legislation. This I believe would have been a truly "unethical" remedy, for it would have struck at the root of one of the most fundamental principles not only of the *Rechtsstaat* alone, but of all modern "free" and "liberal" society, the principle *nulla poena sine lege.* Why did you indulge in this after-thought after having so clearly indicated the correct solution on p.660, first paragraph?'; Alexander d'Entrèves to Fuller, 8 April 1958, The Papers of Lon Fuller, Harvard Law School Library, box 2, folder 13.

> I genuinely do not have the philosophic insight to know just how to reproduce my own convictions properly, and if I did, I would not know what language to use to convey those convictions undistorted to my readers.[124]

The End of the Affair

As the dust of the debate settled, the relationship between Hart and Fuller improved, thanks in part to the activities of the student editors of the *Harvard Law Review*.[125] In the context of this more friendly atmosphere, Fuller took Hart's robustly critical review of Fuller's *The Morality of Law*[126] (more or less) on the chin:

> I was delighted to see so sharp a joinder of issue ... All I can say of Miss Purpose is that the Old Girl still looks good to me. One of her enduring charms is that she is a very complex creature indeed, subject to unpredictable moods of surrender and withdrawal. I believe deeply in her without pretending that I really understand her. So the high romance of which you complain will probably continue despite your thoughtful warning that our liaison promises trouble.[127]

From now on, the two men's correspondence settled into a friendly, co-operative and often jocular pattern, a transition assisted not only by Fuller's helpful intervention with the *Law Review* but, perhaps, by their shared sense of bewilderment at the rapidly developing critique which both were experiencing at the hands of Ronald Dworkin. Fuller, for example, wrote to Hart about the symposium which had caused so much trouble between him, Cohen and Dworkin:[128]

> I thought you might be interested in this symposium on my book. As you will see, Dworkin takes a new tack—vague and self-contradictory laws can do no harm because they are not laws at all. The absurdity of this view—*reached abstractly and outside any institutional context*—suggests to my prejudiced mind doubts about the whole attack on my conception of legal morality.[129]

They exchanged views about this and about plans for the wider dissemination of jurisprudential ideas in forms accessible to students;[130] they quizzed each other

[124] Fuller to Boris I Bittker, 4 April 1960, The Papers of Lon Fuller, Harvard Law School Library, box 14, folder 1.

[125] About which there are a number of amusing blogs on the internet: see, eg volokh.com/posts/1155511746.shtml

[126] 'Book Review of *The Morality of Law*' (1965) 78 *Harvard Law Review* 1281.

[127] Fuller to Hart, 3 February 1965, The Papers of Lon Fuller, Harvard Law School Library, box 3, folder 14.

[128] Published in the *Villanova Law Review*: see references at n 9 above.

[129] Fuller to Hart, 18 October 1965, The Papers of Lon Fuller, Harvard Law School Library, box 3, folder 14; the emphasis is mine, and is designed to draw attention to the fact that Fuller's way of approaching questions of legal theory, unlike either Hart's or Dworkin's, was contextual rather than abstract.

[130] See, eg Fuller to Hart, 27 April 1964; Hart to Fuller, 5 May 1964, The Papers of Lon Fuller, Harvard Law School Library, each from box 3, folder 14.

for references (tellingly, Hart seeks Fuller's help in tracing a quotation from Nietzsche, while Fuller seeks Hart's for one from Bentham).[131] Fuller could never resist the odd dig at Hart:

> In the current issue of the *Journal of Legal Education* there is a review by a man who has studied under both of us. At this distance in time it is a little hard for me to estimate how much damage my course did to him, but the review seems to me to reveal the truly devastating effects on a mediocre mind of too much exposure to ordinary-language philosophy.[132]

But the tone remained fundamentally friendly. The surviving correspondence peters out in 1971, not long before Fuller's retirement, during which his hitherto robust epistolary output was diminished by his rapidly declining health. There is a tinge of nostalgia in Fuller's side of this last exchange:

> Are you by any chance going to the World Congress on Legal and Social Philosophy (grandiose title!) [in Brussels] ... I hope so, for I would most enjoy another get-together with you.
>
> Sincerely,
>
> Lon Fuller[133]
>
> No, I'll not be in Brussels in September—but almost certainly at a conference in S. Francisco about that time. Some sociological-cum-philosophical concern with criteria of responsibility. If you pass through Oxford and/or London in summer do let me know. I'd love a talk.
>
> Best wishes, Yours,
>
> Herbert Hart[134]

So ends the story of their relationship. Their work, of course, continues to shape contemporary jurisprudence to a quite remarkable degree. But the philosophical paradigm which Hart made so influential dominates the jurisprudential field; while the broader interests which Fuller enjoyed have yet to find an equally central place on the agenda of legal theory.[135] Perhaps we should attribute this to his reputation having become so inseparably intertwined with the debate with Hart. Or perhaps we should attribute it to his failure to put his procedural work into the form of a fully synthesised monograph or series of articles in his lifetime.

[131] Hart to Fuller, 6 February 1965; Fuller to Hart, 17 February 1971, The Papers of Lon Fuller, Harvard Law School Library, each from box 3, folder 14.

[132] Fuller to Hart, 18 October 1965, The Papers of Lon Fuller, Harvard Law School Library, box 3, folder 14.

[133] Fuller to Hart, 17 February 1971, The Papers of Lon Fuller, Harvard Law School Library, box 3, folder 14.

[134] Hart to Fuller, 23 March 1971, The Papers of Lon Fuller, Harvard Law School Library, box 3, folder 14.

[135] Fuller's contracts scholarship, and to some extent his work on legal processes, have on the other hand had a significant impact, particularly on American legal scholarship. This broader legacy is strongly reflected in the most recent collection reappraising his work: see Witteveen and van der Burg, n 5 above; see also nn 48–9 above).

William Twining once summed up Hart's career as that of 'a luminous mind with a narrow agenda'.[136] It would be unfair to Fuller to suggest that the opposite applies to him; but it would perhaps not be far off the mark to suggest that his was an imaginative mind whose published output was significantly, and not entirely positively, affected by the occasionally unmanageable ambition of his agenda. While trusting that the extraordinarily prosperous fortunes of his debate with Hart will continue, I venture to hope that Fuller's vision of a theorised legal scholarship which engages in a serious way with law's institutional forms, and which draws on the insights of other disciplines in doing so, will experience the greater prosperity which it merits in years to come.

[136] Lacey, n 3 above, at 361.

2

Human Rights and the Rule of Law After Conflict

HILARY CHARLESWORTH*

Introduction

The 1958 Hart–Fuller debate concerned the conceptual relationship between moral standards and law. Hart's positivism operated to keep the concept of law (largely) distinct from morality; while for Fuller the rule of law had an inextricably moral dimension.[1] Among other things, Hart and Fuller focused on the example of Nazi laws that made criticism of Germany's leadership a criminal offence: were these rightly called 'laws'? The Nazi government's intimidation and destruction of sections of its own population was the major impetus for international concern with human rights, first set out in the United Nations Charter in 1945.[2] It is thus striking that international human rights standards have no place in the debate. There is no reference, for example, to the relevance of the Universal Declaration of Human Rights, which by 1958 was 10 years old. The silence is reciprocated by human rights lawyers who have generally bypassed the debate between Hart and Fuller.[3]

* I thank Karen Knop and Martin Krygier for their generous engagements with this paper, although neither would agree fully with its direction. Thanks also to Susan Harris Rimmer and Jeremy Farrall for their comments and help.

[1] N Lacey, 'Philosophy, Political Morality, and History: Explaining the Enduring Resonance of the Hart-Fuller Debate' (2008) 83 *New York University Law Review* 1059, 1064, 1080.

[2] Articles 1, 55, 56.

[3] One area where there has been some discussion of the designation 'law' and whether it is a neutral or moral one is in the context of terms in human rights instruments such as 'established by law'. See, eg. International Covenant on Civil and Political Rights (ICCPR), Art 9.1: 'No one shall be subjected to arbitrary arrest or detention. No one shall be deprived of his liberty except on such grounds and in accordance with such procedure as are established by law'. See the discussion by the UN Human Rights Committee in *Van Alphen v The Netherlands*, 305/88. The Committee said that 'arbitrariness' was not the same as 'against the law' 'but must be interpreted more broadly to include elements of inappropriateness, injustice and lack of predictability' (para 5.8). The Hart–Fuller debate

A point of connection between the Hart–Fuller debate and human rights is the idea of the rule of law, a concept that is found in the debate and which has a complex relationship with human rights. Its essence is typically identified as limiting the use and abuse of power.[4] Hart did not employ the language of the 'rule of law', preferring concepts such as 'principles of legality', which required that law be made according to a settled process. Hart's positivism can, however, be understood as a basis for the rule of law in the sense that it understood the law as a system of rules generated not by arbitrary power but through proper procedures.[5] For Hart, a bad or immoral law deserved the description 'law' even though we may be morally compelled to disobey it. He wrote:

> [I]f we … make our protest against evil law in the form of an assertion that certain rules cannot be law because of their moral iniquity, we confuse one of the most powerful, because it is the simplest, forms of moral criticism. If with the Utilitarians we speak plainly, we say that laws may be law but too evil to be obeyed.[6]

Hart nevertheless endorsed a natural minimum content of law 'in a world like ours', comprising 'rules forbidding the free use of violence and rules constituting the minimum form of property—with its rights and duties sufficient to enable food to grow and be retained until eaten' which 'overlap[ped] with basic moral principles vetoing murder, violence and theft'.[7] These principles have counterparts in catalogues of international human rights. Ngaire Naffine points out that Hart also assumes that a legal system will operate in a context of freedom of critical debate, another aspect of human rights.[8] Despite these links, Hart's positivism is consistent with the view that human rights are not closely linked to the rule of law,[9] although, as Karen Knop noted in her original comments on this chapter, they may well be relevant to the moral criticism Hart believed should be made of valid but iniquitous laws.

has, however, engaged international criminal lawyers See, eg, M Osiel, 'Dialogue with Dictators: Judicial Resistance in Argentina and Brazil' (2006) 20 *Law and Social Inquiry* 481 and Larry May, Chapter 4.

[4] P Allott, *The Health of Nations* (Cambridge, Cambridge University Press, 2002) 419; R Unger, *What Should Legal Analysis Become?* (London and New York, Verso, 1996) 64. See generally B Tamanaha, *On the Rule of Law: History, Politics, Theory* (Cambridge, Cambridge University Press, 2004).

[5] Lacey, n 1 above, at 1065.

[6] HLA Hart, 'Positivism and the Separation of Law and Morals' (1958) 71 *Harvard Law Review* 593, 620.

[7] *Ibid* 623.

[8] See Ngaire Naffine, Chapter 12.

[9] This approach is made explicit in Joseph Raz's observation that '[a] non-democratic legal system, based on the denial of human rights, on extensive poverty, on racial segregation, sexual inequalities, and religious persecution may, in principle, conform to the requirements of the rule of law better than any of the legal systems of the more enlightened Western democracies'. J Raz, *The Authority of Law* (Oxford, Oxford University Press, 1979) 211.

Fuller too did not use the term 'rule of law' in his response to Hart,[10] but his account of law's 'internal morality' has influenced the accepted ingredients of the rule of law, both in national legal systems and by international institutions.[11] Internal morality was based on the values of accountability of legal authority and the participation of law's subjects in its determination.[12] It prevented the use of law to entrench the powerful and generated a law commanding fidelity. Internal morality was the product of a series of requirements for legal status: that laws be generally applicable, publicly available, prospective, not retrospective, stable through time, understandable, coherent rather than contradictory, susceptible of compliance, and that there be congruence between the law and official action.[13] While these criteria dealt mainly with the form rather than the content of law, they could also affect its substance by refining it, propelling it towards moral goodness,[14] or, in Nicola Lacey's phrase, 'working it pure'.[15] For Fuller, internal morality was concerned with 'a procedural version of natural law, though to avoid misunderstanding the word 'procedural' should be assigned a special and expanded sense so that it would include, for example, a substantive accord between official action and enacted law'.[16] In Fuller's view, if a law was inconsistent with the principles of inner morality, its claim to legality would be compromised, although it would not necessarily be invalid.[17] While at least one of the elements of the 'inner morality' approach to law, the prohibition on retrospective laws, is reflected in human rights standards, Fuller did not refer to any substantive human rights principles. Indeed, Fuller wrote in his response to Hart that '[i]nsofar as is possible, substantive aims should be achieved procedurally, on the principle that if men are compelled to act in the right way, they will generally do the right things'.[18] There has been a suggestion, however, that Fuller's internal morality is based on the same Kantian notion of human agency that grounds human rights principles.[19] On this reading of Fuller, both the internal morality of law and human rights protect us from the arbitrary power of others.[20]

[10] LL Fuller, however, use the term 'rule of law' in his 'Reply to Critics' in *The Morality of Law*, revised edn, New Haven, CT: Yale University Press, 1964).

[11] See, eg, A Magen, 'The Rule of Law and its Promotion Abroad: Three Problems of Scope' (2009) 45 *Stanford Journal of International Law* 51, 60–1; K Davis and M Trebilcock, *The Relationship Between Law and Development: Optimists Versus Skeptics*, New York University Public Law and Legal Theory Working Paper 72 (2008) 23–4.

[12] D Dyzenhaus, 'Aspiring to the Rule of Law' in T Campbell, J Goldsworthy and A Stone (eds), *Protecting Human Rights: Instruments and Institutions* (Oxford, Oxford University Press, 2003) 207–8.

[13] Fuller in *The Morality of Law*, n 10 above, at 187–253.

[14] LL Fuller, 'Positivism and Fidelity to the Law: A Reply to Professor Hart' (1958) 71 *Harvard Law Review* 630, 636.

[15] Lacey, n 1 above, at 1070.

[16] Fuller, *The Morality of Law*, n 10 above, at 996–7.

[17] See the discussion in Dyzenhaus, n 12 above, at 207.

[18] Fuller, 'Positivism and Fidelity to the Law: A Reply to Professor Hart', n 14 above, at 643.

[19] See E Fox-Decent, 'Is the Rule of Law Really Indifferent to Human Rights?' (2008) 27 *Law and Philosophy* 533, 536, 537–8.

[20] *Ibid* 577.

In this chapter I examine the relationship of the rule of law and human rights in a context that has become increasingly familiar: the rebuilding of 'post-conflict' societies by the international community. The rhetoric of the rule of law has become a staple in international rebuilding projects after conflict, and huge resources have been devoted to 'rule of law assistance programmes' more generally. Between 1990–2006, the World Bank approved 330 rule of law projects and spent $US 2.9 billion on them.[21] In 2007 alone, the World Bank allocated US$424.5 million to such projects.[22]

The protection of human rights has an uncertain status in rule of law programmes which focus on creating legal institutions; overall the language of the rule of law has tended to displace or consume the language of human rights, or allow the recognition of only a limited concept of civil and political rights. I suggest that these are negative developments and argue that rule of law projects should be reoriented from the technocratic, leading to an engagement with a full account of human rights, civil and political and economic, social and cultural rights. One benefit of such an approach would be to reduce the focus on law and legal institutions as the methods of achieving the goal of the rule of law—constraining arbitrary power. Neither Hart nor Fuller would necessarily endorse this proposal, although aspects of their writings may be sympathetic to its goals.

Post-Conflict Peace-Building and The Rule of Law

Post-conflict peace-building has become a growth industry in the early twenty-first century. Indeed, it has been said that peace-, democracy- or state-building has 'become one of the critical all-consuming strategic and moral imperatives of our terrorised time'.[23] The term 'post-conflict' masks great complexity. It suggests a neat transition from a state of conflict to peace, while the reality is, as East Timor, Afghanistan and Iraq, for example, all show, that conflict continues long into the formal peace. The peace-building enterprise involves international institutions, both intergovernmental and non-governmental, designing and implementing systems of governance in states that have become dysfunctional through conflict. While the international community has often been wary of engagement in rebuilding after conflict, such activities are now viewed as a form

[21] MJ Trebilcock and RJ Daniels, *Rule of Law Reform and Development: Charting the Fragile Path of Progress* (Cheltenham, Edward Elgar, 2008).

[22] VL Taylor, 'Frequently Asked Questions about Rule of Law Assistance (and Why Better Answers Matter)' (2009) 1 *Hague Journal on the Rule of Law* 46.

[23] R Rotberg, 'The Failure and Collapse of Nation-States: Breakdown, Prevention and Repair' in R Rotberg (ed), *When States Fail: Causes and Consequences* (Princeton University Press, 2004) 42. See also R Paris 'Post-Conflict Peacebuilding' in T Weiss and S Daws (eds), *The Oxford Handbook on the United Nations* (Oxford, Oxford University Press, 2007) 404.

of insurance against terrorism and insecurity.[24] They are also presented as a way of promoting development and human rights, a method of creating model members of the international community out of chaos.

The notion of the rule of law became tainted in the international community after the Nazi era, through the association of law with those atrocities. It was taken as a shorthand term for what might be now termed 'rule by law'.[25] The language of the rule of law does not appear, for example, in the United Nations Charter adopted in 1945. The Universal Declaration of Human Rights refers to the rule of law only once, in its Preamble, stating:

> It is essential, if a man is not to be compelled to have recourse ... to rebellion against tyranny and oppression, that human rights should be protected by the rule of law.

The two major human rights treaties, the 1966 International Covenant on Civil and Political Rights (ICCPR) and the International Covenant on Economic, Social and Cultural Rights (ICESCR), do not refer to the rule of law as such. They present law as one possible method to secure human rights, but not an exclusive one.[26]

The rule of law re-emerged in the 1960s, as part of the United States-funded law and development movement. In the 1980s, internationally-funded rule of law programmes began in Latin America and, with the end of the Cold War, such programmes proliferated in the former Soviet bloc.[27] At a similar time, the UN Security Council began to refer to the rule of law as an aspect of international peace and security.[28] In the 1990s, international financial institutions such as the World Bank became interested in the rule of law as a critical aspect of international development.[29] The rule of law was seen as the key to stability of market economies.[30]

The language of the rule of law now occupies a central place within the post-conflict rebuilding enterprise. It has become an almost universal prescription for managing post-conflict societies.[31] The Brahimi Report championed the use of police and rule of law elements in peace operations in 2000.[32] In 2004, UN

[24] See, eg President Bush's second inaugural speech 'There is no Justice Without Freedom', 21 January 2005: 'Freedom, by its nature, must be chosen, and defended by citizens, and sustained by the rule of law and the protection of minorities'.

[25] Tamanaha, see n 4 above, at 108.

[26] See ICCPR, Art 2; ICESCR, Art 2. See also B Rajagopal, 'Invoking the Rule of Law in Post-Conflict Rebuilding: A Critical Examination' (2008) 49 *William and Mary Law Review* 1347, 1362.

[27] See generally T Carothers, 'The Rule of Law Revival' (1998) 77 *Foreign Affairs* 95.

[28] See J Farrall, *United Nations Sanctions and the Rule of Law* (Cambridge, Cambridge University Press, 2007) 19–20.

[29] Magen, n 11 above, at 66–7.

[30] *Ibid* 94.

[31] See, eg debates in the UN Security Council in 2003 and 2004 noted in Farrall, n 28 above, at 21–2.

[32] L Brahimi *et al*, *Report of the Panel on United Nations Peace Operations* (New York, United Nations, 2000).

Secretary-General Kofi Annan published a report on the rule of law and transitional justice in conflict and post-conflict societies. He called for 'a common basis in international norms and standards' for transitional justice and the rule of law in conflict and post-conflict societies, with the standard peace-builders' disclaimer that no 'one size fits all' formula would work.[33] The following year at the World Summit marking the sixtieth anniversary of the United Nations, leaders of the United Nations' member states agreed that the rule of law was 'part of the universal and indivisible core values and principles of the United Nations'.[34] Rule of law mandates have been given to many UN peace-building operations, including in Kosovo, East Timor, Haiti, Afghanistan, the Democratic Republic of the Congo and the Sudan.[35]

The attractions of the rule of law are manifold in the international sphere: it has a worthy resonance that no one can plausibly reject and yet it is malleable enough to accommodate many types of legal system, from the repressive to the liberal. Thus, the Burmese dictator Ne Win adopted the slogan 'Peace and the rule of law first'.[36] In other words, the concept of the rule of law has no obvious baggage in the international community, highly sensitive as it is to the whiff of imperialism, but is capacious enough to encompass a wide, indeed contradictory, range of understandings. A US State Department official, commenting on China, summed this up nicely: 'The beauty of the rule of law is that it's neutral. No one—the human rights community, the business community, the Chinese leadership—objects to it'.[37]

The term 'rule of law' has many different meanings in the post-conflict context. One group of meanings presents it in a largely procedural manner. Thus, the International Bar Association typically uses the rule of law to signal a government that accepts standing laws and judicial interpretation of the law.[38] This understanding is consistent with Hart's approach to legality. A slightly more

[33] K Annan, *The Rule of Law and Transitional Justice in Conflict and Post-Conflict Societies*, Report of the Secretary-General, UN Doc. S/2004/616 (3 August 2004).

[34] World Summit Outcome para 3, UN Doc. A/RES/60/1 (24 October 2005). Jeremy Farrall identifies five different sets of meanings of 'rule of law' in Security Council practice: n 28 at 32–5.

[35] For a study of Security Council Resolutions outlining rule of law mandates for these operations see J Farrall, 'Impossible Expectations? The UN Security Council's Promotion of the Rule of Law after Conflict' in B Bowden, H Charlesworth and J Farrall (eds), *The Role of International Law in Rebuilding Societies after Conflict* (Cambridge, Cambridge University Press, 2009).

[36] Quoted in N Cheesman, 'The Rule of Law in Burma' (unpublished paper, 2008).

[37] Quoted in Trebilcock and Daniels, n 21 above, at 13.

[38] See, eg, IBA criticism of Zimbabwe for not adhering to the rule of law in this sense, described by R Kleinfeld, 'Competing Definitions of the Rule of Law' in T Carothers (ed), *Promoting the Rule of Law Abroad: In Search of Knowledge* (Washington, DC, Carnegie Endowment for International Peace, 2006) 31, 32. The new US citizenship test, introduced in October 2008, provides the following 'acceptable answers' to the question: 'What is the "rule of law"'? Everyone must follow the law; Leaders must obey the law; Government must obey the law; No one is above the law'. Available at usgovinfo.about.com/library/blinstst_new.htm

developed example of this type of definition, which has resonance with Lon Fuller's inner morality account of the rule of law, is one used by the Office of the High Representative in Bosnia in 2002:

> Under the rule of law no one is above the law. The law applies equally to government and governed alike. No one is untouchable; no one is outside the law, however rich or well connected. It is the first duty of those elected to make the law to respect the law …
>
> The rule of law requires judges and prosecutors who are fearlessly independent. It requires professional police. It requires competent civil servants. It requires an accessible legal profession … It requires legislation that is fair and impartial, and that commands consent.[39]

These accounts of the rule of law make the competence of legal institutions their hallmark, with only faint suggestions of requirements of the substance of law. Also at the procedural end of the spectrum is a manual, *The Beginner's Guide to Nation-Building*, which aims to record the lessons of international military interventions in the name of nation-building. It presents the rule of law as ensuring 'fairness, justice, and equality before the law … [and] preventing official arbitrariness'.[40] The Guide includes transitional justice as an aspect of the rule of law in post-conflict societies, suggesting a focus on criminal law.

Much of the literature supporting a narrow account of the rule of law in post-conflict societies implies that there are different standards applicable in more settled, or economically developed, states. Thus, Randall Peerenboom argues that a minimalist (or 'thin') conception of the rule of law is of particular value in countries that are yet to establish 'a modern, functional legal system'[41] while a human rights-infused 'rich' conception is acceptable in 'mature legal systems'.[42]

There are definitions somewhere in the middle of the spectrum that offer a limited endorsement of some human rights as part of the rule of law. For example, here is a World Bank account of the rule of law:

> the rule of law prevails where (i) the government itself is bound by the law, (ii) every person in society is treated equally under the law, (iii) the human dignity of each individual is recognized and protected by law, and (iv) justice is accessible to all.[43]

In this formulation, the rule of law encompasses the human rights principle of equal treatment under the law and the vaguer idea of 'human dignity'. Other World Bank definitions emphasise the efficient working of legal and judicial systems, impartial judiciaries, predictability of legal outcomes, well-regulated

[39] Office of the High Representative in Bosnia, Peace Implementation Council, *Our Reform Agenda* (14 October 2002). Available at www.ohr.int/print/?content_id=28072

[40] J Dobbins, SG Jones, K Crane and B Cole DeGrasse, *The Beginner's Guide to Nation-Building* (Santa Monica, Rand, 2007) 72.

[41] R Peerenboom, 'Human Rights and the Rule of Law: What's the Relationship?' (2004–05) 36 *Georgetown Journal of International Law* 809, 826 fn 67.

[42] *Ibid* 825.

[43] World Bank 2002 policy document quoted in Rajagopal, n 26 above, at 1347.

markets, and they tend to merge human and property rights.[44] In this way the rule of law promoted by the Bretton Woods institutions has become harnessed to the goal of creating market economies through reducing business regulation and enabling extensive privatisation.

Another group of meanings presents the rule of law as embracing the observance of human rights standards not only by the state and its agents, but also by private actors. We find an explicit linkage of human rights with the rule of law in Kofi Annan's 2004 definition. He describes the rule of law as:

> a principle of governance in which all persons, institutions and entities, public and private, including the State itself, are accountable to laws that are publicly promulgated, equally enforced and independently adjudicated, and which are consistent with international human rights norms and standards. It requires, as well, measures to ensure adherence to the principles of supremacy of law, equality before the law, accountability to the law, fairness in the application of the law, separation of powers, participation in decision-making, legal certainty, avoidance of arbitrariness and procedural and legal transparency.[45]

Apart from the reference to consistency with human rights standards, the definition incorporates most of Fuller's requirements for inner morality. Despite the broad language in this statement and general reference to international human rights norms, in practice, the United Nations has often considered the rule of law an aspect of policing and penal powers. For example, the UN High Commissioner for Human Rights has used the language of the rule of law to emphasise human rights, publishing a set of 'rule-of-law tools for post-conflict states', but these focus on criminal law issues alone. The tools include monitoring legal systems, creating truth commissions, vetting public officials and prosecuting international crimes.[46]

Rule of law projects favoured by the international community revolve primarily around building and strengthening legal institutions. Davis and Trebilcock associate this with Fuller's account of the rule of law.[47] The burgeoning literature on 'lessons learned' from post-conflict rebuilding is based on international templates for the rule of law that can be pulled off the shelf in any new trouble spot.[48] Rule of law projects tend to reproduce the legal systems of the post-conflict rebuilders with little attention to the local context.[49]

[44] See F Upham's selection of definitions in 'Mythmaking in the Rule-of-Law Orthodoxy' in T Carothers (ed), *Promoting the Rule of Law Abroad: In Search of Knowledge* (Washington, DC, Carnegie Endowment for International Peace, 2006) 75, 78.

[45] Annan, 'n 33 above, at para 6.

[46] See Office of the United Nations High Commissioner for Human Rights, *Rule-of Law Tools for Post-Conflict States*, HR/PUB/06 2–6/ (New York and Geneva, United Nations, 2006).

[47] Davis and Trebilcock, n 11 above, at 23–4.

[48] See Dobbins *et al*, n 40 above.

[49] R Mani, *Beyond Retribution: Seeking Justice in the Shadows of War* (Cambridge, Polity Press, 2002) 79–80 describes the competition between French and American lawyers in Cambodia.

Typical projects include judicial recruitment and training, reform of and support for law enforcement agencies such as ministries of justice and the police, and drafting of new laws.[50] The creation or reform of institutions becomes the criterion of success, whether or not they deliver greater accountability and participation. This has led to a technocratic approach to the rule of law in post-conflict states, where cultural and political factors are set aside as irrelevant.[51] The tendency is to compare local institutions to Western models, whatever the local context. One example of this incongruous approach is the use of moot courts by American lawyers to train law students in civil law systems in adversarial styles of legal argument.[52] The assumption behind many manifestations of the rule of law enterprise is that the social and political impact of law is dependent on its institutions taking a particular form.[53] The narrowness of such programmes has been attributed to the limited education of the lawyers who design them, who rarely have any knowledge of development practice or theory.[54]

Balakrishnan Rajagopal has argued that the international popularity of the rule of law rests on its perceived procedural focus compared with the more contested language of human rights.[55] Its value lies precisely in its vagueness: while human rights principles offer a set of normative commitments, the rule of law does not promise any particular set of political or social goals.[56] It is a technical concept above all and fits in well with ideas of institutional governance that are designed to obscure rather than expose areas of discord and disagreement.

A similar pattern arises in the context of the rule of law and development. The rule of law has become valuable to international financial institutions as the bedrock of predictable and productive free market activity after conflict. The World Bank presents it as the vehicle for enforceable private rights in contract and property, which fosters entrepreneurship and investment.[57] Just as in the human rights field, this understanding of the rule of law reduces the possibility that development could have more radical dimensions.[58]

As noted above, the definitions of the rule of law that include human rights tend to refer to them in very general terms, or confine them to a few civil and political rights such as procedural rights, or the protection of life and property. Human rights such as freedom of speech or economic, social and cultural rights

[50] Kleinfeld, n 38 above, at 47–8; S Kouvo, 'State-building and Rule of Law: Lessons from Afghanistan', Nato Defence College Forum Paper 6 (Rome, March 2009) 83.

[51] Kleinfeld, n 38 above, at 51.

[52] *Ibid* 52.

[53] Davis and Trebilcock, n 11 above, at 23.

[54] Magen, n 11 above, at 85–6.

[55] See also Peerenboom, n 41 above.

[56] Rajagopal, n 26 above, at 1357–9.

[57] *Ibid* 1363. See also K Dam, *The Law-Growth Nexus: The Rule of Law and Economic Development* (Boston, Brookings Institution Press, 2006).

[58] A similar point is made by Jeremy Waldron in 'Legislation and the Rule of Law' (2008) 1 *Legisprudence* 91.

are associated with political choices rather than legal ones. Rachel Kleinfeld illustrates this type of reasoning in her comment that:

> Not any human rights reform would necessarily count as a rule-of-law issue. The idea is not simply the growth of human rights, but the notion that the state should be reined in by the law and that law should have content to it—that is, the state cannot violate intrinsic human rights of individuals. Thus the rule of law is historically about negative rights, not positive rights or so-called economic and social rights. There is also a strong connotation of physical or property violence to human rights as a rule-of-law issue. A state violates the rule of law when it abducts and extrajudicially executes citizens or appropriates citizens' property; it is not as intuitive that a state violates the rule of law when it places curbs on free speech.[59]

If the modern rule of law literature has an ambivalent attitude to human rights, it is also true that international human rights literature pays little attention to the rule of law. Promotion of human rights is presented as having a much broader scope than rule of law projects, which are typically associated with a limited focus on criminal law and procedure.[60]

The Rule of Law Applied

For all the priority accorded to the rule of law in the post-conflict literature and the huge resources devoted to it by international institutions, most studies conclude that attempts to build the rule of law have minimal effect on ensuring governmental accountability or popular participation in law-making.[61] Trubek and Galanter offered an early diagnosis of the problems of international export of rule of law programmes in 1974.[62] They argued that the rule of law embodied liberal legalism's idea of law, premised on a socially and politically pluralist society in which the state was the primary source of power. This model had little purchase in societies that were socially stratified, and where non-state groups, such as the clan or local community, exercised extensive social power. The rule of law allocated a central role to an impartial court system, but such institutions were often absent or insignificant in the host societies. Trubek and Galanter's observations retain their bite today.[63]

[59] Kleinfeld, n 38 above, at 69 fn 47.

[60] See, eg ND White and D Klaasen (eds), *The UN, Human Rights and Post-Conflict Situations* (Manchester University Press, 2005).

[61] There are very few systematic studies of rule of law programmes available. For general critiques see D Chandler, *Empire in Denial: The Politics of State-building* (London, Pluto Press, 2006) ch 8; K Samuels, *Rule of Law Reform in Post-Conflict Countries*, World Bank Conflict Prevention and Reconstruction Working Paper Series no. 37 (October 2006) 15.

[62] D Trubek and M Galanter, 'Scholars in Self-estrangement: Some Reflections on the Crisis in Law and Development Studies in the United States' (1974) 4 *Wisconsin Law Review* 1062.

[63] See, eg Carothers, n 44 above; and R Ehrenreich Brooks, 'The New Imperialism: Violence, Norms and the "Rule of Law"' (2003) 101 *Michigan Law Review* 2280.

There has been extensive criticism of the lack of clarity of the meaning and goals of rule of law projects,[64] their top-down and state-centred character, their dependence on imported legal models, their failure to engage civil society and to deliver redress for the poor.[65] Other problems identified in the rule of law project include the huge financial and human resources required but rarely available in post-conflict societies. This means that rule of law institutions rely on the often fickle support of external donors, which dries up once UN peace-keeping missions conclude. Funding cycles also promote short-term projects, such as the erection of buildings, or the purchase of equipment, rather than longer term work such as education and capacity-building. It is also possible that formal state justice systems have lost support and credibility as a result of being implicated in political repression. Many rule of law exercises tend to sideline traditional or customary approaches to conflict resolution, further reducing their relevance.[66] Aid donors often prefer security sector reform projects, focused on the police, prisons and the judiciary.

Examples of failed rule of law projects can be found in East Timor which, seven years after independence, has a dysfunctional justice sector. The UN transitional administration, UNTAET, was unable to articulate a strategy to develop a viable system of justice after independence. It did not assess the existing legal systems operating in East Timor as a basis for its reforms and rushed into appointing judges before either the court structure or legal system had been designed, and then did not provide adequate training for them. Development of the capacity of the local legal profession was also sidelined. UNTAET focused single-mindedly on criminal justice, at the expense of other aspects of the legal system.[67]

More generally, the limited focus of rule of law projects is sometimes the product of reluctance by external actors to engage with local politics and culture.[68] But there are also cases of international engagement post-conflict predicated on an assumption that the society being rebuilt has no legal culture or traditions at all. One such example was the UN Transitional Administration in Cambodia (UNTAC) in 1992–93, which regarded Cambodia as without any indigenous legal system, a clean slate for the importation of foreign models.[69]

Michael Trebilcock and Ronald Daniels identify three broad, overlapping, categories of impediments to rule of law programmes: technical and resource

[64] Kleinfeld, n 38 above, at 35.

[65] See, eg S Golub, 'A House Without a Foundation' in Carothers, n 44 above, at 105, 108–9. Kouvo, n 50 above, at 83.

[66] See, eg L Grenfell 'Legal Pluralism and the Challenge of Building the Rule of Law in Post-conflict States: A Case Study of Timor-Leste' in B Bowden, H Charlesworth and J Farrall (eds), *The Role of International Law in Rebuilding Societies after Conflict* (Cambridge, Cambridge University Press, 2009) 157; see also Samuels, n 61 above, at 18–19. For discussion of Fuller's views on customary law see Jeremy Waldron, Chapter 7.

[67] See Samuels, n 61 above, at 16; Grenfell, n 66 above, at 176.

[68] Mani, n 49 above, at 78–9.

[69] *Ibid* 79–80.

issues (societies lacking the requisite funds, human capital and institutions); socio-cultural historical factors that make rule of law values suspect or irrelevant; and political economy barriers, where there is no political demand or will for rule of law reforms.[70] In light of such problems, local populations often view international rule of law initiatives as a response to external requirements rather than domestic needs.

The Future of the Rule of Law

The disappointments surrounding international rule of law projects have generated a range of proposals for reform, often described on a 'thin' to 'thick' or 'procedural' to 'substantive' spectrum, although the terminology is not used consistently. Brian Tamanaha, for example, has argued for a 'minimalist' account of the rule of law in the developing world to protect against authoritarian governments, on the ground that a fuller version would be impossible to achieve.[71] Minimalist rule of law consists of government adherence to rules adopted by the political authority, treating citizens with 'basic human dignity' and access to a dispute resolution mechanism that is as fair as possible under the circumstances. The implication is that the rule of law should avoid any substantive commitments and simply provide neutral, procedural rules. Neutrality may be hard to achieve because procedural rules rest on political assumptions, for example about the elevated status of decisions of parliamentary majorities.[72] This is even more so in the case of international engagement in post-conflict states, where rules of procedure will often be understood as Western in essence and inhospitable to local understandings of justice.

Another proposal for reform comes from Trebilcock and Daniels who are anxious to resist a substantive conception of justice and they also endorse a 'procedural' approach to the rule of law as the most conducive to development, although they seem to have a much thicker version in mind than Tamanaha. They use the term 'procedural' to designate normative benchmarks for major legal institutions such as the judiciary and the legal education system, based on Amartya Sen's capability approach to development.[73] They suggest that these benchmarks will 'correlate with a minimal constellation of civil and political rights, and a basic arrangement of economic facilities related to the protection of property and contractual rights'.[74]

70 Trebilcock and Daniels, n 21 above, at 38–9; see also Samuels, n 61 above, at 15–23.

71 B Tamanaha, 'The Lessons of Law and Development Studies' (1995) 89 *American Journal of International Law* 470, 476.

72 Dyzenhaus, n 12 above, at 201–4.

73 Trebilcock and Daniels, n 21 above, at 25.

74 *Ibid* 25.

Jane Stromseth, David Wippman and Rosa Brooks propose a more direct linkage of the rule of law with human rights.[75] They argue that observance of human rights is integral to achieving security and for this reason they support a 'pragmatic' and 'synergistic' human rights-oriented conception of the rule of law that is 'unabashedly substantive'.[76] The substance of their definition involves state monopoly of means of violence and resolution of disputes via fair, neutral and generally-applicable rules in a way that respects 'fundamental human rights norms'.[77] Stromseth *et al* identify these central rights as prohibitions on racial, ethnic, religious and gender discrimination, torture, slavery, prolonged arbitrary detentions and extra-judicial killings.[78] While the approach is substantive, the authors describe it as 'deliberately minimalist' and essentially descriptive of current practice: 'These norms are widely accepted in part because they are relatively bare bones and allow ample room for different societies to define rights in different ways, provided they respect core principles such as prohibitions against … discrimination [etc]'.[79] The authors suggest that this list of norms has been 'universally accepted' by being codified in widely-ratified human rights treaties and has achieved customary international law status.[80] This 'unabashedly substantive' approach is very similar to the 'procedural' notion of the rule of law championed by Trebilcock and Daniels.

Stromseth *et al* and Trebilcock and Daniels also agree on the exclusion of economic, social and cultural rights from rule of law projects. Stromseth *et al* do not explain why explicitly, but the implication is that these rights are less accepted internationally than civil and political rights. The authors rely on wide treaty ratification as one sign of international acceptance. Trebilcock and Daniels simply assert that the ICCPR rights are 'most compatible with a procedural rather than substantive conception of the rule of rule' without more detail.[81]

The exclusion of economic, social and cultural rights from the rule of law agenda is based on a number of contestable assumptions. If treaty ratification is the test of international support for principles, as Stromseth *et al* suggest, we should note that the ratification patterns of the ICCPR and the ICESCR are remarkably similar: in September 2008, the ICCPR had 162 parties, while the ICESCR had 159. This cannot, then, be a plausible basis for the distinction. The rejection of ICESCR rights as part of the rule of law is also based on an unsustainable distinction between negative and positive rights, the assumption

[75] J Stromseth, D Wippman and R Brooks, *Can Might Make Rights?: Building the Rule of Law after Military Interventions* (Cambridge, Cambridge University Press, 2006).

[76] *Ibid* 79.

[77] *Ibid* 58.

[78] *Ibid.*

[79] *Ibid* 79.

[80] *Ibid* 186.

[81] Trebilcock and Daniels, n 21 above, at 27. See also Magen, whose proposal for a substantive 'democratic' understanding of the rule of law includes 'fundamental political and civil rights', but not economic, social and cultural rights, n 11 above, at 63.

that civil and political rights entail only state restraint, while economic, social and cultural rights require state action and expenditure. Most civil and political rights have economic, social and cultural implications, and vice versa. For example, implementation of the right to be free from discrimination requires positive action, such as education and monitoring. Understanding the two sets of rights as qualitatively different makes little sense when applied to a human life. It is not clear, for example, why the right to freedom of expression is considered a civil and political right[82] while the right to education is deemed an economic, social and cultural right.[83] Similarly, the designation of freedom of association as a civil and political right,[84] and the right to form trade unions as an economic, social and cultural right, is not based in principle and makes particularly little sense after conflict.[85] A major problem after conflict is economic and social disparity and insecurity exacerbated by conflict and endemic poverty.[86] This is an issue particularly for women because discrimination against women in areas such as access to land or inheritance of housing and property is common.[87]

Whatever the character of the reform proposals for the international export of the rule of law, they share a premise that the legal sphere is distinct from and superior to politics. Take, for example, Kofi Annan's account of the rule of law quoted above. It emphasises accountability to law, the supremacy of law, fairness in applying law, legal certainty and transparency. This belief in the possibility of separating law from politics in the rule of law literature is often challenged by the evidence. Thus, Frank Upham's study of the United States and Japanese legal systems suggests that law is less a technology than a sociology or politics.[88]

At a more fundamental level, Martin Krygier has pointed out that the rule of law has become so entwined with law, legality and legal institutions that its *telos*, or purpose, has been forgotten. This he identifies as starting with the restraint of the arbitrary exercise of power.[89] From this point, Krygier argues that we need to investigate what mechanisms will actually operate as restraints on power, rather than assuming that law, or at least specific, familiar, legal institutions, will always play such a role. Krygier contends that legal institutions by themselves are not capable of curbing abuses of power: they 'always need supporting circumstances, social and political structures and cultural supports, which are not always available and are difficult to engineer'.[90] The rule of law then cannot simply boil

[82] ICCPR, Art 19.
[83] ICESCR, Art 13.
[84] ICCPR, Art 22.
[85] ICESCR, Art 8. In fact ICCPR, Art 22 also refers to the right to form and join trade unions.
[86] See, eg N Niland, 'Rights, Rhetoric and Reality: A Snapshot from Afghanistan' in White and Klaasen, n 60 above, at 322.
[87] See C Chinkin and H Charlesworth, 'Building Women into Peace: The International Legal Framework' (2006) 27 *Third World Quarterly* 937.
[88] Upham, n 44 above, at 75.
[89] M Krygier, 'The Rule of Law: Legality, Teleology, Sociology' in G Palombella and N Walker (eds), *Re-locating the Rule of Law* (Oxford, Hart Publishing, 2008).
[90] *Ibid.*

down to a claim of law's superiority over politics. Indeed it is possible that establishing the pre-eminence of law can reinforce the marginalisation of groups such as women.[91] The teleological approach to the rule of law suggests the value of attention to economic, social and cultural rights as well as civil and political rights in post-conflict societies, not necessarily as legal standards, but as spheres in which attention must be paid to abuses of power.

Karen Knop points out that Fuller was less interested in specific legal institutions than in achieving the conditions for individual freedom. In this sense, then, Krygier's approach connects to Fuller's concern with the social effects of the rule of law, rather than its institutional manifestation.

If we enlarge the concept of the rule of law in post-conflict societies to include the protection of all human rights as restrictions on the arbitrary use of power, the rights to health, housing, food, shelter and work would be at the centre of post-conflict reconstruction.[92] This could challenge the Western market economic model at the centre of, for example, World Bank accounts of the rule of law.[93] Such a strategy is not an easy one, or one amenable to technological delivery. Even the United Nations, which has made an explicit commitment to uphold economic, social and cultural rights, regularly ignores them in post-conflict societies.[94] But it would give some sharper teeth to the often bland understandings of human rights that inform post-conflict rebuilding. It would also de-emphasise legal institutions as a staple of the rule of law and retain some of the oppositional and radical edge of human rights that can be used by local populations.[95] At the same time, it is important to be wary of the potential for human rights to be ritualised, in the sense that their implementation becomes a ceremonial matter, confined to an internationally-funded cadre of professional experts inaccessible to most of the population.[96]

Conclusion

Nicola Lacey has argued that the Hart–Fuller debate can be understood both as a philosophical dispute and as a 'moral and practical disagreement about which institutional arrangements are likely to maximize the realization of valued social

[91] F Ni Aolain and M Hamilton, 'Gender and the Rule of Law in Transitional Societies', University of Ulster Transitional Justice Institute Research Paper 09–02, (Belfast, 11 March 2009) 108.

[92] Tom Campbell's account of an international right to sustenance is helpful here: see *Rights: A Critical Introduction* (London and New York, Routledge, 2006) ch 9.

[93] Waldron, n 58 above, at 96.

[94] ND White, 'Towards a Strategy for Human Rights Protection in Post-Conflict Situations' in White and Klaasen, n 60 above, at 463, 481–2; see also M Brand, 'Effective Human Rights Protection when the UN "Becomes the State": Lessons from UNMIK' in White and Klaasen, *ibid* 365.

[95] Rajagopal, n 26 above.

[96] See, eg Caroline Hughes describing the ritualisation of international human rights norms in Cambodia in 'Human Rights Out of Context (or, Translating the Universal Declaration into Khmer)' in White and Klaasen, n 60 above, at 191.

ends or ideals under specific social and historical conditions'.[97] For Lacey, the central question in the debate can be understood as 'how to develop legal arrangements capable of constraining abuses of power and of addressing such abuses'.[98] This issue is also at the core of modern debates about the role and content of the rule of law in post-conflict societies.

Following Martin Krygier, I have suggested that a single-minded focus on the law and legal institutions as the source of constraints on the abuse of power is unlikely to be successful. Krygier's proposal that we should be clear about the *telos* of the rule of law enterprise before designing institutional rule of law structures is particularly relevant in post-conflict contexts. If the point of the rule of law is to control the use and abuse of power, different translations of the concept will be necessary in different societies; international 'toolkits' that can be carried from one trouble spot to another are unlikely to respond to the complexities of different situations.

An extension of the rule of law in international post-conflict settings to include economic, social and cultural rights as well as civil and political rights is one way of ensuring that the rule of law can influence the uses of power that affect all aspects of human lives. It would require close attention to the way power is distributed in a particular context and reduce reliance on legal mechanisms as the answer to imbalances and abuses. I take Stephen Golub's proposal that the concept of justice become the organising principle of the rule of law field to be on similar lines.[99]

What relevance does the Hart–Fuller debate have to the invocation of the rule of law in post-conflict settings? Karen Knop's initial response to this chapter observed that human rights norms have sometimes come to take the role of morality in the Hart–Fuller debate. On the one hand, Hart's insistence on the analytic separation of law from morality parallels the proponents of the thinnest internationally-sponsored rule of law projects in post-conflict societies. His minimum content of law—rules against violence and for the protection of property—is also reflected in some modern rule of law prescriptions in post-conflict societies. On the other hand, Hart's understanding of the limits of law in achieving moral ends is consistent with decentring the law and legal institutions as mechanisms for achieving restraints on power. Hart's positivism, as noted above, encouraged engagement with the moral dimensions of law and the possibility of civil disobedience when laws were immoral: the claim that 'if laws reached a certain degree of iniquity then there would be a plain moral obligation to resist them and to withhold obedience'.[100] Today, it is possible to argue that

[97] Lacey, n 1 above, at 1072.

[98] *Ibid.*

[99] S Golub, 'Make Justice the Organizing Principle of the Rule of Law Field' (2009) 1 *Hague Journal on the Rule of Law* 1. See too Magen's suggestion that the rule of law is a 'key dimension of democratic quality', n 11 above, at 59.

[100] Hart, 'Positivism and the Separation of Law and Morals', n 6 above, at 617.

international human rights standards can contribute to the identification of, or even define, morally compromised laws.[101]

In his response to Hart, Fuller considered the task of drafting a constitution for a post-conflict society.[102] He recommended that the constitution be essentially a procedural document: '[s]ubstantive limitations on the power of government should be kept to a minimum and should generally be confined to those for which a need can be generally appreciated'.[103] This suggests a caution about pursuing human rights through the rule of law, although Evan Fox-Decent reads Fuller's inner morality to support not only civil and political rights but also possibly economic, social and cultural rights.[104]

How might these different approaches respond to a recent post-conflict situation? In April 2009, Afghanistan's government adopted a law that required a Shiite woman to obtain a male relative's permission to leave her house, seek employment or education, and to have sex with her husband every four days unless she was ill. The law also granted custody of children to fathers or grandfathers only. Its purpose was apparently to shore up Shia support for Hamid Karzai's re-election campaign for the presidency.[105] Hart might propose that civil disobedience as the best course to protest against an iniquitous law, as measured by human rights standards. Indeed, the law prompted large demonstrations in Kabul, and significant international opposition, on the basis that it violated women's human rights,[106] and President Karzai agreed to review the legislation.[107] Civil disobedience, however, carries particular dangers in post-conflict societies, as the violent responses to the demonstrations showed. Fuller might observe that the law did not fulfil the requirements of inner morality (for example, it was applicable only to the Shiite community, it was enacted in great haste and secrecy and was not publically promulgated) and thus its legality was suspect. A teleological approach to the rule of law suggests a different focus: an investigation of what mechanisms in Afghan society could be used to restrain the power of a male elite to oppress women.

The approach I have sketched to the rule of law in post-conflict societies relies on international human rights not so much as a set of legal rules but as a mechanism to draw attention to power abuses in all spheres of life. This proposal may be criticised as overloading the rule of law with human rights norms. Martin Krygier would make this point. His approach rests on a sociological rather than normative claim about what is likely to restrain power. He would prefer to distinguish between that aim and the pursuit of other human rights objectives, for fear that the distinctive, modest but precious virtue of restraint on power

[101] A point made by Karen Knop in Chapter 3.

[102] Fuller, 'Positivism and Fidelity to the Law: A Reply to Professor Hart', n 14 above, at 642–3.

[103] *Ibid* 643.

[104] Fox-Decent, n 19 above, at 577–80.

[105] 'Law "Worse than the Taliban"', *Guardian Weekly*, 3 April 2009, 10.

[106] 'Afghanistan's Women Find their Voice', *Guardian Weekly*, 24 April 2009, 6.

[107] See further www.stopvaw.org/Karzai_Pledges_Changes_to_Shia_Personal_Status_Law.html

might otherwise be obscured. My argument, however, also rests on a sociological claim that the language of economic and social rights is useful in identifying broader, systemic asymmetries of power that can undermine fragile post-conflict settlements.[108]

An alternative is to abandon the vocabulary of the rule of law as a way of limiting the abuse of power after conflict in economic and social fields and argue instead for a rich account of human rights. Rajagopal, for example, takes this course.[109] My preference, however, is to hold onto the concept of the rule of law but to resist a monolithic institutional translation by emphasising the protection of human rights as a mechanism to curb arbitrary power. Recognising the political and social aspects of the rule of law and the variable strategies required to achieve it in any particular context may reduce its appeal to international post-conflict peace-builders, but increase its value to local populations.

[108] For a discussion of this point in the context of Zimbabwe, see I Muvingi, 'Sitting on Powder Kegs: Socioeconomic Rights in Transitional Societies' (2009) 3 *International Journal of Transitional Justice* 163.

[109] See, eg Rajagopal, n 26 above, at 1375.

3

The Hart–Fuller Debate's Silence on Human Rights

KAREN KNOP*

> Since 1946 when the signatories of the United Nations Charter affirmed their faith in fundamental human rights and the dignity and worth of the human person, no state can claim that the denial of such rights to its own citizens is solely its own business … the conception of basic human rights has deeply affected the style of diplomacy, the morality and the political ideology of our time, even though thousands of innocent persons still imprisoned or oppressed have not yet felt its benefits.[1]

Thus wrote HLA Hart in 1979. But as Hilary Charlesworth begins by noting, in Hart's 1958 debate with Lon L Fuller,[2] neither referred to human rights—her assigned theme.[3] 'The silence', she goes on to say, 'is reciprocated by human rights lawyers who have generally bypassed the debate between Hart and Fuller'.[4] Charlesworth, herself an outstanding scholar of international human rights law, rises to the occasion by forging a characteristically elegant linkage: she relates the debate to human rights via its treatment of the rule of law. Tracking the emergence of rule of law programmes as a major export to so-called 'post-conflict' societies, Charlesworth takes issue with the ideas of the rule of law

* I am grateful to Jutta Brunnée, Hans Baade, Hilary Charlesworth, David Dyzenhaus, Nicola Lacey, Mayo Moran and Kristen Rundle for their generosity in commenting on drafts of this chapter and assisting with key sources. The final section of the chapter has benefitted from ongoing work with Ralf Michaels and Annelise Riles on conflict of laws and 'theory through technique', and I owe them special thanks. I am also grateful to the Fellows of Harvard College for permission to quote from The Papers of Lon Fuller held in the Special Collections Room of the Law School Library.

1 HLA Hart, 'Utilitarianism and Natural Rights' (1979) 53 *Tulane Law Review* 663, 680.

2 HLA Hart, 'Positivism and the Separation of Law and Morals' (1958) 71 *Harvard Law Review* 593; LL Fuller, 'Positivism and Fidelity to Law: A Reply to Professor Hart' (1958) 71 *Harvard Law Review* 630.

3 Hilary Charlesworth, ch 2. The only treatment of rights found in the debate is Hart's criticism of the command theory for failing to give a place to rights, by which he meant private rights. Hart, 'Positivism and the Separation of Law and Morals', n 2 above, at 604–6.

4 See Hilary Charlesworth, ch 2.

driving these initiatives. She argues instead for a more substantial concept of the rule of law that would include international human rights, specifically economic, social and cultural rights. In this light, she examines whether either Hart or Fuller developed an approach to law that is potentially hospitable to her argument.

Charlesworth's observation about the Hart–Fuller debate's silence on international[5] human rights is also a discreet criticism,[6] or at least presents a puzzle about the debate, since she adds that the Universal Declaration of Human Rights,[7] for example, had been in existence for a decade. Thus her paper can be seen as diplomatically deflecting from and compensating for the debate's insularity, a feature elaborated on in this volume by Ngaire Naffine.[8] By moving to whether international human rights can be *added*, Charlesworth has given us a fascinating and original paper, but one that—because it takes silence as silence—leaves us without a sense of the debate's more straightforward relevance for international human rights law.

In these comments I seek to show how the Hart–Fuller debate is directly relevant. At the time, the conceptions of law developed by Hart and Fuller contributed to the questions whether international (human rights) law was *law* and whether it should be adjudicated. In the intervening 50 years, ironically, it was the correspondence between the role of *morality* debated by Hart and Fuller and the growing role of international human rights law that gave their exchange its greatest relevance for concrete cases. Finally, I suggest that by shifting the focus of their disagreement from the concept of law to relationships between legal systems, including international, foreign and non-state legal systems, we might begin to develop a new legacy for the debate.

International Law and Adjudication

Charlesworth's example of the Universal Declaration of Human Rights suggests that international human rights ought to have leaped to mind for Hart and Fuller. But what exactly was the general state of Anglo-American legal consciousness about international human rights in 1958? The Universal Declaration was not yet considered binding,[9] and its influence had not yet grown. For instance, in its first decade, the Universal Declaration was referred to by US courts in only

[5] In keeping with Charlesworth's main focus, I will confine my comments to international human rights.

[6] See Ngaire Naffine, ch 12 (interpreting it as such).

[7] Universal Declaration of Human Rights (adopted 10 December 1948), UNGA Res 217 A(III).

[8] See Ngaire Naffine, ch 12.

[9] For a 1959 account of the Universal Declaration's influence, see E Schwelb, 'The Influence of the Universal Declaration of Human Rights on International and National Law' (1959) 53 *American Society of International Law Proceedings* 217 (much, if not most, of what Schwelb describes would not have been stock knowledge for non-international lawyers). On the Universal Declaration's progress toward bindingness, see LB Sohn 'The New International Law: Protection of the Rights of Individuals Rather than States' (1982) 32 *American University Law Review* 1, 16–17.

three cases, as compared to 133 cases from 1998 to 2008.[10] There were new universal human rights treaties covering such subjects as genocide (1948),[11] refugees (1951),[12] the political rights of women (1952),[13] stateless persons (1954),[14] forced labour (1957),[15] and employment discrimination (1958).[16] Then again, not all were yet in force, and the United Kingdom was party to just two,[17] the United States to none. Moreover, none of the 'core' treaties, each with a committee of experts to monitor its implementation by states and some with a right of individual petition, was yet in existence.[18] Thus, the quasi-adjudicative bodies and the jurisprudence characteristic of the contemporary international human rights system still lay ahead.

What of the more developed European system of human rights? The European Convention on Human Rights,[19] then eight years old, is another human rights development contemporaneous with the Hart–Fuller debate and one especially salient for Hart, who was British. On the one hand, by 1958, fundamental issues of government and human rights related to Cyprus, the Irish Republican Army and the West German Communist Party had arisen under the Convention.[20] The insurrection in Cyprus, then a British colony, had led Greece to bring the first inter-state case under the Convention, against the United Kingdom, and caused considerable interest in the Convention both among the British public and in British political circles.[21] On the other hand, the Hart–Fuller debate appeared in print before the European Court of Human Rights had handed down its first judgment. One of the Council of Europe's 15 member states, France, had not ratified the Convention at all. Although the other 14 countries were bound internationally by the Convention, it had the force of law domestically in only eight, the United Kingdom not among them. Nine of the 14 (again not including

[10] T-H Cheng, 'The Universal Declaration of Human Rights at Sixty: Is It Still Right for the United States?' (2008) 41 *Cornell International Law Journal* 251, 273.

[11] Convention on the Prevention and Punishment of the Crime of Genocide (adopted 9 December 1948, entered into force 12 January 1951), 78 UNTS 277.

[12] Convention Relating to the Status of Refugees (adopted 28 July 1951, entered into force 22 April 1954), 189 UNTS 137.

[13] Convention on the Political Rights of Women (opened for signature 20 December 1952, entered into force 7 July 1954), 193 UNTS 135.

[14] Convention Relating to the Status of Stateless Persons (adopted 28 September 1954, entered into force 6 June 1960), 360 UNTS 117.

[15] Convention Concerning the Abolition of Forced Labour (ILO no 105) (adopted on 25 June 1957, entered into force 17 January 1959), 320 UNTS 291.

[16] Convention Concerning Discrimination in respect of Employment and Occupation (ILO no 111) (adopted on 25 June 1958, entered into force 15 June 1960), 362 UNTS 31.

[17] The Conventions on refugees and forced labour.

[18] The core international human rights instruments are listed at www2.ohchr.org/english/law/

[19] Convention for the Protection of Human Rights and Fundamental Freedoms (4 November 1950), 213 UNTS 221.

[20] See AWB Simpson, *Human Rights and the End of Empire: Britain and the Genesis of the European Convention* (Oxford, Oxford University Press, 2001) 884–1052, 1081–2; CHM Waldock, 'The European Convention for the Protection of Human Rights and Fundamental Freedoms' (1958) 34 *British Year Book of International Law* 356, 357.

[21] See Simpson, n 20 above, at 923, 1074.

the United Kingdom) recognised the right of individual petition under the Convention. By 1958, the European Commission on Human Rights had dealt with about 360 cases from individuals; however, all but nine were declared inadmissible without reference to the government concerned.[22]

'[T]he legal significance of the Convention seems to have made very little impact on lawyers' in the United Kingdom, wrote the Commission's President, Humphrey Waldock, in the same year as the debate, 'Is it not a matter of the greatest interest that these written guarantees are now superimposed on the British constitution by a legal instrument operating within the larger framework of the Council of Europe? I believe it is, but I do not think that you will find any mention of it in English works on constitutional law'.[23] As for Oxford University, Hart's academic home, Brian Simpson wryly commented that he did not recall the Convention ever being mentioned when he was a student there from 1951 to 1954, nor was there a professor in the subject of human rights at Oxford until 1999.[24] In contrast, Fuller's colleagues at Harvard Law School included Louis Sohn, a leading scholar and advocate in the field of international human rights, who offered a seminar in human rights as early as 1952[25] —although Sohn has been depicted as somewhat apart from the theoretical debates that dominated the Harvard faculty.[26]

Seen in context, then, it is not particularly puzzling that two legal philosophers said nothing about human rights in 1958. If there is a puzzle, it is that the very phrase does not appear in Hart's writings until 1979,[27] while Fuller never picked up on rights.[28]

Despite its silence on human rights, the Hart–Fuller debate, together with other writings by Hart and Fuller around that time, relate directly to two important aspects of the then-emerging international system of human rights law: in Hart's case the status of international human rights law, and in Fuller's the existence of adjudicative processes. In one of the debate's signal contributions, Hart offered a version of legal positivism that refutes Austin's command theory of law and hence provides a positivism capable of seeing international law as law. Indeed, in *The Concept of Law*, published three years later in 1961, Hart devoted a

[22] Waldock, n 20 above, at 358–60.

[23] *Ibid* 361.

[24] Simpson, n 20 above, at 809.

[25] JM Pasqualucci, 'Louis Sohn: Grandfather of International Human Rights Law in the United States' (1998) 20 *Human Rights Quarterly* 924, 933.

[26] D Kennedy, 'Louis B. Sohn: Recollections of a Co-conspirator' (2007) 48 *Harvard International Law Journal* 25, 27.

[27] See J Mikhail, '"Plucking the Mask of Mystery from Its Face": Jurisprudence and H.L.A. Hart' (book review of N Lacey, *A Life of H.L.A. Hart: The Nightmare and the Noble Dream*) (2007) 95 *Georgetown Law Journal* 733, 761 ('human rights is "the idea of our time," and yet the twentieth century's leading English-language legal philosopher had virtually nothing to say about them').

[28] See P Cliteur, 'Fuller's Faith' in WJ Witteveen and W van der Burg (eds), *Rediscovering Fuller: Essays on Implicit Law and Institutional Design* (Amsterdam University Press, 1999) 100, 113–23 (speculating as to why Fuller never developed his idea of law's morality in terms of rights).

chapter to this view of international law, a chapter that has become canonical among international lawyers, if not among international human rights lawyers.[29]

Almost no international lawyer knows or remembers, however, that Fuller also took an interest in international law around the time of the debate. And insofar as the few Fullerian international lawyers allude to Fuller's discussion of international law in his pivotal article 'The Forms and Limits of Adjudication' ('FLA'), which was circulating in draft by the late 1950s,[30] they find it disappointingly brief and negative, reading him as 'seem[ing] to deny that international society could aspire to a rule of law'.[31] By adding biographical context, I suggest rather that Fuller had an active interest in international law around the time of the debate. In his later work international law appears occasionally as a device to challenge assumptions about the character of domestic law[32] or an illustration of the appropriateness of certain legal forms to certain social contexts,[33] but in this earlier period he was interested in international law as such.[34] '[E]stablishing "the rule of law" in international relations' was becoming one of 'the most urgent [problems] of our times', he wrote in a 1959 letter.[35] Nevertheless, to see Fuller as other than a nay-sayer—and as making common cause with current Fuller-inspired international lawyers let alone more broadly—it is necessary to put into

[29] See, eg B Kingsbury, 'The Concept of "Law" in Global Administrative Law' (2009) 20 *European Journal of International Law* 23 (developing Hartian positivism in international law). On Hart's impact, see also J Brunnée and SJ Toope, 'International Law and Constructivism: Elements of an Interactional Theory of International Law' (2000) 39 *Columbia Journal of Transnational Law* 19. Kingsbury notes: 'The dominant line among international lawyers now is to update chapter 10 by proposing a rule of recognition and developing the institutional capacities for adjudication and change, so as to render international law as a unified system, rather than the mere set of rules Hart concluded it was': *ibid* 28 fn 15. See also Larry May, ch 4.

[30] I will refer to the 1959 typescript of FLA available at the Harvard Law School Library (hereinafter Fuller, 1959 FLA draft) with parallel citation to the published article, which is substantially the same: LL Fuller, 'The Forms and Limits of Adjudication' (1978) 92 *Harvard Law Review* 353. On the successive versions of FLA, see Nicola Lacey, ch 1.

[31] See Brunnée and Toope, n 29 above, at 65 fn 194; J Brunnée and SJ Toope, 'An Interactional Theory of International Legal Obligation' (July 2008), University of Toronto Faculty of Law, Legal Studies Research Series no 08–16, 22 fn 103, available at http://ssrn.com/abstract=1162882. See also J Klabbers, 'Constitutionalism and the Making of International Law: Fuller's Procedural Natural Law' (2008) 5 *No Foundations: Journal of Extreme Legal Positivism* (April) 84, 85, available at www.helsinki.fi/nofo/

[32] See LL Fuller, *The Morality of Law*, revised edn (New Haven, CT, Yale University Press, 1969) 232–4; LL Fuller, 'Human Interaction and the Law' (1969) 14 *American Journal of Jurisprudence* 1. Brunnée and Toope find Fuller's treatment of international law in *The Morality of Law* more congenial. Brunnée and Toope, n 29 above, at 65 fn 19; Brunnée and Toope, n 31 above, at 22 fn 103.

[33] See Fuller, 'Human Interaction and the Law', n 32 above; LL Fuller 'The Law's Precarious Hold on Life' (1969) 3 *Georgia Law Review* 530, 542.

[34] I distinguish earlier from later work based on date of writing rather than date of publication.

[35] Letter from LL Fuller to then Vice-President Richard Nixon, 9 October 1959, The Papers of Lon Fuller, Harvard Law School Library, box 14, folder 1, at 1. The other urgent problem mentioned by Fuller is the proper organisation of economic regulation, *ibid* 1–2.

context his intervention *against* prominent public proposals to strengthen international adjudication, most notably by repealing the so-called Connally amendment, which detracted from US acceptance of the compulsory jurisdiction of the International Court of Justice.[36]

As with Hart, what drew Fuller to international law were the issues it presented for legal philosophy, including the problem 'what is law?' explored in their debate. In Fuller's remarks on international adjudication from that period, this concern with clarifying the meaning of the 'rule of law' converged with his concern to articulate 'the limits of adjudication', which arose from his interest in the practical problems of labour relations and administrative law.[37] Fuller's practical concern extended easily to international law because for him it shared with labour relations and administrative law 'the characteristic that in them if law exists at all, it exists imperfectly—it is still in process of being born'.[38] He thus shared Hart's view of international law as undeveloped.

Already in the 1959 draft of FLA (published posthumously in 1978), Fuller used international law as an illustration of the limits of adjudication. The fact that one of the only two portions of FLA to appear in print during Fuller's lifetime is a paper he delivered to an audience of international lawyers at the 1960 annual meeting of the American Society of International Law suggests that methods of international dispute settlement were more than just grist for his mill.[39] Further evidence of Fuller's concern about international adjudication is found in a 1959 letter he wrote to then Vice-President Richard Nixon.[40] Nixon had been Fuller's student at Duke Law School and, although a long-time Democrat, Fuller became active in Nixon's 1960 presidential campaign.[41]

In the letter, Fuller reported that Nixon's talk on the rule of law,[42] which he had sent to Fuller, was 'highly regarded by the experts here, the only doubt being whether there was not a little too much optimism in the assumption that the problem of Berlin could have been solved if the relevant treaties and agreements had contained a stipulation for the arbitration of disputes arising out of them'.[43] These 'experts' are not mentioned by name, but the doubt is certainly Fuller's own. In an intriguing gambit, he contrasted his high regard for Nixon's talk with

[36] See generally M Pomerance, *The United States and the World Court as a 'Supreme Court of the Nations': Dreams, Illusions and Disillusion* (The Hague, Martinus Nijhoff Publishers, 1996) 222–37, 261–332.

[37] LL Fuller, 'Adjudication and the Rule of Law' (1960) 54 *American Society of International Law Proceedings* 1, 1.

[38] *Ibid.*

[39] *Ibid.*

[40] Fuller letter, n 35 above.

[41] RS Summers, *Lon L. Fuller* (Stanford University Press, 1984) 11.

[42] The talk Nixon sent to Fuller is probably 'Developing the Rule of Law for the Settlement of International Disputes', Address by Vice-President Nixon, made before the Academy of Political Science at New York, 13 April 1959, reproduced in (1959) 40 (1036) *Department of State Bulletin* 622 (4 May).

[43] Fuller letter, n 35 above, at 2.

his 'great dismay' at the stance taken by Charles Rhyne and Arthur Larson, both mentioned positively by Nixon in his talk.[44] The immediate past president of the American Bar Association, Rhyne had made the use of law in international disputes a major platform of his presidency and was continuing his advocacy as chair of the ABA's newly established Special Committee on World Peace Through Law. Larson was a moderate Republican who had recently left the Eisenhower-Nixon administration to establish the World Rule of Law Center at Duke Law School.[45] While Nixon's talk was less evangelical and sweepingly programmatic than Rhyne's and Larson's agendas,[46] he similarly used the crisis over Berlin to urge that future agreements with the Soviet Union provide for binding adjudication by the International Court of Justice, recommended greater recourse to the Court through the modification of the Connally amendment, thereby setting an example to other states, and generally advocated finding practical methods to establish the rule of law as a way of settling disputes among nations.[47]

Although 'I have hitherto refrained from inflicting my writings on you', Fuller wrote to Nixon, he made an exception in enclosing a copy of FLA.[48] 'To speak of moving quickly to establish international courts without the slightest attention being paid to the kind of "law" they will apply is to do a great disservice to the ideal of the rule of law itself', Fuller went on to say, directing Nixon to the section of FLA in which he dealt with this problem.[49]

Fuller opposed international adjudication firstly because he viewed adjudication as always unsuitable to deciding polycentric, socio-political questions, by which he meant many-centred policy issues where 'a pull on one strand will distribute tensions after a complicated pattern on the web as a whole'.[50] While he

[44] Nixon talk, n 42 above, at 623–4. Nixon's mention of Rhyne and Larson may explain why Fuller singled them out and did not also take issue with various legal scholars advocating world peace, most notably his colleague Louis Sohn who had published *World Peace Through World Law* with Grenville Clark in 1958.

[45] A Larson, *Eisenhower: The President Nobody Knew* (New York, Charles Scribner's Sons, 1968) 108–12; DL Stebenne, *Modern Republican: Arthur Larson and the Eisenhower Years* (Bloomington, IN, Indiana University Press, 2006) 218–20. Larson spoke on the same panel as Fuller at the American Society of International Law meeting the following year. A Larson, 'Peace Through Law: The Rôle and Limits of Adjudication—Some Contemporary Applications' (1960) 54 *American Society of International Law Proceedings* 8.

[46] See, eg A Larson, *The International Rule of Law* (New York, Institute for International Order, 1961); A Larson, *When Nations Disagree: A Handbook on Peace Through Law* (Baton Rouge, Louisiana State University Press, 1961); A Larson, 'World Rule of Law: The Time Has Come', Address on the occasion of the second annual Law Day observances of Harvard Law School, 1 May 1959 (unpublished, on file with author); CS Rhyne, *Working for Justice in America and Justice in the World* (McLean, VA, Friends of Legal Profession Public Services, 1995) (containing a number of his speeches); CS Rhyne, 'A World-Wide Challenge to Lawyers: Law for Weapons in Resolving Disputes Between Nations' (1958) 24(16) *Vital Speeches of the Day* 483.

[47] Nixon talk, n 42 above, at 623–4, 626.

[48] Fuller letter, n 35 above, at 1.

[49] *Ibid* 2. The reference is to pp 17–28, which correspond to Fuller, 'Forms and Limits of Adjudication', n 30 above, at 372–81.

[50] Fuller, 1959 FLA draft, n 30 above, at 40; Fuller, 'Forms and Limits of Adjudication', n 30 above, at 395.

may not have thought that all international disputes were polycentric, he dwelled on ones that he did, such as the Berlin case and the question of Germany's future (mentioned in Nixon's talk), and the drawing of international boundaries. For Fuller, the adjudication of polycentric questions is inconsistent with the rule of law because it does not enable a party to participate meaningfully in a decision that affects her. The web of issues and hence the multiplicity of solutions are beyond the capacity of an ordinary litigant to address, and the court necessarily decides with an eye to broader considerations than those presented by the litigant. Moreover, the court is operating beyond its problem-solving capacity because, informed only by the parties to the dispute, it cannot anticipate all of the consequences that will flow from its judgment.[51]

Although Fuller's polycentricity analysis has actually been used to argue for the repeal of the UK Human Rights Act 1998, which implements the European Convention on Human Rights domestically,[52] Fuller was out of step with the rise of human rights litigation—domestic, international and transnational—and with influential theories of such processes. Already before the publication of FLA, Fuller's Harvard colleague Abram Chayes (in fact, an international lawyer) argued that Fuller's image of litigation was obsolete in the United States and a new type of 'public law' litigation had emerged, structured by a series of procedural innovations. Litigation had come to involve the 'vindication of constitutional or statutory policies' rather than the solution of 'disputes between private parties about private rights'.[53] Some two decades later, building on Chayes, Harold Koh heralded the arrival of transnational public law litigation, exemplified by international human rights cases brought in US courts under the Alien Tort Statute, and Anne-Marie Slaughter has modelled interactions among national and international courts in the implementation of public law.[54]

The second reason Fuller opposed international adjudication hinged on the undeveloped state of international law. Given that participation is central to the rule of law, Fuller argued, the litigant must have some idea of the basis on which the tribunal will decide, so that she has a meaningful opportunity to present her

[51] Fuller, 'Adjudication and the Rule of Law', n 37 above, at 2–5.

[52] J Morgan, 'Law's British Empire" (2002) 22 *Oxford Journal of Legal Studies* 729, 740–1. In public international law, a rare engagement with Fuller's polycentricity argument, including as applied to Berlin, is found in HW Baade, 'Some Basic Legal Problems Underlying the Berlin Dispute' in SD Metzger, JW Bishop, HW Baade and S Mendlovitz, *West Berlin: The Legal Context* (RJ Stanger (ed), Columbus, OH, Ohio State University Press, 1966) 53, 84–7; TM Franck, 'Structuring Impartiality in International Law' (1963–64) 39 *Indiana Law Journal* 448, 457–61. The occasional general reference to FLA is found, for example, in LR Helfer and A-M Slaughter, 'Toward a Theory of Effective Supranational Adjudication' (1997) 107 *Yale Law Journal* 273, 313, 320.

[53] A Chayes, 'The Role of the Judge in Public Law Litigation' (1976) 89 *Harvard Law Review* 1281, 1284. Compare Nicola Lacey, ch 1 (Fuller received similar criticism when he first circulated the 1959 draft of FLA).

[54] See D Kennedy, 'Abram Chayes' in D Kennedy and WW Fisher, III (eds), *The Canon of American Legal Thought* (Princeton University Press, 2006) 603, 618. See, eg Helfer and Slaughter, n 52 above; HH Koh, 'Transnational Public Law Litigation' (1991) 100 *Yale Law Journal* 2347; A-M Slaughter, 'Judicial Globalization' (2000) 40 *Virginia Journal of International Law* 1103.

case.[55] Since Fuller regarded international law as 'in process of being born', we might imagine his position to be that a more developed body of international law was needed before international adjudication could serve its purpose. However, Fuller took the position that courts could come first if conditions were such that principles of decision could emerge from adjudication without being laid down in advance. One condition was that polycentric disputes not be settled by courts because the adjudication of such disputes, he thought, does not yield a coherent body of doctrine over time. The other condition was the existence of an actual or potential extra-legal community of interest which could furnish courts with a source of principles, just as the common law of contracts developed alongside the economic institution of exchange, and its doctrines derived from the intrinsic demands of this community of interest.[56] This type of community was lacking in international law (a shared interest in avoiding reciprocal destruction was not sufficient),[57] although, as with polycentricity, it is hard to tell whether Fuller regarded it as a universal problem or was only focused on problem areas. Thus, what was most needed to develop the rule of law in international law was more community,[58] and Fuller in this spirit advocated 'every kind of exchange possible' with the USSR.[59]

Whereas Hart's contribution to the question 'is international law law?' has endured and been developed, Fuller's opposition to the international adjudicative process, first articulated in the late 1950s, has largely been forgotten, bypassed or outright discarded. Indeed, biographical context is needed to reconcile contemporary Fullerian international lawyers to his opposition given that they disagree with Fuller's apparent view in FLA that international society could not aspire to a rule of law. Context shows, however, that Fuller was reacting against utopian domestic-style proposals for a world rule of law such as Rhyne's and Larson's[60]

[55] Fuller, 'Adjudication and the Rule of Law', n 37 above, at 2, 5–6.

[56] *Ibid* 5–8.

[57] Fuller, 1959 FLA draft, n 30 above, at 23; Fuller, 'Forms and Limits of Adjudication', n 30 above, at 378.

[58] Fuller, 'Adjudication and the Rule of Law', n 37 above, at 8.

[59] Fuller, 1959 FLA draft, n 30 above, at 23. In the published version of FLA, Fuller added that in practice this community would take the form of relationships of reciprocity, as opposed to association by common aims, and he changed the phrase to 'every possible bond of reciprocity, every kind of useful exchange'. Fuller, 'Forms and Limits of Adjudication', n 30 above, at 378. Fuller's positive example involved the practice of Soviet arbitrators in foreign trade disputes taking their standards of fairness from the bourgeois trading community, suggesting that he may have anticipated that creating bonds of reciprocity between states would, or should, produce the spread of Western capitalist and democratic principles. Fuller, 1959 FLA draft, n 30 above, at 23–4; Fuller, 'Forms and Limits of Adjudication', n 30 above, at 378–9.

[60] Fuller was presumably reacting against the same sort of proposals later on in 'A Reply to Critics' when he referred to American world peace advocates who opt 'for the earliest possible realization of something like a world legal order "vertical style"'. Here he suspected some of them of being 'influenced not by political and sociological realities but by an impulse toward conceptual neatness, by a conviction that nothing counts as law that does not fit our accustomed definition of domestic law': Fuller, *The Morality of Law*, n 32 above, at 236.

and therefore emphasized the negative, but at the same time was committed to fostering the development of the community needed to give intellectual sustenance to international adjudication:

> When this has occurred—or rather *as* this occurs ... the law can act as a gardener who prunes an imperfectly growing tree in order to help the tree realize its own capacity for perfection. This can occur only when all concerned genuinely want the tree to grow and to grow properly. Our task is to make them want this.[61]

Thus situated, Fuller's analysis of international adjudication chimes with the view of Fullerian international legal theorists Jutta Brunnée and Stephen Toope, writing in 2009, that 'law is only possible within specific times and places where actors have developed certain basic understandings about what they hope to achieve together'.[62]

The more basic point here is that although the Hart–Fuller debate's silence on human rights might imply a certain provincialism, the international human rights law system was far from established in 1958, and Hart and Fuller, in fact, were alive to international law in their conceptions of law and thus engaged with questions important to this emerging system.

From Morality to International Human Rights

Perhaps the most obvious relevance of the Hart–Fuller debate for international human rights is that 50 years on, the role of morality in the debate is often played by international human rights law in the context of domestic adjudication. The 'problem posed by the existence of morally evil laws'[63] arises in the form of laws that violate the positive law of international human rights. Although Charlesworth does not pursue this point expressly, it is implicit in her observation that Hart and Fuller focused on the 'Grudge Informer' case, a post-war German case involving Nazi law, yet neither of their analyses reflected the availability of international human rights standards—precisely those standards for which 'the Nazi government's intimidation and destruction of sections of its own population was the major impetus'.[64]

By way of example, consider *Oppenheimer v Cattermole*,[65] a well-known case about a notoriously immoral Nazi law decided by the House of Lords 17 years after the Hart–Fuller debate. Meier Oppenheimer was a German Jew who had

[61] Fuller, 'Adjudication and the Rule of Law', n 37 above, at 8 (emphasis in original).

[62] J Brunnée and SJ Toope, 'An Interactional Theory of International Legal Obligation' (unpublished manuscript on file with author) 19; forthcoming in *Legitimacy and Legality in International Law: An Interactional Account* (Cambridge, Cambridge University Press, 2010).

[63] Hart, 'Positivism and the Separation of Law and Morals', n 2 above, at 616.

[64] Hilary Charlesworth, ch 2.

[65] *Oppenheimer v Cattermole* [1976] AC 249 (HL). The companion case was *Notham v Cooper*. Ms Notham, a teacher in Germany until Nazi persecution caused her to emigrate, 'conducted her own appeal with conspicuous courtesy and ability': *ibid.* 264 (Lord Hailsham of St Marylebone).

emigrated to England in 1939 to escape Nazi persecution and became a British subject in 1948. Under the infamous Nazi denationalisation decree of 1941, Jews lost their German nationality and their property if they were ordinarily resident abroad at the date of the decree. The issue in *Oppenheimer* was whether in addition to being a British subject, Oppenheimer was also a national of the Federal Republic of Germany and therefore exempt from income tax on his German pension under successive tax treaties between the two countries. Oppenheimer argued, inter alia, that the denationalisation decree was 'a flagrant breach of international law by reason of its objects being part of a policy physically and materially to destroy the Jewish sections of the country's population and to take away the means of building up a new life abroad for those Jews who at the risk of life and limb had succeeded in escaping the National Socialist tyranny'.[66] Of the decree, Lord Cross of Chelsea wrote: 'To my mind a law of this sort constitutes so grave an infringement of human rights that the courts of this country ought to refuse to recognise it as a law at all'.[67] Lord Salmon described the decree as 'so great an offence against human rights that it ought not to be recognised by any civilised system of law'.[68]

Lord Cross' often quoted words seem to echo neither Hart nor Fuller, but rather Gustav Radbruch, whose idea of law served as their foil.[69] Radbruch conceived of a law that violates fundamental morality as not being law at all. As such, he is the only one of the three for whom substantive injustice can invalidate a law. For Hart, a legal positivist, there is no necessary connection between law and morality. An unjust law is nevertheless a law and exists until replaced by another law. Whereas Fuller maintained that law has an inner morality, the principles of that morality, for him, are formal or procedural.[70] They include requirements widely associated with the rule of law, such as that laws be public, be prospective rather than retrospective, and be administered congruently with the laws as announced.[71] For Fuller, it has been argued, these principles are moral in nature because they require the law-giver to uphold the moral idea, definitive of the rule of law, that the subjects of a legal order must be respected and enabled as agents.[72] Fuller's position cannot be neatly summed up, but what emerges

[66] *Ibid* 257.

[67] *Ibid* 278.

[68] *Ibid* 283.

[69] Fuller, 'Positivism and Fidelity to Law: A Reply to Professor Hart', n 2 above, at 649–61; Hart, 'Positivism and the Separation of Law and Morals', n 2 above, at 616–21.

[70] I will use the common description of Fuller's principles as 'procedural', although Jeremy Waldron distinguishes them as 'formal', by which he means pertaining to 'the form that legal norms should take' as opposed to 'the broad character of the procedures that should be used in their application'. J Waldron, 'Positivism and Legality: Hart's Equivocal Response to Fuller' (2008) 83 *New York University Law Review* 1135, 1145. Fuller referred to them as 'principles of legality'.

[71] Fuller later listed eight such principles. Fuller, *The Morality of Law*, n 32 above, ch 2.

[72] See K Rundle, '"Forms Liberate": Reclaiming the Legal Philosophy of Lon L. Fuller' (Doctoral dissertation as submitted for examination, 26 June 2009, University of Toronto, on file with author) ch 5.

from his discussion of the 'Grudge Informer' case is that the violations of law's inner morality both in the applicable law and in the Nazi order as a whole might justify treating that law as invalid.[73] Hence, Fuller might have found the denationalisation decree invalid for reasons related to its creation, elaboration or administration,[74] but this is different from arguing, as Radbruch did, that it is invalid on substantive grounds.

In his reply to Hart, Fuller interprets Radbruch as espousing what David Dyzenhaus calls 'positivism with a minus sign': 'simply subtract[ing] extremely unjust laws from the category of the valid laws of the legal order'.[75] On this interpretation, Radbruch's conception of law captures something of the function of international human rights law in domestic legal systems that recognise international law as hierarchically superior and directly applicable. However, 'positivism with a minus sign' does not find expression in *Oppenheimer*, where international human rights law does not serve as this sort of higher law. In *Oppenheimer*, international human rights law instead contributed to the meaning of public policy in English law.[76] The question of Oppenheimer's German nationality fell to be determined under English law. English law, in turn, referred the question to German law. However, it made an exception if the relevant German law was contrary to public policy. Thus, public policy, informed by international human rights law, reflects a morality *internal* to law—which sounds more like Fuller.

If the House of Lords' reasoning in *Oppenheimer* thus falls between two chairs, Radbruch and Fuller, the intervening half century has produced a rich vein of scholarship that expands the relevance of both thinkers to cases such as *Oppenheimer* and thus to a farther-reaching analysis of international human rights law in domestic courts. Alternative interpretations of Radbruch present his idea of law as a 'continuum of connections' between law and justice, rather than 'positivism with a minus sign'.[77] Regarding Fuller, Dyzenhaus has developed the correspondence between common-law reasoning and Fuller's inner morality of

[73] Fuller, 'Positivism and Fidelity to Law: A Reply to Professor Hart', n 2 above, at 650–60.

[74] See Fuller's treatment of South Africa's apartheid laws in *The Morality of Law*, n 32 above, at 160–1 (emphasising the procedural defects of lack of clarity, contradictions and requiring the impossible).

[75] David Dyzenhaus, 'The Juristic Force of Injustice' in D Dyzenhaus and M Moran (eds), *Calling Power to Account: Law, Reparations, and the Chinese Canadian Head Tax Case* (University of Toronto Press, 2005) 256, 265. See D Dyzenhaus, 'The Grudge Informer Case Revisited' (2008) 83 *New York University Law Review* 1000, 1022, citing Fuller, 'Positivism and Fidelity to Law: A Reply to Professor Hart', n 2 above, at 660.

[76] JG Merril, '*Oppenheimer* v. *Cattermole*: The Curtain Falls' (1975) 24 *International and Comparative Law Quarterly Review* 617, 627–8.

[77] See, eg SL Paulson, 'Lon L. Fuller, Gustav Radbruch, and the "Positivist" Theses' (1994) 13(3) *Law and Philosophy* 313, 315–23; J Rivers, 'Gross Statutory Injustice and the Canadian Head Tax Case' in D Dyzenhaus and M Moran (eds), *Calling Power to Account: Law, Reparations, and the Chinese Canadian Head Tax Case* (University of Toronto Press, 2005) 233. The phrase 'continuum of connections' is from Dyzenhaus, 'The Juristic Force of Injustice', n 75 above, at 265 and see also *ibid.* 265–282.

law, in part by adding substantive equality to Fuller's principles of legality. While recognising that Fuller himself might not have agreed, Dyzenhaus argues that equality is needed to make sense of the principles as a whole and in particular to explain Fuller's principle that law be generally applicable.[78] Much more deserves to be said about this important legacy of the Hart–Fuller debate, but I hope this discussion suffices to illustrate its relevance to concrete cases and to the theorisation of the issues before the courts.

From the Concept of Law to Relationships Between Systems

I conclude, in the spirit of this volume, by proposing a new perspective on Hart and Fuller's 1958 exchange. The editor's inclusion of human rights and legal pluralism among the contemporary angles on the debate invites, I suggest, a shift in focus: from the concept of law to what the debate might have to say about the relationship between different legal systems, international and domestic, state and non-state, and so on.[79]

The Hart–Fuller debate, of course, was not about conflicts between these systems, but it was about conflicts between other systems, namely law and morality, and a past legal system and the present one in the 'Grudge Informer' case. Can one sort of conflict shed light on the other? Interestingly, as a private international law case, *Oppenheimer* shifts Nazi-era law from an issue of prior law for the German courts to an issue of foreign law for the English courts. Indeed, although not in relational terms, Mayo Moran has demonstrated that the comparison with private international law's treatment of foreign law should lead us to re-examine our assumptions about retroactivity and other issues in the adjudication of our own historically unjust laws.[80]

I share Moran's sense of the promise held by the idea that 'the past is a foreign country' and propose here that we also explore its converse. What fresh insights might the Hart–Fuller debate bring to private international law as the discipline that developed to deal with relationships between state legal systems, and (although I do not address this) to interactions between other types of legal systems? Not being a legal philosopher, I am clearly not the right person to tackle this question. My modest aim is simply to whet the appetite for it. I will try to do so by returning to *Oppenheimer* as a way to transnationalise Hart and Fuller's example and thereby their debate.

[78] Dyzenhaus, 'The Juristic Force of Injustice', n 75 above, at 258–9, 262–5, 280–1. See also E Fox-Decent, 'Is the Rule of Law Really Indifferent to Human Rights?' (2008) 27 *Law and Philosophy* 533.

[79] *cf* K Knop, R Michaels and A Riles, 'International Law in Domestic Courts: A Conflict of Laws Approach' (2009) 103 *American Society of International Law Proceedings* (forthcoming).

[80] M Moran, 'Time, Place, and Values: *Mack* and the Influence of the *Charter* on Private Law' in Dyzenhaus and Moran, n 75 above, at 378, 399–405.

In *Oppenheimer*, some of the judges considered it impossible or somehow fictitious for English law to attribute German nationality to Oppenheimer if Germany no longer regarded him as a national.[81] This asymmetry would not have troubled Hart, who made recognition and rules of recognition essential to determining the boundaries of a legal system.[82] Hart's view is congruent with an idea central to private international law which these judges resisted, namely, that a country's private international law rules indicate what effect a foreign law has for *that* country's legal system. There is no 'real' nationality within the sole jurisdiction of the national sovereign; there is only that national status recognised by a particular sovereign for a particular purpose. The English courts could not 'restore'[83] Oppenheimer's German nationality, but they could treat him as a German national for the purpose of English taxation.

Similarly, Hart can provide a justification for the common law's position that when English choice-of-law rules point to German law to determine Oppenheimer's status vis-à-vis Germany, what German law says is a question of fact to be proved by expert evidence in each case.[84] For Hart, it makes sense to treat foreign law as a fact because, for him, law *is* a social fact. Its determination rests on knowledge of the attitudes actually held by courts and other key officials.[85] The judge's options are either to apply the law as it would be applied in the foreign legal system or to invoke the public policy exception to choice of law. She cannot interpret the foreign law for herself and thereby lessen its injustice;[86] she can only refuse openly to recognise its effect in her own legal system.

Against Hart, Fuller argued that Nazi law should not be treated as if 'the only difference between Nazi law and, say, English law is that the Nazis used their law to achieve ends that are odious to an Englishman'.[87] For Fuller, whether Nazi law was law could not be addressed absent consideration of the 'truly frightful predicament'[88] presented to post-war Germany by Hitler's degradation of the German legal system through such violations of law's inner morality as resort to

[81] *Oppenheimer v Cattermole*, n 65 above, at 263 (Lord Hailsham of St Marylebone), 265–6 (Lord Pearson, dissenting).

[82] Compare HLA Hart, 'Kelsen's Doctrine of the Unity of Law' in HE Kiefer and MK Munitz (eds), *Ethics and Social Justice* (Albany, NY, State University of New York Press, 1970) 171, 179, 193 (Hart's hypothetical English law that purports to validate all of the laws of a foreign country, but absent recognition by the foreign country's courts and law-enforcement agencies does so only for the purposes of English law).

[83] *Oppenheimer v Cattermole*, n 65 above, at 266 (Lord Pearson, dissenting).

[84] This having been said, foreign law is a question of fact 'of a peculiar kind'. *Parkasho v Singh* [1968] P 223, 250. In *Oppenheimer*, for example, the House of Lords proceeded on the basis that it was open to them, despite being an appellate court, to decide what German law said. *Oppenheimer v Cattermole*, n 65 above, at 270 (Lord Cross of Chelsea).

[85] Indeed, Hart, in passing, differentiates choice-of-law rules as 'derivative' rules of recognition. Hart, 'Kelsen's Doctrine of the Unity of Law', n 82 above, at 196.

[86] The judge's own interpretive principles, of course, might play a role in choosing between the evidence of foreign law presented by the opposing sides.

[87] Fuller, 'Positivism and Fidelity to Law: A Reply to Professor Hart', n 2 above, at 650.

[88] *Ibid* 648.

retroactive laws to cure past legal irregularities, secret laws, bypassing of law and disregard even for their own enactments, and the distortion of statutes by Nazi judges, as in the 'Grudge Informer' case. Fuller expressed the nature of the dilemma thus: 'Germany had to restore both respect for law and respect for justice. Though neither of these could be restored without the other, painful antinomies were encountered in attempting to restore both at once'.[89]

Fuller's analysis suggests an unstated explanation of why the House of Lords dealt with the question of whether to recognise the Nazi decree, the question for which the case is best known. In fact, post-war German case law had declared the decree void *ab initio*. The relevant German law was instead the Basic Law, the 1949 Constitution, which essentially provided that the nationality of denationalised Jewish Germans was not automatically restored, but that they could reclaim it by way of application.[90] Applying the Basic Law, the House of Lords found that since Oppenheimer had not applied to have his German nationality restored, he was not a German national and was therefore subject to taxation on his German pension.[91] The House of Lords nevertheless addressed the Nazi decree because the issue had been argued and decided in the courts below.[92] In the Court of Appeal, Buckley LJ had written: 'whether or not the person is a national or citizen of the country must be answered in light of the law of that country however inequitable, oppressive or objectionable it may be'.[93]

Although not in terms of Fuller's inner morality of law, a number of the judges in *Oppenheimer* recognised the predicament he discussed and expressed respect for the German Constitution's solution to the problem that its framers 'were unwilling to admit that the 1941 decree had ever been part of the law of Germany but at the same time they did not wish to thrust German nationality on people who did not want it'.[94] Similarly, in deciding to address the hypothetical question whether to recognise the Nazi denationalisation decree, the judges may have sought to support Germany's invalidating of the decree by showing that English law and also international law would find it invalid.

Perhaps less obviously, Fuller's perspective has implications for the English legal system. In counterpoint to the Hart–Fuller debate, David Fraser has shown that whereas the German courts were confronted with the problem of Nazi law after the war, the courts of other countries faced the problem while Hitler was still in power. He portrays the resulting case law in the United Kingdom and the United States as 'confused and confusing': sometimes Nazi law was recognised as

[89] *Ibid* 657.

[90] The House of Lords assumed in Oppenheimer's favour that he did not lose his German nationality on becoming a British subject in 1948. *Oppenheimer v Cattermole*, n 65 above, at 270 (Lord Cross of Chelsea).

[91] *Ibid* 269–72.

[92] *Ibid* 275 (Lord Cross of Chelsea).

[93] *Oppenheimer v Cattermole* [1973] 1 Ch 264, 273 (Buckely LJ), 274 (Orr LJ concurring) (CA).

[94] *Oppenheimer v Cattermole*, n 65 above, at 271 (Lord Cross of Chelsea). See also *ibid* 262–3 (Lord Hailsham of St Marylebone), 284 (Lord Salmon).

law, sometimes it was not.[95] It is possible that the House of Lords in *Oppenheimer* was concerned not only to set the doctrine straight, as against the Court of Appeal, but to address implicitly any taint to their own legal system from its treatment of Nazi-era law—to effect what Fuller called a 'kind of cleanup operation'.[96] A judicial hypothetical was the only way to do so because Germany had already found the decree void *ab initio* and therefore the question of its recognition would not otherwise come before either the Parliament or the courts in the United Kingdom. And this clean-up could only be implicit because no taint arose in *Oppenheimer* insofar as English law for the duration of a war did not recognise a change in nationality brought about by the enemy state.[97]

More generally, a transnationalised Fullerian perspective might invite us to consider how a legal system that respects his inner morality of law can interact with the laws of a system that does not, without itself being affected. Private international law has a long experience with this question; for example, procedural issues are always governed by the forum's law, and, in English common law, breach of natural justice is a bar to the recognition of a foreign judgment. However, English common-law private international law does not factor Fuller's principles of legality into a choice-of-law analysis. Fuller's question about a prior law can equally be asked about a foreign law:

> Can it be argued seriously that it would have been more beseeming to the judicial process if the postwar [substitute 'forum'] courts had undertaken a study of 'the interpretive principles' in force during Hitler's rule and had then solemnly applied those 'principles' to ascertain the meaning of this statute? On the other hand, would the courts really have been showing respect for Nazi [substitute 'foreign'] law if they had construed the Nazi [substitute 'foreign'] statutes by their own, quite different, standards of interpretation?[98]

English private international law opts for the former, as would Hart. It does not ask generally about a foreign law whether, to cite from Fuller's list of principles, it is secret, highly unclear or self-contradictory, or requires the impossible.[99] Hence, in the case of procedurally unjust foreign laws that fall short of the public policy

[95] D Fraser, '"This is Not Like Any Other Legal Question": A Brief History of Nazi Law Before U.K. and U.S. Courts' (2003) 19 *Connecticut Journal of International Law* 59, 125.

[96] Fuller, 'Positivism and Fidelity to Law: A Reply to Professor Hart', n 2 above, at 661.

[97] *Oppenheimer v Cattermole*, n 65 above, at 275 (Lord Cross of Chelsea).

[98] *Ibid* 655.

[99] Interestingly, Fuller's perspective highlights Lord Hailsham's implicit application, in obiter, of one of Fuller's principles of legality: the impossibility principle that a law should not require conduct beyond the power of the affected party. Given that English law would not recognise the 1941 denationalisation decree, the further hypothetical issue was whether English law would treat Oppenheimer instead as having lost his German nationality under a 1913 German law that required him to obtain the permission of the German authorities before he became a British subject if he wanted to retain his German nationality. German jurisprudence seemed to say 'no' and although this would have been sufficient answer for English private international law, Lord Hailsham went on to emphasise that the relevant authorities 'did not then exist, and ... if they had existed, would almost certainly have refused the application on the ground that they had no jurisdiction to grant it': *Oppenheimer v Cattermole*, n 65 above, at 264.

exception, the English courts may apply a foreign law that contains within it the violation of Fuller's inner morality. It is a nice question whether Fuller would approve, given that his discussion is actually of a judgment as opposed to a law. Leaving aside general questions about how to apply his principles of legality to a single law, private international law also raises questions about context for Fuller's imperatives. If a law is invalid in part for reasons that pertain to the legal system as a whole, then how do we approach the question of its validity when it arises through choice of law in a legal system without these systemic defects?

While Fuller's inner morality of law does not lump all laws in a foreign legal system together as either law or not law,[100] we may also ask whether it is consistent with recognising a particular foreign law for certain purposes and not others. In some cases it was a greater disadvantage for Jewish German émigrés to have their loss of German nationality recognised and perhaps be found stateless, and in other cases it was worse to be treated as having retained it, for example, when that meant being classified as an enemy alien.[101] Despite the impact on Oppenheimer (who would be taxed on his German pension), Lord Cross of Chelsea and Lord Salmon maintained that the 1941 Nazi denationalisation decree should not be recognised as law under any circumstances.[102] However, Lord Hailsham gave greater importance to the fact that the effect on individuals was often negative: 'There would seem small value in adding hardship to injustice in order to emphasise the cruel nature of the injustice'. In this light, he noted that 'It may well be that English law will not give a single and unequivocal answer to the problems raised by the unjust and discriminatory legislation of a foreign country'.[103] François Rigaux presents this ability to give a 'yes and no' answer as a virtue of a private international law approach.[104]

In these comments, I have suggested three ways to read the Hart–Fuller debate's silence on international human rights as other than silence. First, if we interpret international human rights concretely to mean the system of international human rights *law*, including its status as law and processes of adjudication, then not only were Hart's and Fuller's competing conceptions of law in the debate both relevant, but they themselves made these connections in other writings around the same time, Hart with more lasting impact than Fuller. Secondly, by recognising the role of international human rights as *morality*, we find a ready-made place for international human rights in an exchange structured around positivism and the separation of law and morals. As I have illustrated, this is a correspondence visible in judicial decisions and enriched by the analytical literature. Finally, reframing the debate in terms of relationships between legal

[100] See Fuller, 'Positivism and Fidelity to Law: A Reply to Professor Hart', n 2 above, at 660–1.

[101] See FA Mann, 'The Present Validity of Nazi Nationality Laws' (1973) 89 *Law Quarterly Review* 194, 202–7.

[102] *Oppenheimer v Cattermole*, n 65 above, at 278 (Lord Cross of Chelsea), 283–4 (Lord Salmon).

[103] *Ibid*, 263.

[104] F Rigaux, *La Loi des Juges* (Paris, Éditions Odile Jacob, 1997) 120.

systems offers a way to unify a number of the contemporary angles on the debate explored in this volume: transitional justice (past and present), international human rights (international and domestic), and legal pluralism (state and non-state). Using private international law—the field of law that developed to deal with relationships between state legal systems—and specifically *Oppenheimer* as a private international law variant of the 'Grudge Informer' case, I have sought to connect the Hart–Fuller debate to some of the issues that arise when legal systems interact and thereby to propose a new reading for our time.

4

International Criminal Law and the Inner Morality of Law

LARRY MAY

In Book V of the *Nicomachean Ethics*, Aristotle gives one of the first statements of the rule of law when he says: 'we allow only reason, not a human being, to be ruler'.[1] Aristotle then divides political justice into two parts. 'One part of the politically just is natural, and the other part legal. The natural has the same validity everywhere alike, independent of its seeming so or not.'[2] This characterisation of the natural part of justice is sometimes associated with the so-called natural duties of justice, specifically with the substantive duties to promote just institutions. But, it seems that Aristotle, at least at that point in his *Ethics*, is referring to something procedural, what might be called 'natural fairness'.

In my view, the debate between Hart and Fuller about the internal aspect of rules or the inner morality of law concerns an issue that is similar to what Aristotle meant by the natural part of justice, namely that part of natural fairness that stays the same from society to society, and perhaps even outside of particular societies, for instance, in the international arena. In this respect one could ask whether there is something like a natural duty to support procedures, such as habeas corpus, that provide minimal fairness for those who have been incarcerated or detained. And if there is such a duty, is it part of the inner morality of law? In his eighth desideratum of the rule of law, Fuller mentions such things as habeas corpus as an aspect of procedural due process, but he does little more than mention it; Hart does not mention it at all. But both legal theorists are focused more on procedural than substantive justice.

In what follows I will investigate what Fuller called 'procedural natural law' in contemporary international criminal law. Most of the theoretical and normative writings about international criminal law have so far been about substantive law, focusing on the four crimes over which the International Criminal Court (ICC)

1 Aristotle, *Nicomachean Ethics*, 1134a35.
2 *Ibid.* 1134b20.

has jurisdiction: crimes against humanity, war crimes, genocide and the crime of aggression.[3] International justice is thought to have come to maturity as these four substantive crimes have been prosecuted by international tribunals and courts. In my view, it is time for international legal theorists and practitioners to take into account procedural issues in as much detail as has been given to substantive ones. I will argue that procedural rights are part of what constitutes the rule of law and are especially important as gap-fillers in creating an international rule of law that respects fundamental fairness. International criminal law will not come to maturity as a system of law unless protections of fundamental fairness, such as a global right of habeas corpus, are put in place.

In this chapter I will use the Hart–Fuller debate as a springboard for assessing procedural rights within the context of the international rule of law. In the first two sections I will rehearse the relevant part of the Hart–Fuller debate as it pertains to the subject of international law and also to the inner morality of law. In the third section I will set out some of my views on these matters, drawing on both Hart and Fuller, concerning the value of fundamental procedural rights. In the fourth section I will discuss the right of habeas corpus, as a good test case of how to think about these issues. In the final sections I will expand on these remarks and argue that procedural rights need to be better protected in international law, if it is to have a claim to legitimacy as a mature legal system.

Hart on International Law and The Rule of Law

HLA Hart draws a distinction between primary rules, in which 'human beings are required to do or abstain from certain actions', and secondary rules, which may introduce, extinguish or modify primary rules.[4] Hart is often interpreted as requiring a rule of recognition, which involves secondary rules that establish how primary rules are to be recognised as valid law; indeed Ronald Dworkin talks about the rule of recognition as a 'master rule' for Hart.[5] Yet, in his treatment of international law in the final chapter of his book, *The Concept of Law*, Hart does not deny that international law is law, even though international law, at least in the early 1960s, seemed to Hart to lack a rule of recognition. In this respect, consider the final sentence of his book:

> Bentham, the inventor of the expression 'international law', defended it simply by saying that it was 'sufficiently analogous' to municipal law. To this two comments are perhaps

[3] I have written studies of each of these substantive international crimes: *Crimes Against Humanity: A Normative Account* (Cambridge, Cambridge University Press, 2005); *War Crimes and Just War* (Cambridge, Cambridge University Press, 2007); *Aggression and Crimes Against Peace* (Cambridge, Cambridge University Press, 2008); and *Genocide: A Normative Account* (Cambridge, Cambridge University Press, forthcoming 2010).

[4] HLA Hart, *The Concept of Law* (Oxford, Oxford University Press, 1961; revised edn 1994) 81.

[5] See Ronald Dworkin, 'The Model of Rules I' in *Taking Rights Seriously* (London, Duckworth, 1977) 41.

> worth adding. First, that the analogy is one of content not of form; secondly, that in the analogy of content, no other social rules are so close to municipal law as those of international law.[6]

This is not to say that formal features of a system of rules were unimportant to Hart. But on the penultimate page of his book, Hart spoke of emancipating 'ourselves from the assumption that international law *must* contain a basic rule'.[7]

Hart himself often says that law is best understood as the 'union of primary and secondary rules'. But by the last chapter of his book, the chapter on international law, Hart is at pains to point out that while this union provides a 'sufficient condition for the application of the expression "legal system"' he has not claimed 'that the word "law" must be defined in its terms'. Instead, he says that the 'idea of a union of primary and secondary rules ... may be regarded as a mean between juristic extremes'.[8] Arguably, what is even more important for Hart for establishing that a set of rules is a legal system is whether the people who live under the set of rules have an internal perspective or point of view toward these rules, where one is concerned with rules 'as a member of a group which accepts and uses them as guides to conduct'.[9]

For Hart, the internal perspective is crucial for legal systems, but there are arguably two candidates for this perspective, only one of which is truly so. What is crucial for distinguishing 'social rules from mere group habits' 'is that there should be a critical reflective attitude to certain patterns of behavior as a common standard, and that this should display itself in criticism (including self-criticism), demands for conformity, and in acknowledgement that such criticism and demands are justified'.[10] Taking this internal perspective is crucial for the proper functioning of a system of rules that is considered authoritative and deserving of obedience.

In Hart's view, international law can be law properly so-called. In the early 1960s, Hart already recognised that international law very closely resembled domestic municipal law in its content, although not in its form, since international law lacked a rule of recognition. Indeed, Hart probably would say something different today, especially with the institution of the International Criminal Court and its complex statute, as well as with the growing recognition and acceptance of the legitimacy of international law in nearly all quarters. But there is another way to understand the legitimacy of the claim that international law is law properly so called.

International law is easier to understand if one focuses on such things as 'the internal aspect of rules' rather than sovereignty which creates or enforces a

[6] *Ibid.* 237.
[7] *Ibid.* 236.
[8] *Ibid.* 212.
[9] *Ibid.* 89.
[10] *Ibid.* 57.

master rule. As Hart recognised, there is an 'absence of an international legislature, courts with compulsory jurisdiction, and centrally organized sanctions'. These absences have inspired 'misgivings' about whether international law is properly called law, especially since the absence of such things seems to indicate lack of a rule of recognition.[11] Hart was seemingly not one of the people who had these misgivings, at least not in a way that made him doubt that international law could be law properly so called. The fact that Hart recognised that many saw international law as a 'doubtful case',[12] and that he placed international law in his last chapter, indicates that he also saw it as a hard case. But as I have been arguing, he probably also saw international law as a good example for discussing the relative importance of the internal point of view as opposed to the union of primary and secondary rules in identifying when there is a system of law.

In eventually taking up the case of procedural rights like habeas corpus it will be important to remember that Hart stressed the importance of 'demands for conformity' with primary rules, as well as a 'centrally organized system of sanctions'. In international law, especially international criminal law, both of these factors are currently hard to satisfy in a rigorous way since there is no sovereign international state that can accomplish or facilitate these things. But gaps in sanctions can be filled without a fully centralised system in place, especially if the relevant officials take an internal perspective toward the law. Especially in high profile cases, indictment and arrest procedures that are piecemeal can go a long way, as can other piecemeal techniques for protecting substantive rights internationally.

At the end of the chapter, I will take up the case of the Guantanamo detainees who tried to get their substantive rights protected even though there was no centrally organised international sanctioning power. The Guantanamo detainees filed habeas corpus petitions in order to put public pressure on the US government to protect their substantive rights. And in addition, habeas corpus appeals sought to prevent the 'legal black holes' that had seemingly opened because of gaps in the international legal system. In this sense, habeas corpus was a gap-filler that helped establish an international rule of law even though there are still not executive and legislative branches of an international government.

Hart was right to think that as international law comes to have more institutional arrangements that are like municipal law, it will resemble municipal law in form as well as in content. And we are certainly moving in this direction with the creation of the International Criminal Court with some compulsory jurisdiction and centrally organised sanctions, at least for those states which have ratified the Rome Treaty. And as the Security Council acts more and more like a world legislature, similarly international law moves closer to municipal law. There is still a lack of fully centralised sanctions in international law, although the various

[11] *Ibid.* 214.
[12] *Ibid.* 3.

appellate courts at the ICTY, ICTR and ICC have been striving valiantly to create a piecemeal uniformity of sanctions, despite lacking a fully centralised mechanism of enforcement of its indictments and judgments. But in the mean time, what has been most striking since the early 1960s, when Hart wrote his book, is how far the world community has moved in developing an internal perspective on international law, especially international criminal law. And with the development of this perspective, some of Hart's worries about international law have been addressed.

In chapter 9 of *The Concept of Law*, Hart launches his own positive discussion of natural law by explaining that there is a 'rational connection between natural facts and the content of legal and moral rules'. Without a minimal natural content to the law, 'men, as they are, would have no reason for obeying voluntarily any rules'.[13] At least some members of the society must voluntarily accept the rules. 'Without their voluntary cooperation, thus creating *authority*, the coercive power of law and government cannot be established'.[14] And for the system to be most stable, these people 'must conceive of themselves as morally bound to do so'.[15] The natural facts must be satisfied for such an acceptance, and their acceptance is expressed in 'internal statements'; but this does not mean that they 'are thereby committed to a moral judgment'.[16]

So for Hart there is a relationship between the minimal content of natural law and the internal perspective; but what is unclear is exactly what the relationship is. And more importantly for this chapter, why restrict the relevant natural facts to the content of rules instead of also to the minimal form of these rules? Would Hart recognise the kind of procedural natural law that Fuller discussed, and that Aristotle seemed also to embrace? Hart seems to suggest that the form also matters when he addresses Fuller directly by claiming that 'in general [rules] must not be retrospective, though exceptionally they may be'.[17] Hart even allows that such considerations may properly be called 'the inner morality of law' yet he couches this acceptance of Lon Fuller's terminology by then stipulating 'It is unfortunately compatible with very great iniquity'.[18]

Some content and also some form seems to be required for law to attain the voluntary acceptance of some of the population. Hart has put his finger on a crucial point: certain things are required for any system of rules to attain sufficient voluntary acceptance in a population to be called a system of law. And Hart's own emphasis on secondary rules as involving largely procedural matters points us toward what must be better secured in international law if there is to be a system of law in the international domain that achieves acceptance as well. Or

[13] *Ibid.* 93.
[14] *Ibid.* 201.
[15] *Ibid.* 203.
[16] *Ibid.*
[17] *Ibid.*
[18] *Ibid.* 207.

at least this is one way to interpret Hart's claim that international law resembles municipal law in content but not yet in form. When international law acquires municipal law's form it will then have a claim to be a mature system of law. As I will indicate in the ensuing discussion of Fuller, the form that is most important is that there is a guarantee of formal fairness that largely comes from the protection of procedural rights.

Fuller on Procedural Natural Law

Lon Fuller was critical of many of the theses and arguments advanced by Hart, but there is nonetheless a striking similarity in how they regarded the internal perspective of a system of law. Hart does recognise the connection between this internal perspective and what he called the minimal content of the natural law, and Fuller makes this connection more explicit and in that sense moves us forward in understanding what needs to happen for international law to become a mature system of law. Whether or not Fuller really does fit into the natural law tradition, he does link something like Hart's internal perspective to certain minimal natural law, and what he also calls moral, considerations that have historically been identified with the rule of law.

For Fuller, there are eight desiderata that, when not satisfied, lead to disaster for the rule of law. Here are the ways failure can occur:

(1) a failure to have rules at all;
(2) a failure to publicise the rules;
(3) the abuse of retroactive legislation;
(4) a failure to make rules understandable;
(5) the enactment of contradictory rules;
(6) rules that require conduct beyond the powers of the affected party;
(7) introducing such frequent changes in the rules that the subject cannot orient his action by them;
(8) a failure of congruence between the rules as announced and their actual administration.[19]

And Fuller helps us understand what is necessary for a set of rules to be a legal system when he says that his eight desiderata concern:

> a procedural, as distinguished from a substantive, natural law. What I have called the internal morality of law is in this sense a procedural version of natural law, though to avoid misunderstanding the word 'procedural' should be assigned a special and expanded sense so that it would include, for example, a substantive accord between official action and enacted law.[20]

[19] Lon Fuller, *The Morality of Law* (New Haven, CT, Yale University Press, 1964; revised edn 1969) 39 and 96.
[20] *Ibid.* 96–7.

For Fuller, 'substantive natural law' concerns 'the proper ends to be sought through legal rules'.[21] Procedural natural law is necessary for rules to be rules at all, and for them to form a system. In this respect there appears to be a connection between the internal perspective on rules that Hart identified and Fuller's inner morality of law.

The inner morality of law is a set of procedures, such as non-retroactivity, that rules must conform to in order for there to be a system of rules at all. As Hart pointed out, to call this an inner 'morality' is questionable, especially since it is compatible with great iniquity. Fuller contends that a system of rules that satisfied his eight desiderata would not be a system that could be gravely iniquitous. Whether properly moral or not, there is no doubt that these desiderata are procedural constraints on rules that when adhered to make of these rules a system of rules that is deserving of respect. And in that sense they satisfy Hart's concern that law appeal at least to some members of society as fair and just and hence deserving of their voluntary co-operation and recognition as being authoritative. One way to begin to understand the possibility of common ground between Hart and Fuller is to see that the inner morality of law must be satisfied in order for people within the system of rules to take an internal perspective toward these rules.

In my view, Hart and Fuller did not really disagree much about what constitutes the inner morality of law. Rather they disagreed about whether and to what extent it really was a 'morality' that connected to ideas such as justice and fairness in a way that blocks iniquity within a system of law. In another place I have suggested that this was at best a minimal moral notion, but that is not to denigrate its moral character nonetheless.[22] Perhaps this is merely to say that these requirements must be satisfied for a system of law to deserve our fidelity to it, where this might capture what both Hart and Fuller wanted, although they both failed to recognise an important aspect of these procedures.

For Fuller, concerning any legal system the procedural natural law can be summarised in one expression, 'due process of law'.[23] Fuller gives as an example 'judicial review'.[24] And he says 'What law must foreseeably do to achieve its aims, is something quite different from law itself'.[25] But why does Fuller think that certain procedural matters are not properly part of the legal system, rather than merely being different types of procedure within a system of law? Perhaps some procedures directly protect substantive rights and others do so in a less direct, although no less important way. Indeed that is what he says of the eighth desideratum. There may be due process rights that guarantee that legal systems

[21] *Ibid.* 98.

[22] See my treatment of this topic in the first few chapters of my book, *Crimes Against Humanity: A Normative Account* (Cambridge, Cambridge University Press, 2005).

[23] Fuller, *The Morality of Law*, n 19 above, at 103.

[24] *Ibid.* 104.

[25] *Ibid* 108.

have a substantive fairness. But also there may be other procedural matters that protect the formal fairness of a system of law without having much to do with any particular substantive right.

Fuller says, 'It is precisely when the legal system takes up weapons of violence that we impose on it the most stringent requirements of due process'. Fuller then says that whenever people embark on 'subjecting certain kinds of human conduct to the explicit control of rules' 'they come to see that this enterprise contains a certain inner logic of its own, that it imposes demands that must be met (sometimes with considerable inconvenience) if its objectives are to be attained'.[26] But Fuller did not seem to see that some rules, like those of habeas corpus, could be very important and yet not necessarily protect any substantive rights. Indeed, habeas corpus is just the kind of procedural right that would protect the formal as opposed to the substantive fairness of a system of law, since what habeas corpus primarily protects against is arbitrariness of decisions, as we will see.

For Fuller, following his eight desiderata would require that there be stringent rules of due process for there to be international criminal law. And this includes judicial review, something currently lacking. As I will argue later, I believe that one of the best things to do to begin to bridge this gap is for there to be an institutionalised international version of procedural natural law, including a right of habeas corpus. In criminal matters, habeas corpus functions as a rudimentary basis of something like judicial review. Interestingly, Fuller does mention habeas corpus once in *The Morality of Law*, and links it to 'procedural due process' under his eighth desideratum, the 'Congruence Between Official Action and Declared Rule'.[27] And he did recognise that it is in this eighth desideratum that there would be rules that were not necessarily themselves part of the legal system. But he didn't put these pieces together and hence missed an important point for the analysis of law in general and international law in particular.

Valuing Visibleness and The Rule Of Law

In considering the idea of formal or procedural natural law, one wonders whether Hart would recognise a 'minimal *form* of natural law' similar to the 'minimal *content* of natural law'. Would Hart regard certain procedural matters, such as the right to habeas corpus, as similar to the substantive prohibitions on murder or theft, as key components for any legal system, given what we know of humans? While neither Hart nor Fuller addressed this issue directly, I believe that key components of the rule of law would indeed be seen by both theorists as important for the natural justice of a legal system. In what follows, I am sympathetic to Fuller's brief suggestion that a version of procedural natural law

[26] *Ibid* 150–1.
[27] *Ibid* 81.

involves a right of habeas corpus, among other basic due process rights. In criminal matters, habeas corpus functions as a rudimentary basis of something like judicial review.

The value of habeas corpus concerns what I call the normative *principle of visibleness*[28] in detention and incarceration as a counter to the secrecy that masks arbitrary exercise of power in this domain. Habeas corpus stands for the proposition at its most minimal, but also at its most powerful, that no one can be hidden in jail or prison. And the reason for this is that such secrecy is too likely to hide mistreatment and abuse. Henry Maine said that 'substantive law has at first the look of being gradually secreted in the interstices of procedure'.[29] It is fitting that what is secreted in the interstices of the procedural right of habeas corpus is the moral principle against secrecy in confinement. Habeas corpus is in one respect the idea that the body of the prisoner must literally be made publicly visible, but this very rudimentary procedure has very great value.

For several thousand years, philosophers have embraced the idea that if one were invisible the normal moral constraints would not be operative. This is presumably as true of Plato's Lydian shepherd who could make himself invisible and hence avoid detection of his crimes, as of the jailer who can make the prisoner invisible and hence hide the jailer's crimes as well. Arbitrariness often seems to need the cloak of secrecy and invisibility. The Lydian shepherd may use his new power for the good of his people, but if he then chooses to use it for ill, there is no stopping him from doing so. The ruler, or jailer, who discovers that he can render a person invisible from public view, may also use this power for wrongdoing, or for hiding wrongdoing, and such abuse of power is at least partially stopped by the anticipation of habeas corpus appeals.

The principle of visibleness does not guarantee that those who are detained or incarcerated will not be treated wrongly or even that they will be treated fairly, but only that if they are to be treated unfairly it cannot be done completely in secret. Blackstone, writing in the eighteenth century, put this point quite well:

> But confinement of the person, by secretly hurrying him to gaol, where his sufferings are unknown and forgotten; is a less public, a less striking, and therefore a more dangerous engine of arbitrary government.[30]

Security of the person is often a key by-product of habeas corpus. The principle of visibleness is a protection of personal security, which, as Justice Kennedy said, 'subsists, too, in fidelity to freedom's first principles'.[31]

[28] The OED lists, as one of the earliest uses of the term visibleness, a sixteenth century reference to the fact that the Catholic Church did not maintain open procedures.

[29] Sir Henry Maine, *Dissertations on Early Law and Custom* (New York, Henry Holt and Company, 1886) 389.

[30] William Blackstone, *Commentaries on the Laws of England* (1765, facsimile of the 1st edn, University of Chicago Press, 1979) vol I, 132.

[31] *Boumediene v Bush*, 128 SCt 2229 (2008) at 2239

The prospect of the revelation of the wrongdoing through even a very rudimentary habeas corpus procedure may act as a deterrent against the wrongdoing occurring at all, or against similar wrongdoings occurring in the future. And in this sense, habeas corpus is clearly related to a human good, namely that wrongdoing should not occur. But habeas corpus is indirectly, not directly related to this good. And it is my view that this is the way that procedural rights are normally related to substantive ones. Procedural rights do not normally have value in themselves, but only as they somehow support substantive rights. There is one exception to this idea and that concerns the so-called rule of law.

Merely having some procedural rules that govern human affairs is often thought to be of value insofar as rule by these rules is better than rule by 'man'. In this sense rule by rules is definitive of the rule of law and against the kind of arbitrariness that comes when people make decisions unconstrained by rules. Procedural rules have value here because they are constitutive of a norm, not merely because they support some other norm. The norm that these procedural rules constitute is itself a procedure. Procedural rights can have intrinsic value in that they are constitutive of a rule of law which promotes fairness. In this sense, procedural rights do not necessarily have content, and while they aim at a certain good, that good, fairness and non-arbitrariness, need not have content, unlike the goods that substantive rights aim at, such as property rights or free speech rights, which have content and aim at a particular human good.

Non-arbitrariness is related to a type of fairness that involves complying with a rule, conjoined with a system of overseeing that the rule is complied with. Political orders are arbitrary, both by having rule by the whim of a person or persons, instead of by a rule, and by having no oversight. The value of non-arbitrariness is hard to characterise. There is a kind of formal fairness that is achieved when procedural rights are respected. Habeas corpus provides a minimal rule for how jailers and rulers should behave, and also a rudimentary system for oversight. In this sense, habeas corpus epitomises procedural fairness. Of course, there is also value to procedural rights in the various ways that they are means to substantive ends.

Habeas corpus was initially thought of as merely the right to be brought from the dungeon and publicly told of the charges against one. At nearly the same time, the right also came to be seen as a right to have those charges assessed to see if there was a prima facie reason to think that they had any basis, and this was understood as the right not to be arbitrarily incarcerated. Later, habeas corpus came to stand for the right to due process in general. And later still, habeas corpus was understood, as it is today in the American system of law, as a right to challenge an incarceration on the basis of any of one's significant constitutional liberties. So, the history of habeas corpus incorporates at least three different ways to understand this right. In the first instance, habeas corpus is a non-derivative procedural right, since the right to be brought into the light of day and told of the charges against one does not address the substantive charges or the eventual trial of the accused. In the second instance, the right becomes a derivative procedural right, especially when it is seen as protecting certain substantive rights such as the right against arbitrary denial of liberty. Finally, habeas corpus comes to be seen as a substantive right, to particular constitutional liberties.

Habeas corpus can be constitutive of the rule of law in that it is clearly better that prisoners be treated according to a regime that has the habeas corpus rule than subject to the possibly arbitrary rule of their jailers. Habeas corpus is a paradigmatic constituent of the rule of law insofar as it stands against the arbitrary exercise of authority. Generally, the rule of law concerns the limitation on a ruler's authority by rules imposed on rulers, not made by them. The value of the rule of law, as with the value of habeas corpus which is itself part of the rule of law, is not merely in the substantive values it advances but also, in a curious way, in the value that inheres in a system of rules that restricts, or places 'stops' in the way of, arbitrariness. Arbitrariness is a disvalue in itself that is not necessarily connected to a specific human good, at least not in a direct way.

Concerning rights like habeas corpus, Larry Alexander has argued that these procedural rights have value only as that value derives from the substantive right 'to liberty from confinement'.[32] I do not deny that sometimes this is true of procedural rights like habeas corpus. But I think that the more important and more interesting value of habeas corpus has to do with its intrinsic value as part of the rule of law. And here what is important is protecting people against arbitrariness that may not support any other substantive right. It may be that the liberty from confinement is unaffected by habeas corpus rights since the prisoner gains only very temporary removal from confinement associated with this right, as I have indicated above. Alexander may be right that there is a worry about certain risks, but specifying what the risk is in the case of a denial of habeas rights is not always easy to do. And it is sometimes unclear what substantive right is risked when the rule of law is denied. I follow Fuller in thinking that a version of procedural natural law involves a rudimentary right of habeas corpus, among other basic procedural rights, and that such rights form the basis for at least a minimal moral fairness in a system of law.

Fundamental Procedural Rights

When there is no constitution, fundamental law typically refers to certain long-standing customs, perhaps even being 'fixed and unalterable'.[33] The customs themselves may articulate principles, but they are not the same as the principles,

[32] Larry Alexander, 'Are Procedural Rights Derivative Substantive Rights?' (1998) 17 *Law and Philosophy* 19 at 31.

[33] JW Gough, *Fundamental Law in English History* (Oxford, Oxford University Press, 1955), 15.

and certainly do not gain their authoritativeness merely from being long-standing.[34] The principles are moral principles that derive their authority in the way all moral principles do, because of their claim to legitimacy. Typically, there are a small set of substantive principles that are thought to be definitive of a particular political society, such as freedom of speech, press, and association, or non-discrimination on the basis of race or gender. Like the principles that undergird a constitution, in a society without a constitution there are principles that also provide a foundation for the political and legal system.

'Fundamental law' is a phrase that came to have its most important meaning in seventeenth century England. Habeas corpus is not itself fundamental law in the sense of being a body of substantive principles undergirding a legal system, but habeas corpus can be significantly intertwined with fundamental law. Procedural, not merely substantive, rights are significant in fundamental law because of the two important roles procedural rights play. As we saw above, some procedural rights are instrumentally valuable as they complement substantive rights. One way that they can do this is by gap-filling. Again following Aristotle, equity relies on such gap-filling insofar as the substantive rules of any system of rules will not always fit the specific case in the way the drafters of the rules envisioned. In particular, habeas corpus can be a gap-filler in that its requirement of visibleness may inhibit kings and presidents from finding loopholes by which prisoners can be abused, or where other forms of unfairness can creep into the system of law.

Habeas corpus minimally involves a deceptively simple procedure, namely, that a person must be brought out of the dungeon and have the charges against him or her publicly recited. This procedure is a bulwark against some of the most serious forms of oppression. Individuals are more secure because governments are deterred from incarcerating indefinitely, or threatening to do so, those who exercise their substantive rights to speech, press or assembly. The procedural right of habeas corpus helps secure these substantive rights. Indeed, whatever the substantive rights are, habeas corpus will help secure them. Whatever the substantive rights, habeas corpus appeals make sure that there is a minimum of protection in a system of law that has those substantive rights at its core.

As fundamental law, procedural rights like habeas corpus are also valued intrinsically in that they support basic fairness within the legal system. Such rights do not specify any right to a particular form of treatment or liberty that the state must protect. Rather, these rights are what minimally must be done so that arbitrariness does not creep into the way that people are deprived of their liberty by being incarcerated. And minimal procedural fairness translates into the embodiment of the moral fairness that is necessary for a system of law to be deserving of fidelity on the part of the population at large. When there is arbitrariness in the system of law, the rule of law is disrupted and the system of

[34] See my discussion of the problems with custom in my book, *Crimes Against Humanity*, n 3 above.

law becomes fundamentally undermined. In this respect, Fuller was on the right track, although he seemed somewhat unsure where to place habeas corpus rights within his schema of procedural natural law.

While it may be that substantive rights undergo change over time, having procedural rights remain constant is crucial, especially since there is much less need for procedural rights to change over time. Habeas corpus is of this sort: a procedural right that can remain fixed even as the particular substantive crimes that could lead to arrest and incarceration might vary over time. Basic moral fairness is achieved in the system of law when there is such a fixed set of procedural guarantees as that provided by habeas corpus. Here, habeas corpus that guarantees that no prisoner is locked away for arbitrary reasons, or as a way to deny other important moral rights of the prisoner, helps secure a foundational moral minimum.

Both Hart and Fuller recognised the importance of procedural considerations to the rule of law. Hart saw these procedures as secondary rules and Fuller saw them as desiderata for the rule of law. Arguably, both theorists saw these procedures as a minimal moral core, although Hart continued to downplay the sense of morality here. In taking as my point of departure this part of the Hart–Fuller debate, what I have stressed, though, is the point of seeming agreement between them that if there is to be a *system* of criminal law (whether domestic or international), not merely a *set* of laws, then attention needs to be placed on procedural not merely substantive rights.

The Hart–Fuller debate highlights the importance of procedural rights and also raises the question of whether there is a sense that fundamental fairness requires certain procedures, placing limits on constructivist approaches to procedural justice. Whether we call the fundamental rights properly moral or not, certain procedural rights must be contained as secondary rules if there is to be a fair system of law. As I will next argue, in international law in general, and international criminal law in particular, attention needs to be placed as much on procedural or secondary rules and rights as on primary or substantive rules and rights. And there is a very practical benefit to this attention. Looking to the global right of habeas corpus provides a way to fill gaps and prevent legal black holes such as existed at Guantanamo Bay.

Habeas Corpus and International Law

Several recent international criminal decisions have addressed habeas corpus rights, but only in the context of specific proceedings already begun at The Hague, not in a broader context that would apply habeas to cases like that at Guantanamo Bay where a gap existed in the system of international law. In the *Kanyabashi* case, the International Criminal Tribunal for Rwanda (ICTR) recognised the international right of habeas corpus, but confined it to 'a review of the legality of detention' of those accused who are currently held by the ICTR.[35] In this way, habeas corpus is restricted in two significant respects. First, there is an attempt to restrict the scope of habeas proceedings so that it only concerns the prima facie legality of the arrest and incarceration, not allowing habeas corpus petitions to be granted where there is a prima facie case for the conviction of the person incarcerated. Secondly, habeas is restricted only to arrest and detention of those who are currently held by international tribunals and courts. I take up the first issue in the current section and the second issue in the next section.

Two very important things come out of the ICTR decisions in the early part of the first decade in the twenty-first century. First, the right of habeas corpus was there recognised as a fundamental, or *jus cogens*, that is, a non-derogable, right. This in effect gives habeas corpus the status of fundamental international law. But secondly, this right was greatly limited, making it a much more restricted procedural right than is true in Anglo-American common law.

For my purposes, one of the most important findings of the string of cases at the ICTR is that habeas corpus is a fundamental right of international humanitarian law. It is not surprising that there was such a ruling, given that the International Covenant of Civil and Political Rights had listed the right against arbitrary arrest. But it is one thing to have the substantive right against arbitrary arrest recognised, and quite another matter to have a specific procedure, like habeas corpus, protected as a fundamental right as well. There is in my view a significant difference between the recognition that people have a substantive right not to be arbitrarily incarcerated, and the procedural right to what is necessary to enforce the substantive right through a review to determine if one has been arbitrarily incarcerated. In the case of habeas corpus, there is also a non-instrumental reason to elevate it to *jus cogens* status as well.

Christian Tomuschat, a very well respected international legal theorist, talks of *jus cogens* norms, as the most fundamental norms of international law, and describes them as 'rules of conduct which proscribe certain attacks on a number of particularly cherished goods of the international community'.[36] Democracy and the rule of law are goods, even if not the sort of goods that are typically listed as important human goods, such as health and wellbeing. Rather than goods of bodily integrity, for instance, the rule of law is a good of fairness. Indeed, fairness is cherished by the international community as is true of all communities. Insofar as it is an important good, the rule of law should be promoted, as should those things that are constitutive of it, such as habeas corpus.

[35] *Prosecutor v Kanyabashi*, International Criminal Tribunal for Rwanda, Trial Chamber II, Case no ICTR-96-15-I, 23 May 2000, Decision on the Defence Extremely Urgent Motion on Habeas Corpus and for Stoppage of the Proceedings, para 28.

[36] Christian Tomuschat, 'Concluding Remarks' in C Tomuschat and J-M Thouvenin (eds), *The Fundamental Rules of the International Legal Order: Jus Cogens and Obligations Erga Omnes* (Leiden, Martinus Nijhof, 2006). 430.

One author has summarised the state of procedural rights in terms of the idea of internationally recognised *jus cogens* norms as follows:

> in addition to the substantive rights expressly declared to be non-derogable, a number of procedural rights which are instrumental to the effective protection of non-derogable rights, must also be respected in all circumstances. Among them is the right to have access to the domestic courts for violations of non-derogable rights, and the right of habeas corpus. Some fundamental aspects of the right to fair trial are also generally considered as non-derogable.[37]

I would only add that some procedural rights, such as habeas corpus, should be seen as *jus cogens* even if not strongly instrumental in this way. The intrinsic value of habeas corpus also needs to be recognised.

If there is to be an international rule of law, certain core rights will have to be protected against abuse wherever in the world that abuse occurs. And a good example is the failure of the US government to provide core procedural rights at the prison in Guantanamo Bay, Cuba. It seemed as if there was a legal black hole, and indeed that was just what certain members of George Bush's administration actually advocated. If human rights are to be protected globally, and if there is to be a system of international criminal law, protecting such procedural rights as habeas corpus across the world is crucial.

Habeas Corpus and Guantanamo Bay

I wish finally to turn to the much more controversial and much richer global habeas right that would apply to all accused, not just those held at The Hague, to have their cases reviewed by the ICC or some comparable international court that has compulsory jurisdiction. I will begin by briefly rehearsing some of the facts of the Guantanamo case that has motivated my study.

After 11 September 2001, the United States and its allies arrested hundreds of supposed enemies of the United States in Afghanistan. Starting in January of 2002, many of those arrested were transferred to a prison at Guantanamo Bay. The detainees were held in captivity without access to legal counsel and without even having their names released or the charges against them publicly proclaimed. One administration official said that the principal motivation for transfer to Guantanamo was that it was 'the legal equivalent of outer space'. And a British judge referred to Guantanamo detainees as existing in a United States created 'legal black hole'.[38]

In 2002, the Inter-American Commission on Human Rights (IACHR) considered a petition from some of the detainees at Guantanamo who argued that their

[37] Silvia Borelli, 'Casting Light on the Legal Black Hole: International Law and Detentions Abroad in the "War on Terror"' (2005) 87 *International Review of the Red Cross* 39 at 55.

[38] *Ibid* 45 fn 22, 41 fn 6.

habeas corpus rights had been violated. On 22 March of that year, the Commission issued 'precautionary measures in favor of the detainees being held by the United States at Guantanamo Bay, Cuba'. The Commission 'decided to request that the United States take urgent measures necessary to have the legal status of the detainees at Guantanamo Bay determined by a competent tribunal'. The United States disputed the Commission's jurisdiction. The Commission rejected the United States' objections and maintained its request. The matter was never resolved as the 'Commission did not subsequently receive any information indicating that its request for precautionary measures had been complied with'. But despite the Inter-American Commission reiterating its concern about the Guantanamo detainees each year after its initial issuing of precautionary measures, there is little evidence that the United States changed its behaviour or policies. The only solace for the IACHR came when the US Supreme Court ruled similarly to it in 2005 and again in 2008, although to this date most detainees have still not been 'produced' or had the charges against them publicly proclaimed by their jailers.

The habeas corpus petitions of several Guantanamo detainees were also filed in US courts. Initially, in *Rasul v Bush*[39] (2004) the US Supreme Court ruled that habeas corpus petitions could be filed by these detainees. Some lower courts affirmed and other courts denied their appeals. Congress then passed the Detainee Treatment Act of 2005, attempting to strip Guantanamo detainees of habeas corpus rights. In *Hamdan v Rumsfeld*[40] (2006) the US Supreme Court reaffirmed the importance of habeas corpus and ruled that the Detainee Treatment Act was not relevant to cases already pending before it. Congress then passed the Military Commissions Act of 2006, stripping habeas and other judicial appeals from all Guantanamo detainees regardless of whether their cases were pending before US courts or not. In *Boumedienne v Bush*[41] (2008), a deeply divided US Supreme Court ruled that the Military Commissions Act was unconstitutional because of its denial of the fundamental right of habeas corpus as an instrument of the protection of individual liberty and the rule of law.

What is most significant, as a matter of international law, is that the Inter-American Commission did not feel it could take stronger measures against the United States in the Guantanamo case. Indeed, even after it became clear that the United States would ignore the Commission's precautionary measures, the Commission did not seek further measures to protect the Guantanamo detainees, who the Commission admitted were at grave risk. It is striking that there has never been a decision of the IACHR against the United States on this issue or anything stronger from the Commission than the 'request' that was articulated above. So, while it is true that the Inter-American Commission at least took up the issue of the deprivation of rights of the Guantanamo detainees, the result is quite far from

[39] 542 U.S. 466 (2004).
[40] 548 U.S. 557 (2006)
[41] 128 SCt 2229 (2008).

minimally satisfactory, calling into question the ability of at least this particular regional human rights commission, if not the entire structure of human rights commissions, to protect procedural rights such as those of habeas corpus.

My view is that more is needed to enforce such procedural rights than is currently on offer. Part of the difficulty is that violations of procedural rights simply do not capture people's imagination the way that violations of substantive rights do. When the substantive crimes of genocide or ethnic cleansing occur, the 'conscience' of the world's community is easily aroused. And so it matters less whether the protections offered are regional or global, although with the institution of the ICC, there is what promises to be an effective global enforcement mechanism for these substantive rights violations to go along with the regional bases of protection.

So far, procedural rights have been protected, if at all, largely through regional human rights commissions and courts. The regional human rights commissions and courts are not part of the international criminal justice system but form their own separate system of international human rights law. Yet there are international institutions that operate globally, not merely regionally, and secure substantive rights. The UN Security Council is empowered to sanction states which would violate the global norm against aggression. The International Criminal Court provides sanctions for violations of the global norms against genocide, crimes against humanity and war crimes. Piracy and slavery have been condemned in large multilateral treaties that are enforced by *aut dedere aut judicare* principles mandating that states either prosecute or extradite those responsible for such violations of global norms.[42] Procedural rights need a similarly global protection institution.

What I envision could be simply understood as an international court of appeals from the regional courts and commissions of human rights; or such a court could also, in a limited set of contexts, be an international court of first impression where one did not have to exhaust all other remedies before these regional courts; or the court could also be a court handling appeals from decisions rendered by domestic or regional courts. Whatever its form, something like a Global Court of Equity is needed to deal with the procedural rights that must be protected for an international rule of law. The upshot would be that there would no longer be legal black holes where detainees could languish in prison for years without ever having charges against them publicly proclaimed.

Many who have written on the rule of law have not recognised the central role of habeas corpus. Lon Fuller only mentions habeas corpus once in his lengthy chapter on the rule of law in his book *The Morality of Law*,[43] and Hart does not mention it at all. And even Fuller does not give to habeas corpus the sort of role in procedural due process that I have argued that it should have. But both Hart

[42] MC Bassiouni and EM Wise, *Aut Dedere Aut Judicare: The Duty to Prosecute or Extradite in International Law* (Ardsley, NY, Transnational Publishers, 1995).

[43] Fuller, *The Morality of Law*, n 19 above, at 81.

and Fuller certainly supply the theoretical basis for supporting habeas corpus rights, especially at the international level. The seemingly innocuous right that a prisoner be brought out of the dungeon and have the charges against him or her publicly proclaimed is indeed crucial for the protection of many other substantive rights, but it is also a value in itself insofar as it is a crucial component of the rule of law. And when thinking about the international rule of law, habeas corpus should be one of the first rights protected. Natural justice, as understood from Aristotle's time to the present, demands as much.

5

On Visibility and Secrecy in International Criminal Law

CHRISTOPHER KUTZ

Larry May's superb contribution in Chapter 4 simultaneously looks at the Hart–Fuller debate with fresh eyes while responding to one of the most pressing issues in justice today: the apparent sacrifice of the rule of law to the claimed needs of anti-terrorist policy, epitomised by US efforts, especially during the George W Bush administration, to restrict the ability of terrorism-related detainees to challenge their detentions in court.[1] May proposes that a right of judicial review of executive detention systems, known as the right of habeas corpus in the Anglo-American tradition, be recognised as fundamental to the idea of a system of criminal law, and that it be further institutionalised through an international court with the power to demand the production of detainees from any national jurisdiction. With respect to the Hart–Fuller debate, May argues that while Fuller certainly made procedural values the core of his account of law's nature, the specific (and, to May, fundamental) value that state detention be justified in court fails to receive its due. The proposal is provocative, to say the least, and indeed casts light on some important issues about the nature of law. While I shall express doubts about institutionalising this principle through a new court system, I think May is right in noting the peculiar lack of attention in Lon Fuller's view (as well as, but less peculiarly, in HLA Hart's), to the special significance of procedural rights in criminal law. Indeed, I think one can take May's principle of visibility further yet, from a demand that executive action be rendered visible, to a demand that the law itself be made visible.

[1] Larry May, Chapter 4.

Procedural Rights and Natural Law

Larry May proposes that we think about the components of an 'international rule of criminal law', to give voice to the transnational principles that seem prerequisites of criminal justice. May's perspective here is that of a classical natural lawyer, like Gentili or Grotius, looking for principles of natural, or intrinsic, justice that cut across the legal traditions and that thus can serve as a transnational basis of criticism of actions taken in domestic courts. It is an ambitious claim, in two respects, and far more so than the basis he cites in the new international substantive jurisprudence of crimes against humanity. First, the sharp differences between different systems of criminal law, especially between civilian and common law systems, but also between Shari'a and secular systems, might suggest that only the most general common principles could be found. Secondly, given the uneasy status of much international law, which seems to hover between aspirational rhetoric and commanding norms, May's hope of identifying a sovereignty-piercing international right of habeas corpus is doubly daunting. For May's argument to succeed, he needs to show that a right to force a judicial hearing of the charges against one is not merely a right won on various diplomatic battlefields, but an intrinsic part of the very idea of law.

May's proposal operates in a space between the views of Hart and Fuller on the ineluctably moral content of any legal system, since both theorists make room for a non-sceptical conception of international law—a conception capable of containing a moralised core. May's proposal is clearly more ambitious than Hart would countenance: Hart argued only that, given actual human vulnerabilities, any realisable legal system would, as a substantive matter, protect against harms to self and essential external resources.[2] For Hart, this response to contingent vulnerability reflected the most that could be said about a 'natural' morality of law, and thus he rejected Fuller's efforts to find morality, as opposed to administrative efficiency, in further considerations. But, as May notes, the dispute between Hart and Fuller about the extent of law's inner morality has no bearing on the status of international law, since both are sympathetic to its claims. While writers in the positivist tradition, such as Austin, have frequently expressed doubts about the status of international law, especially customary international law, their doubts come from the fact that there is no sovereign identified with the promulgation and execution of the international legal order, nor any system of sanctions. From that perspective, for both Hart and Fuller, the international legal system looks more like a pre-legal culture than like a body of domestic law.

Hart's great step forward in *The Concept of Law* was to discard the notion of a sovereign, at least as an analytical building block, and have recourse instead to a rule of recognition, which provides the criteria for distinguishing valid from invalid law. For Hart, the normative social practice supporting that master rule,

[2] HLA Hart, *The Concept of Law*, 2nd edn (New York, Oxford University Press, 1997) 193–9.

rather than the decree of a sovereign, is the foundation stone of legal validity.[3] As Hart himself recognised, his recasting of positivism makes it especially congenial to international law, where the validation of legal norms bears no relation to the command of a unitary sovereign and owes much to a complex social practice of opinion-mongering by learned jurists, whereby an *opinio juris* in support of a convergent international practice can be discerned.[4] Hart provides an interesting example in arguing for the incomplete role of state consent: when Israel came to be, in 1948, it could not plausibly be said that the leaders of the new state had *consented* to their obligations under international law.[5] International legal norms, including non-derogable *jus cogens* norms, may be discerned through a practice that looks much like moral reasoning. But in principle, for Hart, such norms are still thoroughly positivistic, since their validity rests on a contingent, if highly general, social practice.

For Fuller, the uneasy status of international law provides no conceptual trouble. Indeed, the blurry line between moral argument and discernment of an international norm argues strongly in favour of his own proposal, although such arguments are frequently substantive rather than procedural.[6] The notion of the good to be achieved by law—the co-ordination of state and individual behaviour through a system of rules—plays an orienting role in the interpretive task, for example in distinguishing between convergent state practice at the foundation of a norm, and merely parallel state practice. Locating the good served by the practice is in fact key to identifying the convergence, as well as explaining the supporting *opinio juris* that this convergence constitutes law.

Thus, both Hart and Fuller provide room for May's project: in Hart's case, simply because uniformity in the practices governing domestic criminal procedure can be invoked as evidence of an international legal norm; and in Fuller's case because functional questions about what a system of criminal justice must be (as opposed to a system of executive internment) can provide an alternative starting point. One might thus proceed with both Hart and Fuller together, relying on a sense of common practice in domestic courts, coupled with an intuitive sense of the demands of fairness, thus identifying elements of a common core of international legal principles.

The trouble is that this will be a very short list, if one looks beyond formal treaty agreements to respect certain principles of criminal procedure and at actual state practice. To take the most obvious example, the widespread acceptance (across time and space) of torture, despite its universal condemnation by treaty, means that any attempt to identify valid procedural norms from actual

[3] *Ibid* ch 6.

[4] Sovereignty matters to the validity of international norms, but through a concordance of co-ordinate sovereign wills, thus backing a convention or treaty.

[5] Hart, *The Concept of Law*, n 2 above, at 226.

[6] See Lon Fuller, *The Morality of Law* (New Haven, CT, Yale University Press, 1964) 232–4.

practice will need a strongly moralised criterion to leave torture off the list.[7] Rights to speedy trials are largely illusory even in the richest states; and rights to counsel are of recent vintage, narrowly shared, and largely formalistic even when honoured—witness the difficulty death penalty defendants have in the United States showing that even alcoholic, narcoleptic defense lawyers constitute 'ineffective' counsel as a matter of constitutional principle.[8] More generally, the right May is most concerned with, the right to have a judge determine the validity of one's detention, is routinely abrogated in cases of civil emergency. Indeed, the abrogability of that right, rather than its inviolability, is what wins mention in the US Constitution's Suspension Clause; and the International Convention on Civil and Political Rights (ICCPR) fails to list the right of review as one impervious to derogation.[9]

So if we are to join May in arguing for a transnational right of habeas corpus, we will need to go beyond both practice and treaty and look to the good to be provided by a system of criminal procedure, a good he identifies with non-arbitrariness. Such a good is intrinsically linked to the concept of law and an international legal system. This is a moral inquiry, but one for which he thinks there is room in both Hart and Fuller. For Fuller, the right of judicial review follows straightforwardly from Fuller's eighth constitutive requirement of the rule of law: that there be congruence between the announced rules and their implementation.[10] As for Hart, May suggests that it is a conceptual demand of the internal perspective of law (the positive attitude that participants take towards a convergent practice in endorsing it as normative) that the participants regard the system as fair, hence worthy of their allegiance.[11] And hence for Hart too, May suggests that basic principles of fairness form the ground of any realised legal system.

For what it is worth, I think this suggestion may overstate the role of fairness in the establishment and stability of a legal system. First, the relevant criterion is fairness in the eyes of the participants, not in our eyes; and as I have said, the propriety of torturing suspects has long been seen as part of a system of justice, as has the emergency suspension of rights. Secondly, it is a notable feature of Hart's account that the participants in the practice constituting the rule of recognition need not be numerous, only powerful. Their sense of justice, or of the propriety of their legal order, is what counts, as long as the rest of the population generally obeys. And their sense of justice, again, might easily call for the disregard of

[7] Progress away from torture even within the modern liberal tradition has been painstakingly slow. See, eg John Langbein, *Torture and the Law of Proof* (University of Chicago Press, 2006); Darius Rejali, *Torture and Democracy* (Princeton University Press, 2007).

[8] See, eg *Burdine v Johnson*, 262 F.3d 336 (C.A. 5, 2001) (*en banc* decision reversing panel holding that alcoholic, sleeping counsel's performance did not prejudice defendant, since there was no evidence a competent lawyer would have brought about a different outcome).

[9] US Constitution, Art I cl 2; International Convention on Civil and Political Rights, Art 4.

[10] Fuller, *The Morality of Law*, above n 6, at 39, 81.

[11] See Larry May, Chapter 4 at 83.

procedural niceties against a class of social enemies. The participants with power in the system might well see emergency, right-less, detentions as a reasonable balance between civil liberties (for them) and security needs. Argentina, during the dirty war, had a rule of law even if the legitimacy of its legal system was mainly appreciated by the junta themselves and their clients. We simply cannot argue, from within *The Concept of Law* anyway, from the existence of a legal system to universal rights to procedural justice.

Note, however, that Fuller's functionalism is unlikely to get us there either. While it must be generally true that announced laws coincide with their implementation (else no one would have reason to follow announced law), and while a system of judicial review may be necessary to achieve that desideratum, these functional considerations only apply at the wholesale level. They are consistent with derogations from the practice, as in the Argentine example. So while Fuller might move us towards a non-contingent foundation for the right of judicial review, it will not explain its exigency. For that we need May.

Towards a Principle of Visibility

I have suggested that May's argument for a right to judicial review, grounded in the very concept of an international rule of law, cannot be read off Hart's argument, but must rather rest on Fuller's broader view of the values inherent in a legal system. And here we might well think that Hart has the better of the position, given the observed procedural iniquities in domestic legal systems. But if we are to take the aspiration to the rule of law as a moral rather than conceptual commitment, then May's proposal stands on firm ground. Leaving aside for now the special case of emergency rule, one cannot treat criminal law as a system worth maintaining without treating as foundational the right to ensure that one's detention is in accord with law.

May's account of the reason this is so, of the values protected by judicial review, is especially illuminating. A crucial point for May is that procedural rights have not just instrumental value in protecting a set of separate substantive interests, but also a kind of intrinsic value. To be sure, the instrumental value of procedural rights is central to their justification. A right to judicial review of a detention decision reduces (ideally) the probability that one was detained without legal cause, and hence probably reduces the probability that one is detained at all, or for as long. Assuming that we have a positive interest in liberty, judicial review facilitates this substantive value. On the other hand, as May notes, the procedural right may not have any actual effect in a particular case of detention, as when, say, the judicial review simply endorses the executive's decision. Put aside the point that an institution can have value across an aggregate of cases even if it lacks value in a particular case. May's claim is that even in the particular case, judicial review has value: the value of ensuring the 'fairness' and 'non-arbitrariness' of the detention decision.[12] Thus, Larry Alexander's substantive account of procedural rights misses the special value we attach to non-arbitrariness.[13]

I believe May is right about the importance of fairness but sells its value short by describing it as content-less. For fairness and non-arbitrariness themselves are substantive, not merely formal, values even as they attach to form, not substance, in adjudication. Fairness, after all, is a property of decisions or institutions that affect only certain kinds of things: persons, or more generally beings meriting respect. It makes no sense to predicate fairness of other decisions. I need not be fair in my choice between two sandwich meats, ensuring that each is represented in my lunchtime diet. Nor is fairness the right category of value in deciding how I should treat my cats, whether to give more attention to the one whose behaviour I prefer. Fairness matters because the people to whom one is fair matter, and they matter because their intrinsic moral worth places constraints on the way I may treat them. A judicial process that ensures fairness, in the sense of an adequately reasoned decision, consistent with facts and legal norms, and cohering with decisions made about similar cases, implicitly recognises the demand the detainee makes to treatment whose underlying principle can, and will, be articulated to him.

We might also put the point in the vocabulary of republicanism, where the value of non-arbitrariness is central. Arbitrariness as towards people, rather than cats or sandwich meats, matters because it manifests the dependence of the legal subject on the will of the authority.[14] Judicial review, in principle, channels the will of the executive through the law. It thereby renders that will non-arbitrary, something fixed at the boundaries, not simply the will of the executive but something more complex. Although May says that 'arbitrariness is a disvalue in itself that is not necessarily connected to a specific human good', we might well see it as connected to the specific good in which people themselves participate, as beings entitled to dignity and the exercise of their own wills.[15]

I do not mean to overstate the case, to suggest that a system of judicial review within a system of criminal law is sufficient for recognition of dignity in any meaningful sense. At the limit, judicial review can, of course, approve the application of quite horrendous law. Were states to take up the suggestion of Alan Dershowitz, that torture be authorised subject to warrants and judicial review, a victim of state torture might well insist on the right to a judicial determination of the legitimacy of the torture. Would such a decision enhance the dignity of the

[12] See *ibid* 88.

[13] Larry Alexander, 'Are Procedural Rights Derivative of Substantive Rights' (1998) 17 *Law and Philosophy* 19 (cited by May).

[14] This is a prominent theme in Phillip Pettit's work. See, eg *Republicanism: A Theory of Freedom and Government* (New York, Oxford University Press, 2000).

[15] See Larry May, Chapter 4 at 89.

person being tortured? Perhaps there is some sense in which non-arbitrary torture is better than arbitrary torture, by depersonalising the violence of the state. But one might also think it worse in another way. Thomas Nagel remarks that, while it is a terrible thing to be tortured, it is worse yet for it not to be wrong that one is tortured.[16] On this view, it is better that one be conceived by an imagined audience as having a right not be tortured even as that right is violated, than to be tortured without a rights violation. By legitimating one's torture, the state degrades one's dignity.

But one might also see Hart as arguing against this point: not in his jurisprudential work, but in his work on the philosophy of criminal law. Criminal law in a liberal state, in Hart's view, is a 'choosing system': it provides a set of signals to legal subjects concerning the legally preferred (or obliged) course of action, and a general sense of the consequences if one acts counter to those preferences.[17] Because it is a choosing system, Hart argued, criminal law needs a theory of excuse that respects the sometimes limited capacity of citizens to choose—a capacity limited by lack of information, irrationality and the subordination of the will to fear. This is, of course, a substantive view of criminal law, one that orients it contingently, as a matter of our preferences for maximal liberty. It is not a view about the intrinsic role of choice within criminal law. Unlike the minimal content of natural law, where Hart says that certain substantive protections must be in place for law to command fealty (notably, a system of rules protecting bodily integrity), criminal law would seem to have no similar, natural procedural core. General security might, for all that, be best maintained through black-hole detentions. But once the value of choice and liberty are made central, then the value of non-arbitrariness follows, and so comes the right to judicial review.

Implementing an International Procedural Right

So we can follow May towards a right of judicial review, provided we are prepared to defend the substantive values it implements. I now pursue his suggestion that the right be implemented through a distinctive international court, which could hear appeals from claims of arbitrary or unjust detention. May is motivated towards this proposal by the notable weakness of many regional human rights organisations, notably the Inter-American Convention of Human Rights Commission, which investigated the claims of some Guantanamo detainees but found themselves with no power to order trials.

May is surely correct that if we are to take a right of habeas corpus seriously, it needs strong enforcement mechanisms. But I am reluctant to endorse the

[16] Thomas Nagel, 'Personal Rights and Public Space' (1995) 24 *Philosophy and Public Affairs* 83, 93.

[17] See, eg HLA Hart, 'Legal Responsibility and the Excuses' in *Punishment and Responsibility* (New York, Oxford University Press, 1982) 44.

proposal for a new international institution, for several reasons. First, the normal and preferred course for the realisation of international norms is through domestic processes. Something like a right of habeas corpus is already widely recognised through international treaties, not just in the ICCPR, Article 14, but also in the American Convention on Human Rights,[18] the European Convention on Human Rights[19] and, somewhat more weakly, in the African Charter of Human and People's Rights.[20] While the European Court of Human Rights is far ahead of other regional organisations, it provides a model for how transnational claims of rights deprivations might be adjudicated. Given the existence of the treaties, and the development of their implementing bodies, it would be premature to sidestep the regional process and move directly to a new international institution.

Secondly, typical cases of black-hole detentions will likely arise in the course of counter-terrorism or civil unrest. There is in the first place no strong international consensus that the right to a judicial hearing applies in an emergency. Notwithstanding the claims of the International Committee of the Red Cross, we are some way from recognising the right as an element of the *jus cogens*.[21] The international uproar over the lack of judicial review for the Guantanamo detainees arose as much from the unpopularity of the war, the sheer number of detainees, and the widespread prisoner abuse, as it did from the particular claim of a right to habeas corpus. Note that there has been no similar demand that individuals, such as Khalid Sheikh Mohammed, provisionally identified as senior members of al Qaeda, be given an immediate hearing. Claims of the sovereign authority to suspend ordinary criminal processes are at their apogee in relation to terrorism and civil war. It is inconceivable that states would agree to transfer troubling cases to international fora. In any event, no such transfer could take place before the exhaustion of domestic appeals, and so the right would be tremendously slow to be effectuated at the international level. We do better, I think, to work to develop the mechanisms of regional and global diplomacy, to make sure that domestic institutions actually get a chance to review such cases.

Alternatively, a treaty agreement among major players in counter-terrorism would itself be a beginning, replacing the patchwork of institutional accords through police and intelligence services, accords that lead to such co-ordinated travesties as the case of Mahed Arar.[22] In that case, still in dispute in the US courts, Canadian police provided US intelligence with erroneous information about Arar's connections to al Qaeda, which then provided a basis for the United States to send him to Syria where he was tortured for months. Such a treaty need not create an international court for terrorist suspects, but it could specify the

[18] American Convention on Human Rights, Art 7 cls 5, 6 (further specifications in Art 8).

[19] European Convention on Human Rights, Art 5.

[20] African Charter of Human and People's Rights, Arts 6, 7.

[21] There is also, I should say, considerable conceptual space between the international prohibition of arbitrary detention and the specific procedural right of habeas corpus.

[22] Commission of Inquiry, *Report of the Events relating to Maher Arar* (Ottawa, Minister of Public Works, 2006).

procedural requirements for dealing with them, providing rights against both extraordinary rendition and indefinite detention. Even the mere declaration of such rights would go far beyond the ICCPR, and that would seem ambitious enough.

Conclusion: Visibility and the Law Itself

So the value of visibility reveals something about the way in which publicity functions not just as a condition of law's efficacy, but as an essential normative component, part of what makes law law. In this, May shows how the debate between Hart and Fuller can be read more fruitfully as clearing a space for further work on the essential normative commitments of legal systems. Hart's theoretical openness towards a system of law organised around internalised norms rather than force runs with his diffidence about the necessary 'moral' aspects of law. While Hart did not himself take up the possibility that such normative systems might be decentralised, parts of regional networks rather than administrative systems, his understanding of law clearly makes room for the types of legal structures and mixture of soft and hard law that characterise the contemporary international scene.

By contrast, Fuller's lack of interest in the range of structures in which law can reside is complemented by his openness to the expression of values within those structures. The combination of flexibility in both structure and value makes possible the sort of normative investigation May proposes, in which the theorist looks to the ways law has, historically, been itself a source of political value, and not merely a vehicle for values from some other domain. The principle of visibility is at the same time a political and a legal value. Indeed, visibility is only a political value because it is a legal value, for it is only because of the magnification of state power through law that secret systems of detention become possible. I have myself written on the value of publicity in relation to legislation, again a value grounded in law as much historically as conceptually.[23] There I argue that law's significance lies not just in the expanded possibilities of power, but in the way law can anchor the political identity of its subjects. Secrecy in legislation, like secrecy in detention, is troubling in the hypocrisy it enables, between the ideal of a state functioning in accordance with law and the reality of subjection to a ruler's *arbitrio*. Whether the US detention system at Guantanamo constitutes a morally defective legal system, or no legal system whatsoever, is not ultimately a semantic question. It is a question of institutional design and reform. May's philosophical pursuit of the values at stake in international criminal law, both substantive and procedural, is a welcome response to the urgency of that question.

[23] See my 'Secret Law and the Value of Publicity' (2009) 22 *Ratio Juris* 197.

6

The Hart–Fuller Debate, Transitional Societies and the Rule of Law

MARTIN KRYGIER*

Much of the enduring energy and tension in the Hart–Fuller debate stems from the two protagonists' reflections on 'the testimony of those who have descended into Hell, and, like Ulysses or Dante, brought back a message for human beings'.[1] The testimony referred to, of course, was that of witnesses and survivors of Nazism, and, within this context, Nazi law. It raised, in the starkest manner imaginable, questions about the 'laws' of truly evil regimes, and about what adequate responses to such experiences might require. Those are not issues we have left behind us.

Nazism might have been the most satanic of regimes, but it has had more than a few rivals. Perhaps fortuitously, certainly fortunately, many of them exploded or imploded in and since the late 1980s and early 1990s. Their successors, scores of which lost their despots, some more satanic, some less, around that time, were dubbed 'transitional societies' or 'societies in transition'. For many people believed, or hoped, that the worst of the past might be left behind and a new and better future might develop or even be crafted. 'Transition' came to be used to characterise a transformative social space between lamented past and hoped-for future.

The word could, of course, be applied much more broadly. (What society is *not* transitional? Not to mention, when does a transition end? Could it be permanent?) However, it has come to be used of such successor-predecessor social formations in which a lot of recovery, repair, reconstruction and innovation has

* I am grateful to Peter Cane and Kenneth Winston for their comments on an earlier draft of this chapter.

[1] HLA Hart, 'Positivism and the Separation of Law and Morals' (1957–58) 71 *Harvard Law Review* 593, 615.

been attempted, or at least promised. 'Transition' hides manifold differences, to which we will return, but there are similar predicaments and characteristic problems as well.

Anyone familiar with 'societies in transition' reads the Hart–Fuller debate with more than academic interest. The overarching questions discussed there, of course, concerned the relationships between law and morality. Those are not unfamiliar or unimportant matters to subjects and survivors of despotic regimes or civil wars, for example, even if their primary interest is rarely conceptual. Moreover, the collapse of so many political orders, all of a sudden and at roughly the same time, generated a range of specific problems that echo some of those that animated the earlier debate—among them how to deal now with what had happened then. It is also true of most societies in transition, as it was of post-Nazi Germany, that the evils which marked their predecessors were not happenstance, individual or occasional, but deliberate, institutionalised and systematic. Analogies, then, between the legal dilemmas subject of the debate and those that arise in transitional societies are not far to seek. However, there are differences too.

The Hart–Fuller discussion of Nazism had a particular focus: on the legal/moral dilemmas of judges in post-War Germany, faced with complaints of reprehensible acts committed in apparent conformity to the laws or 'laws' passed by the earlier regime. Judges and other officials in many transitional societies have faced parallel dilemmas, at times leading them to diametrically opposed decisions.[2] So that is an obvious subject to discuss, and there are cases for lawyers to debate. However, it has already been well discussed, both in relation to post-Nazi judges,[3] and their 'transitional' successors.[4] Given that discussion and my belief about where some other important issues lie, my own focus is somewhat different.

My brief was to relate the Hart–Fuller debate to 'law in transitional societies'. That is a broader subject than how judges are to 'deal with the past' or do 'transitional justice', to use the current phrases. Many different kinds of societies shelter under the umbrella of 'transition'. They include failed and weak states;

[2] See the unanimous decision of the Hungarian Constitutional Court (11/1992 (III.5) Ab h, striking down a law extending the statute of limitations for certain crimes committed 'but not prosecuted for political reasons' under the communist regime, particularly after the suppression of the 1956 revolution. The court held that would involve retrospectivity and thus be inconsistent with the rule of law. The Czech Court, in similar circumstances, refused to allow its conception of the same concept to be constrained by such 'formalism' (http://angl.concourt.cz/angl_verze/doc/p-19–93.php).

[3] HO Pappe, 'On the Validity of Judicial Decisions in the Nazi Era' (1960) *Modern Law Review* 260; Thomas Mertens, 'Radbruch and Hart on the Grudge Informer: A Reconsideration' (2002) 15(2) *Ratio Juris* 186; Robert Alexy, 'A Defence of Radbruch's Formula' in David Dyzenhaus (ed), *Recrafting the Rule of Law* (Oxford, Hart Publishing, 1999) 15–39; David Dyzenhaus, 'The Grudge Informer Case Revisited' (2008) 83 *New York University Law Review* 1000.

[4] Julian Rivers, 'The Interpretation and Invalidity of Unjust Laws' in Dyzenhaus, n 3 above, at 40–65; Jiří Přibáň, 'Constitutional Justice and Retroactivity of Laws in Postcommunist Central Europe' in J Přibáň *et al* (eds), *Systems of Justice in Transition* (Aldershot, Ashgate, 2003) 29–50; Adam Czarnota, Martin Krygier and Wojciech Sadurski (eds), *Rethinking the Rule of Law after Communism* (Budapest, CEU Press, 2005) pt 2, 'Dealing with the Past'.

states riven by insurrection and civil war; successors of despotisms of various sorts (autocratic, communistic, fascistic, theocratic, paranoiac); and societies in which some people strive to recover from any or all of the above. 'Transitional justice' is only one of the law-related issues facing them. That particular part of it meted out by judges is an even smaller part, which for practical and institutional reasons is rarely able to get to matters or people of the greatest concern.

Of course, judges' dilemmas, and the whole range of issues that surround transitional justice, are important among the legal problems that confront transitional societies. But they receive more attention from scholars, particularly lawyers and philosophers, than many other transitional legal problems, perhaps more than their importance warrants. This is probably because of the dramatic questions of principle they pose, not to mention the apparent familiarity, for those used to looking at legal judgments, of the repertoires and cast of characters involved. But courts have many limitations in dealing with systematic, institutionalised past evils, which is why many transitional societies have chosen to do so in ways other than judicial. These other ways raise problems not considered by Hart and Fuller. Moreover, particularly where they attempt to generate or regenerate a satisfactory legal order, transitional societies confront many law-related problems other than what to do about past evil-doers. Does the Hart–Fuller debate have any resonance in relation to them?

I believe it does. More particularly, I think that Fuller has much to say that is of relevance to transitional societies. Hart offers less. That is not necessarily a criticism, since he really has no concern to offer more. He had other interests. But also there is less available in his way of looking at law. A consequence is that those concerned with law in transitional societies have much to learn from Fuller; less from his interlocutor. And since some of the most important lessons Fuller teaches were subjected to withering criticism, or ignored, by Hart, I guess my argument is implicitly critical of him after all. But in the end it also is critical of Fuller, for not following far enough key insights of his own.

I begin by sketching the approach of each of the participants to Nazi 'law' and subsequent reactions to it. I say more about Fuller, because there is more to say. I then discuss Fuller's conception of the 'internal morality of law', and compare his treatment of it with that of Hart and those (many) legal positivists who took his lead. Thirdly, I discuss some distinctive matters of 'social architecture' that arise in transitional societies. Fourthly, I question some tendencies of the original debate to ignore matters of context and variation. I conclude with reflections on how this debate, refracted through the experience of transitional societies, illuminates or clouds our understanding of the rule of law. Though I criticise Fuller here, I do so in what I imagine to be a Fullerian spirit.

Law or 'law'?

Though the phrase is Hart's, 'testimonies from Hell' are of less concern to his project than to that of Fuller. Indeed, Hart doesn't really seem to consider them central to his sort of activity at all. His article is primarily concerned with the conceptual relationships between law and morals, and so too his discussion of Nazi law and its successors. These are cases for testing and application of his theory; occasions for analysis, not illuminations.[5] However, he does hazard more than a few opinions about the practical dilemmas raised by the Nazi experience and its aftermath, enough to suggest that he believes his conceptual analysis captures and clarifies issues of crucial intellectual, moral and practical import. He just doesn't believe those issues need more than he gives them.

Revolted by the experience of Nazism, convinced that Nazi judges were able to apply obnoxious law because of their trained instinct to separate legal from moral questions, jurists such as Gustav Radbruch had reconsidered their earlier positivist commitments at the War's end. Hart 'feels their pain', as we now say, but he also believes it has led them astray. In his response to their apprehension about the consequences of separating law from morals, he notes that it is 'of a very different character' from the other criticisms he discusses. It 'certainly is less an intellectual argument against the Utilitarian distinction [between law and morals] than a passionate appeal supported not by detailed reasoning but by reminders of a terrible experience'.[6] One gets the sense that in his view, while the hearts of his interlocutors are in the right place, their heads have been somewhat knocked about by their 'terrible experience'.

Radbruch had been a legal positivist before the War. He emerged from it concluding, as Hart understands him:

> from the ease with which the Nazi regime had exploited subservience to mere law … and from the failure of the German legal profession to protest against the enormities which they were required to perpetrate in the name of law, that 'positivism' (meaning here the insistence on the separation of law as it is from law as it ought to be) had

[5] I take the distinction from Avishai Margalit, *The Ethics of Memory* (Cambridge, MA, Harvard University Press, 2002) ix: 'There are two styles of philosophers: e.g. philosophers and i.e. philosophers—illustrators and explicators. Illustrators trust, first and foremost, striking examples, in contrast with explicators, who trust, first and foremost, definitions and general principles. Explicators may use examples, but their examples are stylized and are more like those that appear after i.e. than the genuine examples that follow e.g. The illustrators, for their part, run the risk of using examples as little anecdotes that serve no philosophical purpose. The dangers of each style in philosophy are clear and almost unavoidable; yet, I believe that style in philosophy matters greatly. When examples are apt, they are illuminations, not just didactic illustrations. When definitions are good, they are explications, not mere stipulations. I see merit in both styles, but in temperament if not by conviction I subscribe to e.g. philosophy'.

There would be point in explicating this distinction between ie and eg philosophers as one that captures much about the differences in intellectual sensibility between Hart and Fuller. This article merely illustrates it.

[6] Hart, 'Positivism and the Separation of Law and Morals', n 1 above, at 615.

> powerfully contributed to the horrors. His considered reflections led him to the doctrine that the fundamental principles of humanitarian morality were part of the very concept of *Recht* or Legality and that no positive enactment or statute … could be valid if it contravened basic principles of morality … it is clear that the doctrine meant that every lawyer and judge should denounce statutes that transgressed the fundamental principles not as merely immoral or wrong but as having no legal character.[7]

This 'Radbruch principle', Hart claims, was the basis on which post-Nazi German courts dealt with cases where evil people in an evil regime (local war criminals, spies and informers) had used evil laws for evil purposes. Should a later court allow these 'laws' to shield evil-doers seeking to hide behind them? The courts Hart discusses answered 'no', convicted (some) evil-doers and invalidated those laws that the accused claimed had authorised their acts. The ground, as Hart understood it, was that the content of those laws was so evil that it disqualified them from being treated as laws properly so called.

Hart is full of human sympathy for Radbruch's revulsion and the courts' predicament, but he is not particularly impressed by their reasons. He laments, in the nicest possible way, the 'extraordinary naïveté in the view that insensitiveness to the demands of morality and subservience to state power in a people like the Germans should have arisen from the belief that law might be law though it failed to conform with the minimum requirements of morality'.[8] Not only is Radbruch naive, but, 'more disturbing', he has 'only half digested' the message of the liberalism that he seeks to convey: what law and what morality require are different questions. Neither decides the other. Similarly, the celebration of the courts' refusal to acknowledge certain Nazi laws to be law 'seems to me to be hysteria'. To say that what would otherwise be law is not because it is 'utterly immoral … will serve to cloak the true nature of the problems with which we are faced'.

Now one thing distinctive of Hart's approach is that he has almost nothing to say about the context in which the laws he discussed operated, nor about that in which the post-Nazi courts were operating. He also says nothing about the *character* of Nazi laws, the way they were applied, or the specific characteristics and interrelations of the institutions applying them. He does not appear to think it necessary to examine the particular, peculiar, nature of the Nazi legal order or even the particular Nazi laws he discusses, other than to observe that the latter appear to have been formally legitimate, and they were nasty in content. Of a specific law that he does mention, he merely reports its stated aim (and notes that since it had been in force since 1934, a whole 10 Nazi years!, there was reason to doubt the wisdom of declaring it invalid). It's not that what else went on is of no

[7] *Ibid* 617. For argument that Hart had misconstrued both the cases he discusses and the 'Radbruch formula', see Pappe and Mertens, n 3 above.

[8] Hart, 'Positivism and the Separation of Law and Morals', n 1 above, at 618.

account to him morally, but that he thinks it counts for nothing *legally*, and he is talking about law. Nazis had laws, and they were immoral; not a happy story but a simple one.

Fuller's approach is different, from the start. At issue for him are not only conceptual matters but matters of fact, context and specific character of the laws and legal institutions involved. He stresses these matters in relation both to the courts of Nazi Germany and of its successors.

Thus, the character of Nazi 'law', he argues, cannot be adequately understood without moving 'a little closer within smelling distance of the witches' cauldron than we have been brought so far by Professor Hart'.[9] Instead, however:

> Without any inquiry into the actual workings of whatever remained of a legal system under the Nazis, Professor Hart assumes that something must have persisted that still deserved the name of law in a sense that would make meaningful the ideal of fidelity to law. Not that Professor Hart believes the Nazis' laws should have been obeyed. Rather he considers that a decision to disobey them presented not a mere question of prudence or courage, but a genuine moral dilemma in which the ideal of fidelity to law had to be sacrificed in favor of more fundamental goals. I should have thought it unwise to pass such a judgment without first inquiring with more particularity what 'law' itself meant under the Nazi regime.[10]

Fuller suggests that '[t]hroughout his discussion Professor Hart seems to assume that the only difference between Nazi law and, say, English law is that the Nazis used their laws to achieve ends that are odious to an Englishman'.[11] In saying this, he is not just recommending that Hart get out more. For Fuller details several of the many ways in which the Nazis had undermined the character and role that an Englishman might expect law and legal institutions to play. They had corrupted the instrument, not merely wielded it for unsalutary purposes, so that what was called law was frequently not merely perverse in its effects but deformed and perverse at its core and in its character.

Thus he writes of the profusion of retrospective laws, and of Hitler's declaration after the murder of over 70 Nazis in the Roehm purge, that 'the supreme court of the German people … consisted of myself'.[12] He acknowledges that occasional 'curative' retrospective laws can be tolerated, and might be appropriate (even necessary) in any civilised legal order. However, '[a] general increase in the resort to statutes curative of past legal irregularities represents a deterioration in that form of legal morality without which law itself cannot exist. The threat of such statutes hangs over the whole legal system, and robs every law on the books of some of its significance. And surely a general threat of this sort is implied when

[9] *Ibid* 650.

[10] Lon Fuller, 'Positivism and Fidelity to Law: A Reply to Professor Hart' (1957–58) 71 *Harvard Law Review* 630.

[11] *Ibid* 650. See Jeremy Waldron, 'Positivism and Legality: Hart's Equivocal Response to Fuller' (2008) 83 *New York University Law Review* 1135.

[12] Fuller, 'Positivism and Fidelity to Law: A Reply to Professor Hart', n 10 above, at 650.

a government is willing to use such a statute to transform into lawful execution what was simple murder when it happened'.[13]

Again he writes of 'repeated rumors of "secret laws"', and of the shadow that hung over all law that it could be dishonoured, reversed or ignored at will by its makers. In the article Hart had criticised, Radbruch had mentioned a report that killings in concentration camps had been 'made "lawful" by a secret enactment'. Fuller comments that 'there can be no greater legal monstrosity than a secret statute. Would anyone seriously recommend that following the war the German courts should have searched for unpublished laws among the files left by Hitler's government so that citizens' rights could be determined by a reference to these laws?'[14] Again, no legal order promulgates everything that might affect citizens' rights and that might be cause for complaint, but:

> as with retroactivity what in most societies is kept under control by the tacit restraints of legal decency broke out in monstrous form under Hitler. Indeed, so loose was the whole Nazi morality of law that it is not easy to know just what should be regarded as an unpublished or secret law. Since unpublished instructions to those administering the law could destroy the letter of any published law by imposing on it an outrageous interpretation, there was a sense in which the meaning of every law was 'secret'. Even a verbal order from Hitler that a thousand prisoners in concentration camps be put to death was at once an administrative direction and a validation of everything done under it as being 'lawful'.

Finally, he writes of 'the most important affronts to the morality of law by Hitler's government [that] took no such subtle forms'. One such was to act 'through the party in the streets' rather than allow legal forms to present any hindrance; 'There was no one who dared bring them to account for whatever outrages might thus be committed'. Another was the preparedness of 'Nazi-dominated courts' 'to disregard any statute, even those enacted by the Nazis themselves, if this suited their convenience or if they feared that a lawyer-like interpretation might incur displeasure "above"'.[15]

He follows these general appraisals with a detailed interpretation of the particular laws that Hart had mentioned. He regards them as 'legislative monstrosities', but even they, Fuller argued, could not reasonably be interpreted to justify the decisions at which the Nazi courts had arrived.

In none of this is Fuller saying that, the content of the law being unjust, Nazi 'laws' are not law. Rather he is saying that the Nazi 'legal' system was so degraded and degenerate in the *character* of its rules, its institutions, its output, their relationship to the dictates of the Nazi leadership, in its systematic violation of what he calls the 'internal morality' of law, that to think of its products as laws like any other, which merely happen to point in the wrong direction, is radically

[13] *Ibid* 651.
[14] *Ibid.*
[15] *Ibid* 652.

misconceived. These qualitative considerations, indeed these questions of what Nazi 'law' was, as distinct from what it enacted, do not disturb Hart's discussion. But they did disturb Fuller.

Moreover, his attention to the role of post-Nazi legal officials, of their predicament, was altogether more careful than Hart's. Again here, Hart's post-Nazi judges are like English judges with an unsavoury caseload. They have to judge past acts, on the basis of laws then applicable. Unfortunately, some of those laws were horrible, so this might lead to moral problems for the judges; but not to any difference in their legal roles or responsibilities.

Again, Fuller sees things differently. The difference is already signalled in the heading he gives to that part of his article dealing with these cases: 'the problem of restoring respect for law and justice after the collapse of a regime that respected neither'. This is not a routine job for English judges, even when they run across an unpleasant law. It has as much to do with shaping the future as dealing with the past, and it is undertaken with knowledge that how one deals with the past is one of the most potent ways one has of affecting that future. Fuller describes it well:

> After the collapse of the Nazi regime the German courts were faced with a truly frightful predicament. It was impossible for them to declare the whole dictatorship illegal or to treat as void every decision and legal enactment that had emanated from Hitler's government. Intolerable dislocations would have resulted from any such wholesale outlawing of all that had occurred over a span of twelve years. On the other hand, it was equally impossible to carry forward into the new government the effects of every Nazi perversity that had been committed in the name of law; any such course would have tainted an indefinite future with the poisons of Nazism.[16]

This aptly portrays the predicament of post-despotic, 'transitional' governments throughout the world. Nothing of this predicament is captured in Hart's discussion, or considered relevant to it, as Fuller rightly notes.

The Internal Morality of Law

To repeat, and as is well known, Fuller did not argue that what Nazis claimed, and Hart accepted, as law was not, simply because it was evil. Rather, he argued that, given the pervasively corrupting character of the Nazi legal order, the lawfulness of many Nazi 'laws' (not all—Aryan marriages were still marriages) was degraded. Many of them were so debased *in their formal qualities*, that their character as laws suffered. This was a matter of degree, to be assessed in particular cases, but in the most extreme cases they might not rightly be considered laws at all. The key criteria on which legality depended were found in what he called the 'internal morality of law'.

[16] *Ibid* 648.

That morality, briefly rehearsed here but insightfully explored in *The Morality of Law*, required that the law be made up of general rules, rather than simply ad hoc pronouncements; be publicly available to affected parties; prospective not retrospective; comprehensible; not contradictory; not require the impossible; not change so often that they cannot provide guides to action; be administered in ways that conform to their terms. No legal system achieves perfection in any of these dimensions, nor is perfection a salutary ideal for a practical art. All depends on degree, and overachievement is not necessarily superior achievement. However:

> A total failure in any one of these eight directions does not simply result in a bad system of law; it results in something that is not properly called a legal system at all, except perhaps in the Pickwickian sense in which a void contract can still be said to be one kind of contract. Certainly there can be no rational ground for asserting that a man can have a moral obligation to obey a legal rule that does not exist, or is kept secret from him, or that came into existence only after he had acted, or was unintelligible, or was contradicted by another rule of the same system, or commanded the impossible, or changed every minute.[17]

In the debates between Fuller and his critics, the most common question asked of this 'internal morality' was whether it actually amounted to a morality at all. Were these not merely principles of legal efficacy, necessary for the law to serve any purpose, but equally open to moral and immoral uses. Much mirth was had speculating about the internal morality of the poisoner, the blackmailer, the golfer or the safecracker, for example.[18] Perhaps Fuller's principles did have special purchase on law, but why dignify them as moral if law that conforms to them can be equally used to serve bad purposes as well as good?

That is an important debate, and we will return to it. However, somewhat left in the shade is the qualifier 'internal'. Fuller is moving attention from what traditional natural lawyers took to be essential to law, its substantive moral content; that, in his terms is *external* to the law (though morally no less important for that). He insists that the internal morality, by contrast, is latent within the overarching purpose he attributes to law, 'the enterprise of subjecting human conduct to the governance of rules'.[19]

[17] Lon Fuller, *The Morality of Law* (New Haven, CT, Yale University Press, 1964) 39.

[18] For poison, see Hart's review in (1965) 78 *Harvard Law Review* 1286: 'Poisoning is no doubt a purposive activity, and reflections on its purpose may show that it has its internal principles ("Avoid poisons however lethal if they cause the victim to vomit", or "Avoid poisons however lethal if their shape, color, or size is likely to attract notice")'. Ronald Dworkin makes the same point with a different blaggard: 'A blackmailer would fail in his dastardly objective unless he made his instructions clear and unambiguous': 'The Elusive Morality of Law' (1965) 10 *Villanova Law Review* 634. In his *Philosophy of Law* (Englewood Cliffs, NJ, Prentice-Hall, 1975) 49–50, Martin Golding offers golf and safecracking. And see Fuller's comments in his 'reply to critics' in *The Morality of Law*, revised edn (New Haven, CT, Yale University Press, 1969) 200.

[19] Fuller, *The Morality of Law*, n 17 above, at 96.

A key word is 'enterprise', for law in Fuller's view is not 'a piece of inert matter'[20] that either exists or does not, whatever is done with it and to it. Rather it is purposeful activity that can be better realised by institutions that exhibit some characteristics and competences rather than others. This directs us to the character of the institutions and practices that produce them, and in particular to their 'integrity'. Kenneth Winston cites Fuller's observation that 'the really enduring part of ethics is found, not in the substantive ends we pursue, but in sustaining the integrity of the forms of order by which we pursue them'.[21] And Fuller himself writes that it is 'a great mistake to treat questions of the design and administration of our institutions as if the problem were merely one of weighing substantive ends against one another. For institutions have an integrity of their own which must be respected if they are to be effective at all'.[22]

Fuller believed the integrity of law as a practice depended crucially upon the degree to which it observed the inner morality of law. As Philip Selznick has written:

> For Fuller the 'internal' morality of law consists of standards that emerge as we learn the crafts of judging and legislating. These crafts are accountable to the larger purposes of law, which include doing justice, settling disputes, maintaining public order, and enhancing prosperity. But as crafts they have distinctive criteria of excellence and integrity, and they suffer from distinctive sources of malfunction and debasement.[23]

Pursuing legality, then, is the 'practical art'[24] of developing institutions fit to achieve the purpose(s) latent in the enterprise of law; it is 'social architecture'. The internal morality is a specification of central principles of that art, central pillars of that architecture. These are, in other words, immanent principles of a practice, 'the natural laws of a particular kind of human undertaking ... not "higher" laws; if any metaphor of elevation is appropriate they should be called "lower" laws. They are like the natural laws of carpentry, or at least those laws respected by a carpenter who wants the house he builds to remain standing and serve the purpose of those who live in it'.[25] They can be achieved more or less well, and so 'the existence of a legal system is a matter of degree'.[26]

But what has any of this to do with morality? Here Fuller's answers are various and some critics might have been legitimately misled. Others were just careless. The most common objection, as we saw, is that the 'internal morality' is simply a

[20] *Ibid* 123.

[21] Kenneth I Winston, 'Three Models for the Study of Law' in Willem J Witteveen and Wibren van der Burg (eds), *Rediscovering Fuller: Essays on Implicit Law and Institutional Design* (Amsterdam University Press, 1999) 77.

[22] Fuller, *The Morality of Law*, n 17 above, at 180.

[23] Preface to Witteveen and Wibren van der Burg, n 21 above, at 9.

[24] Fuller, *The Morality of Law*, n 17 above, at 91.

[25] *Ibid* 96.

[26] *Ibid* 39.

general principle of efficacy, and is in fact compatible with any ends, whether moral or iniquitous. These are actually two separate criticisms. I will start with the second.

Fuller, as befits his intellectual character, is less interested in questions of logical compatibility, though he essays some reflections on them, than in real-world likelihoods. And there he disagrees strongly with his critics. He believes that, while 'over a wide range of issues' internal morality is 'indifferent toward the substantive aims of law and is ready to serve a variety of such aims with equal efficacy',[27] it is not indifferent to every aim, and particularly not to systematically evil aims. In response to Hart's curt dismissal of a connection ('It is unfortunately compatible with very great iniquity')[28] Fuller asks for examples:

> Does Hart mean merely that it is possible, by stretching the imagination, to conceive the case of an evil monarch who pursues the most iniquitous ends but at all times preserves a genuine respect for the principles of legality? If so, the observation seems out of place in a book that aims at bringing 'the concept of law' into closer relation with life. Does Hart mean to assert that history does in fact afford significant examples of regimes that have combined a faithful adherence to the internal morality of law with a brutal indifference to justice and human welfare? If so, one would have been grateful for examples about which some meaningful discussion might turn.[29]

It is indeed hard, perhaps not impossible but hard,[30] to find such examples. More deeply, and I will return to this point, it is hard to find *reasons* why such examples should be plentiful.

Joseph Raz comes to admit that there is virtue in the rule of law, which he characterises in terms heavily indebted to Fuller's internal morality, but his praise of it is somewhat tepid (two cheers). He describes it as 'a purely negative value … merely designed to minimise the harms to freedom and dignity which the law might cause in its pursuit of its goals however laudable these might be'.[31] Fuller did not live to see this modest tribute, but he might well answer that it is too modest. The harms for which the rule of law is a suggested antidote are abuses of *power*, not merely of law. There are many ways in which power can be exercised, used and abused, without the intervention of law. Requiring that governments conform to the 'internal morality' in their acts is intended to exclude all those other ways from the start. More is necessary, but that exclusion is no small matter where arbitrary power is a concern.

[27] *Ibid* 153.

[28] HLA Hart, *The Concept of Law* (Oxford, Clarendon Press, 1961) 202. Hart does not always maintain this position, but when he doesn't he appears, as Jeremy Waldron has argued, uneasy that he might be dropping his guard against Fuller. See Waldron, n 11 above.

[29] Fuller, *The Morality of Law*, n 17 above, at 154.

[30] See Kristen Rundle, 'The Impossibility of an Exterminatory Legality: Law and the Holocaust' (2009) 59 *University of Toronto Law Journal* 65.

[31] J Raz, 'The Rule of Law and its Virtue' in *The Authority of Law* (Oxford, Clarendon Press, 1979) 228.

As to efficacy, it matters a lot what one's purposes are whether the internal morality will help achieve them. Here there is a possible ambiguity in Fuller which can mislead. For Fuller specifies the purpose of law both broadly and narrowly. Most generally and neutrally put, as we have seen, the purpose of law is to subject 'human conduct to the governance of rules'. There are many ways this can be done, as Fuller recognises, indeed emphasises, and some have more to do with morality, and specifically the internal morality of law, than others. Parodoxically, however, if we follow this definition, the notion of Fuller's many critics, that the internal morality is just a list of ways in which law can be effective, is odd.

For if your wish is to terrorise, the internal morality can get in the way; and a reflective tyrant will avoid it systematically.[32] Ask Stalin. If it is to shake things up so no one trusts anyone and no one can do anything you don't want, ditto. Ask Mao. If it is to eliminate millions of citizens and others, ditto again. Ask Hitler[33] or Pol Pot. If it is to give your regime maximum unaccountable flexibility and your people a minimum of the same, ditto once more. The list could easily be extended. Tyrants don't like too much light. Even Max Weber's ideal typical charismatic leader, we might recall, used to say, 'it is written, but *I* say unto you'. That is in effect a pledge to override or ignore the internal morality of law at one's will. It accurately describes the ways charismatic rulers behave. And leaders don't have to be very charismatic to feel the temptation.

However, Fuller has a more particular specification of the purpose of law, which involves a special, moral, connection, between it and the internal morality. He insists on a distinction between 'managerial direction', a 'one-way projection of authority, originating with government and imposing itself upon the citizen',[34] and law properly so-called, which depends upon *interaction* between law-giver and citizen. He believes that positivists only grasp the managerial view. They abstract from 'the social dimension' of law, exhibit 'a distaste for phenomena of interaction',[35] and are attuned only to 'efficacy'. The manager wants jobs done at least cost to best effect; efficacy refers to the degree of success in achieving managerial goals. Principles of institutional character are subservient to such goals, and are therefore contingent; appropriate to, and only to, the extent to which they help in the achievement of centrally directed goals. If it helps to keep things quiet, allow unfettered discretion to decision-makers, or change rules rapidly, there is no intrinsic managerial reason to object.

Interaction has a different logic. Unlike managerial direction, interaction requires adherence to the internal morality of law as a matter of principle, not contingent and revisable practice. Partly the point involves a hypothesis about

[32] *cf* Jeremy Waldron, 'Why Law: Efficacy, Freedom, or Fidelity?' (1994) 13(3) *Law and Philosophy* 263; Colleen Murphy, 'Lon Fuller and the Moral Value of the Rule of Law' (2005) 24 *Law and Philosophy* 239.

[33] See Rundle, n 30 above.

[34] Fuller, *The Morality of Law*, n 17 above, at 207.

[35] *Ibid.*

what might be called the sociology of fidelity. People might obey laws that ignore the internal morality, but they won't feel (or have) an obligation of fidelity to them. In a passage worth quoting at length, for it again is animated by the Nazi example, Fuller argues:

> there is a kind of reciprocity between government and the citizen with respect to the observance of rules. Government says to the citizen in effect, 'These are the rules we expect you to follow. If you follow them, you have our assurance that they are the rules that will be applied to your conduct'. When this bond of reciprocity is finally and completely ruptured by government, nothing is left on which to ground the citizen's duty to observe the rules.
>
> The citizen's predicament becomes more difficult when, though there is no total failure in any direction, there is a general and drastic deterioration in legality, such as occurred in Germany under Hitler. A situation begins to develop, for example, in which though some laws are published, others, including the most important, are not. Though most laws are prospective in effect, so free a use is made of retrospective legislation that no law is immune to change ex post facto if it suits the convenience of those in power. For the trial of criminal cases concerned with loyalty to the regime, special military tribunals are established and these tribunals disregard, whenever it suits their convenience, the rules that are supposed to control their decisions. Increasingly the principal object of government seems to be, not that of giving the citizen rules by which to shape his conduct, but to frighten him into impotence.[36]

This distinction between ways in which governments treat citizens in turn rests upon a deeper, less instrumental, more deontological, moral claim. It has to do with what Fuller calls 'the view of man implicit in legal morality'.[37] Here the objection to deviation from the internal morality has not to do with the external substantive purposes that might be pursued. Rather it concerns whether one treats persons with respect:

> Every departure from the principles of the law's inner morality is an affront to man's dignity as a responsible agent. To judge his actions by unpublished or retrospective laws, or to order him to do an act that is impossible, is to convey to him your *indifference* to his powers of self-determination. Conversely, when the view is accepted that man is incapable of responsible action, legal morality loses its reason for being. To judge his actions by unpublished or retrospective laws is no longer an affront, for there is nothing left to affront—indeed, even the verb 'to judge' becomes itself incongruous in this context: we no longer judge a man, we act upon him. (emphasis added)[38]

'Indifference' is a good word to use here, since it can span both well-meaning authoritarian direction and intentional oppression or repression. There is a lot of the former about in modern societies, even those governed with the best of intentions. But there are also many elements that affirm and reaffirm human dignity: a high degree of the internal morality of law, defences in criminal law,

[36] *Ibid* 40.
[37] *Ibid* 162.
[38] *Ibid* 162–3.

provisions concerned with due process, publicity, rights, including rights of appeal, and so on.[39] Imagine societies which are systematically low in all those things. As it happens, citizens of many transitional societies do not need much imagination. A good memory will serve.

Transitional Architecture

One frequent element of the despotic past of many transitional societies, as it relates to law, was the remarkable degree to which law was instrumentalised, and internal morality violated, at every turn. I am not expert on every form of despotism, but I do know something about communism. It was in many ways a unique political formation, particularly in its centralised monopoly over so many domains of life, its systematised pervasiveness, and the pervasiveness of its secret police. Nevertheless, many of the ways communists denied the internal morality of law are widespread among pre-transitional despotisms. I tried to summarise a few characteristic ways, shortly after the collapse of European communism:

> A central characteristic of the exercise of power under 'really existing socialism' was its arbitrariness … At different times, extralegal 'administrative measures', special invisible sentencing boards, secret tribunals, police, informers, torturers commonly took the place of the law; 'partiinost' [Party loyalty], 'socialist legal consciousness', 'analogy', 'campaigns', and 'telephone law' ensured that law itself was politically pliable. And quite apart from these special effects, such law as there was was ignored when expedient and was otherwise long treated purely instrumentally by the Party. Rules of the game were changed unpredictably, subject to no formal procedures of consequence, while the game was still being played. The extent of the state's resulting lawlessness and arbitrariness varied within communist polities according to floating distinctions between 'political' offences and others, between such polities and over time. But compared with 'normal' polities, arbitrariness was enormous, was widely felt and rightly resented. It also came to be expected.[40]

Not much internal morality there! The abuses of law's internal morality, common to the past of so many transitional societies, make it impossible, one might almost say immoral, to treat Fuller's discussions of law's internal morality as lightly as some have. And note that the problem is not necessarily the *absence* of law. Under communism, law was often, alas, plentiful and unavoidable. The problem was its character and how it was used. Character and use are not unrelated. It appears that many despotisms find law very useful, precisely to the extent that it flouts Fuller's criteria and renders rulers, but not their subjects, legally unaccountable. 'Under the rule of [Soviet] strict apparatchiks', as Marina

[39] These are subjects of some of Jeremy Waldron's recent reflections on Fuller.

[40] 'Marxism and the Rule of Law. Reflections after the Collapse of Communism' (1990) 15(4) *Law and Social Inquiry* 647.

Kurkchiyan has vividly demonstrated, 'the bureaucratic invention known as "the power of paper" became a highly developed art form'.[41] And the power of paper was power indeed.

The best of transitional law reformers are keen to put such pasts behind them. Knowing the difference, they would endorse Fuller's insistence that 'we are not interested merely in order—the order, say, of a concentration camp—but in an order that is just, fair, workable, effective, and respectful of human dignity'.[42] To transform law, to make it serve citizens rather than merely their overlords; to develop legal orders which routinely, or even at all, treat persons with respect; to enable civil interactions to occur between citizens and the state and among citizens themselves; these are among the great ambitions of many in transitional societies. If ever there were a need for inspired social architecture, it is there. But it is not easy work.

The discourse of transition has been, I have argued elsewhere, at the same time teleological and imitative, but not especially descriptive.[43] People had a good idea of what they had left behind, and many were confident where they wanted to end up. Where they actually were was left as a somewhat ill-defined space of impatient movement between these two poles. Denizens of post-communist transitions were determined to make 'no experiments'; they had seen the communist future and it hadn't worked. They wanted the other one. And elsewhere too promoters of 'transitional rule of law' strive to emulate 'best practice' rather than build Utopia. Perhaps it is no coincidence that 'transition' and 'transplant' share a prefix.

However, as Stephen Holmes once remarked,[44] and Fuller would surely have agreed, 'an interaction technology is harder to transplant than a production technology'. What do you need to know? How a good legal institution works, where it works? That itself is not a simple thing to understand. And transplanted laws and institutions are typically uprooted from much of what their working might depend on, when they are called upon to travel. They land in territory where much that is already firmly embedded is often unfamiliar and unwelcoming. Are there examples of successful transplantations elsewhere? But why imagine that every transplant will encounter the same reception, wherever it is sent? Should we then stick to local knowledge? But 'the way we do things here' is often the problem. Moreover, changes happen and can be made to happen, and often it is better that they do. We are not always impotent, nor is history just a recycling of familiar patterns. And among the things that can be learned from history is

[41] See Marina Kurkchiyan, 'The Illegitimacy of Law' in Denis Galligan and Marina Kurkchiyan (eds), *Law and Informal Practices* (Oxford, Oxford University Press, 2003) 36.

[42] 'Means and Ends' in Kenneth L Winston (ed), revised edn *The Principles of Social Order: Selected Essays of Lon L. Fuller* (Durham, NC, Duke University Press, 2001) 61.

[43] Martin Krygier and Adam Czarnota, 'After Postcommunism: The Next Phase' (2006) 2 *Annual Review of Law and Social Science* 299, 304.

[44] In a workshop on 'Rethinking the Rule of Law after Communism', European University, Institute, Florence, 2003.

that some things long done are better undone. But how? And if it is hard to know what to do to get to the future, it is equally hard to know how to deal with the past, which often means how to ditch it, or parts of it. Not a simple task.

There is a real gulf between the tinkering renovation required of lawyers and even legal theorists who work within established, well-arranged legal orders, with long legal traditions, institutions and professions, and what is asked of social architects in the conditions prevalent in many 'transitional societies'. And for all the depth of his insights, to engage with some of the deepest problems of law in such societies, one needs to move beyond Fuller's observations on the morality of state law. For these problems run deeper than the character and use of that law.

Social architects, after all, should know a good deal about the terrain for which they design. The quality of their materials will not always compensate for the swamps or sands on which they must try to build, the barrenness and inhospitable nature of some terrains, the treacherousness of others, the presence of uncongenial structures, among them social structures, difficult to remove and yet also difficult to replace. Architects should also know something of the tastes, preferences, understandings and purposes of those for whom, ostensibly, they are building. If in some countries (Bulgaria as a matter of fact), law is thought of as 'like a door in the middle of an open meadow. Of course you could go through the door, but why bother?', this presents a challenge to an architect who would like his building to be useful. A major problem of transitional architecture is to get people to approach the door, let alone go through it; and that for a range of different reasons: some think the door leads nowhere; others that one can get lost, or lose, in there; others that danger lies there; others still that it is not designed for people like them. Again, if, as in many Soviet republics, 'politics [and equally law] was not something you did; it was something other people did to you',[45] the task of making the law inviting might be challenging. And if the law or citizens themselves are surrounded by predatory beasts, that too might affect issues of institutional design and construction. It would be an odd architect who proudly disdained knowledge of where and for whom his buildings are likely to be erected. Legal philosophers, however, do it all the time, and not accidentally. Many consider such matters none of their business.

Fuller was different. In scattered essays in which he elaborates elements of what he called 'eunomics', 'the science, theory, or study of good order and workable social arrangements',[46] he frequently emphasises the importance of extra-legal conditions of legal effectiveness. Thus, he writes, '[i]f made law is divorced from its context, it may be projected upon a social terrain incapable of supporting it, in which case tacit modifications or outright evasions of the law will ensue'.[47] He repeatedly inveighs against overestimation of the power or significance of state

[45] S Neil MacFarlane, in Galligan and Kurkchiyan, n 41 above, at 72.

[46] 'Means and Ends' in Kenneth Winston (ed), *The Principles of Social Order*, revised edn (Oxford, Hart Publishing, 2001) 62.

[47] 'Human Interaction and the Law' in *ibid* 231 and see 257.

law. His Oakeshottian tendency to conceive of institutional design as 'pursuing the intimations' of existing traditions moves in the same direction, though like Oakeshott he has little to say about what to do if it is precisely these intimations that are the problem. Nevertheless, he has a deep feeling for institutional variety, plurality and complexity, a real commitment to recognition of legal contexts and forms of law, as much as the internal features of legal forms.

However, in his debate with Hart and more generally when he discusses the internal morality, Fuller remains a lawyer, for all his interest in social purposes and consequences. The internal morality, on which the possibility of interaction and dignity are said to rest, is expressed in the formal character of legal rules. That is important, but so much else matters for the effectiveness of law as an ingredient in human interaction, much of it out of the reach of lawyers or legal architects.

It is a truism of legal pluralism, yet still important to acknowledge, that the major effects of central legal institutions, where they *have* major effects (which is not everywhere), occur outside those institutions.[48] That being the case, it should be just as obvious, but is rarely so to lawyers, that those effects are to variable extents and in varying manners dependent on the ways state laws interrelate with, are refracted, amplified, nullified by, existing non-state structures, norms, networks and attitudes. Nowhere is everyone waiting to hear just what the legislature and the courts have to say; and, whatever they are listening to, there are many other generators of noise, some of it often louder and closer at hand than that generated by the law of the state. This is generally true, but especially so in many transitional societies, where the state and its law are weak and other forms of normative ordering (or disordering) are strong.

Whenever law stakes a claim to rule there are many sources of potential normative, structural, cultural, institutional collaboration and competition in every society. They, and their interplay, differ markedly between (and often within) societies. How people will interpret the state's law and respond to it, how highly it will rate for them in comparison with other influences—these things depend only partly on what it says, how it says it, and what the law is intended by its makers to do. In complex and variable ways, people's responses to state law depend on how, in what form, with what salience and force, that law is able to penetrate all these intervening media, how attuned to it putative recipients are, how dense, how competitive, resistant, hostile to its messages they might turn out to be.

This is not to say that state law and the character of its rules are unimportant. They are often crucially important. How much and in what ways their effects work out in the world are, nevertheless, heavily dependent on the various and often complex contexts into which they intervene. That is a universal truth.

[48] This and the next two paragraphs are taken from my 'The Rule of Law and the "Three Integrations"' (2009) 1(1) *Hague Journal on the Rule of Law* 25.

Recognition of it requires from many people a major reconceptualisation of what it might mean for law to rule, where we might find it, what it depends upon, and what we need to know to understand it.

Transitional societies and their law commonly have different pasts, presents and likely futures from many of those in which Western legal philosophy is at home, and from which it takes its examples. They also differ equally and for the same reasons from their major sources of legal advice and aid. And they themselves are, like Tolstoy's unhappy families, each unhappy in their own way. They differ from each other not only in their legal institutions, but in the roles they play; the extent, indeed, to which they matter at all in a society. In some states, particularly communist ones, the state was everywhere, into everything and in the wrong ways. The aftermath of that has its own patterns. In others, for most of the time and for most problems, it was nowhere to be seen. That has other implications. And there are multiple options in between. Should these differences matter to philosophy? Should they matter to law, to 'the concept of law', 'the morality of law' or 'the rule of law'?

Context and Variation

I believe so. One need not simply join the familiar anthropologists' chorus, 'This is all very well, but it doesn't apply to the Bongo-Bongo',[49] to worry about the excessively abstract and universalistic character in which much of the Hart–Fuller debate was conducted; in particular, the way in which Hart's discussion surveys, smooths over, and homogenises the conceptual, moral, political and institutional variables to which it purports in its Olympian way to apply. Too much that is specific to particular contexts and circumstances is rendered invisible and insubstantial by the crisp and apparently exhaustive choices (legal questions/moral questions) that Hart poses in the debate. As Nicola Lacey has suggested, 'philosophical analysis of key legal and political concepts needs to be understood both historically and institutionally and ... Hart's relative lack of interest in this sort of contextualization marks a certain limit to the insights provided by his legal and political philosophy'.[50] Fuller's instincts and convictions were radically different; institutional variation mattered to him a great deal. However, in debating Hart, and in his discussions of the internal morality of law, he also has little to say about the play of context in the sway of the law.

What might attention to these things involve? One thing is alertness to empirical particularity and variation. In a book, aptly for this chapter, if fortuitously, entitled *Law and Society in Transition*, Philip Selznick suggested that many central jurisprudential issues could profitably be viewed 'in a social-science

[49] Mary Douglas, *Natural Symbols* (Harmondsworth, Penguin, 1973) 15–16.

[50] Nicola Lacey, 'Philosophy, Political Morality, and History: Explaining the Enduring Resonance of the Hart-Fuller Debate' (2008) 83 *New York University Law Review* 1062.

perspective',[51] the hallmark of which was attention to variation and to context. There are several reasons to do this, central among them that it is 'important for scholars to appreciate the full range of legal experience'[52] and in particular 'to grasp the significance of *variation*'.[53] The nature of law, relations between law, morals, politics, and so on, so often treated as single questions with single answers, could benefit from immersion in the ways these relationships vary, often systematically, within and between different legal orders. And, apart from differences among institutional forms and contexts, there are also *qualitative* differences that matter. Shouldn't we have concepts that register the difference between merely surviving and thriving? Fuller, like Selznick, thought so.

And this, finally, raises Fuller's question about 'fidelity to law' and another about the rule of law, with which I will conclude. How would you know what might encourage intelligent fidelity, for example: the sturdy and independent Englishmen's distinction between legal and moral obligation, Teutonic deference to law, rejection of immoral law? (These options are, by the way, commonly beside the point in many recent societies in transition: no English, no Teutons, no fidelity. The problem in so many of those societies is that no one hitherto had related legal and moral obligation much at all, and they still don't;[54] something of an 'internal attitude' deficit, insufficiently registered in Anglophone legal philosophy.)

There are issues of empirical and theoretical sociology here that might usefully be explored. One of them, on which Hart and Fuller speculate, is why so many Germans obeyed Nazi law and officials enforced it.[55] Another, that Fuller discusses, is what were the pressures facing post-Nazi officials, and what would be the social significance of one way of dealing with a case compared to another. Intelligent speculation abounds in the debate; consideration of evidence, or even thought that a search for it might be appropriate, is rare.[56]

It is true that when rebuking Radbruch for his 'extraordinary naïveté', Hart continues that 'this terrible history prompts inquiry into why emphasis on the slogan "law is law", and the distinction between law and morals, acquired a sinister character in Germany, but elsewhere, as with the Utilitarians themselves, went along with the most enlightened liberal attitudes'.[57] But it didn't prompt *him* to make that inquiry. It is not, he appears to believe, relevant to the philosophical case he is making. Nor does he follow up, as one might, his

[51] Philippe Nonet and Philip Selznick, *Law and Society in Transition: Toward Responsive Law* (New York, Harper Torchbooks, 1978; reprinted with a new introduction by Robert A Kagan, Transaction Publishers, New Brunswick, New Jersey, 2001) 3.

[52] *Ibid* 2.

[53] *Ibid* 8.

[54] See Kurkchiyan, n 41 above.

[55] *cf* Lacey, n 50 above, at 1072: 'the question of whether a positivist or a naturalist attitude toward law would best equip a society to resist tyranny is itself historically contingent to some degree'.

[56] For discussions of that evidence as it pertains to judges, see Ingo Müller, *Hitler's Justice: The Courts of the Third Reich* (Cambridge, MA, Harvard University Press, 1991).

[57] *Ibid* 618.

hypothesis that we would behave better morally and legally if we were clear-headedly prepared, like Bentham and himself, to think of these spheres as conceptually quite separate.

Fuller was far more warmly disposed to social investigation than was Hart. His essays in 'eunomics' have rightly been called exercises in moral sociology.[58] He had a strong sociological sensibility,[59] which served him well at times but left him underpowered in argument against Hart's formidable analytical armoury. He also knew more about what they were both discussing in the debate over Nazi law. And yet his accounts of what might lead to fidelity to law, and more broadly to the rule of law, or what is the connection between the 'internal morality of law' and the likelihood of state evil, all of them so important to him for the differences they made *in the world*, are curiously investigation-free zones: altogether richer in assumption and assertion than in evidence. Yet observation of variation in the ways in which law exists, and in its role and significance between and within societies, can tell us much about the sources of fidelity and the rule of law, and relationships between principles of legality and the (external) morality of law. And transitional societies, where concern with precisely these things (by some) is explicit and urgent, offer us many lessons about what they require, if only about how hard they are to achieve from a standing start, and how many are the ways they can fail to be achieved.

The Rule of Law

How might we think about law and the morality of law in ways that both honour what good law can do and take account of the multifarious contexts and circumstances in which it might be called upon to do it. Fuller's notion of 'social architecture' is extremely suggestive, and his 'internal morality' is an important ingredient. However, in his debate with Hart, he focuses almost solely on the character of state rules, whereas, to adapt Eugen Ehrlich, 'the centre of gravity of legal development lies not in legislation, nor in juristic science, nor in judicial decision, but in society itself'.[60]

In this connection, Nicola Lacey has asked an intriguing question:

[58] Introduction to Winston, n 42 above, at 8.

[59] A reason why Philip Selznick felt such affinity for Fuller's work even though their differences, among them political, were considerable, and led them in different scholarly directions at times. See my 'Philip Selznick: Incipient Law, State Law and the Rule of Law' in J van Schooten and JM Verschuuren (eds), *International Governance and Law: State Regulation and Non-State Law* (Cheltenham, Elgar, 2008) 31–55 esp at 53. See also Lacey, n 50 above, at 1067 and *A Life of H.L.A. Hart* (Oxford, Oxford University Press, 2004) 184.

[60] *Ibid* quoting E Ehrlich, *Fundamental Principles of the Sociology of Law* (Cambridge, MA, Harvard University Press, 1936) xv. This translation has been reissued, with a new Introduction by Klaus Ziegert (New Brunswick, NJ, Transaction Press, 2002).

> Is the striking contrast between natural law and positivist positions that forms the centrepiece of the Hart–Fuller debate best understood as a philosophical disagreement? Or is it rather—or equally—a moral and practical disagreement about which institutional arrangements are likely to maximize the realization of valued social ends or ideals under specific social and historical conditions? Does the debate between Hart and Fuller centre on a timeless conceptual distinction? Or is the debate's lasting significance due to the vivid context in which it framed one of the most pressing moral and political questions confronting post-Enlightenment constitutional democracies: how to develop legal arrangements capable of constraining abuses of power and of addressing such abuses?[61]

The questions Lacey refers to are in fact much older than the Enlightenment, and this is significant. Otherwise, however, this is how I read much of the debate as well. Or at least, I would support Lacey's second version of the question, 'rather—or equally'; since the conceptual issues are crucial, and were clearly important to Hart if perhaps less central for Fuller (though it is not clear he realised that). And I further take the question 'how to develop legal arrangements capable of constraining abuses of power and of addressing such abuses?' as asking how to develop the rule of law.

In transitional societies, few have heard of the internal morality of law. However there is a lot of talk of the rule of law. There is widespread support, or at least widespread rhetorical enthusiasm, for the notion that the law should rule, whatever that means. Indeed, the phrase has enjoyed a remarkable, unstoppable, career in these times of transition. Everyone is for it, international agencies spend billions of dollars on it, there are centres, conferences, websites, and recently even a journal devoted to it. The discourse of transition would be bereft without it.

Now, among legal philosophers including Hart, Fuller's account of the internal morality of law is generally taken to spell out the central elements of the rule of law.[62] Accounts by lawyers might differ in level of abstraction, or in particular features emphasised, but they all share the focus on particularities of familiar law and legal institutions. Thus, though Dicey describes the rule of law as a 'trait of national character which is as noticeable as it is hard to portray',[63] he confidently and famously reduces this 'trait' to three distinctive aspects of English law. Transitional rule of law promoters, in their turn, have by and large tended to take what Carothers has called a 'breathtakingly mechanistic approach' based on the notion that 'a country achieves the rule of law by reshaping its key institutions to match those of countries that are considered to have the rule of law'.[64]

61 Lacey, n 50 above, at 1072.

62 See Raz, n 31 above. The list of eight is extended to 12, but the focus on formal characteristics of legal rules is the same, in Geoffrey de Q Walker, *The Rule of Law: Foundations of Constitutional Democracy* (Melbourne University Press, 1988). *cf*, too, Friedrich von Hayek, *The Constitution of Liberty* (London, Routledge and Kegan Paul, 1960) 149–50.

63 AV Dicey, *Introduction to the Study of the Law of the Constitution*, 10th edn (London, Macmillan, 1959, 1st edn 1885) 187.

64 Thomas Carothers, 'The Problem of Knowledge' in *Promoting the Rule of Law Abroad: In Search of Knowledge* (Washington, DC, Carnegie Endowment for International Peace, 2006) 21.

What all these conceptions have in common is: (a) the confident assumption that the central ingredients of the rule of law are state legal institutions, and (b) the equally confident assumption that we are in a position to stipulate in very general terms what aspects and elements of these institutions add up to the rule of law. These assumptions are so common, indeed, that they largely go without saying in discussions of the rule of law, whether among philosophers, lawyers, or the swarms of transitional rule of law promoters who have so contributed to the unprecedented public prominence of the concept. Is this the best way to think about these matters, particularly in the light of the contingency and variety of transitional and other societies?

The strongest assertion that it is not, at least in relation to transitional societies, can be found in Ruti Teitel's well known work, *Transitional Justice*.[65] For Teitel emphasises that transitions are exceptional in character, and claims that mainstream scholars have ignored this. She briefly summarises Hart's and Fuller's arguments about the Nazi cases, for example, but she doesn't spend much time with them either in exposition or criticism, since she believes that, in arguing abstract questions about law and morals in universalistic terms, Hart and Fuller:

> failed to focus … on the distinctive problem of law in the transitional context … A transitional perspective on the postwar debate would clarify what is signified by the rule of law. That is, the content of the rule of law is justified in terms of distinctive conceptions of the nature of injustice of the various alternatives, such as full continuity with the prior legal regime, discontinuity, selective discontinuities, and moving outside the law altogether …
>
> In the postwar debate, the questions arose in the extraordinary political context following totalitarian rule. Yet, the conclusions abstract from the context and generalize as if describing essential, universal attributes of the rule of law, failing to recognize how the problem is particular to the transitional context. Resituating the problem should illuminate our understanding of the rule of law.[66]

Again, according to Teitel:

> theories of adjudication associated with understandings of the rule of law in ordinary times are inapposite to transitional periods. Our ordinary intuitions about the nature and role of adjudication relate to presumptions about the relative competence and capacities of judiciaries and legislatures in ordinary times that simply do not hold in unstable periods.[67]

Why so? Transitions, Teitel suggests, are 'extraordinary' periods of great 'flux', unlike times of 'ordinary' politics when business goes on more or less as usual.

[65] Ruti Teitel, *Transitional Justice* (Oxford, Oxford University Press, 2000). I discuss Teitel's argument at greater length in 'Transitional Questions about the Rule of Law: Why, What, and How?' (2001) 28(1) *East Central Europe/L'Europe du Centre Est: Eine wissenschaftliche Zeitschrift* 1, 25–34, and 'Rethinking the Rule of Law after Communism' in Czarnota, Krygier and Sadurski, n 4 above, at 266–73.

[66] Teitel, n 65 above, at 14–15.

[67] R Teitel, 'Transitional Jurisprudence …' (1997) 106 *Yale Law Journal* 2034.

Secondly, the flux is not just tumultuous but directed, that is it aims (more accurately, some actors within it aim; many others don't care; others want to go back home; still others just want to leave) to move away from the past and to something different. Thirdly, transitions involve 'normative shift', that is, roughly a shift from a now-derided despotism to now-desired democracy and rule of law. Fourthly, transitions differ markedly from each other, and what 'transitional justice' is taken to require will depend particularly on the character of the political order they succeed.

According to Teitel, in such periods law has a special role which is an 'extraordinary constructive' one, in that it doesn't merely provide settled guidelines for the present but exercises its 'transformative potential' to engender the putatively different future which will come at the end of a 'bounded period, spanning two regimes'. The tension between these two functions Teitel calls the 'rule-of-law dilemma'. Since the transition is special, Teitel argues, it should not be judged according to presuppositions derived from 'normal' conditions. On the contrary, circumstances of transition generate 'a distinctive conception of justice and rule of law in the context of political transformation'.

In consequence of all these variations and peculiarities, Teitel does, and by implication we should, eschew 'idealized theorizing about the rule of law in general'[68] and instead recognise 'the tension between idealized conceptions of the rule of law and the contingencies of the extraordinary political context. Struggling with the dilemma of how to adhere to some commitment to the rule of law in such periods leads to alternative constructions, constructions that mediate conceptions of transitional rule of law'.[69] We must recognise that in transitions, 'the rule of law is ultimately contingent',[70] 'partial, contextual, and situated between at least two legal and political orders'.[71] So much so, that 'in transition, the ordinary intuitions and predicates about law simply do not apply. In dynamic periods of political flux, legal responses generate a sui generis paradigm of transformative law'.[72]

Teitel's emphasis on the specificity of moments of transition alerts us helpfully to the inevitable and specific tensions faced by many actors, including legal actors, in such circumstances. In particular (and this is more of a reproach to Hart than to Fuller), she forces us to consider the extent to which, and many of the ways in which, participants, and particularly officials, in the very special circumstances of post-dictatorial transitions (and though special, there have been many such circumstances, each with its own peculiarities) have a lot on their plate, some of it perhaps unimaginable in Oxford or even Cambridge, MA. A lot

[68] Teitel, n 65 above, at 12.
[69] *Ibid* 15.
[70] *Ibid* 11.
[71] *Ibid* 9.
[72] *Ibid* 6.

of what such officials have done and have to do can be explained and often justified (though often it is easier to explain than justify) by where they sit.

However, in reacting against an impoverished 'off-the-shelf blueprint'[73] approach to the rule of law one must guard against so boosting the uniqueness of transitions that one severs their moorings in institutional possibilities and limitations, and more broadly in the human condition and more general human purposes. That not only needlessly limits the repertoire of possibilities and risks time-consuming attempts to reinvent old wheels, but it also makes it hard to know when purposes are achieved or criticism is appropriate. Does whatever is done with and to law in a particular transition contribute to the 'transitional rule of law' for that time and place? If not, why not? Transitions, like most everything that exists, do indeed have distinctive characteristics, but none of that implies either that there is nothing larger to learn from them about non-transitional circumstances, or that we have no larger moral or conceptual frames in which to judge what occurs in them.

I prefer a view of the rule of law that seeks to capture both what is universal and what is particular in it. This view begins with teleology, as does Fuller's, but resists the speed with which he fuses teleology with particular legal anatomy, that is, his suggestion that the rule of law is to be found in legal rules with a particular set of formal characteristics. Instead, the starting point is a generally valuable state of affairs, in the light of which one can appraise particular institutional recommendations for achieving it. These, however, unlike the ideal itself, are likely to be subject to considerable variation.

Specifically, I recommend that we ask three questions about the rule of law, and do so in the following order—both the questions and the order matter.[74] We should begin by asking what we might want the rule of law for, by which I mean not external ends that it might serve, such as economic growth or democracy, but something like its *telos,* the point of the enterprise, goals internal to, immanent in the concept. I argue that this *telos* involves a state of affairs in which (at a minimum, and this could be added to and elaborated) law contributes in salutary ways to constraining and channelling uses of power—political, social and

[73] Wade Jacoby, 'Priest and Penitent: The European Union as a Force in the Domestic Politics of Eastern Europe' (1999) 8(2) *East European Constitutional Review* (Winter/Spring) 62.

[74] The view is developed in a bunch of articles and deployed for a variety of purposes: 'Transitional Questions about the Rule of Law: Why, What, and How?', n 65 above; 'The Grammar of Colonial Legality: Subjects, Objects and the Rule of Law' in Geoffrey Brennan and Francis G Castles (eds), *Australia Reshaped: Essays on 200 Years of Institutional Transformation* (Cambridge, Cambridge University Press, 2002) 220–60; 'False Dichotomies, Real Perplexities, and the Rule of Law' in András Sajó (ed), *Human Rights with Modesty: The Problem of Universalism* (Leiden/Boston, Martinus Nijhoff, 2004) 251–77; 'The Rule of Law: An Abuser's Guide' in András Sajó (ed), *The Dark Side of Fundamental Rights* (Utrecht, Eleven International Publishing, 2006) 129–61. I have tried most recently to distil the argument in 'The Rule of Law: Legality, Teleology, Sociology' in Gianluigi Palombella and Neil Walker (eds), *Relocating the Rule of Law* (Oxford, Hart Publishing, 2008) and to apply it to situations of conflict in (with Whit Mason) 'Violence, Development, and the Rule of Law' in George Mavrotas (ed), *Security for Development* (Edward Elgar, Cheltenham UK, forthcoming 2010).

economic—so that the possibilities of its arbitrary exercise and abuse are significantly diminished. It is *this* salutary state of affairs, or something like it, that most matters to so many desperate denizens of transition who could use some rule of law, not a particular set of institutional prescriptions. I commend this ideal (not especially controversial in the tradition of thought on the rule of law, but open to revision and elaboration) as well nigh universal in application. No one benefits from unrestrained abuse of power, aside (perhaps and not always) from the abuser.

Next we need to ask what conditions institutions need to fulfil to be able to aid in achievement of such an end. These include matters of scope or reach, character, enforcement and, fundamental but not much pursued by legal philosophers, social salience; however well or ill crafted, law needs to *count* as a restraint on social power. Whether it does so or not cannot be read off from its formal qualities. Fuller's internal morality, by contrast, is primarily concerned with just those qualities and just one of these conditions, the character of laws; important but far from the whole. Yet if, as in many transitional societies, state law has very restricted reach, its formal quality may not count for much.

Only in the light of answers to these two questions does it make sense to move, thirdly, to ask precisely what we need in order to get what we want, because the means are more contingent and variable than the ends. That latter question, the bottom line, as it were, will of course involve particular legal institutions and arrangements, but they will vary, and it will involve many other things as well. Indeed, the question cannot be answered without looking beyond legal institutions to the societies in which they function, the ways they function there, and what else happens there which interacts with and affects the sway of law. For the rule of law to exist, still more to flourish and be secure, many things beside the law matter, and since societies differ in many ways, so will those things. How much Fuller's principles make a difference, and what sorts of differences they make, to the closeness to which a society approaches the ideal will also vary. So first, what do we want? Secondly, what do we need to get it? Thirdly, what do we have that can do it? The usual practice in discussing the rule of law is to go the other way, or simply identify a particular institutional arrangement as 'the rule of law'.

In societies where the rule of law has long been secure, the fact that it is misconceived might not matter too much, since to a considerable extent it runs on its own steam. In transitional societies which seek to build the rule of law, however, these problems are acute. For those most urgently seeking the rule of law are in the end concerned not with a package of legal techniques but with an *outcome*: a salutary state of affairs, where law counts as a restraint on power more than it does or has in many places.

The practical problem becomes how to design arrangements that serve such ends in particular circumstances. Since societies, histories, practices, traditions, institutions, differ and many such differences have effects, so too will the answers that make sense at one time or another, one place or another. That, at least, is a lesson that might be gleaned from the manifest challenges in seeking to build the rule of law in 'transitional' societies. The goal can be clear, but means vary and too often we have no idea what they might be. Unfortunately, too much discussion of the rule of law has started and stopped with a particular set of means.

Given that we can do what we like with words, the rule of law is a notoriously contested concept, and no one's *fiat* travels far, why does it matter what we call it? Well partly because what you think the rule of law is can affect where you look for it, and what you might do to find it, still more to nurture it. In much of my 'transitional' observation, I have been struck by the extent to which 'RoL' practitioners (as promoters of the rule of law in benighted countries are called) are obsessed with mimicking metropolitan legal arrangements, while they ignore all that matters around them. That includes structures, practices, traditions, understandings that have great significance for social fidelity to law, for legal culture, and for the feasibility of the rule of law, but have no obvious institutional connection to the state legal system, and therefore, alas, are not within the purview of typical architects of the rule of law. Even were these latter to manage to graft a perfect set of all eight of Fuller's principles onto the state's legal institutions, so much else, I have felt, would lie untouched that nothing would be likely to change in the world.

But whether or not the principles of legality could be observed by institutions in circumstances where it doesn't make sense to speak of the rule of law, there are certainly circumstances in which it makes good sense to speak of the rule of law, but where Fuller's criteria are not satisfied by the law, not merely in the sense that the world is never ideal but rather that the criteria don't deal with the case. Lacey has mentioned several such cases;[75] let me conclude with two more, one older than hers, one younger.

Within Britain, and as inherited by its dependants, the concept of the rule of law is deeply embedded and very old indeed. Dicey believed so, and it has recently been well demonstrated by the American legal historian, John Philip Reid.[76] Reid shows that in English tradition until the eighteenth century, law was identified with misty, murky but ages-old custom, traced to a time when 'the memory of man runneth not to the contrary'. As he writes, 'the medieval constitutional law out of which today's rule of law developed would not have met the requirements of clarity or precision. There was always an air of indefiniteness, a smoky vagueness surrounding this all-embracing restraining "law" of English constitutionalism. Even its authority as law was shrouded in immeasurability'.[77]

On the old view, as Reid puts it, 'what mattered was not its intrinsic qualities but that it was customary practice, not deliberative decision'.[78] The rule of law

[75] See Lacey, n 50 above, at 1072–8.
[76] John Philip Reid, *Rule of Law* (University of Northern Illinois Press, 2004).
[77] *Ibid* 16.
[78] *Ibid* 13.

tamed unruly exercise of power because even the sovereign was not above it; indeed, was not 'sovereign' in Cromwell's or Blackstone's or Austin's sense, but subject to higher law. It is arguable, and Reid does argue, that there is a major shift in the English conception of law from the eighteenth century, from immemorial custom to sovereign legislation. With that shift came a change in how the rule of law was understood: from fidelity to customs allegedly continuous since 'the memory of man runs not to the contrary', to demands that law, even if sovereign, be public, clear, not retrospective, possible of performance, and so on. Paradoxically, the shift distanced the more old-fashioned, newly-to-be-United States, from the novel transformations of law and legal theory that were occurring in Britain. It was partly what the revolution was about.

My other example is more recent. There was a time (1989 to be precise) when I assumed the rule of law was what the 'transitioning' world needed and that it was well captured in Lon Fuller's 'internal morality' or something like it. And so it seemed to me that in all the excitement of the collapse of communism, this was a product ripe for export. So I was shocked in that same year to read an article by Edward Rubin which took this alleged morality apart as it applied, or rather was argued not to apply, to 'Law and Legislation in the Administrative State'.[79] Rubin argues that the bulk of modern legislation is not, as Lon Fuller thought law to be, 'the enterprise of subjecting human conduct to the governance of rules', but rather 'a series of directives issued by the legislature to government-implementation mechanisms, primarily administrative agencies, rather than a set of rules for the governance of human conduct'.[80] A great deal of modern legislation is 'internal', that is, concerned at least initially with administrative agencies rather than individual citizens. Within 'external' legislation, moreover, much is 'intransitive', that is, though concerned ultimately with citizens, it does not specify precisely what rules an agency is expected to apply to them. There is a vast amount of such legislation in the modern state, and it 'did not arise out of some lapse of moral vigilance. It is central to our beliefs about the role of the government in solving problems and delivering services'.[81]

Of this legislation Rubin argues that Fuller's principles are unhelpful, and '[e]ven for transitive statutes, most of Fuller's principles are persuasive only when the statute relies on courts as its primary implementation mechanism. When a transitive statute is enforced by an agency, our normative system simply does not make the demands that Fuller perceives'.[82] It still makes sense to oppose arbitrary uses of power against citizens, but a great deal of law needs to be thought about in other terms, and where the concern *is* appropriate, antidotes to it are often likely to be very different from those that Fuller suggests.

[79] Edward Rubin, in (1989) 89 *Columbia Law Review* 369.
[80] *Ibid* 371–2.
[81] *Ibid* 406–7.
[82] *Ibid* 399.

Now perhaps this is all wrong; or it might be that a closer reading of Fuller than Rubin's would reveal that he was not setting up universal measures simply to be applied, whatever the form of law, whatever the circumstance. I think it is clear that he was not,[83] though he has often been taken in this way and he might still not be able to get off Rubin's specific and rather sharp hooks. But my point is different. Rubin's analysis only threatens the claim that the rule of law exists in the United States if the rule of law is identified with the legal institutional prescriptions summed up in the 'morality of law'. Many lawyers and legal philosophers think it should be, in which case to the extent that Rubin is right, the rule of law is out the window in America. Perhaps it is, but that is not the reason.

The approach to the rule of law suggested here is not embarrassed by either the historical story Reid tells or the institutional arrangements Rubin reveals, for its existence criteria lie elsewhere. And yet it does not leave us waiting for the next transition, to reveal what the rule of law will turn out to be, just for that place at that time. It also allows us to say why we think, as Hart occasionally does, Fuller almost always does, and I do too, that the rule of law is worth a great deal.

[83] See *The Principles of Social Order*, n 42 above, and the insightful introductory essays by Winston.

7

Legal Pluralism and the Contrast Between Hart's Jurisprudence and Fuller's

JEREMY WALDRON

Introduction

The exchange between Lon Fuller and HLA Hart, published in the *Harvard Law Review* in 1958, covered a whole array of questions in general jurisprudence.[1] Yet there were one or two issues that were salient then or have become salient in legal theory since 1958 that they barely touched on. One is the topic of legal pluralism, and that is my topic in this chapter.

I think it is fair to say that there is nothing whatsoever on this topic in the Hart–Fuller exchange—nor do modern debates about legal pluralism appear to be part of the legacy of the Hart–Fuller debate. So much is this so that some jurists have suggested that the Hart–Fuller debate actually skewed the agenda for jurisprudence in unfortunate ways, which we are only now beginning to correct, and that recent emphasis on legal pluralism is part of that process.[2] However, I have no intention of scolding Hart and Fuller for failing to address legal pluralism in 1958. It would be churlish to do so, given the range of topics they did address. But it is interesting that they neglected this topic, and it tells us something perhaps about blind spots in both their jurisprudence. So in what follows I want to look at various missed opportunities (for addressing this topic) from the positivist perspective that Hart's work represents and from the various perspectives that Fuller's work represents—the 'rule of law' perspective and the anti-positivist position. I am also going to speculate a little about what Hart's and

[1] HLA Hart, 'Positivism and the Separation of Law and Morals', Holmes Lecture (1958) 71 *Harvard Law Review* 593 and Lon . Fuller, 'Positivism and Fidelity to Law: A Reply to Professor Hart' (1958) 71 *Harvard Law Review* 630.

[2] See William Twining, 'Schauer on Hart' (2006) 119 *Harvard Law Review Forum* 122.

Fuller's attitudes to legal pluralism might be expected to be, in light of the positions they took up in their subsequent work.

I suspect that most legal theorists have the following view. They assume that HLA Hart and Lon Fuller would be divided on the question of legal pluralism. They assume that Hart, like other legal positivists, would tend to favour a strongly state-centric view of law, leaving little room for genuine legal pluralism. And they assume that Fuller would be much more sympathetic to legal pluralism, partly on account of his anti-positivist commitments and partly on account of some things he said about customary law and about the diversity of legal systems, not in the 1958 piece but in *The Morality of Law*[3] and in some of his later writings.

I shall try to show that on both sides this view is a little simplistic. I do not mean that Hart was a legal pluralist and Fuller was not. But I mean first that, on the Hart side, we need to distinguish between currents in legal positivism that favour legal pluralism (and there are some) and currents in legal positivism that tend to oppose it; we need to understand how the latter currents are permitted to flow through the distinctive channels of the legal theory that Hart set out in his Holmes Lecture and in *The Concept of Law*;[4] and we need to understand the various ways in which the former currents are blocked. And I mean secondly, on the Fuller side, that we need to understand the pressures put on the idea of legal pluralism by Fuller's 'inner morality of law' and the ways in which this might militate in favour of a monistic rather than a pluralistic legal/political system.

Existence and Evaluation

What I have said in the first section is introductory, and of course the language I have used so far is amateurish: I have talked in terms of theories favouring pluralism and theories opposed to it—as though legal pluralism were a policy. Anyone who knows the pluralism literature will say that that is not helpful.

Legal pluralism is usually understood, in the first instance, as a condition or situation in a society. It is a condition or situation that is empirically discernible, ie discernible by careful qualitative empirical observation. As Sally Engle Merry puts it, legal pluralism is 'generally defined as a situation in which two or more legal systems coexist in the same social field'.[5] 'Legal pluralism' is a term used mostly to describe and characterise the existence of several distinct legal systems, or perhaps legal sub-systems, within a single independent political community, like a nation-state.

As a social condition or situation, it is in the first instance something that either obtains or does not. It is not a proposal that one opposes or supports. At

3 Lon L Fuller, *The Morality of Law*, revised edn (New Haven, CT, Yale University Press, 1969).
4 HLA Hart, *The Concept of Law*, 2nd edn (Oxford, Clarendon Press, 1994).
5 Sally Engle Merry, 'Legal Pluralism' (1988) 22 *Law and Society Review* 869, 870.

this descriptive level, then, the first question to be put to a legal theorist is whether his jurisprudence recognises this category and accommodates this phenomenon, or whether his jurisprudence would insist on characterising the phenomena that legal pluralists draw attention to in some other way: as either (1) the absence of a legal system (on account of unreconciled conflict); or (2) the existence of multiple legal systems in the ordinary sense (for example, the sense in which two adjacent countries have separate legal systems); or (3) the existence of ordered complexity within a single legal system (along the lines of the complexity we see in a federal system, like that of the United States, for example); or (4) the coexistence of systems of law and positive morality. That is a question about the categories that a theory uses.

If a legal theory recognises legal pluralism as a category, there is a further question about how much of it there is in the world. Some confine legal pluralism to cases where European countries established colonies that superimposed their legal systems on pre-existing systems.[6] Other theorists of legal pluralism use a much more generous conception. Leopold Pospisil claims that 'every functioning subgroup in a society has its own legal system which is necessarily different in some respects from those of the other subgroups'.[7] What is sometimes called 'the new legal pluralism' sees pluralism as a characteristic of every society.[8]

These are empirical/conceptual questions, and in themselves they have no normative aspect. But even if we grant that legal pluralism exists and that we need to be able to accommodate it in our categorial scheme, indeed even if we grant that it is pervasive, there may be interesting normative and/or evaluative questions to raise.

For example: to the extent that it exists, is legal pluralism a problem? To the extent that it can be channelled or conditioned by official action, what should be done about legal pluralism? For example, should the state encourage minorities to set up their own legal sub-systems and recognise them when they do? Should the state be solicitous of legal pluralism and refrain from doing anything to undermine it or bring it into disrepute?[9] That is another set of normative questions.[10]

[6] This formulation is from Merry, n 5 above, at 871, citing John Griffiths, 'What is Legal Pluralism?' (1986) 24 *Journal of Legal Pluralism* 1, 5–8.

[7] Leopold Pospisil, *The Anthropology of Law: A Comparative Theory of Law* (New York, Harper & Row, 1971) 107.

[8] Merry, n 5 above, at 873.

[9] For a typology of possible relations between state law and other forms of law in society, see Miranda Forsyth, 'A Typology of Relationships between State and Non-State Justice Systems' (2007) 56 *Journal of Legal Pluralism* 67.

[10] Recent discussions have connected the issue of legal pluralism to the normative philosophy of multiculturalism, responding—often critically—to proposals to promote, legitimise or clear space for the emergence of separate legal systems (catering, for example, to Muslim groups) in jurisdictions like England and Ontario. See, eg Abul Taher, 'Revealed: UK's First Official Sharia Courts', *Sunday Times*, 14 September 2008, 2 and Michael Valpy and Karen Howlett, 'Female MPPs' Concerns Delay Sharia

In what follows I shall consider what one might expect to be Hart's answer to factual or conceptual questions. I will briefly consider what one might expect to be Fuller's answer to these questions as well, though, towards the end of my remarks on Fuller, I will focus specifically on the implications of Fuller's inner morality of law for the normative questions about legal pluralism.

Pluralism and Hart's Positivism: Conceptual Issues

In the literature on legal pluralism, it is sometimes assumed that HLA Hart's jurisprudence, as set out in *The Concept of Law*, is a 'legal centralist'[11] theory that understands law in a vertical, top-down manner, and is therefore implicitly hostile to legal pluralism at a conceptual level:

> Pluralism presents a model of the legal universe in which legal systems and institutions can conflict and overlap. The classic model of the legal order, advanced by Hart and Kelsen, resembled a pyramid. At the top of the structure was the Grundnorm, or rule of recognition, which served to both legally validate and identify the remaining rules of the system. The pluralist view, in contrast, suggests that there can be several legal orders in a given territory, each of which asserts its supremacy over the others.[12]

The assumption is that a theory like Hart's is hostile to the possibilities that legal pluralists envisage or that, hostile or not, it simply cannot accommodate these possibilities in the vertically-structured conceptual framework that it provides for understanding the phenomenon of law. Legal pluralism requires us to recognise as law normative orders that do not acquire their legal character by being ordained from on high by the state; it requires us to recognise law on the ground, so to speak, for example in the form of customary social orderings; and it requires us to recognise such orderings as law even while we leave open the question of their relation to official law promulgated by the state. And it is usually thought that a theory like Hart's can make no sense of this.

Decision; Ontario Government Urged to Go Slowly on Proposal to Allow Islamic Tribunals', *Globe and Mail* (Toronto), 8 September 2005, A8. For discussion in the context of pluralism, particularly worries that legal pluralism can disadvantage women and sub-minorities especially in family law, because it tends to privilege conservative religious norms, see Mitra Sharafi 'Justice in Many Rooms since Galanter: De-romanticizing Legal Pluralism through the Cultural Defense' (2008) 71 *Law and Contemporary Problems* 139: 'In the 1970s and 80s, a spirit of aggressive celebration permeated the study of legal pluralism. The romantic assumption that nonstate law was more egalitarian and less coercive than state law subtended terms like "people's law" and "folk law"'. Sharafi insists that '[t]he cultural defense debate should be read not just as a centerpiece of the multiculturalism discussion, but also as an integral part of the legal-pluralist literature' (*ibid* 140), thus importing the normative concerns of the former into what might otherwise have remained the conceptual and analytical concerns of the latter. See also n 94 below.

11 The term 'legal centralist' is taken from Griffiths, n 6 above, at 3.

12 Nick Barber, 'The *Rechtsstaat* and the Rule of Law' (2003) 53 *University of Toronto Law Journal* 443, 450–1.

There is indeed something to this assumption. But this sort of characterisation of Hart's theory as 'top-down' jurisprudence needs to be understood carefully in light of two important points.

Alternatives to Sovereignty

The first point is that Hart made it a distinctive feature of his jurisprudence to oppose and provide an alternative to the 'sovereign-based' jurisprudence of Hobbes, Bentham and Austin. A major legacy of Hart's jurisprudence was his depiction of the 'threadbare' inadequacy of the command theory of law and his demonstration of how much in a legal system is distorted if law is presented as a top-down command.[13] Hart criticised the vertical structure of the traditional model; he insisted that the key to jurisprudence is not the notion of command or the notion of a sovereign,[14] but the notion of the members of a group accepting a rule. This seems less hostile to pluralist possibilities than traditional positivist theories, inasmuch as it is less vertically-structured than they are. Instead of sovereign power, it placed a sort of customary practice at the foundation of a legal system.

In principle this means Hart *is* in a position to recognise as law the sort of normative orderings that pluralists draw attention to. Having refuted the top-down sovereign-dominated definition of law, he can recognise legal systems wherever we find the appropriate sets of (primary) rules packaged together with (secondary) practices of recognising rules. Law does not have to be state law on Hart's account,[15] though he does make the claim that paradigm cases of law will involve some sort of organised coercion.[16]

However, Hart does play down the extent to which law can be characterised as demotic—as a set of practices embedded in shared consciousness of the ordinary members of a social group. He envisages that in normal cases the fundamental secondary rules of a society will be practices shared and participated in by a small élite sub-set (the 'officials') of the social group they dominate.[17] '[W]hat is crucial is that there should be a unified or shared official acceptance of the rule of

[13] Hart, 'Positivism and the Separation of Law and Morals', n 1 above, at 602–3.

[14] *Ibid* 603–4.

[15] See also the discussion in Kenneth Einar Himma, 'Do Philosophy and Sociology Mix? A Non-Essentialist Socio-Legal Positivist Analysis of *The Concept of Law*' (2004) 24 *Oxford Journal of Legal Studies* 717, 729–30. It is also worth considering the way that Hart's jurisprudence has been used to oppose rather than confirm the statist 'positivism' of *Erie Railroad Co v Tompkins*, 304 U.S. 64 (1938). See Jack Goldsmith and Steven Walt, '*Erie* and the Irrelevance of Legal Positivism' (1998) 84 *Virginia Law Review* 673, 694–700 and Jeremy Waldron, 'Foreign Law and the Modern *Ius Gentium*' (2005) 119 *Harvard Law Review* 129, 142 .

[16] Hart, *The Concept of Law*, n 4 above, at 97–8; however, see also his comments *ibid* 217–18 and 227–8.

[17] This is noticed by John Griffiths, 'The Social Working of Legal Rules' (2003) 48 *Journal of Legal Pluralism* 1 fn 122.

recognition containing the system's criteria of validity'.[18] Popular understanding is not in principle precluded, but we are told that in many settings a great proportion of ordinary people '[will] have no general conception of the legal structure or of its criteria of validity'.[19] True, a legal system can hardly be said to exist in a social group, unless the bulk of its members comply with the rules identified as valid by the system's rule of recognition. But according to Hart they need not be involved directly as participants in the practices that constitute the rule of recognition. In a pre-legal setting, no rule can exist in a society except as a practice among its members: as Hart puts, it, '[i]f, there, the internal point of view is not widely disseminated there could not logically be any rules'.[20] We will discuss this difference in more detail shortly.[21] But, he continues:

> where there is a union of primary and secondary rules, ... the acceptance of the rules as common standards for the group may be split off from the relatively passive matter of the ordinary individual acquiescing in the rules by obeying them ... In an extreme case the internal point of view ... might be confined to the official world. In this more complex system, only officials might accept and use the system's criteria of legal validity. The society in which this was so might be deplorably sheeplike; and the sheep might end in the slaughter-house. But there is little reason for thinking that it could not exist or for denying it the title of a legal system.[22]

Now, this point may be of greatest importance, and the 'slaughterhouse' warning that Hart sound may be at its most urgent, when we are talking about the bamboozled population dominated by a unified legal system associated with a highly organised bureaucratic state.[23] But in principle, the same point could apply to a pluralistic situation as well. As Roger Cotterrell points out, there is no particular reason to identify the officials who accept a rule of recognition as *state* officials:

> Nothing in Hart's books seems to indicate that 'officials' for this purpose must be state officials: certainly the judges of an international tribunal and perhaps the priests of a religious group [or] the elders of a cultural or ethnic group ... could qualify. Each of these kinds of group or association could thus have a kind of law of its own according to its members' concept of law.[24]

So, in theory, all this is compatible with legal pluralism. But its underlying spirit is far removed from the spirit of pluralist jurisprudence. And one has to say that

[18] Hart, *The Concept of Law*, n 4 above, at 111.
[19] *Ibid* 114.
[20] *Ibid* 117.
[21] See text accompanying nn 52–5 below.
[22] Hart, *The Concept of Law*, n 4 above, at 117.
[23] See also the discussion in Jeremy Waldron, 'All We Like Sheep' (1999) 12 *Canadian Journal of Law and Jurisprudence* 169.
[24] Roger Cotterrell, *Law, Culture and Society: Legal Ideas in the Mirror of Social Theory* (London, Ashgate Publishing, 2006) 37.

Hart did not seem particularly interested in the fact that, with a bit of pushing and shoving, his jurisprudential framework could accommodate pluralist possibilities.[25]

Taking Customs Seriously[26]

I said there were two important points which might qualify the allegedly top-down character of Hart's jurisprudence. The second point is that Hart insisted on the integrity of custom as a form of law and refuted reductionist accounts that presented customs as law only on account of their tacit adoption by a sovereign.[27] This appears to leave him some room to accommodate the existence of forms of law besides law ordained by the state.

One obvious point is that the rule of recognition itself is like a custom—a custom accepted at least among judges and high officials.[28] Besides this, there are two other ways in which customs might figure in a theory like Hart's: (1) Custom may figure as a form of law or a source of law recognised in a modern well-organised municipal legal system; (2) customs may figure as the building blocks of legal orderings that differ so much in form and character from a modern well-organised municipal legal system that they are best described as 'informal law' or (more or less pejoratively) as primitive law. In both cases, however, Hart makes moves that tend to be rather unaccommodating so far as legal pluralism is concerned.

Legally-Recognised Customs

Hart observes that '[c]ustom in the modern world is not a very important "source" of law'.[29] It is usually subordinate to statute law, he says, and his discussion makes it clear that his interest in custom as a form of law does not really extend beyond situations where custom is fully integrated into a state-dominated legal system—integrated in the sense that there are clear principles for its subordination as well as for its recognition. Legal customs are subject to the

[25] Simon Roberts, 'After Government? On Representing Law Without the State' (2005) 68 *Modern Law Review* 1, 10 says that 'any claim that Hart encourages us to think about law as something other than the law of a centralised polity would be misleading'. This is right only to the extent that Hart is not driven by any urgent concern that we should rivet our attention on non-centralised non-state law.

[26] The notion that legal positivism is essentially statist is probably a mistake. Legislation is not the only form of positive law. Customs and customary law, too, can be characterised in positivistic terms. See Jeremy Waldron, *Law and Disagreement* (Oxford, Clarendon Press, 1999) 46–7.

[27] *Ibid* 44–9.

[28] *Ibid* 111.

[29] *Ibid* 45.

system's overarching rule of recognition, and that rule will determine what the relation is between custom and other forms of law such as statute and precedent.[30]

The idea that certain customs are recognised (by a rule of recognition) as having legal status suggests that others may not be. And this is what Hart says. 'The meaning and good sense of the denial that custom, as such, is law lie in the simple truth that, in any society, there are many customs which form no part of its law'.[31] Some of these will be best regarded as parts of positive morality (ie of 'the social phenomenon often referred to as "the morality" of a given society or the "accepted" or "conventional" morality of an actual social group')[32] which Hart discussed at great length in *The Concept of Law*,[33] and which he was anxious to distinguish from law, just as he was anxious to distinguish critical morality from law (in the so-called 'separability thesis').[34] What he says about positive morality is extremely interesting. Hart has not simply suggested that certain customs may fall beyond the pale of law; he has done a great deal to elaborate other categories for understanding such customs.

True, Hart's notion of positive morality is articulated in a way that is most appropriate for a socially homogenous society, such as England might have seemed to be in 1961. When he talks of non-legal customs, his example is men doffing their hats to ladies,[35] and when he talks of positive morality, he seems to assume that a society with one legal system will have one body of positive morality too. I have always found it irritating that Hart does not explicitly contrast the unity and systematicity of law in a given society with the diversity of moralities practised among its members and that he fails to highlight the disagreements and dissensus that their critical moralising is likely to generate.[36] He came close to emphasising this sort of moral pluralism and dissensus in 1958 when, in his discussion of the distinction between law as it is and law as it ought to be, he emphasised that often there are multiple 'oughts': 'The distinction should be between what is and what *from many different points of view* ought to be'.[37] Unfortunately, what he had in mind was not pluralism in any social sense but something like the difference (even in the mind of a single individual) between the 'ought' associated with morality and the 'oughts' associated with prudence, efficiency, etc.

[30] *Ibid* 95 (on the provision that a rule of recognition is likely to make for the subordination of some forms of law to others).

[31] *Ibid* 44.

[32] *Ibid* 169.

[33] *Ibid* 169–80.

[34] *Ibid* 185–6.

[35] *Ibid* 44.

[36] See Waldron, *Law and Disagreement*, n 26 above, at 1–4.

[37] Hart, 'Positivism and the Separation of Law and Morals', n 1 above, at 613 (emphasis added).

Systems of Customary Law

Hart is certainly interested in the distinction between 'developed' legal systems (with secondary rules and institutions) and 'primitive' social systems of pure custom, unaccompanied by law. He presents his own theory in the context of a story about the development of the latter into the former.[38] And, as a developmental story would suggest, he acknowledges that there must be intermediate cases; indeed in an endnote that references Diamond, Malinowski, and others, he suggests that there may not be any pure cases of social systems without secondary rules.[39] Certainly he appears willing to leave many such societies as intermediate cases where it is simply unclear whether the term 'law' applies.[40] Hart is by no means dogmatic in his distinction between law and not-law, either in this case or in other marginal cases such as (in Hart's view) international law.[41] I labour this point because it is sometimes thought to be an important difference between a theory like Hart's and theories of legal pluralism that the former gives us a sharp distinction between law and non-law, whereas the latter rely on a blurred or equivocal distinction.[42] I think this is wrong, and that in this respect Hart's jurisprudence is reasonably accommodating to the blurrings and hesitations that modern legal pluralism involves.[43]

The developmental story that Hart tells may indicate that he thinks that the growth of developed law, with clear secondary rules and institutions, is a good thing, and that it is bad for societies to remain at the primitive stage.[44] As Leslie Green has suggested, the story presented in chapter 5 of *The Concept of Law* reads like Whig history:[45] a primitive society runs into certainty difficulties (uncertainty, inflexibility and inefficiency), and the emergence of secondary rules is the progressive solution to those difficulties.[46] But it only reads like that if you ignore the other things Hart says about this process, things that are actually quite chilling:

> Reflection on this aspect of things reveals a sobering truth: the step from the simple form of society, where primary rules of obligation are the only means of social control, into the legal world with its centrally organized legislature, courts, officials, and sanctions brings its solid gains at a certain cost. The gains are those of adaptability to

[38] Hart, *The Concept of Law*, n 4 above, at 91–9. For a fine discussion, see Leslie Green, 'The Concept of Law Revisited' (1996) 94 *Michigan Law Review* 1687, 1698.

[39] Hart, *The Concept of Law*, n 4 above, at 291.

[40] *Ibid* 156.

[41] *Ibid* 227–31.

[42] See, eg Brian Z Tamanaha, 'The Folly of the "Social Scientific" Concept of Legal Pluralism' (1993) 20 *Journal of Law and Society* 192, 193–4 and 199–202.

[43] I know this sentence sounds ironic or sarcastic. It is not intended to be. Blurrings and hesitations in complex social theory are often good things.

[44] Many legal pluralists reject 'the notion that custom is a form of primitive law that will gradually develop into state law': Merry, n 5 above, at 875, citing Stanley Diamond, 'The Rule of Law versus the Order of Custom' (1971) 38 *Social Research* 42.

[45] Green, n 38 above, at 1698.

[46] Hart, *The Concept of Law*, n 4 above, at 91–7.

> change, certainty, and efficiency; and these are immense; the cost is the risk that the centrally organized power may well be used for the oppression of numbers with whose support it can dispense, in a way that the simpler regime of primary rules could not.[47]

The point is partly about the alienation that the growth of specifically legal institutions involves.[48] The transition that Hart imagines between a pre-legal and a legal society involves not only the introduction of a new type of rule—secondary rules, such as rules of change and rules of recognition—but with it the introduction of a new type of rule-mentality and new types of rule-related role and expertise, which radically transform the relation between a people and the more important practices of their society. In a 'pre-legal' society, rules are not supposed to have any presence in society apart from their being practicsed and their having a shared normativity (their 'internal aspect') in the minds and actions of those who practise them.[49] They are certainly not conceived to have a verbalised 'rule-book' existence apart from their presence in conduct and attitude.[50]

To say that rules have this immediate presence in the lives of those subject to them does not rule out the possibility that the 'primitive' rules may be cruel, repressive, pointless or exploitative. Still, the development of law may portend something even worse. For secondary rules to evolve, primary rules must become increasingly manipulable apart from their implicit presence in the conduct and attitudes of those whose lives they govern. Gradually, they become detached from ordinary social practice in a way that allows them to be contemplated by specialists as possible objects of deliberate change or as possible objects of explicit interpretation.

As secondary practices of interpretation and rule-change become established in the community, both those practices and the primary rules they validate may begin to seem increasingly distant from ordinary people's ways of life. The primary rules come to have a presence in the lives of those subject to them that is quite different from their role in pre-legal society. On the one hand, ordinary people will not necessarily have the intimate familiarity with the rules that they used to have: they will be, in that sense, alienated from the rules. And the rules will begin to impact on their lives as much through the work of a dedicated apparatus of coercion as through the normative to-and-fro of a shared internal attitude, perhaps even more so. (This accords with the development of secondary rules of enforcement and the specialist executive apparatus associated with the development of law.)

47 *Ibid* 202.

48 What follows in the next few paragraphs is adapted from Waldron, n 23 above, at 177–9.

49 Hart, *The Concept of Law*, n 4 above, at 88–91.

50 Hart's debt to Peter Winch and Ludwig Wittgenstein is well known in this regard. For an acknowledgment of this connection, see Hart, *The Concept of Law*, n 4 above, at 289. See also Peter Winch, *The Idea of a Social Science and its Relation to Philosophy* (London, Routledge, 1958) 57, and Ludwig Wittgenstein, *Philosophical Investigations* (GEM Anscombe (trans), London, Routledge, 1997) esp 81 and 88 (paras 201 and 241).

I mention all this to drive home the point that Hart's attempt to draw some distinction, even a blurred and hesitant distinction, between the sort of legal system that positivists are supposed to privilege and the sort of normative order that pluralists are interested in is *not* associated with the denigration of the latter as problematic. He, as much as the pluralists, sees customary law as just a different kind of normative order from the formal official law of a 'developed' legal system. Both kinds of normative order have their advantages; both have their dangers.

What one does not get from Hart, however, is a useful sense of what things are like when elements of the two kinds of order exist side-by-side in a given social setting. There must be such cases on Hart's account; the dynamics of the story require it, at least for an intermediate stage. But the impression one gets from *The Concept of Law* is that the emerging rule of recognition will set about systematising things pretty smartly,[51] so that one will not get much more in the way of customary law/official law coexistence than we find in the legal systems discussed above under 'legally-recognised customs'. This, I think, is a product of Hart's tendency to exaggerate the unity of modern legal systems, ie to exaggerate how well-organised they tend to be.[52]

By contrast, legal pluralists are extremely interested in this dissensus aspect of law. And they are by no means alone in this. In their different ways, Dworkinians are also preoccupied with this aspect, and so are practitioners of Critical Legal Studies (assuming there are any left).[53]

Pluralism and Lon Fuller's Jurisprudence

I have several different things to say about Lon Fuller's relation to legal pluralism. Some are about the empirical and conceptual structure of his jurisprudence. But I think the most interesting things I have to say concern the relation between legal pluralism and the normative implications of his theory of the inner morality of law. This discussion is located under 'Fuller, pluralism and the inner morality of law' below.

[51] Hart, *The Concept of Law*, n 4 above, at 95.

[52] I am grateful to John Gardner for this point. See also Joseph Raz, *Practical Reason and Norms*, revised edn (Princeton University Press, 1999) 147, for an argument against Hart's implicit assumption that a given legal system has only one rule of recognition.

[53] For Dworkin's interest, see Ronald Dworkin, *Law's Empire* (Cambridge, MA, Harvard University Press, 1986), on the principle of integrity as a response to the tendency of law to produce a non-unified patchwork. For Critical Legal Studies, see, eg Duncan Kennedy, 'Form and Substance in Private Law Adjudication' (1976) 89 *Harvard Law Review* 1685, 1690 and 1774.

Fuller on Custom

In his book *Law, Culture and Society*, Roger Cotterrell observes that '[s]ome jurists ... have found no difficulty and much value in adopting a pluralistic view of law. They have wished to benefit from a sociological broadening of lawyers' perspectives'[54]. Lon Fuller is one of the jurists he cites in this passage. He does so not on account of anything Fuller said in the *Harvard Law Review* exchange with Hart; the only thing there that would make one think he was sympathetic to pluralism is his general opposition to the sort of positivist jurisprudence that (as we have just seen) appears uninterested in pluralist possibilities. Instead, Cotterrell identifies Fuller as a pluralist on account of some articles that Fuller published in the late 1960s.

In an essay entitled 'Human Interaction and the Law,' Fuller criticised the neglect of customary law in contemporary jurisprudence, insisting that 'we cannot understand "ordinary law" (that is, officially declared or enacted law) unless we first obtain an understanding of what is called customary law'.[55] One of the things this understanding would reveal, said Fuller, was the relation between law and social environment: '[L]aw and its social environment stand in a relation of reciprocal influence; any given form of law will not only act upon but be influenced and shaped by, the established forms of interaction that constitute its social milieu'.[56] And he made similar claims in a number of other papers, criticising modern jurisprudence for what he called 'a grotesque caricature of what customary law really means in the lives of those who govern themselves by it'.[57]

This emphasis on custom is certainly hospitable to legal pluralism, particularly the kind of pluralism that emphasises the roots of law in social mores and discerns multiple legal orderings even in advanced modern legal systems.

Fuller on the Transition from Custom to Enacted Law

That said, it is worth noting that Fuller was far from an enthusiast for the persistence of customary legal systems. In one of the articles I have alluded to, there was a section entitled 'Establishing the Rule of Law among Peoples who are not Accustomed to Thinking of Law as Something Made or Enacted',[58] where Fuller discussed the transition from customary law to modern law. He said:

[54] Cotterrell, n 24 above, at 37.

[55] Lon L Fuller, 'Human Interaction and the Law' (1969) 14 *American Journal of Jurisprudence* 1, 2.

[56] *Ibid* 27.

[57] Lon L Fuller, 'The Law's Precarious Hold on Life' (1968–69) 3 *Georgia Law Review* 530, 538. See also Lon L Fuller, 'Law as an Instrument of Social Control and Law as a Facilitation of Human Interaction' (1975) *BYU Law Review* 89.

[58] Fuller, 'The Law's Precarious Hold on Life', n 57 above, at 537.

> [T]he task of the new nation ... is to bring under a single system of rules peoples who have previously been divided legally by tribe, dialect, skin color, caste, occupation and place of residence. Where previously there may have been almost as many legal systems as there were cultural divergencies within the population, the new nation must establish as rapidly and effectively as it can, a common legal order for all its citizens. This is a tremendous undertaking.[59]

He actually criticised those who suggested not trying to undertake this at all, ie those who suggested that new nations should 'stick by their rules of customary law and forego any venture into the unfamiliar field of enacted law'.[60] Such suggestions were hopeless, he maintained, because customary law, being a system for 'intimate face-to-face relations' could not be expected to rise to the challenge of more distant and impersonal dealings. In this context, the reason for his insistence that we have to understand custom is so that we can grasp the scale and depth of the problem involved in its supersession. I do not think this attitude of Fuller's is likely to be congenial to a modern legal pluralist.

Fuller on 'Miniature Legal Systems' in Modern Societies

Legal pluralists will probably be more attracted to Fuller's remarks on the role of custom and clusters of custom in the life of a modern society. In 'Human Interaction and the Law', he said that we should be interested in 'not only the legal systems of states and nations, but also the smaller systems—at least "law-like" in structure and function—to be found in labor unions, professional associations, clubs, churches, and universities'.[61] He called these 'miniature legal systems',[62] and what he said about them indicated considerable sympathy for the project of modern legal pluralism.

So, for example, in *The Morality of Law*, when Fuller discussed what he called 'multiple systems' ('the existence of more than one system of law governing the same population'), the main example he gave was the coexistence of state law and the parietal 'laws' administered by a college.[63] This may not be the sort of example that more ethnically-attuned pluralists have in mind, but what Fuller said about it was certainly congenial to pluralism's abstract project. Ordinary linguistic usage is not determinative, said Fuller; we should consider the impact that bad jurisprudence has had upon it.[64] We should extract from 'law', he said, 'any connotation of the power or authority of the state'. If law is the enterprise of subjecting human conduct to rules, 'then this enterprise is being conducted, not

[59] *Ibid* 542.
[60] *Ibid.*
[61] Fuller, 'Human Interaction and the Law', n 55 above, at 1.
[62] *Ibid.*
[63] Fuller, *The Morality of Law*, n 3 above, at 125–9.
[64] *Ibid* 125, 126–7 and 129.

on two or three fronts, but on thousands'.[65] Any attempt to avoid pluralism by analysing the parietal rules example within the categories of contract rather than as one of several bodies of law operating in society is both question-begging and obfuscating.[66] A sociologist might study the administration of parietal rules as law 'for the insight he might thus obtain into the processes of law generally'.[67] In modern life, these miniature legal systems may be as important to people as state law: the 'imperfectly achieved systems of law within a labor union or a university may often cut more deeply into the life of a man than any court judgement ever likely to be rendered against him'.[68]

Fuller on Communities of Interpretation

Pluralists are, of course, interested in the interaction (and possible conflict) between 'subordinate' and official state-sponsored normative orders. Fuller was too, though at times the mode of his interest was slightly different from that of the pluralists. He was interested in ways in which attention to 'miniature legal systems' or low-level normative orderings might actually be of service to the dominant official state-sponsored legal system, and ways in which the dominant official state-sponsored legal system might be harmed or frustrated by neglecting them.

Here at last we come to something that *was* actually present in the 1958 exchange. In his response to Hart, Fuller considered how important it is for judges interpreting legislation to be aware of the practices and norms of the community that the legislature purported to regulate:

> Let us suppose the case of a trial judge who has had an extensive experience in commercial matters and before whom a great many commercial disputes are tried … [O]ur judge has of course the duty to follow the law laid down by his supreme court. Our imaginary Scrutton has the misfortune, however, to live under a supreme court which he considers woefully ignorant of the ways and needs of commerce. To his mind, many of this court's decisions in the field of commercial law simply do not make sense … So far as his problem arises from the use of particular words, he may well find that the supreme court often uses the ordinary terms of commerce in senses foreign to actual business dealings. If he interprets those words as a business executive or accountant would, he may well reduce the precedents he is bound to apply to a logical shambles.[69]

The immediate force of this point in Fuller's account is that the judge in question 'can never achieve a satisfactory resolution of his dilemma unless he views his duty of fidelity to law in a context which also embraces his responsibility for

[65] *Ibid* 124.
[66] Fuller, *The Morality of Law*, n 3 above, at 127–9.
[67] *Ibid* 125.
[68] *Ibid* 129.
[69] Fuller, 'Positivism and Fidelity to Law', n 1 above, at 646–7.

making law what it ought to be'.[70] But for the purposes of a discussion of pluralism, the point is that a judge cannot approach that task without sensitivity to the normative orderings of the commercial world, which may well not coincide with the normative orderings sponsored directly by the state and its courts.

It is not the most explicit or sustained endorsement of pluralism in the history of jurisprudence, however, and Fuller quickly spoils the effect, in a later section of 'Positivism and Fidelity to Law', by saying that what Hart's approach to interpretation and the resolution of hard cases neglects is not attention to the norms and mores of subordinate communities but attention to legislative purpose.[71] Indeed he suggests that to interpret a word (the example he gives is the word 'improvement') in a statute regulating (say) administrative practice in medicine or schools:

> we do not proceed simply by placing the word in some general context, such as hospital practice, town planning, or education. If this were so, the 'improvement' in the last instance might just as well be that of the teacher as that of the pupil. Rather, we ask ourselves, What can this rule be for? What evil does it seek to avert? What good is it intended to promote?

Here, the perspective that requires attention appears to be the perspective of the central regulator, not that of the community being regulated.

Fuller on the Separation of Law and (Positive) Morality

Beyond these particular hints and evasions, is there anything more general in Fuller's opposition to legal positivism that would tend to favour legal pluralism? Fuller is anxious in his 1958 response and in all his work to blur the allegedly sharp line between law and morality. This *might* mean that, sociologically speaking, he will find it easier than Hart did to recognise entities in between state law and something like Kantian morality. Fuller's comments elsewhere about 'miniature legal systems', systems that were 'at least "law-like" in structure and function' bear this out.[72] He thought a contrast between law and morality was often simplistic. In positivist jurisprudence, he complained:

> the word 'morality' stands indiscriminately for almost every conceivable standard by which human conduct may be judged that is not itself law. The inner voice of conscience, notions of right and wrong based on religious belief, common conceptions of decency and fair play, culturally conditioned prejudices—all of these are grouped together under the heading of 'morality' and are excluded from the domain of law. For the most part Professor Hart follows in the tradition of his predecessors. When he

[70] *Ibid* 647.
[71] *Ibid* 661–9.
[72] Fuller, 'Human Interaction and the Law', n 55 above, at 1.

> speaks of morality he seems generally to have in mind all sorts of extralegal notions about 'what ought to be', regardless of their sources, pretensions, or intrinsic worth.[73]

And elsewhere he also protested that:

> much that is written today seems to assume that our larger society is enabled to function by a combination of the individual's moral sense and social control through the threatened sanctions of state-made law. We need to remind ourselves that we constantly orient our actions toward one another by signposts that are neither set by 'Morals', in the ordinary sense, nor by words in lawbooks.[74]

This protest against the over-use of the term 'morality' complements his own willingness to be quite expansive in his use of the word 'law', but—more than that—to deny the utility of both the alleged separation between the two and the idea that a *dichotomy*, as opposed to a whole array of categories, is what we most need in this area.

Fuller, Pluralism and the Inner Morality of Law

I said earlier that the distinction between law and morality can be understood (1) as a distinction between two positive systems of practised norms (positive law and positive morality); or (2) as a distinction between law and legal judgments, on the one hand, and critical moral judgements on the other. What we have just been discussing is (1). But plainly, Hart cared most about (2), for example, in his famous definition of legal positivism: 'the simple contention that it is by no means a necessary truth that laws reproduce or satisfy certain demands of morality'.[75] And I think Fuller did also: the bulk of his energies both in the 1958 article and in *The Morality of Law* were devoted to a denial or qualification of distinction (2).

Fuller's position was that any claim about the strict separability of law and morality in the second sense was doomed to founder upon the fact that the enterprise of law and law-making already embodied certain moral principles in and of itself, principles which in turn were connected to wider moral concerns. 'Law', he said, 'contains ... its own implicit morality',[76] which we find, for example, in principles prohibiting retroactivity and purely ad hoc adjudication, and principles requiring publicity, generality and coherence in the laws. And these principles have external moral significance as well. For example, Fuller says, if he or Professor Hart found themselves to be members of a despised minority, they might think themselves safer if the community in which they were despised was a community ruled by law (rather than by some other mode of governance):

[73] Fuller, 'Posivitism and Fidelity to Law', n 1 above, at 635.
[74] Fuller, 'Human Interaction and the Law', n 55 above, at 36.
[75] Hart, *The Concept of Law*, n 4 above, at 185–6.
[76] Fuller, 'Postivism and Fidelity to Law', n 1 above, at 645.

> If we felt that the law itself was our safest refuge, would it not be because even in the most perverted regimes there is a certain hesitancy about writing cruelties, intolerances, and inhumanities into law? And is it not clear that this hesitancy itself derives, not from a separation of law and morals, but precisely from an identification of law with those demands of morality that are the most urgent and the most obviously justifiable, which no man need be ashamed to profess?[77]

This is not the place to embark on an evaluation of Fuller's thesis of the inner morality of law (nor of Hart's peremptory dismissal of it).[78] The question is: how does this aspect of Fuller's jurisprudence relate to his sympathy (or otherwise) for legal pluralism?

The first thing to note is that Fuller believed the inner morality of law might apply as much to subordinate legal systems (the miniature legal systems of professions, labour unions and colleges) as to a large-scale official legal system. We should be prepared to ask, for example of the college's parietal rules in our earlier example, 'Did the school in creating and administering its parietal rules respect the internal morality of law?'.[79] And just as Fuller did not flinch from saying that an official state-level system of governance 'which clothes itself with a tinsel of legal form can so far depart from the morality of order, from the inner morality of law itself, that it ceases to be a legal system',[80] so too he presumably would not flinch from saying that certain small-scale orderings might fail the test of law's internal morality as well. He would refuse to recognise them as law, not because they were insufficiently official or coercive, but because they were insufficiently moral (in the sense of the inner morality of law).

An even more interesting issue arises when we consider the application of law's internal morality, not just to the official state-sponsored legal system and not to the miniature legal systems one by one, but to the whole 'big picture' of law in a pluralistic setting. The values lying behind the inner morality of law require that we consider this also: inasmuch as the inner morality of law is concerned about the dignity and freedom of a person confronted with legal demands,[81] and inasmuch as a given person may be impacted by several legal systems (or thousands of them) in a pluralistic setting, we have to be willing to look to how the inner morality of law applies to the overall situation of people who actually have to face these multiple demands.

Here I think we begin to see that there may be some normative tension between Fuller's legal pluralism, such as it is, and his thesis of law's inner morality. One way of understanding Fuller's inner morality of law—indeed one

[77] *Ibid* 637.

[78] But see Jeremy Waldron, 'Hart and Principles of Legality' in Matthew H Kramer *et al* (eds) *The Legacy of HLA Hart: Legal, Political and Moral Philosophy* (Oxford University Press, 2008), 67 and also Jeremy Waldron, 'Positivism and Legality: Hart's Equivocal Response to Fuller' (2008) 83 *New York University Law Review* 1135.

[79] Fuller, *The Morality of Law*, n 3 above, at 126.

[80] Fuller, 'Positivism and Fidelity to Law,' n 1 above, at 660.

[81] *Ibid* 162.

way of understanding the rule of law or principles of legality—is that they serve the function of keeping the law 'in good shape' so far as the formal and procedural ways in which it impacts individual freedom and dignity are concerned.[82] A case can be made that a pluralistic situation is in fact characteristically not one in which law in a society is 'in good shape'.

One obvious aspect of this is the possibility of contradictory demands. Non-contradiction is one of Fuller's eight principles of the internal morality of law.[83] It is not just a technical matter: Fuller thinks that freedom and dignity are impaired when an individual faces contradictory demands. In a single legal system the problem of inconsistency is managed by principles such as *lex posterior derogat priori*; but it is not clear how this can work in a setting where multiple systems are in play. Fuller's jurisprudence, then, seems to imply that legal pluralism should be seen as something of a problem in this regard. He acknowledges this when he concedes that '[p]ractical difficulties can arise when there is a real rub between systems', and he implies that the problem has to be solved by somehow making the overall legal setting more 'systematic' by setting out clear 'boundaries of competence or rules of over-arching adjudication'.[84] This amounts in effect to an attempt to reduce the extent of genuine pluralism, and normatively it counsels against any policy that would seek to promote pluralism in a society. True, conflict between systems is not inevitable and it may be managed informally:

> Historically dual and triple systems have functioned without serious friction and when conflict has arisen it has often been solved by some kind of voluntary accommodation. This happened in England when the common law courts began to absorb into their own system many of the rules developed by the courts of the law merchant though the end of this development was that the merchants' courts were finally supplanted by those of the common law.[85]

But again, this formulation seems to suppose that in the end the problem will be solved by greater systematicity, institutionally if not at the level of the rules themselves.

I think something similar has to be said about Fuller's eighth principle of the inner morality of law: congruence between law on the books and official action.[86] Clearly it can be applied to miniature legal systems one by one: they must take care that their officials (if they have officials) actually follow the rules that are communicated to their constituents. But there is a problem too with regard to the enforcement and administration of conflicting standards in society generally. In a legally pluralistic society, the ordinary person may find himself at the mercy of cross-cutting enforcement by rival gangs of 'judges' and 'officials', and that may

[82] *cf* John Finnis, *Natural Law and Natural Rights* (Oxford, Clarendon Press, 1980) 272.
[83] Fuller, *The Morality of Law*, n 3 above, at 39 and 65–70.
[84] *Ibid* 124.
[85] *Ibid.*
[86] *Ibid* 39 and 81–91.

have just as much impact on his dignity and freedom (probably much more) than problems of incongruence within a single legal system.[87]

I emphasise these points about congruence and consistency, and the ways they might motivate a negative response to legal pluralism (inasmuch as legal pluralism is something one can do anything about), because they help us see that the repudiation of a vertical top-down command theory of law is by no means wholly congenial to legal pluralism. Fuller's position is that we cannot see the point of principles like consistency or congruence until we begin to understand law as a more-or-less horizontal enterprise of reciprocity between law-maker and law-subject.[88] But once we do espouse a conception of law that emphasises reciprocity, then instead of sitting back and enjoying the colourful diversity and dissensus of legal pluralism, we will begin to understand why every participant in every legal enterprise in a given society has reason to try to reduce the number and extent of incompatible demands that a pluralistic situation gives rise to and to try to reduce also the amount of disparate actions in the way of enforcement and administration that the presence in a single society of multiple legal systems is likely to generate.

The last thing I want to say in this regard is to point out the implications of rule-of-law principles of generality and legal equality so far as legal pluralism is concerned. When people have expressed alarm about the prospects of Shari'a courts being set up in (say) England or Ontario or about the admission of 'cultural defences' to criminal charges, some of that alarm has been about substantive matters: for example, the impact that Shari'a might have on the position of Muslim women or about the way in which cultural defences might legitimise domestic violence or sexual abuse.[89] But some of the concerns have been more abstract, concerns about legal equality or a concern that the law should be the same for all in a given society. It is a venerable theme in the rule-of-law tradition. When we talk about the rule of law, said Dicey in 1885, we mean:

> not only that with us no man is above the law, but (what is a different thing) that here every man, whatever be his rank or condition, is subject to the ordinary law of the realm and amenable to the jurisdiction of the ordinary tribunals.[90]

[87] See also Jeremy Waldron, 'Kant's Legal Positivism' (1996) 109 *Harvard Law Review* 1535, 1539–40 and 1556–62.

[88] See Fuller, *The Morality of Law*, n 3 above, at 192–5.

[89] See Sharafi, n 10 above. See also Melissa Spatz, 'A "Lesser" Crime: A Comparative Study of Legal Defenses for Men Who Kill Their Wives' (1991) 24 *Columbia Journal of Law and Social Problems* 597; Taryn F Goldstein, 'Cultural Conflicts in Court: Should the American Criminal Justice System Formally Recognize a "Cultural Defense"?' (1994) 99 *Dickinson Law Review* 141; Leslie Green, 'Internal Minorities and Their Rights' in Will Kymlicka (ed), *The Rights of Minority Cultures* (Oxford University Press, 1995) 270; and Susan Moller Okin, *Is Multiculturalism Bad for Women?* (Princeton University Press, 1989).

[90] *AV Dicey, Introduction to the Study of the Law of the Constitution* (London, Macmillan, 1902) 189.

Our belief in the rule of law commits us to the principle that the law should be the same for everyone: one law for all and no exceptions. 'In England', said Dicey, 'the idea of legal equality, . . . of the universal subjection of all classes to one law' is key to the way we interpret the rule of law.[91]

This notion of legal equality is not exactly what Lon Fuller means when he talks of generality as the first principle of the inner morality of law, but it is connected with it.[92] He was mostly interested in what he called 'the obvious truth that the citizen cannot orient his conduct if what is called law confronts him merely with a series of sporadic and patternless exercises of a state power'.[93] But he did glimpse the connection between generality and the formal justice of treating like cases alike, and just like HLA Hart, he toyed with the idea that this might presage an important connection, at a very abstract level, between the idea of law and the idea of justice.[94]

My point in the present context is that this justice- or fairness-related virtue of law is liable to be lost in circumstances where different members of the same society are dealt with according to different legal systems on the basis of different sets of norms. It will not help to say that those subject to a given legal system or sub-system are being dealt with on the basis that 'like cases are to be treated alike' by the lights of that system or sub-system. For they will be neighbours or colleagues or customers or competitors (or just fellow citizens) of those who are being treated by other standards, and it is inevitable, given that, on the pluralist account, these rival systems are supposed to be operating *in the same social field*, that these discrepancies will seem unfair and invidious. Those who see them in this way, or those who have not deafened themselves to this complaint for the sake of their social-theoretic commitment to the delights of 'diversity', will understand the worry and, to the extent that they can do anything about it, they might want to commit themselves to opposing or reducing or mitigating the legal pluralism of their society.

Conclusion

One of the things I have tried to do in this chapter is dispel the impression that it is the so-called vertical or top-down character of their jurisprudence that makes it difficult for legal positivists like HLA Hart to apprehend the delights of legal pluralism.

Hart did acknowledge and leave room for some of the possibilities that legal pluralism draws attention to. To the extent that he is uninterested in these

[91] *Ibid* 199. This paragraph is adapted from Jeremy Waldron, 'One Law for All: The Logic of Cultural Accommodation' (2002) 59 *Washington and Lee Law Review* 3.

[92] Fuller, *The Morality of* Law, n 3 above, at 39 and 46–9.

[93] *Ibid* 110.

[94] *Ibid* 157–8; *cf* Hart, *The Concept of Law*, n 4 above, at 157–67 and 206.

possibilities, it is not because of the vertical structure of his theory. For one thing, Hart's jurisprudence is not, straightforwardly, a top-down theory. For another, his lack of interest in pluralism is really a product of his thinking that the facts that pluralism draws attention to are not very important. He is just not as excited about those possibilities as they are.

Fuller *is* interested in the possibilities that legal pluralism draws attention to, particularly so far as they relate to the legal and social complexity of modern societies. But in his case, too, I think this interest is independent of whether jurisprudence is conceived in top-down terms. Indeed, the abandonment of top-down jurisprudence is cited by Fuller as a basis for his adoption of principles that—as it turns out—are actually quite hostile to pluralism, principles that regard it as a matter of concern and dismay when people are subject to disparate and incompatible legal demands, vulnerable to the cross-cutting administrative, judicial and enforcement efforts of rival groups of 'officials' and dealt with unequally on the basis of disparate norms and procedures that make a mockery of generality, legal equality and the idea that like cases should be treated alike.

8

The Politics of Defining Law

MARGARET DAVIES

Introduction

At first glance, Jeremy Waldron's argument that both the positivist Hart *and* the more sociologically-minded Fuller are in different ways receptive to the possibility of legal pluralism appears counter-intuitive. As Waldron demonstrates, however, neither Hart nor Fuller is consistently open to pluralism, and both writers exhibit some ambiguity when considered from this perspective. As Waldron suggests, it would be distorting matters to state that Hart was interested in or sympathetic to legal pluralism, but there are one or two elements of his work which at least do not foreclose pluralism, and which might even encourage a pluralistic reading of legal systems. Waldron demonstrates this by a detailed discussion of several pro- and anti-pluralism elements of the work of Hart and Fuller, as reflected in the debate and elsewhere. There is a great deal of merit in Waldron's argument, and I do not want to take issue with it in any major way.

Rather, I want to comment on the political nature of definitions of law by considering the following: first, the distinction between prescriptive and descriptive approaches; secondly, a comparison of the image of pluralism presented by Waldron with a less empirical understanding of pluralism; and thirdly, some questions raised by recognition of multiple legalities, a matter discussed by Waldron at the end of Chapter 7.

Defining 'Law' for Legal Pluralism

As Jeremy Waldron points out, there is little in the debate between Hart and Fuller which directly addresses the matter of legal pluralism. Fuller does raise the image of state law coexisting with some kind of religious law, for instance when he refers to a declaration by some Pope in relation to the duty of judges in divorce cases: 'if you will, it is one kind of law against another'.[1] Fuller's point is that such instances of legal duality do not say anything useful about the relationship between law and 'generally shared views of right conduct' because in essence, it is two different legal systems which have come into conflict.[2] He points to a tendency (not by Hart) to collapse religion into morality or 'views of right conduct', a lapse of logic which is still often evident in our apparently 'secular' legal and political spheres. On the face of it these are, however, trivial references, and do not reflect a concern for legal pluralism in the debate. On the contrary, Fuller seems to be indicating that the law–morality problematic is *not* about pluralism as conventionally understood.

The absence of pluralism in the debate is especially apparent if pluralism is understood—as it normally is—as an empirical fact. Waldron quotes Sally Engle Merry, who says that pluralism is 'generally defined as a situation in which two or more legal systems co-exist in the same social field'.[3] This statement echoes a slightly earlier comment by John Griffiths:

> Any sort of 'pluralism' necessarily implies that more than one of the sort of thing concerned is present within the field described. In the case of legal pluralism, more than one 'law' must be present

Thus, for Griffiths, Merry and many other legal pluralists, pluralism 'is an attribute of a social field and not of law'.[4] Taking this as a starting point, Waldron states that pluralism 'either obtains or does not' and that it 'is not a proposal that one opposes or supports'.[5] Pluralism is said to describe a social field and is not a normative objective or prescription for a legal order.

Here, however, it is easy to sense trouble with both the social-scientific conception of legal pluralism *and* the positivist edifice built upon the distinction between is and ought. Fuller senses a similar kind of trouble in Hart when he comments: 'It is not clear . . . whether in Professor Hart's own thinking the distinction between law and morality simply "is" or is something that "ought to be" and that we should join with him in helping to create and maintain'.[6] Fuller qualifies this statement, but only by questioning whether there is *ever* value in the distinction when it is applied to the so-called 'description' of a legal system (and later, by questioning its utility for judicial decision-making).[7] He says, for instance, that 'in human affairs what men mistakenly accept as real tends, by the very act of their acceptance, to become real'.[8] As I have said elsewhere, this has

[1] Lon Fuller 'Positivism and Fidelity to Law: A Reply to Professor Hart' (1957–58) 71 *Harvard Law Review* 630, 638.

[2] *Ibid.*

[3] Sally Engle Merry, 'Legal Pluralism' (1988) 22 *Law and Society Review* 869, 870, as quoted by Jeremy Waldron in Ch7.

[4] John Griffiths, 'What is Legal Pluralism?' (1986) 24 *Journal of Legal Pluralism* 1.

[5] Jeremy Waldron, Ch 7 at 136.

[6] Lon Fuller, 'Positivism and Fidelity to Law: A Reply to Professor Hart', above n 1.

[7] *Ibid* 647.

[8] *Ibid* 631.

been and remains the fate of legal positivism:[9] it is 'true' because it is assumed to be so on a broad scale, and because people act in accordance with this presumption. Positivism is a self-fulfilling prophecy or ideology which so influences behaviour that it has become true. But that does not mean that positivism covers the field as far as understanding law is concerned; there are also alternative readings of law and many practices which compromise the positivist boundaries.

So is a pluralistic understanding of law simply something that 'obtains or does not'? Personally, I think that depends on how law is defined, which seems also to be Waldron's view.[10] However, as I will explain shortly, even where state law is the only law that is recognised, I think that too can be regarded as pluralistic. First though, in order to work out whether legal pluralism exists, we need a definition of law. But a definition or concept of law is not prescriptively innocent. A definition of law is itself a type of normative ordering of social facts or 'reality' and carries with it political and ethical consequences, as indeed indicated in the debate. There are normative reasons for choosing one concept of law over another.[11] Here I depart from Waldron, who suggests that the identification and description of a social field as legally plural (or not) is an 'empirical/conceptual' point with 'no normative aspect'.[12] This is not to say that he sidelines the normative implications of legal pluralism, just that he sees them as independent from its descriptive and empirical aspect.

To illustrate my point, consider the following questions. Is Australia a legally plural nation? Are we a legally plural society? 'Nation' already implicates a particular legal system and possibly a particular view of law, whereas 'society' seems more neutral regarding the concept of law. There are many ways of answering these questions, some of them suggested by Waldron's overview of pluralism. I will comment on these possibilities in a moment. But in order even to approach the question openly, we need a definition of law. An understanding of 'law' that harnesses society to the state and operates exclusively over a geopolitical terrain, forecloses the possibility of legal pluralism. On this view, we can have pluralism of custom, religion, belief, morality, and so forth, but not of law. Law is singular and exclusive. The term 'law' could also, however, be seen to be capable of many different definitions (as suggested by Brian Tamanaha)[13] or even as in some way exceeding definition. There is nothing benign or neutral about the decision to name norms derived from the state 'law', while others are

9 'Feminism and the Flat Law Theory' (2008) 16 *Feminist Legal Studies* 281.

10 Jeremy Waldron, Ch 7 at 137: 'the first question to be put to a legal theorist is whether his jurisprudence recognises this category and accommodates this phenomenon, or whether his jurisprudence would insist on characterising the phenomena that legal pluralists draw attention to in some other way'.

11 A point also made explicit by Tom Campbell in *The Legal Theory of Ethical Positivism* (Aldershot, Dartmouth,1996).

12 Jeremy Waldron, Ch 7 at 137.

13 Brian Tamanaha, *A General Jurisprudence of Law and Society* (Oxford, Oxford University Press, 2001) 194.

downgraded to custom or practice. The 'objective' material of institutions, norms and practices underdetermines its conceptualisation and description, meaning that the choice between calling something 'law' and calling it 'custom' or 'belief' is framed by a politics of naming:[14] a highly contestable terrain which *prescribes* (not just describes) the spaces of legitimacy. When political leaders insist, for instance, that law is singular and by definition excludes 'other' forms of normative ordering, they invoke and enforce a particular conceptual framework with far-reaching ethical consequences. In spite of this reinforcement of legal monism, it has recently become commonplace to hear Indigenous normative practice referred to as 'law' rather than simply 'custom' or 'belief'. This change is partly due to a better understanding among the non-Indigenous of Indigenous society, but also because of a deliberate political choice, reiterated countless times, that Indigenous law deserves the status of that name.

To return to the two questions posed above, we can see these normative choices playing out in notions of what it means to be plural, what it means to be legal, and what spaces these concepts are intended to shape and depict. Undoubtedly, we are a plural *society*, and this can easily be extended to a claim that we are a *legally* plural society. In addition to the law of the Australian state, there is at a minimum Indigenous law and the various religious laws which govern certain communities. Moreover, taking the so-called 'new' pluralism of the late 1980s, which identified obligatory normative structures across education, labour organisations, corporate life and multiple private sectors, there is no question that a pluralism of normative environments is a necessary characteristic of contemporary human society.[15] Whether or not such normative orders are properly termed 'legal' is another matter, one which has seriously exercised the minds of scholars in the field. It would be thinkable, if not plausible, to say that *only* Australian state law is obligatory: individuals can choose whether to adhere to religious laws and, to a lesser extent, Indigenous law, and where there is a conflict, state law always prevails. A practical assessment of which legality has the social and political power to enforce itself publicly and universally over other legalities would clearly suggest that state law is more often 'obligatory' where others are not. But to deduce that Australian law is therefore the only or even the primary source of legal obligation would be a completely hegemonic and one-sided position, a position which assumes that the enforced universality of Australian law supplants the more personal and identity-forming obligation felt as a consequence of heritage and belief.

[14] See generally Boaventura de Sousa Santos, *Toward a New Legal Common Sense*, 2nd edn (London, Butterworths, 2002) 91.

[15] Merry, n 3 above, at 869–96.

Critical Pluralism

This all takes as its point of departure the notion that legal pluralism is about positive fact, the description of a social scientific field, empirical investigation, and so forth, traditionally the realm of sociologists, anthropologists and ethnographers rather than lawyers and legal theorists. As Waldron suggests, the role of legal philosophy is essentially limited to developing a conception of law against which the existence or otherwise of legal pluralism can be measured. However, questioning the distinction between the descriptive and the prescriptive challenges not only legal positivism but also the socio-legal account of pluralism. Beyond the empirically positivistic legal pluralism described by Waldron, recent debate has seen the movement towards another 'new' pluralism, one which critiques the simple 'factual' basis of traditional legal pluralism, and which contests singular definitions of law, abstract notions of legal subjectivity, and non-dynamic accounts of the relationship between law and its social 'others'.[16] No single new theory of legal pluralism has emerged from this debate, but there are certainly some areas where the limitations of a more positivistic pluralism have been exposed.

This is not the place to enter into a detailed exposition of this critical, alternative or post-pluralism, so I will just comment on a few angles which have some relationship to the debate and Waldron's critique. In particular, I was struck by Fuller's description of Hart and like-minded scholars as being concerned primarily 'to preserve the integrity of the concept of law' without necessarily knowing or even caring what 'other' is excluded. Certainly, unless I am mistaken, Hart offers no sensible definition of 'morality'. Fuller continues:[17]

> They are like men building a wall for the defense of a village, who must know what it is they wish to protect, but who need not, and indeed cannot, know what invading forces those walls may have to turn back.

A defensive wall constructed without knowledge of the nature of the threat seems obviously useless, though an intuitive desire for integrity, coherence and firm boundaries is a common enough fixation. Desmond Manderson has referred to the need for some kind of orderly conception of law as an aesthetic preference:[18] legal theorists prefer their conception of law to look logical, contained, coherent and singular. What happens if we abandon or relax this obsession with knowing what the law is and identifying with empirical certainty the spaces in which it operates? What if we try to appreciate the interrelationship of multiple normative

[16] See, eg Desmond Manderson, 'Beyond the Provincial: Space, Aesthetics, and Modernist Legal Theory' (1996) 20 *Melbourne University Law Review* 1048; Martha-Marie Kleinhans and Roderick A Macdonald, 'What is a *Critical* Legal Pluralism?' (1997) 12(2) *Canadian Journal of Law and Society / Revue Canadienne de droit et societe* 25; Margaret Davies, 'Pluralism and Legal Philosophy' (2006) *Northern Ireland Legal Quarterly* 577; 'Feminism and the Flat Law Theory', n 9 above .

[17] Fuller, 'Positivism and Fidelity to Law: A Reply to Professor Hart', above n 1, at 635.

[18] Manderson, above n 16.

environments which are connected differently in different contexts, and exist in multiple complex locations? And what if the subjects of law are regarded not just as its passive recipients, but as agents who construct the contexts and the practices of law (if not its 'content')? Law need not look like a village surrounded by a wall or even like some integrated network: it can just as easily be regarded as disorderly, multi-vocal and located in many inseparable but highly complex communities and sub-communities. On this view, law (including state law) inhabits plural spaces, not just a single geographical terrain, and it cannot be reduced to a single system derived from a set of criteria or general rule, much less a bounded and exclusive entity. The traditional pluralistic image of multiple (but each singularly-defined) legal systems coexisting in a single space simply does not capture this pluralism of spaces, interpretations, subjects and normative contexts.

To relate this alternative or 'pluralistic' pluralism[19] to the debate and to Jeremy Waldron's Chapter 7, I will simply pick up one point. Most interesting is the tantalising thought raised by Hart's notion that it is the officials of the legal system who are empowered to recognise and thereby (in some sense) legitimate the law. As Waldron puts it, Hart:

> insisted that the key to jurisprudence is not the notion of command or the notion of a sovereign, but the notion of the members of a group accepting a rule. This seems less hostile to pluralist possibilities than traditional positivist theories, inasmuch as it is less vertically structured than they are. Instead of sovereign power, it placed a sort of customary practice at the foundation of a legal system[20]

This is an important point. The basis of law becomes a custom or usage accepted by a group. Unfortunately for pluralism, Hart limits those who can 'recognise' the rule of recognition to officials within the system, thereby rather quickly reinstating the vertical character of law. For Hart, the group was not the washed or unwashed masses as this 'would involve putting into the heads of ordinary citizens an understanding of constitutional matters which they might not have'.[21] The role of ordinary people in the existence of law is thus limited to their general acquiescence to it. Nonetheless, in theoretical terms, as Waldron implies, the move towards the 'customary practice' of officials is potentially radical. Rather than locate the source of norm-construction in some mysterious pinnacle, 'natural' world, deity or hierarchical end-point of a legal system, the order is inverted: the source of authority comes from below, even if in Hart's case it is a 'below' already constituted by the practice of law. But as Waldron suggests, Hart does not make the most of this theoretical insight.

What *more* might be made of this consensus basis to law? First, as Waldron points out by reference to Roger Cotterrell, 'officials' could mean the privileged

[19] Mellisaris 'The More the Merrier: A New Take on Legal Pluralism' (2004) 13 *Social and Legal Studies* 57

[20] Jeremy Waldron, Ch 7 at 139.

[21] HLA Hart, *The Concept of Law*, revised edn (Oxford, Oxford University Press, 1994) 60.

interpreters within many different types of group: elders, priests, and so forth. Such groups can each recognise their own types of law. But why limit such recognition to officials? Hart's justification is surely patronising and unnecessarily elitist. Secondly, therefore, there are possibilities for understanding state law in a dynamic and pluralistic way if the category of readers and recognisers of law is fully democratised. And thirdly, why focus only on the separate normative systems which may arise when similarly-minded people act in common? When people act together, even when they are relatively like-minded, the outcome is not only consensus, but also conflict and ambiguity. A 'consensus' may mask a number of different voices and perspectives. Diverse perspectives may, of course, be brought together in a pragmatic compromise. Apparent unity may also be the product of powerful interests and discourses that can suppress the less powerful or marginal voices within a community. The idea of bounded unity in a community may also downplay the intersections and dissonances between one normative system and another. Perhaps legal theorists ought to focus as much on pluralism, ambiguity and relationality as we do on that which is mainstream and central.

Plurality within state law is arguably generated by the diversity of individuals and groups within a society. Robert Cover noted that each religious sectarian community inhabits a distinct normative environment or *nomos*.[22] Such *nomoi* in turn inform group-members' understandings of state law: different meanings arise from the intersections of state law with different normative fields. When state law is explicitly brought into play (a relatively rare occurrence) it imposes order on this bottom up 'jurisgenerative' process since the official processes of dispute resolution must decide between competing legal meanings. To put it simply, people generate a plurality of interpretations of state law, but the process of adjudication requires judges to choose between conflicting meanings so that order can be maintained. With the benefit of several extra decades of critical and feminist theory, Cover's approach might be extended so that it also takes account of differences *within* social groups. Social and religious normativity is itself complex, diverse and interconnected with larger social patterns, and the mainstream meanings engendered by leaders of a group may themselves suppress dissident voices within a community, for instance those based on a specifically women's or feminist consciousness.[23]

The essential issue, however, is that *subjects* are central to the process of norm construction. To quote MacDonald and Sandomierski, 'How do *legal subjects* imagine, invent, and interpret legal rules? … How do the actions and practices of *legal subjects* instantiate the rules they conceive and perceive?'[24] To say that law is

[22] Robert Cover, 'Nomos and Narrative' (1983) 97 *Harvard Law Review* 4.

[23] Judith Resnik 'Living their Legal Commitments: Paideic, Communities, Courts, and Robert Cover' (2005) 17 *Yale Journal of Law and the Humanities* 17, 47.

[24] Roderick MacDonald and David Sandomierski, 'Against Nomopolies' (2006) 57 *Northern Ireland Legal Quarterly* 610, 614.

'living', or subject–driven, or based in community (including religious) practice undermines law's singular identity because subjects are necessarily plural, and construct plural legal narratives.[25]

Something tending in this direction, although not nearly as bold as Cover's work, is also tentatively identified by Fuller in the debate with Hart. Waldron indicates that there is at least one part of the debate which has a relationship to legal pluralism, if only a tangential one.[26] It is found in Fuller's comments about the way in which the normative environment of commercial practice can be (and ought to be) used to inform judicial decisions.[27] The implication of Fuller's comments is that the law is fully embedded in a social setting, and that the normative contexts of the law, in particular the practices developed in particular settings, are part of the law. As Waldron comments this 'is not the most explicit or sustained endorsement of pluralism in the history of jurisprudence' and Fuller does not (here at least) explore the insight to its full potential. Its most interesting aspect is, perhaps, once again the challenge to the is/ought distinction which underlies it.

Justice and Coexistence

I hope I have said enough above to indicate that recognition of multiple positive legal orders is not the *only* or even the most important expression of legal pluralism. However, it is still a very significant issue and Waldron points to two common objections to any recognition of plural positive legal orders, for instance in relation to the use of Shari'a courts or, one might add in the Australian context, the separate recognition of Indigenous law. First, there are 'substantive matters' or problems that might arise when the values of one form of law clash with the values of another: in Waldron's words, 'for example the impact that Shari'a might have on the position of Muslim women or about the way in which cultural defences might legitimise domestic violence or sexual abuse'.[28] This issue is not specifically connected to the Hart–Fuller debate, although it is of course intrinsically concerned with the boundaries of state law, and its relationship with its own heritage and other cultural contexts. Secondly, there are matters of principle, relating to the need to have the same law for all citizens. This issue relates to Fuller's concern for the internal morality of law and more particularly the imperative towards consistency and transparency in application of law.

Waldron is right to note that serious concern is often raised over the impact which greater recognition of non-Western law might have on women. Waldron does not express an opinion on this either way, but I feel that more needs to be

[25] See also Manderson, above n 16, at 1064.
[26] Jeremy Waldron, Ch7 at 149.
[27] Fuller, 'Positivism and Fidelity to Law: A Reply to Professor Hart', above n 1, at 646–7.
[28] Jeremy Waldron, Ch 7 at 53.

said about this matter, which always haunts any discussion of pluralism and gender. First of all, it is not only non-Western cultures which 'legitimise domestic violence or sexual abuse'. Rape and sexual assault conviction rates and the prevalence of domestic homicides indicate that Western legal cultures also fail to offer effective deterrence against domestic violence, rape and sexual assault (and therefore tolerate and even 'legitimise' such behaviour).[29] Of course, tolerance of violence against women is not reflected in legal doctrine as it was once in the common law (and as it might be in other cultural contexts), but it would be a serious mistake to assume that what the positive law says about these crimes reflects the way they are treated by our law and more broadly by elements within our culture. As Mary Heath has commented in relation to South Australia, 'there is little evidence that [rape] *is* illegal except a few words tucked away in the Criminal Law Consolidation Act'.[30] South Australia is by no means unusual in this respect. In this context, as in many others, positivism fails to understand the enmeshing of law and socio-cultural factors and sometimes promotes simple law reform where broader and ongoing cultural strategies are needed. Moreover, identifying violence against women as a problem with 'other' cultures can mask it within our own.

It is true, however, that there are also very serious questions about the way women are treated in some non-Western legal cultures and that we need to be careful about uncritical importation of normative orders through forms such as a cultural defence to crime. But even here, it is easy to essentialise and therefore dismiss legal 'others'.[31] When an entire culture is seen through Western eyes to be inherently oppressive, we need to be certain that we have asked women, minorities and dissidents within that culture to interpret it and to construct their own picture of its values and norms. By relying on the versions of a culture provided by powerful voices within it, we entrench the authority of the culturally powerful to interpret it at the expense of others who have an equally valid stake in determining cultural norms. Cultures are not static, univocal and orderly systems, but rather composed of a multitude of diverse voices, views and practices. For instance, accessing women's perspectives, as occurs from time to time through minority women's advocacy organisations, is a vital part of this process. Far too often the (male) holders of cultural authority are given unique power to represent and interpret it and we collaborate in the oppression of women when

[29] Mary Heath, 'Lack of Conviction: A Proposal to Make Rape Illegal in South Australia' (2007) 27 *Australian Feminist Law Journal* 175; *cf* Wendy Larcombe, 'The "Ideal" Victim v Successful Rape Complainants: Not What You Might Expect' (2002) 10 *Feminist Legal Studies* 131.

[30] Heath, n 29 above, at 176.

[31] Sherene H Razack, 'Imperilled Muslim Women, Dangerous Muslim Men and Civilised Europeans: Legal and Social Responses to Forced Marriages' (2004) 12 *Feminist Legal Studies* 129. Razack uses the idea of 'culturalisation of violence' to refer the way in which violence against women is seen as a cultural characteristic of Muslim populations, meaning that its presence in Western culture is masked. For one attempt to compare violence against women in American and Islamic society see Rana Lehr-Lehnardt, 'Treat Your Women Well: Comparisons and Lessons from an Imperfect Example Across the Waters' (2002) 26 *Southern Illinois University Law Journal* 403.

we accept a univocal narrative about a culture which may have different interpretations.[32] After all, it is only because of the persistence of Western women in making alternative views about our own culture heard that we have made the progress that we have over the past several decades.

But for me the issue is not only whether substantive values and norms within a cultural setting sufficiently protect women or are oppressive. There is also a pragmatic question. Are women's interests better protected by allowing minority law into the mainstream where it can be subject to broad scrutiny or, alternatively, by promoting 'one law for all' which may result simply in the privatisation of minority law and a lack of transparency in its operation? There are certainly risks associated with the recognition of cultural norms which invoke different values from those of the liberal West. However, women's interests are manifestly *not* served by simply assuming that the mainstream positive law promotes their material wellbeing or that it grants rights which are in practice enforceable.

The internal diversity of different groups is ultimately related to Waldron's second, rule-of-law related, comment concerning the need to treat like cases alike: 'this justice- or fairness-related virtue of law is liable to be lost in circumstances where different members of the same society are dealt with according to different legal systems on the basis of different sets of norms'.[33] Waldron invokes 'our belief in the rule of law [which] commits us to the principle that the law should be the same for everyone: one law for all and no exceptions'.[34] Clearly 'our' belief in the rule of law is a significant element of the general protection of freedoms, equality and legal transparency which, while not perfect, is a major achievement of Western legal systems. But our belief must surely sound hollow or even hypocritical to those for whom the law is not applied equally: when, for instance, it is the well-connected and wealthy who can obtain the greatest protection under the law or when racial discrimination legislation can be unilaterally set aside.[35] Moreover, as Michael Detmold pointed out some years ago (and to paraphrase), we may all be equal under the (Australian state) law, but what happens to equality if two people with two different laws are nonetheless treated as equal under only one of those laws?[36] Assuming for the moment that justice requires that people be treated on the basis of formal equality, if the rule or measure applied is not

[32] See Hannah McGlade, 'Aboriginal Women, Girls, and Sexual Assault', *ACSSA Newsletter*, 12 September (2006), 6–13; Heather Douglas, '"She Knew What was Expected of Her": The White Legal System's Encounter with Traditional Marriage' (2005) 13 *Feminist Legal Studies* 181; Wendy Shaw, '(Post) Colonial Encounters: Gendered Racialisations in Australian Courtrooms' (2002) 10 *Gender, Place and Culture* 315.

[33] Jeremy Waldron, Chapter 7 at 154.

[34] Jeremy Waldron, Chapter 7 at 154.

[35] As it has been done in the Northern Territory since the beginning of the 'intervention' there, thereby allowing a range of measures in relation to Indigenous people which clearly do not operate on the principle of equality.

[36] Michael Detmold, 'Law and Difference: Reflections on Mabo's Case' (1993) 15 *Sydney Law Review* 159, 163.

recognised by one party on whom it is enforced, then 'justice' is quickly transformed into a one-sided exercise of power.

Conclusion

In conclusion, Jeremy Waldron states that one of his aims was to 'dispel the impression that it is the so-called vertical or top-down character of their jurisprudence that makes it difficult for legal positivists like HLA Hart to apprehend the delights of legal pluralism'. This is a conclusion with which I concur. It is possible to see vertical conceptions of law, for instance those which harness the concept of law to a state, as one crystallised element of a much more plural legal environment or, alternatively, as one perception which can coexist with more expansive and less coherent understandings of law and legal practices.[37]

[37] On which further see my 'Feminism and the Flat Law Theory', n 9 above.

9

Law as a Means

LESLIE GREEN*

The Instrumentalist Thesis

No one doubts that individual laws often serve as means to promote or secure certain ends. The rule against perpetuities is a means of setting temporal limitations on the grant of an estate. Bundles of laws working through statutes or fields of doctrine are also means to ends, including ends that are, under other descriptions, means to further ends. Enacting the Fewer School Boards Act,[1] for example, was intended as a means to the end of reducing the number of school boards, which was in turn intended as a means of uncoupling education from property tax, which was intended as a means of asserting financial discipline (and other sorts of discipline) over local schools, which the government of the day considered a desirable end. Examples like that make the instrumentality of laws sound like a top-down affair. Just as often it is bottom-up. It is not only legislatures and courts but also individuals who use laws as means to their ends. Leona Helmsley wanted her dog to be adequately provided for after her own death. So she left it US$12 million in trust, through the helpful instrumentality of the laws of New York State. And every day lots of sensible people make wills, contracts and powers of attorney; they marry, sue and incorporate, all using the special means that laws provide. None of this is remotely controversial.

The same cannot be said of the following thesis: '[L]aw is a means, a specific social means, not an end'.[2] In fact, few propositions in general jurisprudence are as controversial as that one. For Kelsen is not just saying that particular laws are instruments for securing collective or individual ends. He is saying that this is true of *law itself*: it is part of its specific nature, of how we identify law. And he

* I thank Anthony Sebok, who was a generous respondent at the ANU conference, Andrei Marmor and others at a a University of Southern California Colloquium, and Dori Kimel, Joseph Raz and, especially, Julie Dickson for helpful discussions.

[1] Fewer School Boards Act, SO 1997, c 3.

[2] Hans Kelsen, *General Theory of Law and State* (A Wedberg (trans), Cambridge, MA, Harvard University Press, 1949) 20.

goes further: law can only be identified as a means of a special sort, and *not* as an end of any sort. I am going to call that the *instrumentalist thesis* about law, and I am going to defend a qualified version of it here.

Lon Fuller considered some such thesis to lie at the core of his disputes with HLA Hart (and others) over the nature of law. Fuller writes, 'A statute is obviously a purposive thing, serving some end or congeries of related ends. What is objected to [by Hart] is not the assignment of purposes to particular laws, but to law as a whole'.[3] And if law does have a purpose as a whole, then why not organise our theories of law around that purpose, instead of focusing so much on the means, procedures and structures characteristic of legal systems? Is the instrumentalist not putting the cart before the horse?

Hart, on the other hand, agrees with Kelsen: we cannot assign significant ends or purposes to law 'as a whole'.[4] Undeniably, there are things that law necessarily *does*. For example, law provides institutions that authenticate and apply norms. But that sort of thing is not law's *end*—it is the means by which law *goes about* its (various) ends. Hart thought law's means fell into two broad classes: those that are 'means of social control', and those that provide individuals with 'facilities for the realization of wishes and choices'.[5] Law does both through the creation, recognition and application of rules. Other social institutions pursue law's ends by other means, for example, by creating economic incentives to which people are likely to respond, by altering the physical environment to change their feasible options, or by assassinating them before they can interfere with the government's plans. Law is distinguished from them less by what it does than by how it does it: law is less a functional kind than it is a modal kind.[6]

Of course, this is not the only idea about law that has ever been called 'instrumentalist'. Brian Tamanaha assembles quite a list of others, covering most of the alleged sins of the American legal system.[7] He complains that, in the United States, law is widely practised with indifference to the social good, judges reason from the bottom line up, lawyers care more for wealth and power than for humanity or justice, 'cause lawyering' corrupts legality, and so on. The thread linking his miscellany is the alleged fact that in the United States, 'law is widely viewed as an empty vessel to be filled as desired, and to be manipulated, invoked,

[3] Lon L Fuller, *The Morality of Law* (New Haven, CT, Yale University Press, 1969) 146.

[4] Clearly stated in Hart's 'Postscript' to The *Concept of Law*, 2nd edn (Oxford, Clarendon Press, 1994) 248–50; but also pervading his review essay, 'Lon L. Fuller "The Morality of Law"' in *Essays in Jurisprudence and Philosophy* (Oxford, Oxford University Press, 1983) 343–64.

[5] HLA Hart, 'Positivism and the Separation of Law and Morals' (1958) 71(4) *Harvard Law Review* 600, 604.

[6] I am not claiming a sharp distinction here. If L is distinguished by the fact that it ϕ-s by χ-ing, then it is a mixed kind. I am claiming an explanatory *priority* for the modalities in identifying legal systems : (a) law and other social institutions ϕ, but (b) among the ϕ-ers, law is the institution that ϕ-s *by* χ*-ing*.

[7] Brian Z Tamanaha, *Law as a Means to an End: Threat to the Rule of Law* (New York, Cambridge University Press, 2006) 1.

and utilized in the furtherance of ends'.[8] That view is not the thesis advanced by legal instrumentalists like Kelsen or Hart. And what makes it repugnant has little to do with the idea that law is a means to an end, and much to do with the alleged popularity of the view that law may be 'filled as desired', and the chilling hint that any sort of manipulation in service of such desires would be just fine. Those attitudes do not express a thesis in general jurisprudence; they betoken a vice, one that in plain speech is usually called *selfishness.*

Another complex of attitudes not here relevant but sometimes called instrumentalist is a view, not about *law*, but about *jurisprudence.* This view holds that a theory of law should be oriented, not to the truth about law, but to the promotion of socially desirable ends. There are strains of that idea in Fuller, who thinks that jurisprudence should above all provide 'direction posts for the application of human energies'.[9] Now, if that is the game, instrumentalism begins with a handicap. As publicity material, 'Law is a means!' would flop. It would not inspire lawyers or judges; it would not awaken the student who already finds the law boring enough without leaden interventions by legal philosophers. But I do not think it the job of general jurisprudence to inspire; its job is to produce a correct (philosophical) explanation of the nature of law.

In this fragment of that large task, I approach the work as follows. First, I argue that the instrumentalist thesis, though controversial, is a rendering of a view of law that is actually *not* controversial. That gets instrumentalism on the table as a candidate interpretation of that view. Then, I try to clear what seem to be the leading falsehoods and fallacies standing in the way of accepting the thesis. Naturally, this approach cannot amount to a demonstrative proof. But it should make a view that many intuitively accept more perspicuous, more plausible, and more secure.

The Instrumentalist Conception of Law

Law is not a surd feature of the universe, like the speed of light or Planck's constant. Law belongs to the meaningful world of ends and means. By 'meaningful' I refer to the fact that we can make sense of a lot of human action by understanding it as adopting means to achieve certain ends in light of the situation as the agents see it. The view of law as primarily a matter of means to ends is the foundation of Jeremy Bentham's entire legal philosophy. It is elaborated, crudely and at length, in Rudolf von Ihering's late works.[10] It structures Max Weber's analysis of the state and law, and in a different way, Karl Marx's theory of law (to the extent that he can be said to have a theory of law). It is

[8] *Ibid.*

[9] *Ibid* 632.

[10] Rudolf von Ihering, *Law as a Means to an End* (I Husik (trans) New York, Macmillan, 1921; 1st edn 1877–83, 2 vols).

implicit in HLA Hart's idea that law is an institutionalised system of social rules aimed at securing some basic goods, for at least some people. And it is explicit in Joseph Raz's observation that, 'The law is not just a fact of life. It is a form of social organization which should be used properly and for the proper ends', an expression of what he calls 'an instrumental conception of law'.[11]

Now, those names might lead you to suspect that only positivists and fellow-travellers adopt an instrumental conception of law. Nothing could be further from the truth. There is no other way to understand Aquinas, who says, 'A law, properly speaking, regards first and foremost the order to the common good'.[12] Law is thus oriented to that good. Admittedly, law has other species-typical features: it is a general kind of order, issued by an authoritative source, and promulgated to its subjects. But for Aquinas, these features are all explained by the fact that law is a means in the service of a particular end:

> Whenever a thing is for an end, its form must be determined proportionately to that end; as the form of a saw is such as to be suitable for cutting. Again, everything that is ruled and measured must have a form proportionate to its rule and measure. Now both these conditions are verified of human law: since it is both something ordained to an end; and is a rule or measure ruled or measured by a higher measure.[13]

Aquinas' view thus parts company with the instrumental *thesis* set out in Section 1, which denies that law is 'for an end'; but it just as obviously embraces an instrumental *conception* of law. One cannot have teleology without *teloi*, and in law the relevant ends are brought about through means to which Aquinas paid careful attention. The false association between an instrumental conception of law and legal positivism—the thesis that all law is a human artifact, a social construction—flows from the false assumption that nothing can be an instrument unless it is also an artifact. Not so. An instrument may be an *objet trouvé*, a conveniently chipped piece of flint, made by no one, but picked up and put to some use. And even if an artifactual rule may be measured by a 'higher measure' that is not itself an artifact, the artifactual rule will nonetheless remain primarily a means of directing and assessing conduct.

Teleological instrumentalism of Aquinas' sort lives on, overtly and covertly, in many contemporary theories of law. It is vigorously asserted by Fuller, who, while agreeing with Hart that law is 'the enterprise of subjecting human conduct to the governance of rules',[14] thinks that Hart misses the upshot that law must therefore be a 'purposeful enterprise'.[15] Now, 'purposes' and 'enterprises' have, it is true, nuances absent from 'ends' and 'means', and Fuller often prefers the former terms

[11] Joseph Raz, *The Authority of Law* (Oxford, Oxford University Press, 1979) 226; and Joseph Raz, *Between Authority and Interpretation* (Oxford, Oxford University Press, 2009) 102–6.

[12] Thomas Aquinas, *Suma Theologica* (Fathers of the English Dominican Province (trans) New York, Benziger Brothers, Inc, 1947) vol 1, Pt I-II, Q 90, art 3, 995.

[13] *Ibid* Pt I-II, Q 95, art 3, 1015.

[14] Fuller, *The Morality of Law*, n 3 above, at 74.

[15] *Ibid* 145.

in order to emphasise the special features of his own brand of legal instrumentalism. But at other times he is just as happy to speak bluntly. Of his famous desiderata of legality—the 'inner morality' of law—Fuller simply says, 'All of them are means toward a single end'.[16] Law, on Fuller's account, is an institution on a mission.

All these writers share an instrumental conception of law. What divides them is (inter alia) the instrumental *thesis* about law, the claim that *within* an instrumental conception, law can only be identified by focusing on its (species-typical) means rather than on its ends. I suspect that thesis marks a more significant division in legal philosophy than do many of the more familiar ones, including the distinction between positivism and anti-positivism. But I cannot pursue that hypothesis here. In preparation for the argument, let me instead turn to some abstract, but necessary, observations about the nature of instruments and values.

Means, Instruments and Ends

Kelsen says that law is a means, not an end. The hard part is the second, negative, proposition: law is *not* an end. We cannot decide whether that is false unless we have some grasp of how it could be true. But the affirmative claim is no less puzzling: What would it take for law *to be* 'an end'?

The creation of particular laws is among the ends of law, in both legislation and adjudication. So those *laws* can be ends. One might make it one's end to establish legal systems where there are none, or to improve or protect them where they already exist. But that will not show that *law is an end*; it will show that *law-establishing* and *law-protecting* can be ends, which hardly seems controversial. Could Kelsen be suggesting that we can understand law *without reference* to ends? Surely not. He repeatedly affirms that law is a means; but in the context 'means' is a relational term, and the relevant relata are *means* and *ends* (which is why we can speak of a 'means-ends relation'). If law is a means at all, there must be some ends to which it is, or is taken to be, a means.

A more promising interpretation is this: law's means are more important in identifying law as a social institution than are law's ends. Law *has* ends and law should serve *good* ends. Perhaps law should serve good ends as part of the nature of law. But what makes law special are the means by which it serves those ends. Moreover, law's ends, even if they are proper ideals for law, are not distinctive: there are no ends universal among or unique to all legal systems, no ends that unify and explain all features of its means. This helps interpret Kelsen's cryptic remark that 'legal norms may have any kind of content'.[17] Kelsen does not mean that a law could be a rock or a slug. Indeed, he asserts that every law has features

[16] *Ibid* 104.

[17] Kelsen, n 2 above, at 113. Could this be the thought that gets garbled in Tamanaha's remark about seeing law as an 'empty vessel'?

that could quite naturally be called the 'content' of law (eg delicts and sanctions). His substantive point is this: the same means that gave us the Fewer School Boards Act could also have given us a More School Boards Act, or a School Boards (Restoration) Act, and all of these Acts would have been law, and they would have been law in virtue of the means by which they were produced, rather than the character (moral or otherwise) of the ends at which they were aimed. But isn't that legal positivism after all? No. To get positivism we need to add at least the proposition that *the ultimate law-producing means are artifacts.* We have not added that.

What, then, of 'means'? To the extent that there is any difference between means and instruments, the instrumentalist thesis interprets law as an *instrument.* It is perfectly acceptable to say, 'Drawing an equilateral triangle is a means of drawing an equiangular triangle'. After all, to do the second, you need only do the first, and having done the first, you have an iron-clad guarantee that you have achieved the second. But that is not a means in the instrumentalists' sense. The instruments with which one might draw an equiangular triangle include things like protractors and pencils, not equilateral triangles. This has nothing to do with the concreteness of the former. Many instruments are abstract objects, including mnemonic devices, truth-tables, and, of special interest to jurisprudence, norms and systems of norms. What is important is that these instruments are distinct from the ends to which they are put, are capable of being brought under intentional control, and can be assessed as being more or less well adapted to produce their ends.[18]

This explains why there is often a close relationship between L being instrumental to E and L being causally efficacious in helping to bring about E. The role of causal efficacy tempted some, including Weber, to suppose that instrumental reasoning, in law or elsewhere, is somehow more objective or scientific than is any reasoning about value. That could at best be true of the causal premises in instrumental reasoning. It is not true of all the premises or of the conclusions. We reason: (1) *L most effectively produces E,* and we enthymematically conclude, (3) *Someone ought to adopt L.* The suppressed crucial premise is (2): *E is worth producing.* But neither (2) nor (3) are 'objective' or 'scientific' in any way that would have impressed Weber. That is evident with respect to (2), since it is about what values merit pursuit; but it is also true of (3), since that is a deontic statement telling someone what to do.

This is worth mentioning because it highlights a central issue about instrumental value. Some find it tempting to say that if L* is *better* able to produce E than is L', then L* has *greater* instrumental value than L', on the ground that it

[18] Law may also have *unintended* ends; it may have what Robert K Merton called 'latent' as well as 'manifest' functions, in his *Social Theory and Social Structure,* revised and enlarged edn (New York, The Free Press, 1968) 60–4. There are theories of law that regard its unintended consequences as more important than its intended uses, but I do not explore them here. For some brief remarks on that issue see Leslie Green, 'The Functions of Law' (1998) 12(2) *Cogito* 117.

gives more E-bang for one's L-buck. But this does not follow. Nothing has instrumental value that lacks value. Something inherits its instrumental value from the end to which it is a means. If that end is worthless, then it has no value to pass on to L. So L* may be more effective than L' in producing E and yet at the same time utterly valueless. This sounds odd only because it can be useful to speak of L* *as if* it had instrumental value, prescinding from any assessment of its ends. That is how we often talk about people's reasoning when we are uncommitted to, or uncertain about, the value of the ends they pursue. It is how the bureaucrat or economist or democrat might speak when considering how to attain an end taken as 'given' by the government, the client or the people.

Kelsen is aware of this issue, but mistakenly thinks it shows that all effective means have *relative* value: if L efficiently produces E, then L has some positive value, relative to E.[19] Now, relative values certainly exist. American dollars have relative value, for their value as a medium of exchange or store of value varies *in relation to* the demand for other currencies. But the fact that L stands in a means-end relationship to some E does not show anything about L's value. What gives dollars their value is their *use* as a medium of exchange or store of value, which media and stores are themselves valuable, and therefore worth pursuing as (intermediate) ends. In contrast, if E is worthless (eg the satisfaction of a desire for a saucer of mud, for no further reason),[20] then L does not get relative value from E, for E has no value to contribute. The most effective pump draws no water from an empty well.

Of course, not all ends are instrumental. On plausible assumptions about value, chains of instrumental reasoning must ultimately bottom in ends that are *not* of value only as means to further ends. I shall follow traditional usage and say that non-instrumental ends are *intrinsically* valuable. Unfortunately, this term is also in use to pick out ends that are *absolutely* or *inexplicably* valuable. I want to leave open the possibility that intrinsic values may be relative to time and place and in that sense not absolute, and also the possibility that even intrinsic values are all liable to philosophical explanation. These are not matters we need to settle here. But it will be useful to mark a distinction within the realm of intrinsic value. I am going to call it the difference between dependent and free-standing values.[21] An intrinsic value is *dependent* if the explanation for why it is of value necessarily includes reference to the fact that it is of value *to* or *for* someone (or something) capable of appreciating the value that it has. A beautiful sunset is of

[19] Hans Kelsen, *Introduction to the Problems of Legal Theory: A Translation of the first edition of the Reine Rechstlehre or Pure Theory of Law* (BL Paulson and SL Paulson (trans), Oxford, Oxford University Press, 1992; 1st edn 1934) 16. And compare Kelsen, n 2 above, at 436.

[20] I adapt Elizabeth Anscombe's famous example, in *Intention*, 2nd edn (Oxford, Blackwell, 1966; 1st edn 1963) 70–1. (But note that *pleasure* derived from satisfaction of this desire would be a further reason.)

[21] For a discussion of a similar division, though with a different terminology and to a different purpose, see Joseph Raz, *Value, Respect, and Attachment* (Oxford, Oxford University Press, 2001), which influenced my thinking at several points in this section.

intrinsic value because it is of value *to* people (or animals) that have the capacity to take sensual pleasure in its colours or to respond to it under the aspect of beauty. Doesn't that turn sunsets into instrumental values? No. The *way* in which sunsets are of value to their responders is not as something that can be brought under intentional control so as to produce more or less of the value in question. Sunsets are not instruments. We value them for what they contribute to our lives, not for what we can do or attain by 'using' them.

Any things whose intrinsic value is *not* explained in that sort of way (ie by the fact that they are of value *to or for* an appreciating subject) I shall call 'free-standing'. As such, they would be of value, not as means to some end, like income, and not of value to or for someone or other, like sunsets. They would be of value for their own sake, in themselves. This last idea is difficult to explain, though many, including Kant, think it easy to exemplify: *persons* have that sort of value. Someone who is not only of no use to anyone or for anything, and who is not loved, admired or even considered by anyone, even he has value in himself. Kant called such things 'ends in themselves'.[22]

Into these murky waters I wade no further. I do not think that law is or could be an 'end in itself,' nor am I aware of any opponent of the instrumentalist thesis who coherently advances the contrary view. My focus will be on law's instrumental or dependent-intrinsic value, and on how law's means stand in relation to such values.

Five Fallacies About Instrumentalism

As I said, the instrumentalist thesis is one interpretation of a commonplace view about law, a view shared by philosophers as different as Aquinas and Bentham. But it is also an interpretation so encrusted with errors and fallacies that it can be difficult to see the thesis for what it is.

Kelsen himself is responsible for some of these. In the first edition of the *Pure Theory of Law* he elaborated the instrumentalist thesis in this way: 'The law is a coercive apparatus having in and of itself no political or ethical value, a coercive apparatus whose value depends, rather, on ends that transcend the law *qua* means'.[23] The elaboration spins out two further claims. The first is that law is not only a means, but a *coercive means*. The second is that, because law is a means, it can have no moral or political value 'in and of itself'. Otherwise put, law is a *mere means*.

Both elaborations are mistaken. It is not necessary to repeat here the familiar arguments establishing that the use of coercive force is neither essential nor

[22] *Ibid.*
[23] Kelsen, n 19 above, at 31.

unique to law. That work has been done for us.[24] But Kelsen's second elaboration, that law has 'in and of itself no political or ethical value' is equally doubtful, though it has rarely come under scrutiny.

Law is (or can be) a means to valuable ends, so law has (or can have) instrumental value. But why does that commit us to denying that law can have *non*-instrumental value? Consider the general claim:

> *(F1) If law is an instrument, then it is a mere instrument and can have no non-instrumental value.*

As it stands, (F1) is a plain non-sequitur; yet arguments have occasionally been offered for it. John McTaggart criticised the idea that the state might have non-instrumental value, and there is no reason to think he would have spared (or even distinguished) its legal system. In a warning to his fellow idealists who, he feared, were stumbling down the path to state-worship, McTaggart wrote:

> [W]hatever activity it is desirable for the State to have, it will only be desirable as a means … Compared with worship of the State, zoolatry is rational and dignified. A bull or crocodile may not have much intrinsic value, but it has some, for it is a conscious being. The State has none. It would be as reasonable to worship a sewage pipe, which also possesses considerable value as a means.[25]

Fine mockery; and in its day possibly therapeutic. But the argument does not accomplish much without the implied assumption that only conscious beings can have intrinsic value. Possibly McTaggart is concerned with that because he is trying to show that the state does not merit *worship*. But worship, taken literally, is a *very* special way of engaging with things of intrinsic value. Many things that are not worship-worthy are nonetheless of immense intrinsic value: Ben Nevis, the great redwoods, the Goldberg Variations, *Guernica*.[26]

Of course, mountains, forests and works of art are not instruments, so although they help us understand intrinsic value they do not test (F1). But many things are, and do. The Victoria and Albert Museum has an eighteenth-century flute made by Peter Bressan.[27] New, it was a superb instrument, of such good acoustical design that copies are still made and played today. Yet none of that explains why Bressan's flute is under glass in a museum. That has to do with a different aspect of its value. The Bressan flute is a splendid example of the woodturner's craft. Its ebony is sectioned by elegantly proportioned silver bands, and into the wood the maker insinuated, in tiny hand-cut channels, strands of silver wire, achieving the effect of a delicate engraving on the wood's surface. The

[24] See Hart, *Concept of Law*, n 4 above, at 26–42; Fuller, *Morality of Law*, n 3 above, 106–11; Joseph Raz, *Practical Reason and Norms* (Oxford, Oxford University Press, 1999) 154–62; John Finnis, *Natural Law and Natural Rights* (Oxford, Oxford University Press, 1980) 266–70, 325–32.

[25] JME McTaggart, 'The Individualism of Value' in his *Philosophical Studies* (SV Keeling (ed), London, Edward Arnold, 1934) 109.

[26] Or, at any rate, if their value merits some kind of worship, it is not the kind that worried McTaggart.

[27] Museum no 452–1898.

Bressan flute is certainly an instrument; that was (and remains) its primary role in human culture. But it is no *mere* instrument; for it has further value that cannot be explained by the fact that it could be played easily and in tune.

Could (F1) be false in general yet true of law? I doubt that law has aesthetic value, though I have heard proud draftspersons speak as if their work does, and some civilians and code-enthusiasts revere the orderly arrangement of legal materials as if they shared the spare beauty of Wittgenstein's *Tractatus*. Those attitudes seem misplaced, but perhaps that betrays my own insensitivities: if a proof can be elegant, why can't a legal system, abstractly considered, be beautiful? In any event, there are other possibilities to consider.[28]

The first is genealogical. The law now in force did not spring into existence a moment ago. It developed and evolved over long periods, subject to many influences, and bears the imprint of crucial junctures in our history. Drawing-board constitutions and legal systems sketched out by philosophers or law professors tend to remain on the drawing boards—when we are lucky. If they take life without causing social catastrophe, it is usually because they have adapted to their societies in ways unanticipated, and perhaps unwelcomed, by their authors. Law's *adaptability* is of instrumental value; but the path-dependent *adaptations* can come to be constituent aspects of the society law regulates. When people are aware of these they may become attached to them, and these attachments come to have intrinsic value. That a legal system developed particular techniques, honoured particular values, vested authority in certain institutions—these are all culture- and path-dependent features of law, and they can give law value independent of its success at serving the ends it is meant to serve. Its legacies, ceremonies and formalities can be valued in themselves and can even merit honour. When things go well, the legal system itself will deserve respect, even when it includes rules that are sub-optimal and rulings that are off-mark.

To forestall possible misunderstanding, I am arguing, against (F1), that this much is possible, not that it is necessary. And I am not suggesting that intrinsic value in a legal system's history is its *dominant* value, or that it should always be honoured, efficiency be damned. That would be silly. But exaggerating genealogical value is not the only way of being silly. Holmes complained, 'It is revolting to have no better reason for a rule of law than that so it was laid down in the time of Henry IV'.[29] Does anyone really argue that a complete reason for applying an old rule lies in the fact that it is old? Most who emphasise the value of old rules stress two things: first, the fact that a rule is old may be a reason for thinking it serves us well—it has stood the test of time; secondly, to preserve it lends stability to law. But others go beyond any instrumental considerations. They are attached to their law, and thus take pride in the fact that a still-existing rule *was* laid down in

[28] I do not contend that these are the *only* sorts of intrinsic value law may have.

[29] Oliver Wendell Holmes, Jr, 'The Path of the Law' (1897) 10 *Harvard Law Review* 469.

the time of Henry IV. This would have struck Holmes, if not as repugnant, at least as nonsense, for it recognises values that cannot get past his self-imposed blinkers. In the continuation of that famous passage, the blinkers let in no other light:

> for our purposes our only interest in the past is for the light it throws upon the present. I look forward to a time when the part played by history in the explanation of dogma shall be very small, and instead of ingenious research we shall spend our energy on a study of the ends sought to be attained and the reasons for desiring them.[30]

If one responds to history only 'for the light it throws upon the present', and if the only aspect of the present one cares about is the 'explanation of [legal] dogma', then a lot of good, and evil, in one's history is bound to pass one by. But there are reasons for caring about the history of law that are not (now) reasons for adopting that law, and there are reasons for concern about our law's history that have nothing to do with how we should write a treatise or advise a client. We have become attached to it and its ways; it has become part of our collective life. We value old books, old languages and old houses, in part because of their antiquity. There are societies (not, regrettably, our own) that venerate old people. No one thinks this is best explained in terms of their use value.

The second sort of intrinsic value in law is a time-slice of the first. Law may have organic value as an aspect and expression of the society it serves.[31] Our legal system can be of value to our society because it is *our* law. It is now easy to lose sight of this amid the flurry of cosmopolitan enthusiasms. And in open, mobile, pluralist societies, the word 'our' sounds unpleasantly nativist, essentialist and exclusionary. Yet it need be none of those things. The law of an open and tolerant society is still *its law*,[32] and the involvement of such a society in creating and administering its law is something that is of value even when (instrumentally) better results might have been produced by different means, for example, by rule of an imperial master. The extent to which law has organic value varies,[33] as do the aspects of the legal system that most express it. In the nineteenth-century, the English used to hold the common law in this sort of regard, in the United States it has mostly been reserved for the Constitution, in Québec for the Civil Code, and in Scotland for any aspect of the legal system that is certifiably not-English.

As I said, genealogical and organic values are not present in all legal systems (never mind all *possible* legal systems). They are contingent on aspects of the political culture and on the content of the laws. Nor, when present, are they the

[30] *Ibid* 474.

[31] See Raz, *The Authority of Law*, n 11 above, at 258–60.

[32] And thus the openness of a legal system to foreign or international law does not show that it has ceased to be 'our law'.

[33] It is possible for law not to have organic value at all, to be totally *alienated* from its society. See Hart, *The Concept of Law*, n 4 above, at 117. Indeed, this is a standing risk that flows from the nature of law itself: See Leslie Green, 'Positivism and the Inseparability of Law and Morals' (2008) 83(4) *NYU Law Review* 1035.

most important values that those systems have—that would be to confuse *intrinsic* value with *great* value. Acknowledging the reality of law's non-instrumental value therefore requires reforming the instrumentalist thesis. We need to drop Kelsen's idea that law can have no value in and of itself. But at the same time, it is improbable that law would *have* intrinsic value if it did not *also* have instrumental value—if it were an 'idle ceremonial'.[34] Law's (potential for) great instrumental value makes it a central political institution, and that centrality sustains its (dependent) intrinsic value for the society whose law it is.

(F2) If law is an instrument, then law always has some instrumental value.

I turn now to an objection that comes from the other direction. We laid the ground for it above. Off-hand, (F2) seems out of place. Isn't the message of the instrumentalist thesis that whether law has any value, and what value it has, *depends on the ends* that law serves, and on how well it serves them? What instrumentalist would even moot a proposition like (F2)?

Kelsen comes close. He begins on the footing that a law exists only when it is *valid*: an invalid law is not a law that has the property of invalidity; it is no law at all: '[b]y the word "validity" we designate the specific existence of a norm'.[35] But then Kelsen maintains that a valid norm is not merely one that *belongs* to the legal system, but also one that is *binding* (ie is such that its subjects ought to do as it requires) in virtue of its membership in the system. He obviously needs an escape route, not only because some actually-existing laws are awful and ought to be disobeyed, but also because the question whether any law ought to be obeyed is a moral question, and on his own account to be excluded from a pure theory of law.

Here is Kelsen's (F2)-style solution. Whenever we use a norm (however stupid, inhumane or unjust) to assess conduct as being in or out of conformity with that norm, we assess it from the point of view of one kind of value, namely, *relative value*. Hence, since law regulates its own creation, a valid law *always* has value relative to the higher norms that authorise, permit or require its creation. This does not give law the absolute value that Kelsen thought natural lawyers impute to valid law: 'no absolute value is claimed for law. It is taken to have entirely hypothetical-relative validity'.[36] All the same, relative value *is* a kind of value, and Kelsen invokes it again when he explains the lawyer's notion of justice: 'judging something to be just is simply to express the relative value of conformity to a norm'.[37]

[34] I borrow the phrase from David Hume, who uses it to describe what would become of justice when respect for its rules no longer served human ends, in his *An Enquiry Concerning the Principles of Morals* (Charles W Hendel (ed), New York, Liberal Arts Press, 1957) 15.

[35] Hans Kelsen, *Pure Theory of Law* (M Knight (ed) Berkley, CA, University of California Press, 1967) 10. This does not deny that some invalid laws and legal transactions are used *as if they were* valid. (For example, courts sometimes give people the benefits of a void marriage *as if it were valid*, on equitable or other grounds.)

[36] Kelsen, n 2 above, at 436.

[37] Kelsen, n 19 above, at 16.

Even Hart was guilty of this error, if only in the second degree. He never followed Kelsen in denying absolute values, or in denying that there are moral values that may conflict with law's demands and, in that event, prevail over them. But residue of (F2) infects his controversy with Fuller. When Fuller says the desiderata of legality add up to an internal *morality* of law, Hart bridles. His first line of defence is concessive: Fuller's desiderata require rules, and when rules are steadfastly applied we may not have substantive justice, but we do have like cases being treated alike, and thus 'one essential element of the concept of justice'. 'So there is, in the very notion of law consisting of general rules, something which prevents us from treating it as if it is utterly neutral, without any necessary contact with moral principles'.[38] Some legal positivists grumble about that concession, since it does not sound like something a positivist should concede. But that is trivial compared to the fact that the concession is wrong. If the rules are bad *enough*, no justice of any kind, administrative, formal or otherwise, results from their steadfast application. When an evil rule is *not* applied to someone covered by its terms, there is no one to whom an injustice is done, no one entitled to demand that the evil be perpetuated.[39] There is no injustice 'in the air'.

Hart's second line of defence is offence. He says Fuller moves illicitly from what 'ought' to be done *relative to some standard or other*, to what 'ought' to be done *morally speaking*: 'We say to our neighbour, "you ought not to lie", and that may certainly be a moral judgment, but we should remember that the baffled poisoner may say, "I ought to have given her a second dose"'.[40] So when we think about the principles that 'ought' to be followed in order to regulate society by law, it does not follow that we are engaged in moral reasoning. Nor does it follow from the fact that we freely talk about how a law 'ought' to be interpreted, that we have found a moral basis to legal interpretation. There are lots of oughts. The 'inner morality of law' falls among the non-moral ones, alongside the oughts of cookery and carpentry.

But Fuller need not suppose that the injunction 'Laws ought to be promulgated!' is *itself* a moral norm. He can say that when law conforms to this norm of legal craftsmanship, moral good tends to follow or, more weakly, harm is prevented.[41] Whether this saves (F2) is uncertain. For in order actually to do good, or prevent harms, the principles of legality, all of them matters of degree, need to reach a certain threshold, which threshold, for Fuller, coincides with the existence conditions for a legal system. But there is notoriously *quite a lot* of retrospectivity, vagueness and normative conflict in legal systems. Unless we are going to say that many actually existing legal systems are not what they appear to

[38] Hart, 'Positivism and the Separation of Law and Morals', n 5 above, at 624.

[39] See David Lyons, 'On Formal Justice' (1973) 58(5) *Cornell Law Review* 833; and Leslie Green, 'The Germ of Justice' (forthcoming).

[40] Hart, 'Positivism and the Separation of Law and Morals', n 5 above, at 613.

[41] For the weaker version, see Joseph Raz, *The Authority of Law*, n 11 above, at 223–4.

be, the threshold of minimal conformity to the desiderata of legality will need to be set quite low, and at that low level may not, after all, prevent harm, let alone do good. At this point, Fuller may be tempted to rely on one of his more extreme theses: that *every* single departure from the principles of legality constitutes an insult to the dignity of people as responsible beings.[42] So while there may be no harm, there will always be a wrong. Yet surely that is just too extreme. It is as unreasonable as saying any failure to say 'thank you' to the bar-tender is an insult to his dignity. Disrespect, insults, etc are all subject to threshold conditions, and minor slights do not undermine our very humanity as responsible beings. In any case, this move is inconsistent with Fuller's own view that some retroactivity and some unclarity can actually make law *better*, not just all-things-considered, but *pro tanto*, for there comes a point when prospectivity and clarity become vices, and a move to reduce them is therefore an improvement.

There is something depressing in these arguments, on both sides. Hart and Fuller both neglect the point stressed above: nothing has instrumental value unless the ends it serves also have value. Probably they take this for granted, sharing the common view that all existing legal systems achieve some good ends, even if only in helping to co-ordinate road traffic. All the same, that common view is not a universal view, and it would not be pointless to offer, or expect, some defence of it. Kropotkin appraised three centuries of the rule of law thus:

> The millions of laws which exist for the regulation of humanity, appear upon investigation to be divided into three principal categories—protection of property, protection of persons, protection of government. And by analysing each of these three categories, we arrive at the same logical and necessary conclusion: *the uselessness and hurtfulness of law*.[43]

Kropotkin's judgement is swift and harsh. But for the legal instrumentalist, it is the territory on which the (F2) needs to be fought, not amongst 'relative' values, multiple 'oughts' or 'inner' moralities. And the result will be that we must modify (F2) so that it is conditioned on the ends that law actually pursues, and on its actual success in pursuing them.

(F3) If law is an instrument, then there is a generic end that law necessarily serves.

I turn now to the main ground for divorce, or at least separation, between the two great families of instrumentalist views. (F3) is denied by the negative limb of the instrumentalist thesis. (F3) is a thesis that marks an important division between Fuller and Hart, and between Hart and Dworkin.

I frame (F3) as if instrumentalism commits one to the existence of a generic end for law. In truth, Fuller only says that it is *ironical* to affirm that individual

[42] Fuller, *The Morality of Law*, n 3 above, at 162.

[43] Petr Alekseevich Kropotkin, *Law and Authority: An Anarchist Essay* (London, International Publishing Co, 1886) 18.

laws or statutes can have a purpose while holding that law as such does not.[44] He does not explicitly deny that the irony could result from a correct assessment of the nature of things (as in 'It's ironic that the government's enthusiasm for deregulation led to the nationalisation of banks'). And, as I mentioned, one of the difficulties in interpreting Fuller on this point is that he sometimes treats as the end of law what everyone else counts as its species-typical means: ie the guidance of human action by norms, rules or principles of a particular sort. Is it possible that Fuller thought the instrumentalists' error was to take for law's means what is really its end? That would render (F3) true but trivial. We should not impute that view to Fuller, for if he really held it he would not have gambled so much on his fragile claim that there is a *correlation* between law's means being in good order (inasmuch as they satisfy the desiderata of law's 'inner' or 'internal' morality) and law satisfying its proper ends as identified by 'external morality'.[45]

I tend to think that Fuller is simply groping towards the point we took from Aquinas: 'Whenever a thing is for an end, its form must be determined proportionately to that end; as the form of a saw is such as to be suitable for cutting'.[46] That accords with Fuller's observation that, when legal philosophers try to distinguish legal order from 'the gunman situation writ large', they fail to see that 'It is ... precisely because law is a purposeful enterprise that it displays structural constancies which the legal theorist can discover and treat as uniformities in the factually given'.[47] The 'structural constancies', for example the fact that law regulates human conduct by rules and similar standards, that these rules form some kind of system, and so on, *are* 'constancies' only *because* law is a 'purposeful enterprise' striving for a definite end.

It is curious that Fuller thinks positivists must deny this, but a lot depends on precisely what he intends by a 'purposive enterprise', and that is not an idea he tries to make very precise. As we have seen, anyone who thinks law is a means thinks it a means to *some* ends or other. Perhaps Fuller assumes that unless law serves a *generic* purpose—an overall end that itself distinguishes law from other social institutions, law's very *own* end—then law's means would not be 'constancies' but variabilities. Without a generic end, there would be nothing to explain why law has the means it has, nothing to unify them, and nothing that makes them features of law *as such*.

Even within such an account, however, we do not need the hypothesis of a generic end. Different mid-range ends can do the work piecemeal. The fact that law contains the sort of rules that are potentially knowable by their subjects, can be explained if we assume that law aims to help a variety of people attain a variety of ends. Other features desirable in the law, and at some modest threshold

[44] Fuller, *The Morality of Law*, n 3 above, at 150.

[45] Lon L Fuller, 'Positivism and Fidelity to Law: A Reply to Professor Hart' (1958) 71(4) *Harvard Law Review* 630, 636 and, much less tentatively, in his *Morality of Law*, n 3 above, at 95–151.

[46] See n 11 above.

[47] Fuller, *The Morality of Law*, n 3 above, at 151.

possibly necessary (eg that laws be clear and prospective) can be explained on the assumption that law is trying to pursue its ends while ensuring that it also conforms to important independent values (such as protecting legitimate expectations, respecting persons, and so on). These are plausible ideals for law, and also for many other forms of social organisation.

I have argued that the hypothesis of a generic end for law is not needed to explain why all legal systems have certain common features. But I have not shown the hypothesis to be false. On that issue I shall say only this: it is perhaps a warning sign that many of the candidates that have been offered for law's generic end (eg protecting human rights, securing respect for persons, keeping the peace) are attractive ideals for law that are neither common to all legal systems nor unique to them, while others (eg maintaining order, co-ordinating activity) are so vague as to be useless to jurisprudence and, when specified more precisely, quickly lose their claims to universality.

It is worth noting, however, that rejecting the hypothesis of a generic end is compatible with accepting that law typically serves certain (plural) ends. Hart thought so, and thought that without reference to what he sometimes called the 'minimum content' of natural law, we would be without a complete criterion for distinguishing legal systems from other institutionalised rule-systems effective in a society.[48] A full-fledged legal system would typically aim to regulate violence, property, kinship and promises. Fuller seems largely uninterested in this issue, because he denies any significant difference between the 'enterprise' of law and the enterprise involved in the internal regulation of clubs, churches, schools or agricultural fairs.[49] Anyone running such institutions according to rules ought to be concerned about the character as well as the content of those rules: both universities and unions should try to keep their regulations clear, prospective, stable, and so forth. Of course, there may be *additional* requirements that apply to legal systems (eg in virtue of the fact that they exercise compulsory jurisdiction over their subjects), and there may be *additional urgency* to some of the shared requirements (eg in virtue of the scope of authority that legal systems claim).

Perhaps law is less like Aquinas' saw than it is like a Swiss-Army knife: a multi-purpose tool handy for lots of ends, but not necessarily an all-purpose tool. Many of these ends have structural ramifications of the sort Aquinas mentions, but the ramifications are complex and variable. Inasmuch as law aims at *guiding* conduct, then its action-guiding rules will need to be laid down in advance of the conduct they are to guide. Inasmuch as law aims at *evaluating* conduct (as right or wrong, good or bad), then there is no conceptual requirement that the standards be prospective, but there is a requirement that they not be hopelessly vague. And inasmuch law is to *educate* its subjects about the moral significance of the standards it declares, then the reasons for these standards will

[48] Hart, *The Concept of Law*, n 4 above, at 193–200. See also n 6 above.

[49] Fuller, *Morality of Law*, n 3 above, at 124–5.

need to be more transparent than they would if law's aim were simply to secure co-ordination and conformity around them. What we do not need, and what I doubt we will find, is what (F3) proposes: a generic end of law that explains the leading features of law's means.

(F4) If law is an instrument, then it is a neutral instrument.

Much ink has been wasted proving the non-neutrality of *law*, especially when that is taken to involve such easily dispatched theses as the following: (a) law is neutral among all sorts of conduct; (b) law is neutral among all political ideologies; or (c) law is neutrally applied to all its subjects. The first is absurd, the second hovers on the margins of absurdity, and the third is a possible ideal rarely satisfied in fact. I therefore disregard these and other possible interpretations of (F4) in favour of one that is at least linked to the instrumentalist thesis. Raz writes:

> Like other instruments, the law has a specific virtue which is morally neutral in being neutral as to the end to which the instrument is put. It is the virtue of efficiency; the virtue of an instrument as an instrument. For the law this virtue is the rule of law.[50]

Notice that this does not make any claim about the neutrality *of law*. The claim is about the neutrality of *law's specific virtue*, ie legality, or the rule of law. That virtue is said to be neutral with respect to law's pursuit of its decidedly non-neutral ends. This suggests that the problem with (F4) lies in an ambiguity: is it the law that the instrumentalist believes neutral, or the principles of legality that govern the creation and operation of law?

Fuller concedes that, over a wide range, his principles of legality are 'ready to serve a variety of such aims with equal efficiency'.[51] That sounds like a qualified endorsement of the instrumentalist thesis. The qualifications are as follows. First, Fuller says that there is a *tendency* for any instrument satisfying his principles to do good, for example by encouraging open government and public scrutiny, and ensuring that there are certain evils that governments cannot perpetrate.[52] Secondly, as noted above, Fuller thinks that *every* departure from his principles is an insult to human dignity. Thirdly, he also thinks that law, even when well-ordered, is a *limited*-purpose instrument. He says that law is bad at economic allocation. He says that adjudication as a social technique is trustworthy only when confined to the traditional role of deciding cases between two (or a few) parties, avoiding what he calls 'polycentric' issues: moral problems involving complex principles and consequences for many people, including non-parties.

These points are all disputable. The effective capacities of law as an instrument of governance are hard to assess, and probably vary amongst societies. Law's

[50] Raz, *The Authority of Law*, n 11 above, at 226.

[51] Fuller, *The Morality of Law*, n 3 above, at 153.

[52] Strangely, Fuller thinks that racial discrimination is among them, for to *target* a given race for ill treatment requires defining the indefinable, whereas a statute prohibiting discrimination on *grounds of race* is safe from any such vagueness. *Ibid* 160–1.

capacity to produce desirable economic outcomes depends on the content of the law, and on the way it goes about securing those allocations. And the idea that traditional adjudication is somehow insulated from 'polycentric' issues is false in fact and dubious as an aspiration.[53] But the key point is this: no one needs to be converted to (F4) to think that we should use law's instruments only when they stand a fair chance of being effective, or that when they are effective, they will not be neutral amongst ends or ideologies.

I said that law is more like a Swiss-Army knife than like Aquinas' saw. I meant, of course, that it is not so much a single instrument as a union of various instruments: mandatory rules, power-conferring rules, individual norms, and much more. However, it is not a union of every *possible* instrument, and in trying to order one's own affairs, let alone those of others, one may find oneself stuck with a task for which none of the existing legal instruments are very good. Each of law's tools has its limits, and there are some things that probably cannot be directly achieved by any of law's tools. ('You can't legislate love'—which is not to say that you shouldn't try.)

(F5) If law is an instrument, then law is subject only to instrumental evaluation.

The final claim saddles the instrumentalist with exclusively instrumental standards for *evaluating* law: the end (and only the end) justifies the means.

If L is a valuable instrument, then *one* important question is how effective L is, compared to the feasible alternatives, in achieving the valued ends. The criteria of effectiveness vary with the instrument and the end: an effective knife should cut well, an effective algorithm should compute well, an effective flute should play well. When an instrument is partly identified by its intended or typical end, the criteria of effectiveness take on a special caste: they are criteria that must be met (allowing for some adjustment or repair) if the instrument is to count as a full-fledged member of the class. A baseball is not an ineffective knife; it is not a knife at all, though a blunt or bent knife certainly is. We can speak of these, as Fuller does, as 'internal' criteria of evaluation: instrumental standards called up by the nature of the instrument itself. Law has such criteria, and Fuller identifies several of them. But as Fuller also admits, they do not pick out law as a social institution, for they are mostly the criteria that apply to other rule-governed enterprises.

What is most pertinent here, however, is that the existence of such internal criteria of evaluation does not establish any of the following propositions:

(1) The internal criteria are the most *morally important* criteria for evaluating law.
(2) The moral significance of the internal criteria is *exhausted by* their instrumental contribution to the value of the law.

[53] Jeff King, 'The Pervasiveness of Polycentricity' (2008) *Public Law* 101.

(3) Moral criticism of law may be *ousted by* showing that it is not based on one of the internal criteria for evaluating law.
(4) With respect to any internal criterion, *any change that improves its effectiveness is morally desirable.*

Some of these propositions are more obviously wrong than others. Both (1) and (2) confuse functional importance with moral importance. Proposition (3) suggests the comforting but implausible view that a social institution gets to choose the moral standards that it would like to meet—that it can face an examination board best suited to its nature and ambitions. Occasionally, this thought gets reversed, so that from the premise that there *is* a standard that law must meet (say, that its allocative norms should be just) it is held to follow law must meet that standard *in virtue of the fact that it is law.* The claim is made often enough about justice.[54] Now, it is true that law must answer to justice, but that is not because a modicum of justice is required for something to count as law (not even Fuller goes that far) but because, as an institution that allocates burdens and benefits among people, law is *apt for* appraisal as being just or unjust. In the same way, a market, whose internal virtue is efficiency, cannot oust appraisals of its foreseeable distributive effects by pleading, 'I wasn't *trying* to do justice!'

Finally, (4) simply omits all other moral constraints to which any valuable instrument must conform. Nothing in the conceptual claim that law is a means licenses this omission. On the way to securing its ends, law must respect all sound deontological constraints; it must treat its subjects with respect, and so on. To the extent that Fuller wants us not only to keep this in mind, but also to take it to heart, his reminder is welcome. But it is not as if the instrumentalists named at the outset express any sympathy for (4), not even Bentham or Ihering, who came closer than any to supposing that 'the end justifies the means'. Kelsen actually held that, 'the end cannot "justify" the means, even if the end itself is "justified", i.e., obligatory. The means to a justified end can be quite unjustified'.[55] And Hart's theory of law is, on the normative side, quite surrounded by non-instrumental constraints: his case for duty to obey the law rests on the principles of reciprocity and fairness; his case for punishment includes distributive constraints on who may be punished; his account of justice acknowledges, though admittedly with little elaboration, the principles of legality that Fuller so prizes.

Fuller accuses Hart's theory of law of being 'managerialist', epitomising it as a 'one-way projection of authority … simply acting on the citizen—morally or immorally, justly of unjustly, as the case may be'.[56] The final clause intimates, absurdly, that Hart cares less about whether the law acts morally or immorally than he does about the conceptual distinction between the moral and the

[54] See, eg Robert Alexy, *The Argument from Injustice: A Reply to Legal Positivism* (BL Paulson and SL Paulson (trans), Oxford, Clarendon Press, 2002).
[55] Hans Kelsen, *General Theory of Norms* (M Hartney (trans), (Oxford, Oxford University Press, 1991) 17–18.
[56] Fuller, *The Morality of Law*, n 3 above, at 191–2.

immoral. The penultimate clause asserts, falsely, that Hart is unaware that law is not only top-down but bottom-up, as seen in the facilities it provides for private individuals to arrange their affairs, but also in the voluntary co-operation of large numbers of people without which law could not exist at all. And the initial charge, associating a rule-based instrumentalism with something called 'managerialism', is a bare stipulation, or an indication that Fuller either misunderstands Hart or misunderstands how managers actually run enterprises.

Conclusion

I have tried to make the instrumentalist thesis about law—or at any rate *an* instrumentalist thesis about law—plausible, first, by showing that it belongs to an instrumental conception of law that, if not undeniable, is in any case not denied by most legal philosophers, whether they be positivists or not. I then tried to make it seem a plausible interpretation of that conception by showing how the most influential charges against it cannot stand. At the same time, not all versions of instrumentalism survive unscathed. We had to abandon the claim that law is a coercive instrument, and also the claim that law can only have instrumental value. In other respects, however, the familiar charges against instrumentalism mostly turn out to be a matters of guilt by mistaken association. All this does not prove that law's means contribute more to the identification of law than do its ends—but it makes it a lot harder to doubt.

10

Comment on 'Law as a Means'

ANTHONY J SEBOK

Leslie Green's Chapter 9, 'Law as a Means', is an engaging and subtle analysis of an underexplored aspect of modern jurisprudential argument.[1] Green's subject—'the instrumentalist thesis'—is a peculiarly modern one. In fact, I would hazard that it is a subject peculiar to a certain sub-set of modern jurisprudential scholars, namely modern analytic positivists and their critics.

This is not to say that there have not been instrumentalist theories of law prior to modern positivism. Green's brief discussion of Brian Tamanaha's work on instrumentalism gives the reader only a glimpse of the major American debate over instrumentalism, namely the rise of, and reaction to, legal realism.[2] Legal realism, which self-consciously developed in response to something it called 'legal formalism', was much concerned with theories of adjudication as opposed to law, and defended a certain approach to adjudication within legal systems.[3] But the historical pedigree of instrumentalism goes back earlier. Legal historians Morton Horwitz and William Nelson, associated with Harvard Law School in the 1970s, promoted the idea that American law in the early nineteenth century was uniquely 'instrumentalist', at least in comparison with the English common law out of which it sprang.[4] These too were historical accounts of the shift in styles of adjudication, buttressed with various social or political explanations for the shift. For Horwitz, common law judges in the newly formed United States selectively inserted negligence-based theories of liability into tort and property law in order to advantage the commercial class over the agricultural class. According to

[1] Leslie Green, Chapter 9.

[2] *Ibid* 170, citing Brian Z Tamanaha, *Law as a Means to an End: Threat to the Rule of Law* (New York, NY, 2007).

[3] See Anthony J Sebok, *Legal Positivism in American Jurisprudence* (1998) 48–112.

[4] See Morton J Horwitz, *The Transformation of American Law, 1780–1890* (Cambridge, MA, 1977) 7–30 and William E Nelson, 'The Impact of the Antislavery Movement upon Styles of Judicial Reasoning in Nineteenth Century America' (1977) 87 *Harvard Law Review* 513.

Nelson, federal and state judges interpreted the doctrines of the conflict of laws in order to advantage an anti-slavery ideology over the institution of slavery in antebellum America.

I agree with Green that Tamanaha's treatment of instrumentalism barely does justice to the concept, but not only because, as Green notes, Tamanaha regards instrumentalism as nothing more than a form of pretextual behaviour (in this respect, Tamanaha's concept of instrumentalism is remarkably similar to that propounded by Critical Legal Studies). The legal realists and the nineteenth century instrumentalist judges (as depicted by Horwitz and Nelson) were not really concerned with the definition of law, but only with the role of the judge within a settled legal system. They certainly would have baulked at the idea that they were acting pretextually. It is possible that, had they been pressed, they would have articulated a theory of law that was, roughly speaking, instrumentalist, but it simply was not the question that concerned them or which their work engaged.

As Green notes, beginning with Kelsen, the question of whether law is an instrument becomes a subject of inquiry and debate. Kelsen said, 'Law is a means . . . not an end'.[5] Fuller disagreed. As Green carefully notes, Fuller does not ever come out and state, baldly, that law is an end, not a means (although, as I note below, Green argues persuasively that Fuller could make such a claim). But Fuller comes very close at various points in his writings. Green cites Fuller's backhanded argument in *The Morality of Law* where he attributes to the positivist the position that while *a law* may have a purpose, *law* does not.[6] Presumably, Green concludes, Fuller thinks the opposite is true—law has a purpose. Fuller make a similarly negative argument in *Positivism and Fidelity to Law*, where he attributes to the positivist the view that law is 'nothing' more than a 'social reality'.[7] This makes law even less than a means: it is nothing but a social fact which may or may not have instrumental value, and certainly no value as an end in itself.

I have been careful to avoid placing Hart in this debate, because Hart clearly thought that law served a variety of ends. In *Positivism and the Separation of Law and Morals*, before he got around to criticising Fuller, Hart first cleared away some troubling claims that had been made by the Legal Realists.[8] According to Hart, the Realists did not understand that 'law' was a practice, and that it required the interpretation of statutes and the common law in light of certain rules and principles. In the 'penumbra', for example, judges had to exercise discretion in light of 'social aims', while in the 'core' they were required to stick to settled

[5] Hans Kelsen, *General Theory of Law and the State* (1949) 20, cited by Leslie Green, ch 9 at 169.

[6] Lon Fuller, *The Morality of Law* (New Haven, CT,1969) 146.

[7] Lon Fuller, 'Positivism and Fidelity to Law: A Reply to Professor Hart' (1957) 71 *Harvard Law Review* 629, 631.

[8] HLA Hart, 'Positivism and the Separation of Law and Morals' (1957) 71 *Harvard Law Review* 592.

meanings.[9] The point here is not to remind the reader that Hart was comfortable talking about 'social policies and purposes' in law,[10] but rather to note that Hart's picture of law was very similar to the theory of 'reasoned elaboration' developed by the Legal Process school.[11] According to Hart and Sacks' *The Legal Process*, the 'ultimate' purpose of law is '[the task of] establishing, maintaining, and perfecting the conditions necessary for community life to perform its role in the complete development of man'.[12] The practice of reasoned elaboration (the 'legal process' promoted by post-war legal scholars in response to the sceptical attack of the Legal Realists) was based on attributing to law the thinnest of aims: the goal of 'institutional settlement'.[13]

I bring up Hart's affinity to Legal Process because it strengthens and underscores a point made by Green early in his chapter, which is that Fuller and Hart were not really disagreeing over the concept of 'law as a means' as much as they were disagreeing over the conception of law as a means.[14] This can be seen from either side of the problem.

Hart, like the Legal Process theorists, thought that law had an end, and that this end was, roughly speaking, to co-ordinate and secure the purposes of a society, whatever those purposes might be. Hart famously argued that the Nazis could have had a legal system whose ends included terrorising citizens and killing innocent persons. Hart and Sacks argued that their theory that law was nothing more than the achievement of a system of institutional settlement was based on a moral concept, but not the kind of moral concept that was typically associated with natural lawyers: 'the proposition that a settled law should be respected . . . that it is in some sense "right" *simply because it has been duly made*—itself an ethical concept'.[15]

Fuller, on the other hand, did not believe that a law was right 'simply because it has been duly made', unless the word 'duly' contained moral content that exceeded the basic biological requirements Hart described as the 'minimum content of natural law'.[16] Fuller tried to enlist the Legal Process school to his side, but, given their adoption of the value-free language of social science and their scepticism that values were any more than the product of interest group competition, it is hard to see why, in the end, they would invest in the principle of institutional settlement any more moral content than HLA Hart. It is worth noting that Henry Hart deeply opposed *Baker v Carr*, which, under Fuller's

[9] *Ibid* 609–11.

[10] *Ibid* 612.

[11] I try to establish the connection between HLA Hart and the Legal Process school in Sebok, *Legal Positivism in American Jurisprudence* (Cambridge, UK, 1998) 120–40.

[12] Henry Hart and Albert Sacks, *The Legal Process* (St. Paul, MN, 1994) 110–11.

[13] *Ibid* 112.

[14] Leslie Green, Chapter 9 at 173.

[15] Hart and Sacks, n 12 above, at 118 (emphasis added).

[16] Hart, 'Positivism and the Separation of Law and Morals', n 8 above, at 622–3.

approach, should (arguably) have been an easy case.[17] Similarly, the Legal Process school were highly critical of the Warren Court's equal protection decisions of the 1950s, including all of their school desegregation decisions.[18] For Fuller, law's end was the 'internal morality of law', and while he denied that this end state was mimetic to a specific state of affairs, he certainly believed that it excluded certain end states from coming into existence. Fuller could not imagine how the Nazis would have been able to secure the end state they desired—domestic terror and genocide—without violating the relatively concrete demands of the internal morality of law. As he famously claimed: 'Hart seems to assume that evil aims may have as much coherence and inner logic as good ones. I for one, refuse to accept that assumption'.[19]

Green is absolutely correct when he notes that the key difference between Hart, Kelsen (and, I would add, the Legal Process school) and Fuller (and Dworkin) is their conception of the law as means. The positivists claim that law is 'better understood' by focusing on its means while Fuller and Dworkin think that the law is better understood by focusing on its ends.[20]

The remainder of Green's Chapter 9 is structured as follows. After demonstrating that Fuller *et al* really accepted the position that law is a means, but disagreed with the conception of means adopted by their rivals, the positivists, Green then argues that no 'opponent of the instrumentalist thesis . . . coherently advances' the view that law is an 'end in itself'.[21] This conclusion is unsurprising, given that in the previous section Green established that all of the proponents of the 'law as ends' thesis also believed that law was a means. In other words, while it makes sense to believe that law is a means to certain ends, it makes no sense to believe that (a) law is not a means to *any* end and (b) is nonetheless valuable because it is an 'end-in-itself'.

Next, Green refines the position that law is a means. He points out five fallacies which might be held by those who take seriously the idea that law is a means for certain ends (that is, everybody). The net result of this paring away of misconceptions leaves us with the following picture of the idea that law is a means. (1) Law may have non-instrumental value as well as instrumental value,[22] but if it does not secure an end that has value, it has no instrumental value.[23] (2) Law does not secure a 'generic' (eg universal) end,[24] and because law is a means to securing non-universal ends, it can be evaluated from a moral perspective that

[17] 369 U.S. 186 (1962). *See* Albert Sacks, 'Henry Hart' (1969) 82 *Harvard Law Review* 1593, 1594.

[18] Anthony J Sebok, *Legal Positivism in American Jurisprudence* (1998) 133, 152 and see Gary Peller, 'Neutral Principles in the 1950s' (1988) 21 *U Mich JL Ref* 561.

[19] Fuller, 'Positivism and Fidelity to Law: A Reply to Professor Hart', n 7 above, at 636.

[20] Leslie Green, Chapter 9 at 173.

[21] *Ibid* 176.

[22] *Ibid* 179–80.

[23] *Ibid* 182.

[24] *Ibid* 185.

takes into account the value of the ends it secures.[25] (3) Although law's 'ends' are not neutral,[26] law's 'ends' are neutral with respect to the ends law secures.[27] By this, Green means simply that an instrumentalist need not be committed to the fallacy that the 'law is a neutral instrument' in order to believe that 'the principles of legality that govern the creation and operation of law' may be neutral as between the ends (political, economic, etc) that are promoted by the operation of any specific law or legal system.[28]

Finally, Green tries to understand Fuller's objections to the positivist's conception of instrumentalism, and his best reconstruction of Fuller's motivation is political and psychological. The fear is that a theory of law informed by Green's cleaned-up instrumentalism will not motivate legal reform and will not provide a sufficient bulwark against injustice. So, the argument goes, Fuller refocuses the attention of his audience to the ends served by law, where much more direct debate over moral questions can occur.[29]

I would like to introduce another explanation for Fuller's resistance. I raise it not because I want to endorse Fuller's position (I do not) but because I feel that Green's analysis will be strengthened if we take the best possible argument Fuller might mount.

I am not sure that Green clearly states the difference between the two conceptions of instrumentalism that he argues occupy the ground between the positivists and Fuller. Green describes a spectrum: the former emphasise means over ends, while the latter emphasise ends over means. Green explicitly rejects that anyone might seriously adopt a 'purist' position such as valuing law as 'end-in-itself' and he argues that unless means secure ends which are valuable, those means lack 'instrumental value'. This suggests to me that both purist positions—taking either ends or means as valuable 'in themselves' (or, as Green puts it, as 'surds')[30]—is off the table for Green, and I agree with him.

However, taking the extreme purist position 'off the table' still leaves a choice between two versions of the middle position, namely that law is the pursuit of ends by means. As Green notes, one can emphasise the former or the latter (or, I suppose, view both in equipoise). A brief review of the three claims above, which summarise the results of Green's five fallacies about instrumentalism, suggests that, like Hart, Green thinks that the right way to approach the analysis of the concept of law is to focus on the law's means. If, for example, law does not secure a 'generic' (eg universal) end, then what benefit can the jurisprude derive from studying law's ends? They will be contingent and varied. On the other hand, if there is such as thing as a set of law's 'ends', why not try to identify what they are,

25 *Ibid* 187.
26 *Ibid* 186.
27 *Ibid* 185.
28 *Ibid* 185.
29 *Ibid* 187.
30 See Paul Carus, *The Surd of Metaphysics (Are There Things in Themselves?)* (Chicago, IL, 1903).

even if they are not neutral? Just because they are not neutral does not mean that are not susceptible to rational study by the jurisprude.

Fuller's response to this, I think, is to go on the offensive and to argue that Green underestimates the role that ends play in identifying means. I think that Fuller would agree with Green that there is a limited set of law's 'ends', but he would disagree that they can be identified without regard to the ends that law secures.

An analogy would be Dworkin's argument about voting systems. Dworkin concedes that typically we view democracy as a means by which we secure our ends (although it may also have non-instrumental value). However, in certain cases where a majority vote produces a result that is unjust, we then have to review whether or not we have the correct understanding of democracy.[31] We do not discard our commitment to the concept of democracy, but we test our definition (majoritarianism) against the end state that has been produced: 'there can be no objection *in the name of democracy*, to other procedures that protect ['democratic conditions'] better [than democracy]'.[32] If someone were to insist, however, that we were illegitimately changing the meaning of the word 'democracy' by insisting that it did not always require majoritarianism, then Dworkin's response is simple: 'we should have to rephrase our question to ask why we should have democracy'.[33]

I think that Fuller (who deeply influenced Dworkin) would adopt the structure of Dworkin's argument over the conception of democratic conditions in his defence of his conception of instrumentalism. He would not deny that the law has 'ends'. He would deny that we can know the law's 'ends' without reference to the ends law serves. So, for example, the reason why prospectivity (or non-retroactivity) is an end of the law (or what Fuller calls part of the 'morality of law') is because the subject of a law must be able to comply with it, and that requires fair notice.[34] But of course, the common law is replete with results that could not have been anticipated and for which no fair notice has been given. Legislatures sometimes pass laws which have a retroactive effect. Fuller knows that it is not logically impossible for a legal system to pass retroactive laws. Sometimes he speaks as if it might be practically impossible for a society to function if there were too many such laws.[35] But in his key example against Hart ('the Roehm Purge') he does not make the case that the selective use of retroactive laws to eliminate political rivals would introduce so much uncertainty into the legal system that people would be unsure about whether their contracts would be upheld by the courts.[36]

[31] See Ronald Dworkin, *Law's Empire* (Cambridge, MA, 1986) 17.
[32] *Ibid* 17.
[33] Ronald Dworkin, *Taking Rights Seriously* (Cambridge, MA, 1977) 141.
[34] Fuller, *The Morality of Law*, n 6 above, at 51.
[35] Fuller, 'Positivism and Fidelity to Law: A Reply to Professor Hart', n 7 above, at 645.
[36] *Ibid* 650.

Fuller's main argument against retroactive laws is that they produce end states that are manifestly unjust. One could imagine that if a Nazi lawyer persisted in insisting that the virtue of the retroactive laws used by the government was that there was finality, or, to borrow from the Legal Process school, 'institutional settlement', Fuller would look at the lawyer and say, 'Let me rephrase the question: why should we have institutional settlement?'. A legal virtue (or an 'end' of law) that does not produce an end-state that is just, is, for Fuller, a defective legal virtue and should be redefined until it is a means towards securing the end-states we desire.

I want to be clear that I do not necessarily agree with the argument that I have just suggested. However, I think that it represents a serious response by Fuller to Green within the boundaries of Green's early and powerful argument that even Fuller is an instrumentalist. Just because Fuller cannot seriously claim to view law as a 'end-in-itself' does not mean that he must accept the instrumentalism outlined by Green in Chapter 9. There may be other reasons for Green (and myself) to prefer an instrumentalism that stresses means over ends, but I think they must be further elaborated.

11

Two Turns of the Screw

DESMOND MANDERSON

'If the child gives the effect another turn of the screw, what do you say to two children—?'
['We say, of course', somebody exclaimed, 'that they give two turns! Also that we want to hear about them'.[1]

Performing Stories, Performing Law

Henry James' short novel *The Turn of the Screw* appeared in 1898. It is a ghost story, uncanny both in content and in form. It relates such uneventful events that the reader is left turning from interpretation to interpretation, trying to determine just what is going on. Yet like the ghosts themselves, wherever we look, there is nothing to see. 'And what did this strain of trouble matter when my eyes went back to the window only to see that the air was clear again and—by my personal triumph—the influence quenched? There was nothing there.'[2] This 'nothing', ironically, establishes the ghosts' menace. Until the very last sentence of the book, which hits one like a fist, nothing happens, nothing is proved, and yet a palpable feeling of tension and anxiety builds. It is therefore not fanciful to suggest that the real power of the story lies not in its narrative but in its rhetoric. The book creates a mood of anxiety that infects the reader's reading. This is what one might call the 'performative' dimension of the story. James' tale constitutes a reader, alert but confused, who thereby experiences the feeling of being *part of* a ghost story rather than merely reading *about* one.

Sixty years later, HLA Hart and Lon Fuller likewise do not merely describe two different approaches to legal interpretation: in their style, rhetoric and structure they perform these approaches. This chapter similarly wishes to connect *its*

[1] Henry James, *The Turn of the Screw* (New York, Heritage Press, 1949; 1st edn 1898) Prologue, 2. (For ease of reference amongst many different editions I cite to James with reference both to page numbers and to chapter numbers).

[2] James, n 1 above, XXIV, 140.

argument with its form and for this reason I have chosen to devote considerable space to discussing a work of literature. *The Turn of the Screw* illuminates certain essential features of the Hart–Fuller debate. Both are tales about law, interpretation and ghosts.[3] Through James, this chapter argues that the debate between Hart and Fuller epitomises legal interpretation as haunted. Rhetorically, they present two largely incommensurable visions of law. Yet their efforts to exclude the other's approach fails. But instead of choosing between Hart and Fuller we can gain a richer understanding of legal interpretation if we treat their performance as mutual and interactive. I do not mean that Hart and Fuller can in any way be reconciled through compromise or synthesis. I mean rather that each remains 'haunted', and therefore productively unsettled, by the perspective of the other. To be haunted is never to be comfortable with one's judgement or knowledge, never at peace. This may be 'a horror'[4] in a story, but necessary in a legal system.

There are uncanny parallels between James' story and the debate. In Fuller's article in particular, the metaphor of the 'turn' is strikingly prominent.[5] Hart's metaphors are linear; he insists on clearing the ground, starting afresh, moving ahead. This rhetoric, which aims to make simple what had previously been only 'dimly sensed',[6] corresponds to his notion of clarity and certainty as the function of law and the goal of legal interpretation. Fuller, on the contrary, turns questions over and around like an unusual object we are bent on studying. This corresponds to *his* notion of the purposive nature of law and the practice of legal interpretation. In each case, their talk about legal reasoning is a performance of it.

Accordingly, when Fuller describes Hart's argument as giving positivism 'a new and promising turn', and then later speaks of it 'taking a turn',[7] the implication is that Hart's argument is less linear than he asserts—as if Hart himself were being forced by the unexpected to turn in unforeseen directions. In just this way Fuller believes our assumptions about meaning are necessarily open to the unexpected. So too Fuller's insistence that interpretation 'turns' on this or that appropriates a

[3] For recent work on these themes see Jacques Derrida, *Specters of Marx* (New York, Routledge, 1994); Jacques Derrida, 'Force of Law: The Mystical Foundation of Authority' (1990) *Cardozo Law Review* 920; Shoshana Felman, 'A Ghost in the House of Justice' in *The Juridical Unconscious* (Cambridge, MA, Harvard University Press, 2002) 131–69; Avery Gordon, *Ghostly Matters: Haunting and the Sociological Imagination* (Minneapolis, MN, University of Minnesota Press, 1997); Tatiana Flessas, 'A House Haunted by Justice' in Desmond Manderson (ed), *Legal Spaces* (*Law Text Culture vol 9*) (Sydney, LIRC, 2005) 215–44.

[4] James, n 1 above, V, 35–6.

[5] In Hart's essay, the word turn is used with dramatically less frequency and in virtually none of the senses I have discussed here. 'Turn' or its variants are used five times in Hart, and 17 times in Fuller. Of these, Hart twice says 'let me turn to …' as a way of introducing sections of his argument, but other than that the only metaphor that is used is the phrase 'turn of the century' which also occurs twice. Moreover, Hart never uses the word as a way of analysing Fuller's argument, where it is often precisely to analyse Hart's position that Fuller uses the metaphor of turning.

[6] HLA Hart, 'Positivism and the Separation of Law and Morals' (1958) 71 *Harvard Law Review* 593, 604.

[7] Lon Fuller, 'Positivism and Fidelity to Law' (1958) 71 *Harvard Law Review* 630,632–5, 649.

circular metaphor to capture the work of interpretation itself.[8] 'By pulling our minds first in one direction, then in another, these cases help us understand the fabric of thought before us.'[9] This rhetoric reaches its zenith when Fuller concludes that positivism 'takes a morbid turn',[10] again with its suggestion of a surprise imposed on Hart against his will. Elements of movement, discourse and unease are bound up in Fuller's metaphor.

For Hart, Fuller's twists and turns are merely 'mysterious'. He defends instead the merits of 'speak[ing] plainly'.[11] Further, Hart contrasts 'reason' and 'passion'. Radbruch's critique of Nazi law is characterised as a 'passionate appeal' that is 'supported not by detailed reasoning' but by an 'extraordinary naïveté' and even 'hysteria'.[12] But there is little evidence in Radbruch's texts of unreasoning passion, naivety or hysteria. Indeed, Hart himself defends the Utilitarians precisely because they united their 'passion for reform' and their 'passionate intensity' with 'even-minded sanity'.[13] Yet in the course of the article passion quickly turns from a term of praise to one of condemnation. Hart's rhetoric reframes Fuller and Radbruch as muddled thinkers who have let their passion get the better of them. This too maps directly onto a theory of law which privileges simplicity and certainty as *necessary* aspects of legal meaning 'if we are to communicate with each other at all, as in the most elementary form of law';[14] and from which perspective passion is a pitfall to be avoided.

Hart and Fuller's differing metaphors are not just argumentative tools but a manifestation of their differing ideas of law. For Fuller reflection and circularity are merits of legal analysis. For Hart they are demerits. Thus, it is already an argument against Fuller that his theory 'would seem to raise a whole host of philosophical issues before it can be accepted';[15] such issues 'confuse one of the most powerful, *because* it is the simplest, forms of moral criticism'.[16] Yet for Fuller, law loses its legitimacy when it refuses to engage with just these issues. Law's besetting sin for Hart is uncertainty; clarity is its salvation. Law's besetting sin for Fuller is arrogance—the assumption that we know what we mean; doubt is its salvation. Turning and circularity are sins for Hart and virtues for Fuller. The rhetoric of these two essays place the reader in the position of *experiencing* two radically different voices engaged in legal reasoning, rather than merely reading about them.

There is a paradox in this. The rhetoric of both Hart and Fuller involves an unqualified rejection of the terms, the affect and the priorities of the other. It

8 *Ibid* 662, 666.
9 *Ibid* 667.
10 *Ibid* 670.
11 *Ibid* 614–15, 620–1; see also 594.
12 *Ibid* 615–19.
13 *Ibid* 595–6.
14 *Ibid* 607.
15 *Ibid* 620.
16 *Ibid* 620.

leads, particularly in the case of Hart, to increasingly shrill rhetorical gestures in which his opponents are accused first of passion, and then of naivety, obscurity, hysteria, insincerity and dishonesty. But at the same time their efforts to exclude the other's argument fail. As I will have occasion to illustrate below, Hart's positivism fails to establish the 'reality' of law which is its sole goal, while Fuller's morality constantly falls back on positivism to establish the ethics of law which is its sole goal.

Even on their own terms, the Hart–Fuller debate does not leave one side victorious. But neither can we compromise or balance the two positions, since the *commitment* they demand is absolute: there is no such thing as positivism or purposivism 'now and then' since it is precisely the problem of where to start that is at stake. Nor is a synthesis possible since if we have one we necessarily do not have the other. We need both positions to make sense of law, but it is impossible to acknowledge them both at once. Instead we experience an 'oscillation' from one incommensurable language and approach to the other. The positions they represent are mutually contradictory, and equally necessary. This is the paradox which Derrida discusses in 'Force of Law'.[17] Here, too, there is an ineradicable tension between justice as sameness and justice as difference, between laws as rules and law as irreducible to rules. 'Between justice (infinite, incalculable, rebellious to rule and foreign to symmetry) and the exercise of justice as law or right, legitimacy or legality, stabilizable and statutory, calculable, a system of regulated and coded prescriptions'[18] we cannot *choose* since our commitment is neither synthesisable into a unity nor prioritisable into a hierarchy.

The irresolute relationship dramatised by Hart and Fuller, like the relationship between justice or ethics[19] and law, suggests that legal interpretation is neither 'amoral', as Hart has it, or 'moral', as Fuller has it, but *haunted.* Why do we have ghost stories? Why do they affect us? The ghost is that unsettling figure of some thing which cannot be accommodated within a specific worldview. It hovers on the periphery of our vision and alerts us to an incommensurable reality which we can neither incorporate in our structures *nor* ignore.[20] The rest of this chapter will elaborate this argument and why it matters to the Hart–Fuller debate and to law.

[17] Derrida, 'Force of Law', n 3 above; Drucilla Cornell *et al*, *Deconstruction and the Possibility of Justice* (New York, Routledge, 1994). See Peter Goodrich, *et al* (eds), *Derrida and Legal Philosophy* (London, Palgrave Macmillan, 2008).

[18] Derrida, 'Force of Law', n 3 above, at 959; see also 'Before the Law' in Derek Attridge (ed), *Acts of Literature* (London, Routledge, 1992) 181–220.

[19] Derrida, 'Before the Law', n 18 above, esp at 153–62.

[20] Gordon, n 3 above; Flessas, n 3 above; see Emmanuel Levinas, *Otherwise than Being* (Alphonso Lingis (trans), Duquesne, Pittsburgh University Press, 1981; 1st edn 1974) ch V esp at 165–71.

Certainty and Madness

The Turn of the Screw is about law and this unsettling relationship. A young woman is hired by a man called the Master as governess for two young children. Only one condition attaches to her employment: 'that she should never trouble him—but never, never; neither appeal nor complain nor write about anything; only meet all questions herself'.[21] The governess, like a judge, is confronted by the lack of any ultimate authority, whether human or textual, from whom a *definitive* answer can be wrested. We can stare at the text or talk to God or the Master, but they won't talk back. This is law's condition and the judge's anxiety: never to trouble the Master again.

The Turn of the Screw explores the consequences of a search for an unambiguous interpretation which precisely *because* it eludes us, stimulates our actions. The Master forwards a letter which hints at shameful behaviour by Miles, the young boy in the governess' care. This letter too provides no explanation but only an effect—the boy is expelled—which leaves the governess with a mystery to solve. More than one. Ghosts begin to encircle the estate. But they too are nebulous, like 'nothing' and 'no one', their form indescribable, their aims unspoken. The reader, like the governess, is faced with an interpretative absence. The Master, the letters and the ghosts: all are imperturbable 'figures of silence'.[22]

When the governess finally breaks the only law she was commanded to keep and writes to the Master, Miles steals the letter. But this too turns out to be a silence not an answer.

> 'You opened it?'
> 'I opened it.' ...
> 'And you found nothing!'—I let my elation out.
> He gave me the most mournful, thoughtful little headshake. 'Nothing.'
> 'Nothing, nothing!' I almost shouted in my joy.
> 'Nothing, nothing', he sadly repeated.
> I kissed his forehead; it was drenched. 'So what have you done with it.'
> 'I've burnt it.'[23]

The indecipherable, silent and charred, has no determined meaning, but it nevertheless produces *effects*.[24] As Shoshana Felman insists in a reading of the story to which I am heavily indebted:

> We have seen how the letters become a crucial dramatic element in the narrative plot precisely because of their unreadability ... [I]t is precisely because the letters fail to

[21] James, n 1 above, Prologue, 6.
[22] Shoshana Felman, 'Turning the Screw of Interpretation' (1977) 55/56 *Yale French Studies* 94.
[23] James, n 1 above, XXIV, 140–1.
[24] See Derrida, 'Before the Law', n 18 above.

> narrate, to construct a coherent transparent story, that there is a story at all: there is a story because there is an unreadable, an unconscious.[25]

In other words, the governess' frantic need to make sense of her responsibility in the *absence* of any judgement but her own intensifies her anxious search for certainty.[26] Like a judge, she cannot know, in any absolute way, what is going on around her. And like a judge she nevertheless *must* know and decide. This compulsion or legal obligation increasingly governs her theory—a theory in which doubt becomes impossible and those who oppose her are treated as mad.

The strategy of the governess lies in characterising doubt as an anomaly and an irritation. Time and again, the governess insists on banishing ignorance, on her need to 'have mastered it, to see it all', to 'know everything'.[27] Throughout the novel her narrating voice firmly rejects any interpretative possibilities but hers. She is certain, she is beyond doubt. Events 'can have but one meaning' (a core); 'but one sane inference' (an even-minded sanity). 'If I had ever doubted', she insists, 'all my doubt would at present have gone'.[28]

> 'He was looking for little Miles.' A portentous clearness now possessed me. 'That's whom he was looking for.'
>
> 'But how do you know?'
>
> 'I know, I know, I know!' My exaltation grew. 'And you know, my dear!'[29]

The governess is well aware that she might be thought to be a little mad. 'I go on, I know, as if I were crazy; and it's a wonder I'm not. What I've seen would have made *you* so; but it has only made me more lucid, made me get hold of still other things.'[30] She believes that the only thing that keeps her sane and allows her to 'take hold' of the situation is her insistence on the certainty of what she knows and sees.[31] Her final insistence (and it is Hart's too) is that *someone* has to be mad: and it isn't her.[32]

Yet no one but the governess ever sees these ghosts. Indeed, she is oddly certain of a whole host of details: that the two ghosts have come back to claim the two children; that the children have seen and communicated with them, though they deny it; and that this communication will kill them. All this is merely posited by the governess. But whence comes her authority? 'I just know' is the governess' mantra, and her dogmatic rhetoric dominates the text and quenches doubt just as it dominates Mrs Grose, the governess' trusting confidante. Only in retrospect did I wonder why, in my reading of the tale, having sensed that there was something

[25] Felman, n 22 above.

[26] Edmund Wilson, 'The Ambiguity of Henry James' in *The Triple Thinkers: Twelve Essays on Literary Subjects* (New York, Penguin, 1962).

[27] James, n 1 above, II, 13; III, 17; XXI, 128; XXIV, 141.

[28] *Ibid* II, 17; IV, 29; XX, 119. See also Felman, n 22 above, at 154–5.

[29] James, n 1 above, VI, 40.

[30] *Ibid* XII, 79.

[31] *Ibid* VI, 40. See also *ibid* XX.

[32] *Ibid* XII, 78–9; Felman, n 22 above, at 194–5.

implausible or at least unexplained in the governess' account, I chose instead to take as certain and unambiguous everything I was told. It is in *this* way that the ghost story is experienced by the reader: as a shadow of doubt and of unanswered questions which are sensed but never seen, felt but instantly repressed.

Felman argues that *The Turn of the Screw* is about interpretation:

> The governess's whole adventure turns out to be, essentially, a reading-adventure, a quest for the definite, literal or proper meaning of words and of events.[33]

The ghosts the governess sees are the dead figures of her predecessors, Peter Quint, the estate manager, and Miss Jessel, the governess. Both, like the governess, were given free licence by the Master though we are told that both used that freedom for 'evil' not for good. Now they are back from the dead, to conquer the children 'for the love of all the evil that, in those dreadful days, the pair put into them [a]nd to ply them with that evil still'.[34] The two ghosts are the mirror image of the governess. They gave a corrupting knowledge; the governess provides a protective innocence. Yet the governess and the servants are two sides of the same coin. What haunts the governess is precisely the uncertainty of a different interpretation, of different choices *equally* mandated by the Master's sphinx-like silence. The ghosts represent the excluded, the inexplicable, the unpredictable, the denied, the possibility of error, the threat of otherwise—all those things which a dogmatic literalism rejects as irrelevant to 'the disposition of the ordinary case'.[35]

Hart behaves like the governess. He insists on a 'core of certainty' if we are to have law at all.[36] That which is not certain is for Hart not law in this 'centrally important' and 'necessary' sense.[37] Indeed in Hart's essay, certainty and plainness become the *exclusive* criterion for the validity of an argument, against which ambiguity or doubt is the very best reason simply to dismiss his opponents as mysterious or confused. In relation to Hart's own method of argument, the penumbra is not simply marginalised; it is illegitimate.

But legal certainty comes at a high price. In order to protect the determinate 'core' of legal interpretation, Hart's penumbra becomes very shadowy indeed. His treatment of cases in which meaning is not certain is radically different from cases in which it is. To 'soften this distinction' is, in Hart's view, a terrible error.[38] While the latter is 'necessary' if we are to have law at all, the former is only 'inevitable'.[39] Above all, Hart treats judges' use of 'social policy' or their understanding of the 'growing needs of society' in deciding the meaning of a legal rule as a process entirely unrelated to 'the normal case'. Discovering the 'core' of legal meaning is both utterly different from penumbral reasoning and counts as law,

33 Felman, n 22 above, at 153.
34 James, n 1 above, XII, 79.
35 Hart, 'Positivism and the Separation of Law and Morals', n 6 above, at 620.
36 *Ibid* 607.
37 *Ibid* 615.
38 *Ibid* 615.
39 *Ibid* 607.

moreover, 'in some centrally important sense' *denied* to the penumbra.[40] In attempting to narrow the grey areas that Fuller sees as permeating all of law, Hart's strategy is to bathe the core in a harsh and doubtless light: and to cast out the penumbra as irrelevant to it. At this point Hart and Fuller begin to swap positions before our eyes. Hart looks like the prophet of uncertainty, conceding that in these grey areas judges might be guided by the morality of law, or by something (anything) else.[41] On the other hand, it is Fuller who attempts to bring legality back to *every* part of law, insisting that interpretation in core and penumbra alike are guided by knowable practices of legal reasoning.

Hart's response to Radbruch exemplifies the failure of his strategy to achieve its goals. As Fuller points out, Hart seems to treat the war-time 'informant cases' as the workings of a perfectly ordinary legal system which just happened to be devoted to 'odious' purposes.[42] Hart writes:

> The wife was under no legal duty to report his acts, though what he had said was apparently in violation of statutes making it illegal to make statements detrimental to the government of the Third Reich ... The husband was arrested and sentenced to death, apparently pursuant to these statutes, though he was not executed but was sent to the front ... The wife pleaded that her husband's imprisonment was pursuant to the Nazi statutes and hence that she had committed no crime.[43]

In fact, German courts operated with no such clarity.[44] Indeed, the use of secret and retroactive laws, the politicisation of the judiciary, the abandonment of neutrality, and so on, were well in place by 1935.[45] Part II of the new Criminal Code read:

> Punishment is to be inflicted on anyone who commits an act which has been declared punishable under the law or who deserves to be punished according to the fundamental principles of a criminal statute and healthy popular sentiment.[46]

Of the actual operation of Nazi courts, Hart is blissfully ignorant. This ignorance is not just coincidental; it is intrinsic to his approach to 'core' legal reasoning. Hart's repeated use of the word 'apparently' is significant. The man was '*apparently* in violation of statutes'; he was arrested and punished '*apparently* pursuant to these statutes'. Fuller tells us that things were not as they appeared in Nazi Germany. But for Hart the appearance of law is all that matters. Politics and history are irrelevant to our inquiry. We rely instead on the simple surface and

[40] *Ibid* 612–14.
[41] *Ibid* 607–8.
[42] Fuller, 'Positivism and Fidelity to Law', n 7 above, at 650.
[43] Hart, 'Positivism and the Separation of Law and Morals', n 6 above, at 618–19.
[44] Fuller, 'Positivism and Fidelity to Law', n 7 above, at 650–5.
[45] Otto Kirchheimer, 'State Structure and Law in the Third Reich' in Franz Neumann and Otto Kirchheimer, *The Rule of Law under Seige* (William Scheuerman (ed), Berkeley, CA, University of California Press, 1996) 145–7; see also the posthumous collection of the writing of Franz Neumann, *The Rule of Law* (Leamington Spa, Berg, 1986).
[46] Kirchheimer, n 45 above, at 146.

clear meaning of words—with the result in this case that we are seriously misled as to what those words actually meant to the people who were sentenced to death or (since 'sentenced to death' did not actually mean 'sentenced to death') sent to the Eastern front. As we read Hart's account of the case, it surely seems plausible that the Nazi regime in fact depended on a kind of blindness to anything but the formal semblance of legality in order to gain legitimacy for its actions. Hart himself refuses to look behind the court's statements and treats as legally sufficient the mere 'tinsel of legal form'.[47] The paradox of this is that Hart's positivism wishes to separate 'is' from 'ought', the morality from the reality of law. But his interest in the form rather than the substance of legal processes prevents us from adequately understanding the lived experience of those legal facts, and therefore from understanding just what law truly 'is'. That is the first turn of the screw. Hart's positivism demonstrates its own *ignorance* of legal reality.

The accusation of 'naïveté' Hart levels at Radbruch is better directed at himself. Indeed, naivety is for Hart positivism's greatest *virtue*: its refusal, when words 'apparently' mean one thing, to wonder whether—not just in point of justice but in point of fact—they might actually mean something else. Positivist method glorifies this willful blindness. In consequence, Hart trusts a corrupt legal system's claim that it was 'apparently' just applying the law. Clearly that affords the legal system a respectability it did not deserve. This is the danger which, according to Radbruch and Fuller, lies in positivist reasoning. Hart falls for it himself.

What makes this hard to see is the rhetorical force which is brought to bear to control and limit our interpretations. At the end of *The Turn of the Screw*, Miles and the governess finally confront one another. The governess aims to extract from him the ultimate and most perfect form of knowledge: a confession. This confession will (apparently) establish her authority over the child and destroy forever the ghosts' power.[48] 'The child's confession', says Felman, 'would thus constitute the crowning achievement of the governess's enterprise of reading: the definitive denomination—by means of language—of both truth and meaning'.[49] Felman demonstrates the violence inherent in this 'mastery' and in particular its repression of alternative possibilities. Whether performed by the Master or the governess or an author or interpreter, a literal reading which denies the place of uncertainty in any text works because it blinds us to the ambiguities we thereby choose to ignore, and to the violence which imposes a single, exclusive frame of reference.[50]

The two children in this story are the object of law's interpretative power; for the 'governess' is the government of the child. The narrator's strategy is to possess all knowledge herself and to repress all doubt. When, in the great final scene, she

[47] Fuller, 'Positivism and Fidelity to Law', n 7 above, at 660.
[48] James, n 1 above, XXIV, 139–42.
[49] Felman, n 22 above, at 160.
[50] *Ibid* 190–2.

finally bullies some fractured information from Miles, her reasserted control at 'his supreme surrender of the name and his tribute to my devotion'[51] is profoundly visceral:

> It was like fighting with a demon for a human soul, and when I had fairly so appraised it I saw how the human soul—held out, in the tremor of my hands, at arm's length—had a perfect dew of sweat on a lovely childish forehead. The face that was close to mine was as white as the [ghost's] face against the glass, and out of it presently came a sound, not low nor weak, but as if from much further away, that I drank like a waft of fragrance.
>
> 'Yes—I took it.'
>
> At this, with a moan of joy, I enfolded, I drew him close.[52]

In Hart and James alike, interpretation is no passive reception but the active exertion of control, discipline, limitation and exclusion, shored up by forceful rhetoric and willful blindness. Interpretation is an exercise in control which, like madness, accepts only a single viewpoint and rules out all contradictory evidence:[53]

> To see is therefore paradoxically not only to perceive but also not to perceive: to actively determine an area as invisible, as excluded from perception, as external by definition to visibility.[54]

Madness is the hysterical response of an anxious soul to doubt. The madness of the governess lies not in the ghosts she sees but in the exclusion of alternatives and the dogmatism to which her anxiety drives her. *The Turn of the Screw* is truly remarkable in persuading the reader to *share* in that madness. The madness of Hart's project is similar, and he too marshals exceptional rhetorical resources to ensure our complicity.

Three Dimensions of a Death

Nothing, however, can prepare the reader for the shock of the final page.[55] Miles having finally admitted his knowledge of and communion with Jessel and Quint, the governess is convinced she has triumphed over mystery and uncertainty, the ghostly unknown finally exiled from the law:

[51] James, n 1 above, XXIV.
[52] *Ibid* XXIV, 140.
[53] Felman, n 22 above, at 194–5.
[54] *Ibid* 166.
[55] I apologise to those of my readers who have not yet read *The Turn of the Screw* for I must spoil this effect by revealing it.

> They are in my ears still, his supreme surrender of the name and his tribute to my devotion. 'What does he matter now, my own?—what will he ever matter? I have you', I launched at the beast, 'but he has lost you forever!' Then, for the demonstration of my work, 'There, there!' I said to Miles.
>
> But he had already jerked straight round, stared, glared again, and seen but the quiet day. With the stroke of the loss I was so proud of he uttered the cry of a creature hurled over an abyss, and the grasp with which I recovered him might have been that of catching him in his fall. I caught him, yes, I held him—it may be imagined with what a passion; but at the end of a minute I began to feel what it truly was that I held. We were alone with the quiet day, and his little heart, dispossessed, had stopped.[56]

Has ever one sentence so comprehensively transformed our understanding of a book? The loss of the ghost is the death of the child. Now all our doubts flood in on us with giddying force. It little matters whether the ghost has killed the child or whether the smothering embrace of the governess was responsible; whether indeed the ghosts existed outside the anxious imagination of the impressionable young governess. Either way, her insistence on total control of the child is ill-starred and unjust. The final turn of the screw is the hardest. His little heart, dispossessed, had stopped.

The Morbid Turn

The first dimension of this death is perhaps its depiction of positivism's 'morbid turn'.[57] The effort to extract doubt from the law offers only the certainty of its death. A law which has been dispossessed of what is not strictly derivable from its own text, whether we call that its ghost or its purpose, is a law rendered inorganic. Said JM Portalis, the principal author of the *Code Civil*:

> A Code, however complete it may seem, is no sooner finished than thousands of unexpected questions present themselves to the magistrate. For these laws, once drafted, remain as written. Men, on the other hand, never rest. They are always moving; and this movement, which never ceases and whose effects are variously modified by circumstances, continually produces some new fact, some new outcome.[58]

Fuller describes as morbid and fearful positivism's rejection of an interpretative mode never closed to the challenges of social change. Many writers over the past 50 years[59] have elaborated on this unruly element as a necessary transformative engine *within* legal interpretation.

[56] James, n 1 above, XXIV, 144–5.

[57] Fuller, 'Positivism and Fidelity to Law', n 7 above, at 670.

[58] JM Portalis, *Preliminary Address, delivered on the occasion of the presentation of the draft of the government commission, on 1 Pluviôse IX (21 January 1801)* (International Cooperation Group (trans), Ottawa, Department of Justice of Canada, 2004) 6.

[59] Derrida, 'Force of Law', n 3 above; Levinas, n 20 above; Desmond Manderson, *Proximity, Levinas and the Soul of Law* (Montreal & Kingston, McGill-Queen's University Press, 2006); Philippe

The moment of every legal decision requires us to judge how to apply prior general norms to the new and singular situation before us. A judge trying to decide whether the current dispute fits within established categories must always confront the fact that they have a *choice*: we must still decide if this case is 'the same as' or 'different from' the past, and, obvious or difficult, this is one choice that the past cannot ever help us with. Although the choice is admittedly highly visible 'in the penumbra', every case requires us to make the same kind of decision. Judgement always entails not a choice but the *possibility* of a choice, the ghost of a chance. For Derrida, who uncannily unites both Fuller and James, this problem is not capable of being limited to the penumbra or defined in advance:

> The undecidable remains caught, lodged, at least as a ghost—but an essential ghost—in every decision, in every event of decision. Its ghostliness deconstructs from within any assurance of presence, any certitude or any supposed criteriology that would assure us of the justice of a decision, in truth of the very event of a decision.[60]

So 'the ghost of the undecidable'[61] describes how justice influences our reading of the law without ever being adequately specifiable within the rules, and in fact remaining strictly incommensurable to them.[62]

There are, of course, serious risks posed by such an approach to guard against which positivism responds with morbid anxiety.[63] But 'whoever sought to be just by economizing on anxiety?'[64] The governess strove to keep her charges safe and innocent forever. She attempted to control and know everything, to remove all anxiety and doubt.[65] But the risk posed by the ghost's evil, and the fear of uncertainty that lay over these events, she averted at the cost of Miles' life. As Felman points out, as well as being a ghost story, *The Turn of the Screw* is a murder mystery with a difference: the crime is committed not at the beginning but at the end of the story, and the detective is the culprit:

> The self-proclaimed detective ends up discovering that he himself is the author of the crime he is investigating: that the crime is his, and that he is, himself, the criminal he seeks ... for it is by the very act of forcing her suspect to confess that the governess ends up committing the crime she is investigating.[66]

To me, nothing better explains Fuller's assessment that positivism's desire to protect an interpretative innocence is allied to the death of legality, in Nazi Germany and beyond.

Nonet and Philip Selznick, *Law and Society in Transition: Towards Responsive Law* (New York, Harper & Row, 1978); Olivier Abel, *Paul Ricoeur, La promesse et la regle* (Paris, Michalon, 1996).

60 Derrida, 'Force of Law', n 3 above, at 965.

61 *Ibid* 963.

62 Derrida, *Specters of Marx*, n 3 above, at xix.

63 Fuller, 'Positivism and Fidelity to Law', n 7 above, at 669–71.

64 Derrida, 'Force of Law', n 3 above.

65 For example, James, n 1 above, XXIV, 139; see also *Ibid* VI.

66 Felman, n 22 above, at 175–6.

Losing the Core

A second dimension lies in the form of *The Turn of the Screw*. As I have already noted, the genius of James' story lies in its performativity: the *effect* of ghostliness it produces in the reader. In particular, the unsettling power of that last sentence lies not just in how it requires one to retrospectively reinterpret the whole novel, but in our awareness that these new interpretations had always been there, dormant and repressed as we surrendered to the governess' narrative control. The last sentence, then, works as a kind of ghost: for me it brought forth all the doubts about the governess' tale which, shadowy and unacknowledged, had haunted the edge of my consciousness throughout, and which by force of will I had avoided thinking about.

To read a story is to 'suspend disbelief'. But I thought I knew what disbelief I was supposed to suspend (certain core assumptions were obvious and unassailable), and in that last sentence my own reading and my own certainty suddenly collapsed around me. At that moment, the core meaning of the story was overturned. Yet that is exactly what Hart rules out, because to imagine it as an *ever-present possibility* 'is to assert that there is no central element of actual law to be seen in the core of central meaning which rules have, that there is nothing in the nature of a legal rule inconsistent with all questions being open to reconsideration in the light of social policy'.[67]

Hart is right to draw attention to this issue. For Fuller, all law is about our encounter with the unexpected, and in face of the unexpected even the so-called core of a legal provision ('I know, I know, I know! . . . And *you* know, my dear!')[68] may become 'open to reconsideration'. In that way, Fuller insists that 'core' and 'penumbra' are not two radically divergent paths of attributing meaning but aspects of the one process. As Fuller says, the purpose of reflection on the penumbra lies not just in helping us deal with grey areas, but in clarifying for us what the law was about all along.[69] This clarification may change whether we decide that a 'truck' (and not just a 'roller blade') is a vehicle (for the purposes of a regulation). In short, there are, for Fuller, no '"standard instances" that remain constant regardless of context'.[70]

[67] Hart, 'Positivism and the Separation of Law and Morals', n 6 above, at 615.

[68] James, n 1 above, VI, 40.

[69] Fuller, 'Positivism and Fidelity to Law', n 7 above, at 668.

[70] *Ibid* 663. Once again, Hart comes close to making Fuller's case for him. Hart writes of the formalist, 'He either does not see or pretends not to see that the general terms of this rule are susceptible of different interpretations and that he has a choice left open uncontrolled by linguistic conventions. He ignores, or is blind to, the fact that he is in the area of the penumbra and is not dealing with a standard case' (at 610). The formalist's problem is that he mistakenly treats the penumbra as if it were the core; but according to Hart this does not undermine the correctness of Hart's analysis 'in the core'. But on the next page Hart's example of social and penumbral reasoning is Justice Peckham's decision in *Lochner v New York* (1905) 19 U.S. 45 (US Supreme Court). For Hart this shows that judges do, as they must and whether we like it or not, make 'clear choices in the penumbral area to give effect to policy' (at 611). But this is just what Justice Peckham did *not* think he

For Hart, what is at stake is our ability to control future decisions through 'the notion that rules have authority'.[71] Law looks forward: it prescribes and limits outcomes. For Fuller, what is at stake is our ability to reinterpret past decisions in light of purposes which we do *not* already know and which are in some measure always emergent. Law looks backward: it describes and reassesses our goals. Looking backwards on our prior decisions in light of our present predicament, we notice things to which we previously were blind, yet that on reflection are crucial to our understanding. It would be entirely wrong to say that this is what we 'always' or 'really' meant. Rather, interpretation is the process by which we keep learning and relearning what we mean. Perhaps that is why Hart condemns 'retrospective' laws while Fuller condemns 'retroactive' ones.[72] A retroactive law undermines the rule of law because it *acts* on past behaviour, changing the legal meaning attributed to prior conduct. On the other hand, there is for Fuller something retrospective about *all* laws since our understanding of the meaning of even core terms depends on a ceaseless reflection; what has elsewhere been termed law's 'fabulous retroactivity'.[73]

The Turn of the Screw illustrates precisely how shifts in perspective unsettle the core of a reading. The story lulls us into an interpretative laziness which assumes that some questions are just not 'open for reconsideration', and then traumatically wakes us up. On the very last line, all our prior certainty is retrospectively undone. The core of our interpretation (its 'standard instances', its self-evident assumptions) is revealed to be deeply flawed, which flaw, we now perceive, was already lurking in the shadows of our earlier reading. Doubt or uncertainty is the ghost which necessarily haunts any reading. The ghosts of *The Turn of the Screw* were both invisible and there all along.

In *The Turn of the Screw,* that humbling moment of recognition arrives only in retrospect:

> I held him—it may be imagined with what a passion; but at the end of a minute I began to feel what it truly was that I held.[74]

So sure is the governess that her passion and love is the 'standard instance' of her goodness that Miles is dead before she notices it. Without a ceaseless interrogation of our assumptions—without attending to the penumbra or ghost of the law which hovers unwelcome but insistent on our periphery—there can be no

was doing at all. Rather he believed himself to be applying nothing but the unalterable and acontextual core of the legal regulation in question. Justice Peckham *believed* he had no discretion. If this shows anything, it shows that core and penumbra are never self-identifying, and that consequently the problem that Hart identifies as 'formalism'—to be 'blind to the fact that [one] is in the area of the penumbra and is not dealing with a standard case'—is a much more significant and widespread problem than Hart acknowledges.

71 Hart, 'Positivism and the Separation of Law and Morals', n 6 above, at 615.

72 Hart uses 'retrospective' three times and 'retroactive' never; Fuller 'retroactive' nine times and 'retrospective' never.

73 Jacques Derrida, 'Declarations of Independence' (1986) 15 *New Political Science* 7.

74 James, n 1 above, XXIV, 145.

improvement in our understanding. Keats described 'negative capability' as the essential force that 'went to form a man of achievement, especially in literature'.[75] Law and literature find themselves possessed of the same 'uncertainties, mysteries, doubts'. It is how each in their way struggle to prevent a death.

The Trap of Interpretation

There is a third dimension to our experience, as readers, of Miles' death. In the New York Preface, James declares he has created a trap 'to catch those not easily caught (the fun of the capture of the merely witless being ever small)'.[76] If the repression of doubt is symptomatic of the governess' madness, *The Turn of the Screw* traps us in it. One way it does so is by persuading us to accept the governess' reading of events. But another way is by inviting us to reject it. As Felman explains:

> The reader of the *Turn of the Screw* can choose either to believe the governess and thus to behave like Mrs Grose, or not to believe the governess and thus to behave precisely like the governess ... To demystify the governess is only possible on one condition: the condition of repeating the governess's very gesture ... It is the very gesture of exclusion which includes: to exclude the governess—as mad—from the place of meaning and of truth is precisely to repeat her very gesture of exclusion, to include oneself, in other words, within her very madness.[77]

James' 'trap' is that of *any* categorical reading in which haunting disappears, whether the ghosts are reduced to elements of the governess' material landscape on one reading, or to figments of her psychological landscape on another.[78] We risk either believing the governess or substituting her certainty with another (as she in turn replaced the servants who now haunt her).

Here is a further turn of the screw. While Fuller rejects Hart's reading of events, he too ends up 'repeating the governess's very gestures'. When we look at Fuller's critique of the statutes in question we find that his 'internal morality of law' is based entirely on questions of procedure. Principles such as judicial objectivity, legal clarity of expression, and the impropriety of secret or retrospective

[75] I am grateful to Peter Fitzpatrick for the allusion and the quote.

[76] Henry James, New York Preface to *The Turn of the Screw*, Robert Kimbrough (ed) (New York, WW Norton, Critical Edition, 1966) 120; see Felman, n 22 above, at 185 *et seq*. Here a very brief personal reflection or perhaps, as the governess would have it, confession. The only other story to have had a like effect on me was *Sixth Sense* (M Night Shyamalan director, 1999), another ghost story whose shocking conclusion led me to a most embarrassing and, frankly, uncontrollable fit of crying. I think part of the trauma I experienced in watching this film is attributable in a similar way to narrative instability and the way in which it requires us to retell the whole story, from the beginning, in a new light. There is I think something traumatic in having one's interpretation confronted in this way. See also *The Others* (Alejandro Amenábar director, 2001) which is based, if thinly, on *The Turn of the Screw*.

[77] Felman, n 22 above, at 190, 196. See also Wilson, n 26 above.

[78] Felman, n 22 above, at 185–90.

legislation—are these not the very aspirations of Hart's positivism? For example, Fuller analyses the statute under which the wife reported her husband:

> Extended comment on this legislative monstrosity is scarcely called for, overlarded and undermined as it is by uncontrolled administrative discretion. We may note only: first, that it offers no justification whatever for the death penalty actually imposed on the husband, though never carried out; second, that if the wife's act in informing on her husband made his remarks 'public', there is no such thing as a private utterance under this statute.[79]

Fuller argues that the Nazi courts got it wrong. He thinks that the words used in these laws had some objective and necessary content which the courts ignored. How is this different from Hart's insistence that the meaning of any word (such as 'public') must include 'some standard instance in which no doubts are felt about its application?'.[80] Again, Fuller argues that the Nazi regime's resort to retroactive legislation, to untrammelled administrative discretion, and their willingness to 'disregard any statute … if it suited their convenience', made impossible 'a lawyer-like interpretation'.[81] Fuller's criticism is not that the German regime was too positivist, but on the contrary that it was not 'lawyer-like', rule-bound—in short, not positivist enough.[82]

Fuller faces a further difficulty. He refuses to accept any 'uniform principle of judicial interpretation'[83] in Nazi Germany because of the immorality of those principles. Indeed, Fuller's essay treats the distinction between 'goodness' and 'evil', a word he uses over a dozen times, as self-evident, merely asserting that 'coherence and goodness have more affinity than coherence and evil'.[84] Fuller does not acknowledge Nazism did not merely corrupt a legal system. It realised a *vision* of it informed by the anti-positivist ideologies of German Romanticism up to and including Heidegger and Schmitt.[85] Neither does he acknowledge that the problem is not that law-makers might develop an 'immoral morality' or 'a more

79 Fuller, 'Positivism and Fidelity to Law', n 7 above, at 654–5.

80 Hart, 'Positivism and the Separation of Law and Morals', n 6 above, at 607.

81 Fuller, 'Positivism and Fidelity to Law', n 7 above, at 652.

82 As Prof Macdonald pointed out to me in the course of many helpful conversations I have had with him on this subject, there is nevertheless a distinction between thinking of positivism as about the objective content of meaning, as does Hart, and a lawyer-like 'interpretation' which privileges instead, as does Fuller, the dialogue and protocols of argument. While it might then be said that Fuller's concern with Nazi legality was not their abandonment of the meaning of words but their abandonment of the process of reasoning, I nevertheless think it fair to say that, particularly in light of Fuller's concern with the meaning of the word 'public', above, the line between Hart and Fuller is very fine here.

83 Fuller, 'Positivism and Fidelity to Law', n 7 above, at 654.

84 *Ibid* 636.

85 See in particular George Mosse, *The Crisis of German Ideology: Intellectual Origins of the Third Reich* (New York, Grosset and Dunlap, 1964); and Pierre Bourdieu, *The Political Ontology of Martin Heidegger* (Peter Collier (trans), Stanford University Press, 1991); Carl Schmitt, *Political Theology: Four Chapters on the Concept of Sovereignty* (George Schwab (ed), University of Chicago Press, 2006); *Legality and Legitimacy* (Chapel Hill, NC, Duke University Press, 2004). See also Ian Ward, *Law, Philosophy and National Socialism: Heidegger, Schmitt, and Radbruch* (Bern & Frankfurt, Peter Lang

perfect realization of iniquity',[86] but rather that we disagree about what goodness is in law or in laws. By assuming a core of goodness and a core of evil, which can never be confused, he simplifies the problem which confronts many societies, those who lived during the Third Reich not least.[87]

Fuller's argument therefore ultimately *returns* to positivism. First, he defends clarity and objectivity in law as a necessary interpretative practice. Secondly, he appears to stabilise legal interpretation by resort to an objectivist morality which he had earlier rejected in relation to law. Fuller, like James' critics, merely repeats the gesture of the governor. He tries to make the ghost disappear, to bring them back to the land of the living, simply by replacing one stabilising 'Master signifier'[88] (linguistic meaning) with another (morality). At this moment he falls back on positivism's insistence on the need for mastery over uncertainty. One is either a positivist or one repeats the gestures of positivism; one either believes the governess' totalising worldview or replaces it with one's own. Fuller is caught in James' trap, which is to say Hart's.

Preserving Law's Ghosts

Ghosts haunt every reading. They are figures of shadow and doubt which *interrupt* our certainty, unassimilable within the structure of reasoning mandated by the text or system, and yet unable to be refuted or ignored. The ghost is the relic of another realm which our established framework can neither explain nor explain away.

Yet *The Turn of the Screw* holds an enduring fascination because it does *not* replace one narrative 'truth' with another. James refuses to wrest from his readers *their* interpretative authority. He will not tell us 'the truth':

> But isn't this precisely what the Master does in *The Turn of the Screw*, when, dispossessing the governess of her Master (himself), he gives her nothing less than 'supreme authority'? It is with 'supreme authority' indeed that James, in deconstructing his own mastery, vests his reader. But isn't this gift of supreme authority bestowed upon the reader as upon the governess the very thing that will precisely *drive them mad*?[89]

Our reading remains ineradicably haunted by the undecidability of the text and by the strange way in which its different possibilities continually colour one another.

Verlag, 1992); David Dyzenhaus: *Law as Politics: Carl Schmitt's Critique of Liberalism* (Chapel Hill, NC, Duke University Press, 1998); Mark Antaki, 'Carl Schmitt's *Nomos of the Earth*' (2004) 42 *Osgoode Hall Law Journal* 317.

[86] Fuller, 'Positivism and Fidelity to Law', n 7 above, at 636.

[87] See Hannah Arendt, *Eichmann in Jerusalem* (New York, Penguin, 1994 [1963]).

[88] The phrase is, of course, something of a cliché within deconstruction and post-structural theory, but it is doubly apposite here in its precise reference to the interpretative theories at play in James' ghost story, and in its resonances with theories of law.

[89] Felman, n 22 above, at 206.

The question in the context of legal interpretation is this: How we can respect those ghosts without succumbing to James' trap: either denying their existence (as does Hart) or incorporating them into a new system (as does Fuller) which as we have seen tames and positivises them? What would it mean to preserve Fuller's haunting voice—the still, small, uncomfortable disruptions of 'the ordinary case'—*as* ghosts rather than merely attempting to reduce them into a new and perfected system?[90] Throughout this chapter I have insisted that James' novel is performative. And I have likewise sought to understand Hart and Fuller as each performing distinct visions of legal reasoning. The answer to my question lies in understanding Hart *and* Fuller as providing us with a performance of law; jointly rather than separately, as two actors in the same play jointly create a performance.

Neither Hart nor Fuller is right.[91] But neither can we mix a cocktail composed of bits of each of them. Instead, the *antagonism* between them, and the anxiety that disagreement forges, captures the unique virtue of legal interpretation, for ever caught between simultaneous, contradictory and uncompromisable[92] goals to be faithful to the rules before them and to the promise behind them.[93] Henry James offers us a literature which preserves the tension between different readings and refuses to defuse it. Of recent writers, Derrida has most consistently explored the nature and productivity of such insoluble antagonisms.[94] Thus, responsibility and accountability are not opposites or choices: they are incommensurable forces that provide us with a deeper understanding of each though we are constantly forced to betray them in our attempts to realise them.[95] So too he speaks of a 'tension at the heart of the heritage' between forgiveness as the unconditional pardon of the guilty as such, and forgiveness as a conditional grant, as demanding an economy of repentance:[96]

> These two poles, the *unconditional and the conditional*, are absolutely heterogeneous, and must remain irreducible to one another. They are nonetheless indissociable: if one wants, and it is necessary, forgiveness to become effective, concrete, historic; if one wants it to *arrive*, to happen by changing things, it is necessary that this purity engage

[90] This is the difficult and fundamental question which arises in those attempting to relate Levinasian ethics to law: see Manderson, n 59 above; Marinos Diamantides (ed), *Levinas, Law, Politics* (London/New York, Routledge-Cavendish, 2007); Simon Critchley, *The Ethics of Deconstruction* (Oxford, Blackwell, 1992).

[91] Neither, *ca va de soi,* am I. There could be no conference, or papers, or book, otherwise.

[92] In *Law's Empire,* Dworkin recognises that our goals are uncompromisable in discussing the problem with 'checkerboard solutions'. But his argument for 'integrity' does not recognise that our legal goals are also contradictory: see Ronald Dworkin, *Law's Empire* (Cambridge, MA, Belknap Press, 1986) 178–84, 225–77.

[93] Jean-Francois Rey, *Levinas: le Passeur de justice* (Paris, Michalon, 1997); Critchley, n 90 above; Derrida, 'Force of Law', n 3 above; Jacques Derrida, *Gift of Death,* (David Wills, trans) (Chicago, University of Chicago Press, 1995.

[94] Derrida, 'Force of Law,' n 3 above; *Gift of Death,* n 93 above.

[95] Derrida, *Gift of Death,* n 93 above.

[96] Jacques Derrida, 'Forgiveness' in *On Cosmopolitanism and Forgiveness* (Mark Dooley and Michael Hughes (trans), London, Routledge, 2002) 34–5; see also the Introduction by Simon Critchley and Richard Kearney, eg at x–xi.

> itself in a series of conditions … It is between these two poles, *irreconcilable but indissociable*, that decision and responsibilities are to be taken.[97]

How is it that two ideas can be both 'irreconcilable' and 'indissociable'? Justice, responsibility, language, hospitality, show us that we often need two things that we cannot have at the same time, and find ourselves caught in anxious oscillation between them.[98] Such language perfectly describes, not Hart or Fuller, but the strange experience of reading them both:

> [T]hese two regimes of law, of *the* law and the laws, are thus both contradictory, antinomic, and inseparable. They both imply and exclude each other, simultaneously. They incorporate one another at the moment of excluding one another, they are dissociated at the moment of enveloping one another.[99]

The 'ghost of the undecidable', Derrida writes, is not an idea but an experience—a performance—necessary for any genuine decision. But we can't stay undecidable forever. All decisions must finally return, as does Fuller, to the proper application of a rule, whether modified or reinstated, whose content will inevitably continue to be imperfect and provisional and so continue to be haunted by this ordeal the next time and the next.[100] Law requires an *oscillation* between textual and ethical fidelity in which the ghost of conscience haunts the law, casts doubt upon it, and yet is continually being reified into textual terms which, failing to do justice to it, are haunted in their turn. Clearly this argument for ethical doubt and fractured judgement is much more sympathetic to Fuller's position than to Hart's. The ghost that haunts the law (let us call it, with Hegel, law's *Geist*; at once its ghost, spirit, and essence)[101] is an interpretative model with which Fuller seems highly sympathetic. Nonetheless, it is my reading that in the final analysis Fuller unfortunately falls back into the systematisation of law in ways which fail to do justice to his ambitions.

This is an approach to legal interpretation I have not seen in previous commentary. Legal interpretation should be understood by reading Hart–Fuller together, without giving in to any attempt at resolution or synthesis. Theirs is not an argument we should attempt to settle, or like the governess we will be left holding a corpse.[102] A ghost, on the other hand, is not dead. On the contrary, it represents a dynamic element—an ethic, a scruple—that interrupts any system by reminding us of what that system can neither do without nor incorporate. As

[97] Derrida, n 96 above, at 44–5.

[98] *Ibid* 51, 54.

[99] Jacques Derrida and Anne Dufourmentelle, *Of Hospitality* (Stanford University Press, 2000).

[100] Derrida, 'Force of Law', n 3 above.

[101] I am grateful to David Carlson for this allusion, though I do not have space in this chapter to draw out its implications adequately: see David Gray Carlson, Drucilla Cornell and Michel Rosenfeld (eds), *Hegel and Legal Theory* (New York, Routledge, 1991); David Gray Carlson, *A Commentary on Hegel's Science of Logic* (New York, Macmillan, 2007).

[102] Felman, n 22 above, at 168, 173: 'The grasp of the signified turns out to be the grasp but of a corpse'.

we see in *The Turn of the Screw*, a ghost story is not a truth or a reality, but it generates effects in the same way that the unconscious, which can likewise never be understood by the rational mind, nevertheless generates profound effects. In law these effects are doubt, humility, reflection, growth.

Uncertainty and ambiguity are not then the Achilles heel of law, but Hermes' winged heel, its opportunity for listening, communication and responsiveness. Legal legitimacy is not ultimately about procedures. It is a discourse which *binds* us to law and makes us not merely obedient to it but responsible for it.[103] Fidelity to law requires a legal system in which decision-makers are capable of learning from the unique events they are called upon to decide, while being compelled in the end to give a ruling. Faced with such contradictory ambitions, how could a judge or a governess fail to be haunted? Who would wish it otherwise?

Let us end where we began, with metaphor. Turning in circles is the screw's purpose not its futility. The more resistance it encounters, the more firmly does it support the structure. Each turn manifests a contradiction and simultaneously intensifies a commitment.[104] A system from which doubt and disagreement have been excluded might be thought of as a screw with a stripped thread. Although it might still spin it has ceased to bite, bind and sustain a community. So we should refuse the invitation to choose between Hart and Fuller and instead recall that neither can accommodate or do without the other. That is the last turn of the screw. Hart–Fuller remain lodged in legal thought as ghosts—Hart the governess, Fuller the ghost. In their strange dance, they haunt one another and both of them haunt us. May we never be dispossessed.[105]

[103] On the distinction between obedience and responsibility in law see D Manderson, 'From Hunger to Love' (2003) 16 *Law and Literature* 87; Manderson, n 59 above, ch 7.

[104] Edward Shils, *Tradition* (University of Chicago Press, 1981); Thomas Kuhn, *The Structure of Scientific Revolutions* (University of Chicago Press, 1962).

[105] Emily Dickinson, *Complete Poems* (Boston,Little, Brown, 1924), LXIX in Stephen Axelrod and Camille Roman (eds), *New Anthology of American Poetry* (Rutgers,Rutgers University Press, 2003) 563:

'One need not be a chamber to be haunted,
One need not be a house;
The brain has corridors surpassing
Material place ...The prudent carries a revolver,
He bolts the door,
O'erlooking a superior spectre
More near.'

12

The Common Discourse of Hart and Fuller

NGAIRE NAFFINE

> When you are criticizing the philosophy of an epoch do not chiefly direct your attention to those intellectual positions which its exponents feel it necessary to defend. There will be some fundamental assumptions which adherents of all the variant systems within the epoch unconsciously presuppose. Such assumptions appear so obvious that people do not know what they are assuming because no other way of putting things has ever occurred to them. With these assumptions a certain limited number of types of philosophic systems are possible, and this group of systems constitutes the philosophy of the epoch.[1]

Desmond Manderson contends that the visions of Hart and Fuller are incommensurable. I suggest, on the contrary, that they are quite similar and certainly commensurable. Though they mark out and defend different intellectual positions, Hart and Fuller share a number of fundamental assumptions which appear so obvious to them that they barely need stating. Their important similarities are to be found in the unsaid and the assumed—what does not need proper clarification because so much is already understood and presupposed.

Manderson on Hart and Fuller

Manderson adopts an approach to legal interpretation which is heavily indebted to a variety of literary theory. This theory tends to make extensive use of metaphor and to draw on literary fiction. It also, typically, recommends a certain analytic sequence for coming to understand the relationship between terms within different systems of meaning. When applied to the Hart–Fuller debate, the theory seems to call for the following analytical steps. First, there is a critical

[1] Alfred North Whitehead, *Science and the Modern World* (New York, Macmillan, 1926) ch 3 'The Century of Genius'.

examination of the rhetoric of Hart and Fuller and their 'two incommensurable visions of law'. Secondly, we observe that 'their efforts to exclude the other's approach fails'. Thirdly, we come to see that 'their performance [is] mutual and interactive'. This final step, we are told, does not entail any kind of reconciliation of the two approaches through 'compromise or a synthesis'. Rather each is said to remain 'haunted and therefore productively unsettled, by the perspective of the other'.[2]

The incommensurability of the visions of Hart and Fuller is supposedly evidenced by their dramatically different rhetorical styles which reflect their very understanding of law. Hart, for example, is 'linear'; he aims to 'make simple';[3] indeed he 'privileges simplicity and certainty as necessary aspects of legal meaning'.[4] Fuller, by contrast, 'turns questions over and around'[5] and relies heavily on the 'circular metaphor' of 'the turn' to express his understanding of law. 'For Fuller reflection and circularity are merits of legal analysis.'[6]

The two theorists, it is said, thus perform their understanding of law; they 'dramatise' what they talk about. Although Manderson claims that there is no victor in this debate and that 'both positions' are needed 'to make sense of law', Fuller nevertheless emerges as the more subtle and measured thinker. For in his effort to make law transparent and direct, and to clear away the mystery of law, Hart is obliged to resort to 'increasingly shrill rhetorical gestures', whereas Fuller continues to appreciate that 'doubt is [law's] salvation'. To help us appreciate the intimacy of the relationship between rhetoric and narrative in the work of Hart and Fuller, between their mode of story telling and the story itself, Manderson artfully employs Henry James' novel, *The Turn of the Screw*, a ghost story whose ghostliness is to be found as much in the telling, in its turns and twists, as in its plot and denouement.

There is more sophistication, qualification and refinement in Manderson's analysis than I convey in this brief and perhaps crude summation. But these I think are the important elements. Although he observes a convergence in the thinking of Hart and Fuller in parts of their legal analysis, even a swapping of positions about the significance of proper procedure (his second analytical step), Manderson's far greater interest is in their differences, which he believes are sustained despite various cross-overs of ideas and productive tensions. He believes that their visions of law remain incommensurable and unassimilable, that 'neither can accommodate or do without the other'; that the approach of each haunts the other; and further (perhaps paradoxically) that this creative spooking is good for law.[7]

[2] Desmond Manderson, Chapter 11 at 198.
[3] *Ibid* 199.
[4] *Ibid* 199.
[5] *Ibid* 198.
[6] *Ibid* 199.
[7] *Ibid* 216.

Hart and Fuller in Conversation: Subject, Terms and Assumptions

In reply, I want to suggest that the legal visions of Hart and Fuller have much in common, and are certainly commensurable. However, my account of the discourse between Hart and Fuller, and their commonalties, does not rely on the subtleties of literary theory and its conventions for discourse analysis. Rather it treats the famous debate as a conversation between scholars and asks some fairly straightforward questions about the interlocutors, the questions they pose for themselves, their definition and deployment of terms, and their presuppositions. But, like Manderson, I am also interested in the ghosts in these stories: what remains spectral and in the background; what is unsaid because it is taken to be a given: an assumed commonality which requires no further explication. I am also concentrating on the debate itself, not what Hart and Fuller said before or later came to say and came to stand for.

Even within the confines of this two-article debate, the research questions posed are of remarkable breadth. Indeed, in today's research climate, when there is a financial imperative to devise projects which are clearly delineated and delimited, ideally comprehensible across disciplines, which are suitably focused and manageable, which do not claim too much without substantiation, one wonders how these two scholars would fare if this debate were to be the anticipated outcome of their researches or even the intellectual setting for a project seeking funding.

On the second page of his paper, Hart effectively sets the subject and terms of the debate. He informs us that he will offer a positivist's reply to the proposition that 'law and morals' or differently phrased 'what *is* and what *out* to be are indissolubly fused or inseparable'. He will argue for a distinction rather than a fusion. He concedes from the outset that these phrases concerning 'the point of intersection between law and morals' could have many different meanings and so he will have to be quite clear about what he, as a positivist, means by them and how he intends to refute them.

At this point one could anticipate a careful definition of terms, an explanation of how Hart will employ them, and delimitation of the scope of project: Which law? Which jurisdiction or jurisdictions perhaps? And whose morality? How are these main terms to be deployed? How is analysis thus to be delimited and managed, given the extraordinary sweep of the proposition to be evaluated? This is the level of specificity that I think we would demand of our scholars today.

What is striking about both papers is that neither author ever really answers these very basic questions, but only walks around them. Neither makes himself perfectly clear about what precisely he means by 'law' and 'morals' and yet the conversation does not fall apart. I suspect that it is because of the large measure of their common thinking about law that Hart and Fuller can sustain a meaningful dialogue in the absence of clearly-defined central terms. My point is that Hart and Fuller do not confront each other as alien thinkers offering truly incommensurable visions of law, as Manderson suggests. They do not stare at each other with mutual incomprehension, mouths hanging open. Somehow a great deal is implicitly agreed upon and assumed, without too much explication, and it is these implicit agreements that enable meaningful dialogue to occur. Implicitly, the conversation is confined and constrained by common background assumptions which enable and delimit the debate and sustain the conversation, and make it deeply interesting to the antagonist.

It is true that Hart, in setting the terms of the debate, tells us quite soon what Blackstone, Bentham and Austin all meant by a moral law. The laws of God and the principles of utility are mentioned here (with Bentham the utilitarian, Blackstone and Austin the invokers of higher law). But Hart is far less clear about what *he* means by 'morals'. His paper is peppered with terms which employ the word 'moral' as a qualifying adjective; he refers to 'moral aims', 'moral principles', 'moral rules', 'morally good rules', 'moral factors', 'moral propriety' and 'moral right'. He refers to the converse, to that which is 'morally outrageous' and to 'evil aims'. He gives some illustrations of 'moral factors' which are relevant at the point of sentencing, such as the protection of society from 'wanton attack' and not inflicting 'too much misery'.[8] The setting for this discussion is the aftermath of the Nuremberg trials and the 'moral evil' entailed in the Nazis' treatment of the Jewish people. This gives some specific substance to Hart's idea of evil and of 'morally iniquitous laws' and of departures from what Hart calls 'the fundamental principles of humanitarian morality'.[9]

Hart recognises 'certain fundamental notions which are "necessary" and "bottomed in the common nature of man"', quoting Austin here.[10] He goes on to explain that as we are not 'giant land crabs with an impenetrable carapace' which extract nutrients from the air,[11] there must at least be 'rules forbidding the free use of violence and rules constituting the minimum form of property'; '(s)uch rules overlap with basic moral principles vetoing murder, violence, and theft'.[12] This is his natural minimum moral content of law which he takes to be present in all 'developed legal systems'. He then says that beyond this we cannot agree about what is moral and so the necessary overlap between law and morals cannot be more extensive than this. Thus he suggests great variation in moral thinking, possibly even conjuring up incommensurable moral visions.

But Hart has already assumed that his reader will have little difficulty making sense of all his various usages of the term 'moral': that the reader will know what he means by moral rules, or moral principles, etc; that the reader will be able to

[8] HLA Hart, 'Positivism and the Separation of Law and Morals' (1958) 71 *Harvard Law Review* 593, 613.

[9] *Ibid* 617, 618.

[10] *Ibid* 621.

[11] *Ibid* 623.

[12] *Ibid.*

tell them when he sees them and so they need no further explication. Hart has also assumed that his own legal system conforms to the requirements of at least a natural minimum moral content and certainly that it is a system which permits free and critical debate as to its nature: it is a liberal legal system. There is no supporting evidence for this supposition or anticipation of dispute. It is taken as a given. In other words, he has assumed an interlocutor much like himself.

Fuller is alert to this loose usage by Hart, his failure to define his central term 'moral'. He accuses Hart of being much like his predecessors, Austin and Gray, for whom '"morality" stands indiscriminately for almost every conceivable standard by which human conduct may be judged that is not itself law'.[13] They include 'The inner voice of conscience, notions of right and wrong based on religious belief, common conceptions of decency and fair play, culturally conditioned prejudices'.[14] Hart too, he says, 'seems generally to have in mind all sorts of extra-legal notions about "what ought to be", regardless of their sources, pretensions or intrinsic worth'.[15] But this does not prevent Fuller engaging with Hart *as if* there were a single commonly understood meaning of 'morality', one upon which they could both agree, and which makes sense of the question 'Should law and morals be distinct?' and enables them to debate the question as if they were asking the same question and not talking past each other.

Nor does Fuller's insistence on definitional clarity lead him to define his own meanings or to use his central terms with consistency and precision. Fuller seems to employ several conceptions of morality. First, there is his 'internal morality of law', which seems to comprise such procedural requirements as coherence, consistency, orderliness, prospectivity, explanation and justification. Thus there is 'a moral logic to decision-making processes',[16] as Lacey puts it. To Fuller, law's inner morality will pull legal decisions 'towards goodness, by whatever standards of ultimate goodness there are'.[17] So there is law's 'internal morality', that is its 'procedural framework' and processes, and then there is something else again, some 'ultimate goodness', which has magnetic properties for law that is itself internally moral, in the more procedural sense. Fuller also refers to 'goodness' and 'evil'[18] (both undefined).

There is also reference to what seems to be a more mundane ordinary social common-sense morality, that of 'common decency'.[19] This is said to entail 'generally shared views of right conduct that have grown spontaneously through experience and discussion',[20] though it is not clear who is party to this discussion.

[13] LL Fuller, 'Positivism and Fidelity to Law: A Reply to Professor Hart' (1958) 71 *Harvard Law Review* 630, 635.
[14] *Ibid.*
[15] *Ibid.*
[16] Nicola Lacey, Chapter 1, 31.
[17] Fuller, 'Positivism and Fidelity to Law: A Reply to Professor Hart', n 13 above, at 636.
[18] *Ibid.*
[19] *Ibid* 635.
[20] *Ibid* 638.

It entails 'ordinary standards of decency'[21] and what 'most ordinary citizens would regard as mistaken or evil'.[22] Further there is a religious morality invoked, God's law or higher law, which, according to Fuller, the Roman Catholics have happily been wise enough not to foist on human law.[23]

In Fuller's account, we seem therefore to have at least four varieties of 'morality'. There is ultimate goodness, which is to be distinguished from something called 'evil'. There is the morality of the Catholic Church which is bracketed off from the debate because it does not, in his reckoning, generally intrude on law. There is ordinary decency. And then there is procedural morality; and in Fuller's thinking, procedural morality is naturally drawn towards goodness, whether it be understood as ordinary decency or some ultimate goodness; this is not entirely clear.

Like Hart, Fuller implicitly believes that *his* legal system is moral. He distinguishes it from 'perverted regimes', but even these, he suggests, display a 'certain hesitancy about writing cruelties, intolerances and inhumanities into law'. For there are 'demands of reality that are the most urgent and the most obviously justifiable, which no man need be ashamed to profess'.[24] Thus he invokes a deep universal morality to which even perverted regimes subscribe.

A Common Discourse

Hart and Fuller have much in common. Both display a strong faith in their own legal systems and that of the other. They assume that their laws are not iniquitous; that they are moral in perhaps the deepest sense. Hart refers to the 'developed legal system',[25] taking his own to be one such system.[26] Fuller distinguishes his own legal system from 'perverted' regimes.[27] Fuller also manages to convey to us that his own system possesses an internal procedural morality which naturally gravitates towards the good. Hart too seems to believe implicitly in the procedural justice and fairness of his own system. And both seem to believe that law, in itself, is a good thing. As Leslie Green notes in Chapter 9, both Hart and Fuller share a belief in law and that belief can be distinguished from that of anarchists such as Kropotkin who wrote of 'the uselessness and the hurtfulness of law'.[28]

21 *Ibid* 661.
22 *Ibid* 637.
23 *Ibid* 660.
24 *Ibid* 637.
25 Hart, 'Positivism and the Separation of Law and Morals' n 8, 621.
26 I am suggesting here that 'developed', as Hart uses it, has at least two connotations. One is developed in its complexity and the other is developed in its morality.
27 Fuller, 'Positivism and Fidelity to Law: A Reply to Professor Hart', n 13 above, at 646.
28 Leslie Green, Chapter 9 at 182.

Both theorise at a high level of abstraction about law conceived as a universal phenomenon and as a single idea. Both also take their own law, Anglo-American law, to provide the template for all law. And they share important assumptions about what counts as moral. Though neither supplies a clear and consistent definition of morality, each already knows enough about what the other means to enable coherent dialogue to occur about the law–morals and the is–ought distinctions. Morals therefore do not need clear definition and the debate can proceed nevertheless because each is of a mind with the other: essentially they share a worldview of what is right and wrong, good and evil, decent and indecent, and good and bad law. Neither is facing an incomprehensible and uncomprehending other whose meaning and vision is impossible to come to grips with.

Indeed, each faces an interlocutor who is remarkably similar to himself. They are intellectual elites. They hale from their country's leading law schools and hold academic posts of considerable influence and eminence. As Fuller himself concedes, 'neither Professor Hart nor I belong to anything that could be said in a significant sense to be a "minority group" in our respective countries'.[29] They have played a critical role in setting the terms of their debate. That debate is really about their own legal systems, their respective countries, though it is misleadingly cast in universal terms.

Both Hart and Fuller share the estimable aim of articulating a coherent vision of the appropriate relationship between law and morals and of thereby achieving a moral law. As Nicola Lacey puts it, 'both … [are] committed to theorising the "normativity" as much as the "factivity" of law'.[30] Hart thinks this aim is best achieved by keeping law and morals distinct and then comparing the two and seeing if the law lives up to morals. One then knows whether it is right to obey the law. Fuller thinks it is better to require law itself to display what he terms an internal morality so that it commands fidelity.

But from the entire tenor of their debate, it is clear that both believe that they are writing from within fundamentally decent legal systems, about which they need not be fundamentally ashamed, which permit learned gentlemen freely to express their thoughts. The laws they implicitly write about are developed; they are not perverted; they do not countenance cruelties and atrocities; they are tolerant and humane. And law is always a good to be striven for. They share what Suzanne Langer has called 'implicit "ways"'. These are ways which 'are not avowed … but simply followed … They are what a German would call his "Weltanschauung", his attitude of mind, rather than specific articles of faith. They constitute his outlook; they are deeper than facts he may note or propositions he may moot'.[31]

[29] Fuller, 'Positivism and Fidelity to Law: A Reply to Professor Hart', n 13 above, at 637.
[30] Nicola Lacey, Chapter 1, 23.
[31] Suzanne K Langer, *Philosophy in a New Key: A Study in the Symbolism of Reason, Rite and Art*, 3rd edn (Cambridge, MA, Harvard University Press, 1957) 4.

Both assume a society ordered in a particular way with a certain orderly legal framework and system. Both want moral laws and assume that their laws are in the most fundamental ways already moral. Both have difficulty envisaging truly alien ways of thinking, the truly incommensurable. Hart refers to the undeveloped legal system and leaves it at that. Fuller refers to the perverted legal system but even then he cannot imagine it failing to conform to what he takes to be the fundamental moral precepts.

Who Could Offer An Incommensurable Vision?

I have said that our two debaters are really cut from the one cloth. So who are they unlike? What would an interlocutor be like who possessed genuinely different ways of thinking about the nature of law, its moral basis, and more specifically about the rightness and goodness of the Anglo-American regimes: who would possess an incommensurable vision? We can imagine an interesting and varied cast of characters who might offer real differences of thought. Green speaks of the anarchist Kropotkin. But we need not go far afield to find them, say to Confucian or Shari'a regimes, or say to Aboriginal customary law.

Ordinary citizens within the legal systems which are familiar to our two debaters and who form their natural setting might well have offered incommensurable visions at the time they were writing. An explicitly homosexual Englishman; a married Englishwoman; an African-American; a prisoner on death row, could all offer very different perspectives and might even be said to possess an uncommon vision of law.

The married woman of the 1950s, in conversation with Hart, might say that on a daily basis the law failed to protect both her person (I refer to the spousal immunity from prosecution for marital rape which persisted until the 1990s) and (going back not too long ago, say to her grandmother) her property of which she was essentially divested upon marriage. She could say that she had not been afforded the legal carapace needed by all soft-shelled human crabs unable to draw sustenance from thin air. In other words, the English legal system did not even satisfy her 'species-typical ends', as Green calls them, in the sense of protecting her bodily integrity within marriage and her basic rights as a proprietor.[32] Hart would find that his legal system did not possess the minimum content of natural law and therefore might reassess his implicit positive appraisal of his own system of law. A homosexual Englishman would point to the criminal nature of his most intimate desires. (Though it must be said that elsewhere in his writing, Hart in fact does weigh in against such odious laws.)

An African-American in conversation with Fuller might have reflected on the failings of his system, especially the failure to enable him to participate in it at all,

[32] Leslie Green, Chapter 9 at 172.

to have full franchise. He might therefore question the very framework which supposedly constitutes American law's inner morality. The inmate on death row would no doubt question the legal intolerance and inhumanity entailed in the death penalty.

These are not just minor empirical quibbles about large-scale theories which are not in themselves dependent on specific social instantiations: they are not simply small-scale disputes about specific parts of the law which leave the main part of the theory untouched. They go deeper than this. If, even to a positivist such as Hart who does not otherwise believe in the necessary overlap between law and morality, protection of bodily integrity and confidence about ownership go to the very heart of any civilised legal system, and form its minimal content of good law, then it can be said that the justice concerns of English married women reveal a different face of law and present him with a genuinely different way of thinking. If a fair procedural framework is fundamental to Fuller, then the disenfranchised African-American is excluded from such a law and cannot share his vision. Hart and Fuller therefore have more in common, despite their supposed intellectual differences, than they do with these other more ordinary English and American men and women. The ordinary standards of decency invoked by Fuller did not apply to many ordinary people.

As Hilary Charlesworth observes, the debate occurred in 1958, 10 years after the Declaration of Human Rights, and yet Hart and Fuller took 'little account of contemporary human rights developments'.[33] Nor did they look around to see what was happening in their own backyards, an act which might have shaken their implicit faith in their own law. And certainly they did not look to foreign lands, in any informed or sociological manner. Instead, they worked with ideal types of law: the 'developed legal system' and the 'perverted regime'.

'The past is a foreign country', said LP Hartley.[34] '[T]hey do things differently there.' Fifty years on, after the flourishing of feminist legal theory, critical race theory, and queer theory, with the expansion of international human rights, and with global legal knowledge facilitated by the Internet, it is perhaps too easy to see Hart and Fuller as parochial or provincial in their thinking about the nature of law and the nature of morals: as a sort of caricatured Tweedledum and Tweedledee.[35] It may be harder to appreciate the novelty of their thinking and the real acts of creativity and intellectual bravery demanded of them as they developed, tested and debated the conditions of a moral law.

[33] Hilary Charlesworth, Chapter 2 at 225.

[34] This over-quoted phrase is from Hartley's *The Go-Between* (Harmondsworth, Penguin, , 1958) 7.

[35] As Jeremy Waldron observes in Chapter 7, it would be unreasonable to expect of them the sort of sensitivity to legal pluralism and to the diversity of laws that we would require of a scholar today.

13

How Norms Become Normative

PHILIP PETTIT*

The Norm–Normative Gap

Norms, as I understand them here, are regularities in the behaviour of a population, not mere standards for behaviour. But, more particularly, they are regularities that satisfy three further, plausible conditions.[1] People give acceptance or approval to those who conform with the regularities and/or reject or disapprove of those who deviate. This acceptance rating, as we may call it, helps in some measure to explain the general conformity. And all of this is a matter of more or less common awareness: each is in a position to see that the conditions obtain, to see that others are in a position to see that they obtain, and so on.[2]

* This chapter emerged from discussion of a sketch of related ideas at two conferences, one in the University of Bielefeld in May 2008, the other in the Australian National University in December 2008. The earlier, Bielefeld version of the paper appear as 'Norms, Commitment and Censure' in M Baurman, G Brennan, RE Goodin, and NSouthwood (eds) *Norms and Values. The Role of Social Norms as Instruments of Value Realisation* (Baden-Baden, Nomos Verlag, 2009). I am most grateful for the searching feedback I received, especially from my commentators, Thomas Spitzley in Bielefeld and Richard McAdams at the ANU. I am also grateful for some comments received from Michael Baurmann and Geoffrey Brennan.

[1] P Pettit, '*Virtus Normativa*: Rational Choice Perspectives' (1990) 100 *Ethics* 725 (reprinted in P Pettit, *Rules, Reasons, and Norms* (Oxford, Oxford University Press, 2002)); G Brennan and P Pettit, *The Economy of Esteem: An Essay on Civil and Political Society* (Oxford, Oxford University Press, 2004).

[2] D Lewis, *Convention* (Cambridge, MA, Harvard University Press, 1969). This characterisation of social norms leaves open a range of questions. Does a regularity count as generally instantiated if it is a regularity that applies only to those holding a certain office or meeting a certain qualification? How extensive is the pattern of approval or disapproval envisaged when it is said that the regularity has a high approval rating? Moreover, must the approval or disapproval be associated with the relevant type of behaviour, considered in general, or will it suffice if it reliably appears, instance by instance? And what, finally, is required for the approval rating to help to explain the pattern of behaviour? Must it contribute in some measure to the production of the behaviour, at least among a number of those complying? Or will it do if it is there to reinforce the behaviour, should the motives that normally produce it fail for one or another reason? Will it do, in other words, if it is a virtual or standby force that is triggered to support the behaviour only on a need-to-act basis, when the 'red lights' are

This account of norms is broadly in line with the approach of recent authors on the subject and ought not to generate any deep controversy.[3] Where those accounts vary from that provided here, that is often because they are focused on particular sets of norms, not norms in general. Herbert Hart[4] concentrates, for example, on rules that generally prevail in a society, are supported by serious social pressure, are thought useful in some way for the life of the group, and are individually burdensome, however beneficial in group terms.

There are many different stories about how norms emerge but under most of them, norms come about as a result of rationally intelligible adjustments between the parties. They are regularities that people are naturally motivated to comply with and naturally motivated to enforce, say by retaliation against offenders or by some other form of punishment. Under these stories, however, neither compliance nor enforcement need have any element of the normative. People will comply with a regularity because prudence dictates, not because they ought in an independent sense to do so. And people will enforce the regularity on the same basis, if enforcement is intentional, not because offenders ought in an independent sense to be punished.

These naturalistic theories of norms apply to a wide spectrum of social regularities, ranging from norms of etiquette to norms of decent behaviour. With norms at the etiquette end, it is understandable that they might be sustained from merely prudential motives, but with norms at the decency end it seems that something more strongly normative is relevant. In order to count as decent, after all, people will have to conform to norms of decency because they ought in an independent sense to conform, not just because it is in their rational self-interest to do so. A pressing problem for any naturalistic theory of norms, then, is to explain how some norms come to assume such a normative, more-than-prudential status in the minds of those who uphold them.

The problem might be described, in a way that Herbert Hart made famous,[5] as an issue about how people assume an internal point of view on norms that they instantiate and enforce. He recognised that the norms on the realisation of which

illuminated? (P Pettit, 'The Virtual Reality of Homo Economicus' (1995) 78 *Monist* 308; expanded version in U Maki (ed), *The World of Economics* (Cambridge, Cambridge University Press, 2000); reprinted in P Pettit *Rules, Reasons, and Norms*, n 1 above.) I am happy to leave aside these questions, taking an inclusive view of norms. But there is one further question we cannot avoid.

[3] HLA Hart, *The Concept of Law* (Oxford, Oxford University Press, 1961); P Winch, *The Idea of a Social Science and its Relation to Philosophy* (London, Routledge, 1963); E Ullmann-Margalit, *The Emergence of Norms* (Oxford,Oxford University Press, 1977); J Coleman, *Foundations of Social Theory* (Cambridge, MA, Harvard University Press, 1990); RH McAdams, 'The Origin, Development and Regulation of Norms' (1997) 96 *Michigan Law Review* 338; E Sober and DS Wilson, *Unto Others: The Evolution and Psychology of Unselfish Behavior* (Cambridge, MA, Harvard University Press, 1998); JJ Elster, *Alchemies of the Mind: Rationality and the Emotions* (Cambridge, Cambridge University Press, 1999).

[4] Hart, *The Concept of Law*, n 3 above, at 84–5.

[5] *Ibid.*

a legal system depends—the norms followed and applied by those who administer the system—are ones which insiders treat normatively and that any theory of law ought to make sense of this. Yet he saw that the more or less naturalistic account that he himself sketched of how such norms might emerge and gain a hold did not fully account for this internal perspective. The problem he faced is exactly the problem as to how norms —(naturalistically explicable norms—) gain a normative status in the minds of those who implement them.

But the reference to Hart prompts an important clarification. To say that people develop an internal point of view on a norm, taking it to make a non-prudential demand, does not reduce to saying that they internalise the norm: that they conform to the norm out of internal motives of attachment, not out of the external motives that might be provided by the desire for acceptance or the fear or rejection. Take a prudentially based norm such as that of standing at a certain distance from an interlocutor in conversation. You might abide by that norm out of fear of social sanction, while actually being inclined to stand closer. Or you might internalise the norm, and become attached to standing at the prescribed distance. But even if you internalise the norm in that sense, there won't be any independent basis in which it will command your allegiance. The norm won't have a normative status for you.

The problem before us does not bear directly on the incentives for abiding by a norm and on the factors that lead people to internalise it motivationally. It bears rather on the way that people come to conceptualise the demands of a norm. The norm will assume a normative status in their attitudes (they will see it from an internal point of view) just insofar as they recognizs a non-prudential sense in which it commands their allegiance. The problem of explaining how a naturalistically explicable norm can assume this status is the problem of closing the norm–normative gap.

In this chapter I want to tell a story about how one particular norm, the norm of honesty, might materialise and stabilise on a naturalistic, prudential basis and yet, under a more or less inevitable set of pressures, assume a normative status in the practice of those who conform: a status that is not wholly prudential in character. I think that the story has very general implications but I shall not try to develop these in the present context.[6] The story shows how in principle the norm–normative gap might be closed, even if it does not demonstrate the general significance of the particular manner in which it is closed.

The chapter is in three more sections. In the next I analyse what honesty requires and show how we might expect a norm of honesty to arise on a naturalistic basis. In the following section I explain why such a norm is bound to mobilise attitudes of commitment and censure, thereby assuming a properly normative profile. And then in the last I expand on the significance of this fact,

[6] P Pettit, *Why We Owe Each Other* (Oxford, Wiley-Blackwell, forthcoming). In the current paper I argue that there is a not wholly prudential sense in which the norm of honesty can gain a hold on people. In the book I explore how such a norm can gain a fully moral hold.

looking at two forms of commitment, avowals and promises, that a flourishing norm of honesty may be expected to activate.

The Naturalistic Norm of Honesty

Most accounts of norms concentrate on regularities in non-linguistic behaviour but there is no reason why they should not be extended to regularities of a communicative character as well. There might be a norm (a naturalistically explicable norm) against the use of coercive threats, for example. Or there might be a norm against the manipulative use of speech. In manipulation everything appears to be above board, unlike the case of coercion, but speakers rely on an underhanded power (say, their skill at spin or their intimidating presence) in order to secure a desired uptake. In this chapter I concentrate on perhaps the most basic norm that is likely to arise in the space of words: a norm against deception—a norm of honesty.

The Meaning of Honesty

In order to understand what a norm of honesty would entail, we need to be clear about what counts as deception or dishonesty. The most obvious way in which speech is likely to deceive, or so it may appear, is through conveying an inaccurate or inadequate account of that which it purports to represent. Let us concentrate for the moment on the assertion that reports a public state of affairs: that it is raining, to take an occurrent state of affairs, or that Princeton lies just south of New York, to take one of a standing character. An assertion will be inaccurate if things are not as they are reported to be, and inadequate if the way they are reported to be does not provide all the information that is contextually required for the guidance of the hearer.

If I report things inaccurately or inadequately in making an assertion, does that mean that I am being deceptive and dishonest? And if I report things accurately and adequately does that mean I am being non-deceptive and honest? In each case the answer is 'no'. I may misreport things because of being misinformed or underinformed myself, not out of a deceptive wish to mislead the hearer. And if I report things accurately and adequately I may do so due to the lack of proper information, and may actually have meant to deceive. It is in virtue of the intent of a communication, not its content, that a report counts as non-deceptive or deceptive.

This observation suggests that what is required for non-deception or honesty is not accuracy or adequacy (if you like, truth) but rather sincerity. An assertion will be sincere just in case the belief it purports to express really is the belief of the speaker: one to which the speaker at least assents. My assertion reports that it is raining and expresses, or at least purports to express, my belief that it is raining. Whether or not the report is true, the assertion will be sincere just in case I believe that it is true: just in case it is a true expression of my belief.

What is it for an utterance to express or purport to express a belief as distinct from reporting on a state of affairs? Expressing and reporting are both forms of representation, in a broad sense of that term. When I express a belief that it is raining by reporting that it is raining, then I represent the environment as rainy and I represent myself as holding the belief that it is rainy. And I support both representations with full knowledge and with full consent, in the overt manner that is characteristic of speech; the representation does not occur behind my back. At a single stroke I describe the world and express the belief, where both the description and the expression are forms of linguistic representation.

Why does the self-representation count as expression, and the world-representation count as a report or description? The crucial contrast, as I see it, is the following. I may explain a descriptive misrepresentation of the world on the grounds that I misread the evidence: I thought the water on the glass was rain. But I cannot explain the expressive misrepresentation of my belief (say, the belief that it was raining) on similar evidential grounds. Suppose I spoke insincerely in reporting that it was raining and that I am challenged about this. I cannot explain the expressive misrepresentation of my state of belief—I cannot explain my insincerity—by claiming that I got that belief wrong: I misread the evidence on what I actually believed. Descriptive misrepresentation is explicable on grounds that the evidence that prompted it was misleading, expressive misrepresentation is not explicable in that way. For the moment I take that point of contrast as a given; it will assume a good deal of importance in the later argument.

What honest, non-deceptive assertion requires, then, is that it be sincere. The expressive self-representation that it involves must be accurate and adequate to the facts; the speaker must actually have the belief expressed, whether or not that belief is correct. But what of other speech acts? What of the question that communicates a desire for a certain information, the request that indicates the presence of a wish, the declaration that reveals an intention, or the command that conveys an order: an order, as it happens, that the issuance of the command will itself constitute?

Such speech acts represent attitudes of the speaker on a par with the belief that the assertion represents the speaker as having. And they represent those attitudes in an expressive manner, by the criterion just introduced, not in the manner of a report or description. In normal contexts a speaker cannot plausibly explain a misrepresentation of attitude on evidential grounds: on the grounds that he or she thought wrongly that they had the attitude expressed. As with assertions, these speech acts will be sincere and honest to the extent that the speaker really has the attitudes expressed, insincere and deceptive to the extent that the speaker lacks them.

We can sum up this discussion in three claims. When I represent myself as having a certain attitude, and it is understood on all sides that I cannot give an evidential explanation for having misrepresented myself, the representation at issue counts as an expression. When my expressive self-representation fails to be accurate or adequate to the type of attitude expressed, it counts as insincere. And it is insincerity of this kind that constitutes dishonesty and would be ruled out by a norm of honesty.

Making Honesty a Norm

Honesty is something that each of us is bound to welcome from others. If I communicate with you honestly then I can extend and improve the epistemic representation of your environment and facilitate the achievement of your goals. I can make you aware of opportunities and obstacles of which you may not have been conscious, providing you with a new set of eyes and ears. And I can make you aware of failures in your own practical and theoretical reasoning, providing you with a new set of checks on how you think and plan. Assuming that I do not offend in other ways, say through resort to coercion or manipulation, I will be a friend in the forum of your informational gathering and informational processing: an amicus curiae, a friend of the court.

The welcome character of honest communication appears most vividly in the fact that the service I provide for you in such communication may be exactly like the service you provide for yourself when you stop and reason about the best thing to do or think, or when you seek out extra information.[7] I collaborate with you epistemically, as we might say, when I communicate with you in this mode. I provide you in all sincerity with considerations that bear on how you conduct your thought and action. And assuming that I avoid coercion and manipulation, I offer these on a take-it-or-leave it basis, enabling you to make up your own mind, using your own reason. Other things being equal, there is everything to celebrate about this service (at least if I am reasonably competent) and nothing to regret.[8]

In view of its welcome character, it should not be surprising that we can explain the emergence and survival of a norm of honesty on a purely naturalistic, prudential basis. One straightforward explanation would derive the norm from the appeal of conditional honesty. Consider the tit-for-tat pattern in which people are honest, roughly, with those that they expect to be honest in return; they are honest in a first encounter with another, as the idea is often regimented, and are honest in any later encounters provided that the other was honest in the immediately preceding exchange. Such conditional honesty is bound to be prudentially attractive in recurrent prisoner's-dilemma interactions with random

[7] P Pettit and M Smith, 'The Truth in Deontology' in RJ Wallace, P Pettit, S Scheffler and M Smith (eds), *Reason and Value: Themes from the Moral Philosophy of Joseph Raz* (Oxford, Oxford University Press, 2004); P Pettit, 'Joining the Dots' in M Smith, HG Brennan, RE Goodin and FC Jackson (eds), *Common Minds: Themes from the Philosophy of Philip Pettit* (Oxford, Oxford University Press, 2007).

[8] Other things will not be equal when honest communication plays a role, eg, in activities like blackmail or exploitation.

others. I can tell you about my source of food, you can tell me about yours, but we would each like to know about the other's source without letting the other know about ours. In a single-shot dilemma of this kind, dishonesty may pay dividends, being likely to produce the better result whatever the other does. But when people face an indefinite iteration of such predicaments it makes a great deal of sense if each of them begins by being honest with any new partner and then continues to be honest in later encounters provided that that person was honest in the previous exchange.

Robert Axelrod[9] ran a famous computer simulation that displayed the merits of such a tit-for-tat strategy in a society where such exchanges recur in an open-ended way. The strategy is going to be a viable one to adopt for the first time, even if no one else has done so. It promises to be robustly successful in competition with a wide range of rival strategies, such as permanent honesty, permanent dishonesty, or tit-for-double-tat. And it is going to be resistant (at least in general)[10] to the invasion of the population by numbers of individuals with rival strategies.

The benefits of conditional honesty make it likely that people will find it attractive and even that they are primed by their evolutionary history to find it attractive, as evidence suggests that other species are primed.[11] But if people all display tit-for-tat in the sphere of communication then honesty will become a regular pattern. And this pattern will presumably attract a high acceptance rating, given the benefits it confers. Each will find others appealing insofar as they are reciprocally honest and, under plausible assumptions, each will be reinforced in their honesty by the prospect of proving to have such appeal.[12] Since this will all be accessible as a matter of common knowledge, the upshot will be the appearance of a norm of honesty, under our earlier account of what a norm requires.

I invoke this explanation of why a norm of honesty might emerge in order to show that the appearance and continuation of such a norm is likely to be naturalistically explicable. Other accounts that would bear out the same lesson might appeal to the effects of cultural evolution in addition to the factors invoked

[9] R Axelrod, *The Evolution of Cooperation* (New York, Basic Books, 1984).

[10] M Nowak and K Sigmund, 'A Strategy of Win-Stay, Lose-Shift that Outperforms Tit-for-Tat' (1993) 364 *Nature* 56.

[11] For an example among vampire bats see GS Wilkinson, 'Reciprocal Food Sharing in the Vampire Bat' (1983) 308 *Nature* 181; GS Wilkinson, 'Food Sharing in Vampire Bats' (1990) 262(2) *Scientific America* 64; and among stickleback fish see M Milinski, D Pfluger *et al*, 'Do Stickelbacks Cooperate Repeatedly in Reciprocal Pairs?' (1990) 27 *Behavioral Ecology and Sociobiology* 17. There has been some scepticism about these results (JR Stevens, 'The Selfish Nature of Generosity: Harassment and Food Sharing in Primates' (2004) 271 *Proceedings of the Royal Society, London B* 451), given the cognitive limitations of the creatures involved. But there is also evidence of tit-for-tat behaviour among vervet monkeys (RM Seyfarth and DL Cheney ,'Grooming, Alliances and Reciprocal Altruism in Vervet Monkeys' (1984) 308 *Nature* 541), and among cotton-top, tamarin monkeys (MD Hauser, MK Chen *et al*, 'Give Unto Others' (2003) 270 *Proceedings of the Royal Society, London B* 2363).

[12] McAdams, n 3 above; Brennan and Pettit, n 1 above.

in these accounts, or instead of them.[13] But we need not go into further detail. The point to emphasise is that there is no dearth of naturalistic accounts for why we should expect a norm of honesty to emerge and survive in human society.

This is the important point, because it highlights the problem of the norm–normative gap. The norm of honesty is taken by most of us to have a strong normative status. We do not prescribe honesty for ourselves or others, on the grounds just that honesty pays. That may well be so but we think that there arealso independent grounds for prescribing honesty. We think that people ought not to be honest with one another just because that makes rational, self-interested sense. If the norm of honesty is naturalistically explicable, however, why does it display this extra normative status? Where does that normative status come from? And does its appearance mean that the naturalistic story does not identify all the factors relevant in explaining its appearance and stability?

One way of explaining the gap would be to postulate that the acceptance rating in the case of honesty is inherently normative in character—it involves casting conformity as right or desirable or admirable—where the rating with certain other norms is merely prudential. But this explanation does not give an account of what a normative, non-prudential rating is supposed to involve; it invokes the obscure to explain the obscure. And it does nothing to explain why such a rating appears in the case of honesty but not with other norms. It is unenlightening and ad hoc, and the challenge is to see if we can do better.

I think that we can do better. There are grounds for holding that as a regularity of honest behaviour gets established by a naturalistically explicable norm, it will inevitably give rise to the concept and practice of commitment and to the related concept and practice of censure. And once people begin to think of being committed to honest communication, and being subject to censure for dishonesty, the norm assumes a normative status for them.

Making the Norm of Honesty Normative

Counselling and Consulting

Suppose that we are confronted with a human society in which the norm of honesty has been established on a naturalistic basis. To be concrete, suppose that the norm appears and stabilises on a conditionally co-operative basis, reinforced by a prudential pattern of approval for honesty, disapproval for dishonesty. What sort of behaviour would this sort of explanation lead us to expect?

When the norm is not overridden by other factors (for example, by a salient conflict of interests), we must certainly expect that human beings will counsel

[13] Sober and Wilson, n 3 above; P Richerson and R Boyd, *Not by Genes Alone: How Culture Transformed Human Evolution* (Chicago,University of Chicago Press, 2005).

and consult one another, confident in their mutual honesty, about the lie of the land in which they operate. Rather than just relying on their personal sources of information, and personal styles of reasoning, they will seek and offer one another a wealth of epistemic advice. They will pool their information and put their minds together in exploring its implications. Those implications will bear on what to think and do, whether individually or together.

When I consult with you, under this pattern, I will presumably provide you with information about the opportunities in your natural environment for fulfilling certain desires, and about the opportunities that may arise because of a convergence of interests with third parties. I may tell you, for example, that a third party would be willing to provide you with a reward for choosing A rather than B and that, on the basis of my knowledge of your desires, you ought to approach that person and seek an offer of a reward. And in the same information-providing spirit I may make the same report about myself. I may say that I myself would be willing to provide you with a reward for choosing A rather than B and that you ought to consider approaching me with a view to securing an offer.

But the behaviour that we can expect under a naturalistically explicable norm of honesty is not restricted to the sort of counselling and consulting described here. What we now have to see is that when I provide information about my beliefs or attitudes or intentions, I can go beyond what I do when I provide information about a third party's disposition; I have an important reason in self-interest to do this; and in doing it I give the norm of honesty a distinctive normative cast. What I can and ought in prudence to do, as I shall put it, is to commit to the beliefs or attitudes in question. In this section I shall look at the possibility, rationality and normativity of committing to a belief and in the next section I shall consider how such commitment generalises to other attitudes and, in particular, to intentions.

Expression and Excuse

In order to explore these matters, we have to go back first to a feature of regular assertion that was mentioned earlier. When I make an assertion that turns out to be false—inaccurate or at least inadequate—it is always an open possibility that I can explain why it is false in a way that establishes my sincerity and my honesty. I can show that the evidence at my disposal was misleading and that my assertion expressed the belief that I formed in response to the evidence. I asserted that it was raining and did so perfectly sincerely, taking the water on the windows to be evidence of rain.

Suppose now that I had communicated my belief that it was raining to you and that you took certain steps on the basis of that information. When you discover that I misinformed you, will the naturalistic, prudential norm of honesty lead you to see my communication as dishonest and a fit target of retaliation? Surely not. Or not at any rate if I get the opportunity of explaining to you that though my descriptive report was false, my representation of myself as someone who believed in the rain was not; I made the report sincerely. If I get the chance to explain this to you (or if you just see that I am in a position to provide such an explanation) then you will surely resist retaliation. You will take it that notwithstanding the disservice that I unwittingly performed, still your conditionally co-operative strategy does not require that I be penalised; in fact it requires that I not be penalised. The explanation of my disservice plays the role of cancelling the retaliation that might seem to have been required under a strategy of conditional honesty. It counts in this context as an excuse.

The concept of an excuse may not be strictly definable on the basis of the naturalistic concepts introduced in this story. But a somewhat weaker claim certainly seems plausible. This is that we can explain the appearance of such a concept, invoking only naturalistic elements in the explanation.[14] If we simulate the position of someone who is about to be penalised for dishonesty, within a relationship of manifest, conditional co-operation, we can readily imagine why that person might protest their sincerity; why the other party might accept the explanation provided for their mistake; and why in that context the word 'excuse', as we use it, would become accessible to both. With the sort of meaning that we give the term, the parties are in a position to recognise that what the first person has done is to provide an effective excuse for having told an untruth and on that account that the naturalistic norm of honesty does not support retaliation.

The Possibility of Commitment

The concept of an excuse, and the practice of invoking excuses, is bound to have a place under any norm of honesty, given that honesty requires sincere communication. It will be required in order to mark the crucial difference between speaking falsely but sincerely and speaking falsely and insincerely; it plays the role of showing how the first is not in breach of the norm but the second is. And now the big news. With the appearance of such a notion of an excuse, it will become possible for people to practise what I describe as commitment.

Suppose that you make a report to me, as in our earlier examples, about the current rain or the position of Princeton in relation to New York. You are bound to be aware of the excuse that you can make for the failure of such a descriptive report; this will be a matter of shared linguistic understanding, as I emphasised earlier. And so you can give yourself some comfort in making that report: you can expect to count as sincere and co-operative even if, as it turns out, the report is false. But the salience of this possibility means that you now have a way of playing safe—a way of hedging your bets—in any representation of yourself that looks

[14] P Pettit, 'A Sensible Perspectivism' in M Baghramian and A Dunlop, *Dealing with Diversity* (London, Routledge, 2000).

risky. You can represent your beliefs or any other attitudes in a descriptive way, leaving room for invoking an evidential excuse in the event of the representation proving to be false.

Imagine now that I seek information on what you believe in some domain where you are not so clear about your beliefs. I ask whether you believe that Jones is trustworthy, for example, or whether you believe that the stock market is going to recover soon. You may simply express your belief on the matter, saying that Jones is indeed trustworthy or that the market will recover.[15] In this case you will have no excuse to offer, if it becomes clear from your behaviour (as, plausibly, your caution in dealing with Jones or the market might later make it clear) that you do not really believe this. That emerges from our account of what it is to express such a belief. But anticipating this possibility, you may decline to represent your belief expressively and do so just descriptively. You may say that you believe, so far as you can tell, that Jones is trustworthy or that the market will recover: that that is what you find yourself inclined to say. And if you do opt for the descriptive representation of your belief then you will have an excuse available, as a matter of common awareness, should your later behaviour belie the report. Your self-representation will allow excuses, not exclude them.

We can now introduce the notion of commitment, at least in the domain of belief representation. Assume that the difference in significance between expressive and descriptive representation of a belief is a matter of common awareness, as it will have to be amongst the linguistically competent. And now suppose that, when asked whether Jones is trustworthy, or the market reliable, you express your belief in a way that, as a matter of common awareness, puts evidential excuses for misrepresenting it out of reach.[16] In that case it is natural to say that you commit to the belief. You manifestly forego resort to an evidential excuse for misrepresenting the belief to an addressee; you speak in a way that forecloses the possibility of invoking such an excuse. You put yourself in the hands of the other, denying yourself grounds on which to protest at punishment, should you prove not to hold the belief expressed.

The Rationality of Commitment

Why would people ever commit to beliefs? Why would they ever put excuses beyond reach? It takes only a little reflection to see why committing yourself to a belief, in the sense described, may often be in your rational self-interest.

[15] Consistently with such expression, I may take the content of the belief to be probabilistic, as in saying that the chances are high that Jones is trustworthy or that the market will recover. In the terms that I go on to introduce, there will still be a commitment in that case but the commitment will not be as hazardous as in the case where the content is not probabilistically qualified.

[16] V McGeer, 'Is "Self-knowledge" an Empirical Problem? Renegotiating the Space of Philosophical Explanation' (1996) 93 *Journal of Philosophy* 483; R Moran, *Authority and Estrangement: An Essay on Self-knowledge* (Princeton, NJ, Princeton University Press, 2001); V McGeer, 'The Moral Development of First-Person Authority' (2008) 16 *European Journal of Philosophy* 81.

Talk is cheap, in the old slogan, and to the extent that it remains cheap, it will be less than convincing. But as talk is made more expensive, as the costs of misrepresentation mount, then talk becomes more compelling. You are less likely to speak untruly as the expected costs of doing so rise. This homespun insight is now frequently invoked in the literature on game theory and the evolution of signalling.[17]

The insight directs us to a prudential reason why you might be very willing, not just to report certain beliefs, but to give them expression in a manner that forecloses the possibility of appealing to misleading evidence in excusing misrepresentation. For to the extent that you do foreclose the appeal to such an excuse, you make it more likely that you will have to pay for misrepresentation, suffering retaliatory and indeed reputational costs. And to the extent that you do that, what you say will be more credible and convincing for your audience. Thus, you will have a better chance of inducing that audience to rely on you, guiding their behaviour on the assumption that your representation is correct. And by proving to be reliable, you will have the opportunity to build up mutually beneficial relationships of trust. Commitment is the high road to such community.

But not only are there attractions of this kind attaching to commitment. It turns out that even if you wanted to, you could not indefinitely postpone commitment. At some level of linguistic communication, you will have to represent yourself on the excuse-excluding pattern; you cannot keep excuses available at every level of self-representation.

Suppose you want to hedge your bets on what you believe about Jones. In that case you will say that your impression is that you believe that Jones is trustworthy: that you find yourself inclined to say that he is, or something of that kind.[18] By taking this line you can get yourself off the hook, if you are proved to have misrepresented your belief; you will be able to appeal to a misreading of the evidence that you had about your beliefs at that first level. But is this ploy available at every possible level? Is the second-level belief that you would thereby represent yourself as having had open, for example, to the same possibility? Might you be able to explain having got it wrong by appeal to a misreading of the evidence at that level? And if so, what then of the third-level belief that you would represent yourself as having mistakenly held about the second-level belief? Might it be open to the same possibility as well?

On pain of infinite regress, these progressively higher-level beliefs cannot all be represented in the reportive manner way that would keep the possibility of evidential excuse open. At some level you must express the belief held, foreclosing

[17] J Maynard Smith and D Harper, *Animal Signals* (Oxford, Oxford University Press, 2004).

[18] It will not be enough to say that I believe that Jones is trustworthy, rather than simply saying that he is trustworthy. Shared contextual expectations will mean that even then I am going to be taken to be expressing the belief, not just reporting it. I would be laughed out of court if I claimed, in explaining behaviour which did not reflect the belief, that I had only expressed the higher order belief that I believe that Jones is trustworthy, not the ground-level belief that he is.

any excuse for getting it wrong.[19] The option for expression over description, then, is not a heroic choice in favour of commitment. When you represent what you believe to others you have to commit yourself at some level and have to expose yourself to the possibility of censure at that level. The only choice is whether to commit in the lower reaches of self-representation or in the higher.

The Normativity of Commitment

When you opt to give expression at a certain level to your belief, then we may say that you avow that belief, conveying it in a manner that forecloses evidential excuses for misrepresentation. You assume responsibility, on an evidentially invulnerable basis, for getting that belief right. You assume the position of a spokesperson in relation to yourself, not just that of a third-party observer.

Does the avowal of a belief in this sense mean that there is a non-prudential sense in which you ought to instantiate and display the belief avowed, short at least of a change of mind? I claim that it does. Even when you report a belief you subscribe implicitly to the rules of representation under which you will be guilty of an offence if the report is incorrect. Thus, you expose yourself to the charge that you breached those rules in a case where you, as you implicitly alleged, had the capacity not to do so: you expose yourself to epistemic blame. But this exposure does not make you very vulnerable in the case where you merely report a belief. You can claim, as you might claim in reporting on another's belief, that the evidence was misleading or that you, the subject of the report, changed your mind after the report had been made.

Things change in two related ways, when you avow the belief rather than just reporting it. First, you make the obligation incurred much more directional, since you will be required to perform appropriately or to produce evidence of a change of mind, if you are to not to be blamed under the rules of representation for dishonesty. Appealing to misleading evidence is no longer an option, so that the obligation incurred is that much more constraining. Absent evidence of a change of mind, avowal requires you to display the belief ascribed.

But the second change that avowal signals is even more important. Given that you put aside the possibility of being mistaken about the belief you avow, you cannot put yourself forward as a reliable self-representer just on the basis of your epistemic capacity as a representing subject; otherwise evidential excuses would have to remain open.[20] What is the basis that you implicitly allege for being

[19] D Bar-on, *Speaking My Mind: Expression and Self-knowledge* (Oxford, Oxford University Press, 2004); V McGeer, 'Out of the Mouths of Autistics: Subjective Report and its Role in Cognitive Theorizing' in A Brook and K Akins, *The Philosophy and Neuroscience Movement* (Cambridge, Cambridge University Press, 2005).

[20] One broadly Cartesian alternative might be that we have an infallible access to suitable states of mind and that we generally choose to avow only those attitudes or intentions that show up in the epistemically guaranteed way. But that story is highly dubious, since the idea of epistemic infallibility

reliable to the point of foreclosing such excuses? It can only be that you make up your mind—you determine the belief to have—at one and the same time that you give it expression. Asked whether you believe that p, you make a judgment on whether or not p (you make up your mind on the matter) and you avow the belief that p in giving expression to the belief formed: in saying, 'p'.[21] Thus, the second change signalled by avowal is that you engage the rules of representation, not just in the epistemic guise of a representing subject, but also in the practical guise of the agent represented. If you get things wrong you expose yourself, not just to epistemic blame, but to blame for not being up to the standards of agency: not forming beliefs in such a way that they stay formed and are displayed in action.

With this dual shift, the requirements associated with the rules of representation allow talk of what you ought to do, or ought to have done, that is not itself prudential. Absent a change-of-mind excuse, we may say that as a self-representer with a purported, agentially based capacity to conform to your representation of your belief you ought to have conformed; you ought, under the rules of representation, to have displayed the belief ascribed. And we can say that under those rules you are subject to blame or censure. It may be that in breaching the rules you behaved imprudently, say because of the retaliatory or reputational costs involved. But we can abstract from that charge of imprudence—indeed it may not even apply—when we censure you. We can censure you from within your implicit and purported aspiration to operate under the rules of representation.

There is nothing mysterious going on here. The ought that we invoke is, in Kantian terms, the ought of a hypothetical or conditional imperative. If you subscribe to the rules of representation, so we say, then you ought to display the belief avowed, setting aside the possibility of a change of mind. And assuming that you do indeed subscribe, as you purport to do, we can put those rules in the background and say, without explicit qualification, that you ought to have displayed the belief you avowed and that you are subject to blame or censure for not having done so.

The ought invoked here, as this comment makes clear, is an in-system obligation: a requirement that obtains within the system of representational rules, in particular the system of rules as they apply to self-representers who choose to avow a certain belief as distinct from merely reporting it. But while that in-system ought is not a prudential obligation, of course, our story suggests that if there is an obligation to abide by the system of representational rules itself—if

is so contentious. And in any case it fails to make sense of why we have no choice but to express our beliefs at some level if we are to make assertions. It would seem like an unbelievably happy coincidence that whenever we make an assertion we happen at the appropriate level to enjoy Cartesian infallibility.

[21] G Evans, *The Varieties of Reference* (Oxford, Oxford University Press, 1982).

there is a corresponding out-system obligation—then that is going to be prudential in character. The idea in the story sketched is that prudential agents will opt in general for tit-for-tat co-operation; that they will give rise thereby to a norm of honesty in their communicative dealings with one another; that they will engage this norm in avowing beliefs, not just reporting them; and that in doing this they will expose themselves in a relatively directional, agential manner to certain non-prudential obligations.

Consistently with these observations, of course, it might be that the prudential, out-system reasons for subscribing to the rules of representation are not very strong so that you may be expected to defect on your self-representational obligations as soon as they become costly. But as a matter of fact, the prudential reasons for subscribing to the rules are normally going to be very weighty. You will not be able to proclaim allegiance to the rules and defect opportunistically, as prudential convenience requires. Under almost any plausible circumstances, such defection would be likely to destroy your reputation and the cost would be ostracism from communicative co-operation with others. Thus, you will have to make the hard choice between being in or being out: between subscribing to the rules, and being generally faithful to their requirements, or opting for a state of hostility, or certainly the absence of fellowship, with others in your society.

But it may not be that the rules under which people bind themselves in avowal of their beliefs (or, as we shall see, in other avowals and promises) gain a further, more than prudential hold on people. I spoke earlier of the possibility of internalising certain norms motivationally. The example provided was the move whereby a norm of standing at a certain distance from interlocutors might be adopted in the first place on a prudential basis (say, the basis on which conventions in general may be adopted)[22] but come to be internalised motivationally as people get to like that particular pattern. It is possible, in a parallel way, that people should come to internalise the rules of self-representation motivationally, becoming attached to them in their own right, even if they begin with an adherence that is purely prudential in character. They might be moved, in Hume's terminology, by a feeling of sympathy for the general benefit that the rules provide in facilitating social life. I think that it is wholly plausible to postulate such an internalisation of the rules but nothing in my argument depends on its occurring.

Avowals and Promises

The conclusion of the argument so far is that even when people come to uphold a norm of honesty on a purely naturalistic basis, they are going to get themselves into a position where they are bound to conceive of their compliance with the

[22] Lewis, n 2 above.

norm as a matter of commitment and of the punishment to which offenders are exposed as a matter of censure. They are bound to adopt an internal point of view on the norm: a point of view under which it assumes a normative, not merely prudential status. This result is exciting in itself but it assumes a particular significance in view of the range of cases over which it applies. It turns out that the commitments people have to recognise in the course of honest communication, and the forms of censure that they are bound to license, extend over all forms of attitude and action, not just over beliefs.

Beyond the Avowal of Belief to the Avowal of Other Attitudes

Commitment, by our account, is a form of self-representation in which a speaker forgoes an otherwise available excuse for self-misrepresentation and does so as a matter of shared awareness with the audience. But commitment in this sense need not be limited to the case of belief. A participant in an exchange may commit to any of a variety of attitudes, not just to the attitude of belief. And equally, as we shall see, such a participant may go further and commit to one or another specific course of action.

Questions and requests and orders, as we saw earlier, involve the expression of attitudes, among them attitudes other than belief, not their descriptive attribution. The question expresses the wish to know whether something is the case together with the background belief that things are otherwise thus and so. The request expresses the desire that the addressee do something or other and the belief that this is possible. And the order expresses the act of giving a command as well as the associated belief that the speaker has the requisite authority to do so.

In each of these cases the speaker might have resorted to an excuse-allowing way of communicating the relevant attitudes, though that would have required a good deal of circumlocution. Instead of playing safe, however, the speaker opts for an excuse-excluding form of expression, thereby engaging a commitment and inviting censure for misrepresentation. No one will think that speakers should be censured if they make false background assumptions in asking questions, making requests or giving orders. But everyone will think that they are subject to censure if it turns out that the attitudes they expressed were not actually in place: that the speaker was insincere or dishonest, for example, in pretending to a wish to know something, or pretending to a desire that something be done.

But it is not just in non-assertoric speech acts that speakers commit to attitudes other than belief. Suppose, using an apparently descriptive idiom, that I say 'I approve of white lies in politics'. I will certainly have expressed and committed to the belief that I do indeed hold that attitude of approval. But in normal contexts I will also be taken to have expressed and committed to that attitude of approval itself—and this, again, as a matter of shared understanding.[23] I will have put myself in a position where I cannot excuse myself evidentially if it turns out that I don't actually hold the attitude of approval ascribed. I will have expressed both the belief that I hold an attitude of approval towards political white lies and the attitude of approval itself.

The reason why this is so derives from the principles that govern conversation, and in particular from the principle according to which a speaker is expected to choose words that do not understate or overstate the information to be communicated.[24] When it comes to communicating your attitude of approval, you might have done so in a clearly descriptive manner, expressing your belief that you approve, while indicating that that belief may be mistaken. Given that you do not opt for that manifestly available form of words, you will be taken to be communicating something more (and this, as a matter of common awareness) in saying, baldly, 'I approve of white lies in politics'. The something more that you will be taken to communicate, plausibly, is that you are not hedging your bets on whether you have that attitude or not; you are staking your reputation on your proving to have the attitude, denying yourself access to an evidential excuse for any misrepresentation.

This commissive construal of your words fits with a broader sense of what you are doing in saying 'I approve of white lies in politics'. Why would you have any interest in telling us about your attitudes in a descriptive spirit? You might want to do that with your therapist or confessor. You might want to confess that you seem to hold an attitude of approval towards politically motivated white lies, you know not why. But in normal contexts such a confession would be out of place. And so the words you use are bound to be taken as a commissive expression, not just a descriptive report, of your attitude.

There is another, even better established way in which people commit to attitudes of approval and disapproval, apart from resorting to self-ascription. That is by means of employing evaluative terms, positive and negative. These would include stock examples like 'kind' and 'cruel', 'generous' and 'selfish', 'good' and 'bad'. And, within the practice of commitment, they might also include 'censurable' and 'not censurable'. Even if predications of evaluative terms are used to commit to beliefs, as I take them to be generally used,[25] they serve at the same time to commit to attitudes of approval and disapproval. You would not count as understanding such a term, if you did not understand that to use it of something is to represent yourself as having an attitude of at least qualified approval or disapproval towards the item evaluated. And this self-representation will count as commissive, not just descriptive. If the self-representation proves to be

[23] F Jackson and P Pettit, 'A Question for Expressivists' (1998) 58 *Analysis* 239; F Jackson and P Pettit, 'Locke, Expressivism, Conditionals' (2003) 63 *Analysis* 221.

[24] P Grice, *Studies in the Ways of Words* (Cambridge, MA, Harvard University Press, 1989).

[25] P Pettit, 'Embracing Objectivity in Ethics' in B Leiter (ed), *Objectivity in Law and Morals* (Cambridge,Cambridge University Press, 2001).

inaccurate—if it turns out that you do not actually have the associated attitude of approval or disapproval—the misrepresentation will not be explainable and excusable by appeal to misleading evidence; it will be subject to censure.

Beyond Avowals to Promises

Not only do we routinely commit to attitudes, however, in co-operating with one another conversationally. Even more importantly, we commit with equal regularity to performing specific actions. The point is best demonstrated by considering the contrast between my telling you what a third party is going to do in the event that you make a certain choice and telling you what I am going to do in that event.

Suppose that I tell you in consultative mode that somebody else intends to reward you for choosing A rather than B in a choice that you currently face, indicating therefore that he or she will indeed provide a reward. I thereby express the belief that the person intends to provide the reward, so that I cannot excuse myself if I prove to have misrepresented the belief. But I merely report that the person intends to provide that reward and if I prove to have misrepresented his or her disposition, then I may well be able to explain and excuse the misrepresentation by showing that I had been misled by the evidence available. I may be able to show, for example, that I overheard the person express an intention to reward the choice of A in a context where I wrongly thought that you were the subject of discussion.

But what now if I tell you that I, and not another person, intend to reward your choice of A? In such an address I will have committed to the belief that I so intend, as in the other case; I will not be able to explain or excuse any misrepresentation of that belief. But will I have committed to a belief such that if it proves to be incorrect—if I prove not to have the ascribed intention—I can explain and excuse the misrepresentation of my intention? Will I have made a commitment that has the same thin profile as the commitment in the case with the other person?

Suppose that I tried to explain and excuse my failure to provide the reward for your choosing A, on the grounds that I had misread my own intentions. I made the attribution of intention sincerely, so I might say, and I do not count as insincere and dishonest just because it proved to be false. This explanation would have no plausibility whatsoever—it would make me a laughing stock amongst my audience—in view of considerations that we rehearsed in discussing the commissive aspect of self-ascribing an attitude of approval or disapproval.

With the self-ascription of an attitude there is a clear distinction between reporting, in a fallible spirit, that I think I have the attitude, and ascribing the attitude without reservation. And in the same way there is a clear difference between reporting in a fallible spirit that I think my intention is to do such and such and ascribing that intention without qualification. Under standard principles of conversation, therefore, the choice of the unqualified words means that there is more information to be communicated than what the qualified statement would have conveyed. And that information, plausibly, is that I am committed to the intention. I have put aside appeal to any evidential excuse for misrepresenting the intention, if I prove to have misrepresented it. I have locked myself in.

That makes for a first disanalogy between reporting on someone else's intention to provide a reward and expressing my own intention to provide it. But, importantly, there is a second disanalogy too. This appears when we consider another way in which I might explain why I got the other person's behaviour wrong and misled you about the prospect of a reward. This also is a form of explanation and excuse that is not normally available in the case where I say that I myself, not another person, intend to reward your choice of A.

Where I reported the intention of the other person, predicting a reward, it may be that I got the other person's intention right but that he or she failed to provide the reward because of a later change of mind. I may be able to show that the person gave up on the intention to provide a reward after I made my report to you but before you actually made the choice of A. Perhaps there is some collateral indication of that shift of attitude or perhaps the person is willing to confess that it did indeed occur. If I can explain the failure of my prediction on grounds of such a change of mind, then I will be able to excuse myself just as effectively as if I had been able to explain it on grounds of misleading evidence. Thus, I will be able to continue to present myself to you as a sincere and honest interlocutor.

The second disanalogy between the first-person and the third-person case is that just as I cannot excuse my failure to provide you with a reward on evidential grounds, so I will not be able to excuse it on the grounds of a change of mind. I will be a laughing stock if I try to invoke this excuse just as I will be a laughing stock if I try to invoke the other. I will make a mockery of my words if I try to claim that while I ruled out the possibility of having gotten my intention wrong, I did not mean to rule out the possibility of changing my mind.

Why is this so? Arguably, once again, because of the principles of conversation. Instead of having said 'I will reward you for the choice of A', I might have said something much more qualified. I might have told you that I intended to provide you with a reward for choosing A but that there was a possibility that I could change my mind. In the absence of that qualification, the declaration of an intention to provide a reward, or the declaration that I will provide a reward, is bound to be construed as communicating something more. And the extra information that it is naturally taken to communicate is that I am committed to rewarding your choice of A in a way that denies me access, not just to an evidential excuse for not acting on such an intention, but also to the excuse that invokes a change of mind.

We saw earlier that there is very good reason why I might want to commit to a belief or other attitude, and not hedge my bets. Exposing myself to a penalty for any misrepresentation, I can make it much more credible thereby that I hold that attitude and I can hope to elicit an equally committal response in you. It should be clear on parallel grounds why I might want to commit to a certain action, not just commit to an intention to perform it while retaining the right to change my mind. By committing to the action rather than just the intention I expose myself to penalty for non-performance on even a wider front than before and I give you firmer grounds still for taking me at my word and responding in kind. I make a double commitment, renouncing the possibility of excusing misrepresentation of myself either on evidential grounds or on grounds of a change of mind.

This doubly strong commitment constitutes what we call a promise and is available with actions as distinct from attitudes.[26] I can tie myself to doing something independently of how my mind changes in the meantime; I can guard against changing my mind for good reason or just through a failure of constancy. But I cannot promise you to believe something or desire something, if there is good reason for changing my mind; belief is meant to reflect evidence and fact, and desire to reflect how things appeal in light of my beliefs about them. What I can do in the domain of such attitudes, however, is to promise an action that will guard against the sort of change of mind that comes about as a result of weakness of will or intellect, and not for any good reason. I can go beyond the mere avowal of an attitude and commit myself to the exercise of vigilance in order to reduce the possibility of weakness or inconstancy; and I can do this in a way that guards against any later change of mind.

My Word is My Bond

Whenever I make a commitment, be it an avowal or a promise, I lock myself into a certain performance—I bind or obligate myself—by manifestly abjuring recourse to a certain excuse for not living up to the relevant self-representation. In commitment to an attitude I lock myself into continuing to display the attitude ascribed, putting aside the possibility of invoking an evidential excuse for having misrepresented myself. In commitment to an action I lock myself into actually performing that action, putting aside the possibility of invoking either an evidential or a change-of-mind excuse for proving to have misrepresented myself.

The binding of the self that commitment involves is not absolute, of course, even in the case of the promise. I may excuse self-misrepresentation in the case of an avowal (an attitudinal commitment) by appealing to a change of mind or by appealing to a change of circumstance; it is only the evidential sort of excuse that is set aside. And I may excuse self-misrepresentation in the case of a promise— (a

[26] There are lively debates about the nature of promising to which this discussion can be seen as a contribution. My approach rejects the broadly expectation-based approach defended in TM Scanlon, *What We Owe to Each Other* (Cambridge, MA, Belknap Press of Harvard University, 1998) ch 7. It belongs with approaches that take promising to involve a transfer of rights, though the rights invoked here, those associated with the practice of excusing oneself, are given a naturalistic explanation. See J Jarvis Thompson, *The Realm of Rights* (Cambridge, MA, Harvard University Press, 1990).

commitment to action) by appealing, if not to a lack of evidence or a change of mind, at least to a change of circumstance. I didn't keep the promise, I say, not because I got my intention wrong, nor because I had a change of mind. I failed to keep the promise, so the excuse will go, because circumstances changed from how we assumed in common they were, when I made the commitment: I believed that the change of circumstance effectively negated the terms of understanding on which the promise was made.

The binding aspect of commitment, notice, is always relative to another person. I deny myself access to a certain excuse for misrepresenting my attitude or action in the sense that I allow you, the addressee of my self-representation, to punish any misrepresentation. What denying access to the excuse means is that I deny myself the corresponding grounds for complaining about any punishment you might impose. When I lock myself into the attitude or action, I bind or obligate myself to you; I give you authority to demand performance or to exact redress.[27]

This interpersonal aspect of the binding involved comes out in the fact that you can release me from the bond. You can release me from a promise, either as an act of grace or because you agree that circumstances have changed in a way that undermines the terms on which the promise was made. And while you cannot release me from an avowal, you at least have a unique authority, as you have with promises too, to forgive me any misrepresentation that I may have practised.

Conclusion

As people seek to be honest with one another, they inevitably provide more than the benefits mapped in the counsel-and-consult model. The process of honest communication entails the formation of commitments to attitudes and commitments to actions among the parties; it leads them inescapably into making mutual avowals and promises. Thus, it enables the parties to lock one another into various patterns of thought and action, on pain of a penalty against which they cannot complain—a penalty that counts as censure. And all this is so, no matter how naturalistic the basis on which the norm of honesty emerges and survives. Out of the naturalistic motions of prudential, norm-creating adjustment come the makings of normative, not merely prudential obligation: the commitments that authorise claims and the censure that makes such claims effective.

[27] S Darwall, *The Second-Person Standpoint: Morality, Respect, and Accountability* (Cambridge, MA, Harvard University Press, 2006).

14

Resentment, Excuse and Norms

RICHARD H MCADAMS*

Philip Pettit identifies a 'norm–normative gap' in the naturalistic explanation of social norms and offers a way to fill the gap, at least for norms of honesty in communication. In this brief comment, I describe an alternative way to bridge the gap and suggest that the solution Pettit offers is not as inevitable as he claims.

The Norm–Normative Gap

What is the norm–normative gap? It is *not* the important yet sometimes neglected gap between a *mere* behavioural regularity and a norm. Pettit's appropriate definition of a norm excludes the former.[1] A behavioural regularity is not a norm unless '[p]eople give acceptance or approval to those who conform with the regularit[y] and/or reject or disapprove of those who deviate'.[2] Only when the behavioural regularity enjoys an approval rating that contributes to behavioural conformity and when there is some 'common awareness'[3] of the regularity, the approval rating, and the causal contribution of the latter to the former is the result a norm. So understood, a norm can exist merely because it is in most individuals' rational self-interest to conform, at least most of the time. A norm need not include a 'strongly normative element' by which individuals believe they *ought* to conform in a non-prudential sense. Yet because we know that most people believe there are non-prudential normative reasons for complying with certain norms, there is a gap between mere naturalistic norms and, for want of a better term, normative norms.

* I thank Jim Staihar for conversations about an earlier version of Philip Pettit's Chapter 13.

[1] See also Richard H McAdams and Eric Rasmusen, 'Norms and the Law' in AM Polinsky and SM Shavell (eds), *The Handbook of Law and Economics* (Amsterdam, NL, Elsevier, 2007) 1573–618.

[2] Philip Pettit, Chapter 13 at 227.

[3] *Ibid.*

By 'non-prudential' reasons, Pettit means to exclude not only the avoidance of external sanctions, but also the influence of internalised incentives. A person who internalises a norm may 'become attached'[4] to it without granting it a normative status. Here, I assume Pettit means that a person who internalises a norm might feel something like guilt or anxiety from violating it or positive feelings such as pride or camaraderie from complying. These feelings create additional incentives for compliance. But compliance is still about the rational self-interested response to incentives. Internalisation therefore need not create or constitute a normative status for the norm.

Thus, what Pettit seeks to explain is not incentives or behaviour, but 'the way that people come to conceptualise the demands of a norm'.[5] Pettit mostly avoids discussion of obligation, but a familiar part of what Pettit seeks to explain is why some norms are commonly thought of as constituting moral obligations while others are not. How do individuals move from prudence-talk to obligation-talk? Pettit's phrasing is broader, asking 'how some norms come to assume such a normative, more-than-prudential status in the minds of those who uphold them'.[6]

An Alternative Explanation for How Norms Become Normative: Resentment

To this general question, Pettit does not offer a general answer. Instead, he focuses on one particular norm: that requiring honesty in expression. There is a pertinent empirical question here: how commonly do our social norms command our allegiance in a non-prudential way? My guess is that such commitment is quite common—that most norms of any consequence are normative in the strong sense—and that it is only the exceptional case, such as rules of 'mere' etiquette, where people conceptualise the norm as only a prudential guide. If so, then Pettit's explanation fails to bridge the norm–normative gap for the majority of norms. Of particular interest, the theory does not tell us how *legal* rules assume a 'more-than-prudential' stature in the minds of those who follow them, although this is often the case. Pettit hints that his 'story has very general implications'[7] that he explores in a forthcoming book. No doubt he will make good on his claim. But at least for now, one wonders whether there is a more general theory that explains how most norms become normative.

[4] *Ibid* 229.
[5] *Ibid.*
[6] *Ibid* 228.
[7] *Ibid* 229.

A Preliminary Observation: Narrowing the Gap

Before offering such a theory, let me first identify how the norm–normative gap is *narrower* than it may first appear. There are two points. First, as Pettit poses the problem, people already have the cognitive or neural capacity for making non-prudential 'ought' judgements. Nothing in Pettit's account offers to explain the origin of this mental capacity. In showing how naturalistic norms of honest expression become normative, Pettit merely assumes the capacity of individuals to engage in commitment and censure; he offers to explain the (near) inevitability that the capacity is exploited, not why it exists.

Secondly, for norms to exist even naturalistically, people must evaluate the behaviour of others. This point follows from Pettit's definition of norms, which requires that the behaviour the norm demands has an 'acceptance rating', which means that 'people give acceptance or approval to those who conform with the [behavioural] regularities and/or reject or disapprove of those who deviate'.[8] In other work, Pettit has elaborated (as have I) the power of esteem-seeking to generate naturalistic norms.[9] The acceptance rating is an incentive only because human beings value the good opinion of others intrinsically (as well as instrumentally). But the presence of norms also means, conversely, that human beings have *the capacity and inclination* to form attitudes of approval and disapproval. Developing such attitudes requires that one hold to some criteria of assessing others or the behaviour of others. One grants esteem to another because, say, she satisfies the criterion of being honest; one disapproves a person because, say, he fails the criterion of being thoughtful.

The criteria of assessment underlying esteem-based norms might remain unarticulated and subconscious. One might just have a vague positive or negative feeling towards the behaviour of others, producing an unreflective grunt of approval or disapproval. But one's criteria of assessment for esteem judgements can be and frequently are explicit and subject to conscious reasoning. A person may reflect on the behaviour he is evaluating and consider how it compares to other behaviour or how the presence of unusual circumstances affects the evaluation. This point is consistent with the fact that the granting or withholding of esteem is ultimately a reflexive, not an intentional, act. If one values honesty or industriousness, and observes the presence (or absence) of those qualities in a person, one cannot choose to withhold (or grant) the relevant quantum of esteem anyway. Yet the ultimately involuntary nature of the esteem judgement does not mean that one cannot revise one's criteria for esteem in light of rational criticism, nor reset the bar for behaviour based on new information or a new frame of analysis. A person who loves chess at age 15 may later decide that

8 *Ibid* 227.

9 See Philip Pettit, '*Virtus Normativa*: Rational Choice Perspectives' (1990) 100 *Ethics* 725. See also Richard H McAdams, 'The Origin, Development, and Regulation of Norms' (1997) 96 *Michigan Law Review* 338.

chess-skill is not such an important basis for esteem judgements, or that a certain level of prowess in chess openings is more common and less impressive than he once believed, or that a person's access to chess tutors affects the merit of his performance.

Thus, even with a merely naturalistic norm, as Pettit defines them, individuals may employ explicit, reasoned criteria for granting the approval and disapproval that supports the norm. This narrows but does not eliminate the norm–normative gap; that gap persists because the resulting esteem judgements are still not 'strongly normative', but merely produce an incentive for others to comply with the norm. My reasoned approval for chess prowess in others does not quite entail my thinking that people 'ought' to play chess in a non-prudential sense. However much reasoning goes into my esteem-judgement, in the end, I simply 'like it' when others are good at chess.

Nonetheless, as a result of these two points: (1) that people have the mental capacity of making strongly normative judgements, and (2) that people engage in explicit reasoning about the criteria of their esteem judgements, the norm–normative gap is not as large as it first appears. One only has to explain how individuals' esteem assessments become normative. How do individuals move from making a reasoned judgement of the form 'I dislike and disapprove other people being dishonest' to the form 'I believe people (including myself) ought to be honest independently of their self-interest'. There might be two steps here; one is to move from 'liking' other's norm compliance (based on explicit reasoning about the criteria of assessment) to believing that others 'ought' (in a non-prudential sense) to comply. The second step is applying this judgement about others to oneself.

An Alternative Theory for Bridging the Gap

Let me now offer, briefly and tentatively, an explanation for each step, which together constitute an alternative to Pettit's account. First, there is a tendency to turn one's criteria of assessment for esteem judgements into a non-prudential normative judgement. The motivational spur for this shift is resentment. Robert Sugden posits 'that it is part of normal human psychology for us to feel resentment against individuals whose acts are both contrary to our expectations and contrary to our interests—particularly if we believe that those individuals knew their acts would have those properties'.[10] A self-centred perspective supports A's emotion of resentment towards B for any behaviour that has two qualities: it is unexpected and it harms A (especially if B has knowledge of these

[10] See Robert Sugden, 'Normative Expectations: The Simultaneous Evolution of Institutions and Norms' in A Ben-Ner and L Putterman (eds), *Economics, Values, and Organization* (Cambridge, UK, Cambridge University Press, 1998) 73, 81. See also David Lewis, *Convention* (Cambridge, MA, Harvard University Press, 1969) 99–100; Pettit, n 9 above, at 734.

facts, though that seems not to be essential). Expected behaviour, even if harmful, is generally excused or ignored; it is difficult for an individual to significantly resent a stranger for advancing his own interests in just the way everyone, including the individual, expects. But given that Pettit's definition of a norm requires a corresponding behavioural regularity, the naturalistic norm ordinarily makes everyone expect the behaviour the norm demands. As a result, norm violation is usually unexpected. When another's unexpected norm violation harms an individual, it triggers resentment.

Now consider an empirical claim about human psychology: An individual with the capacity to make non-prudential ought judgements strongly tends to exercise that capacity to censure behaviour that (a) fails his criteria of assessment for esteem judgements *and* (b) causes him to feel resentment (because it is unexpected and personally harmful). It would require an odd selflessness (or perhaps unusual philosophical sophistication) for an individual to resist making negative, non-prudential ought judgements about behaviour that shares all these characteristics: he disapproves of it, he is surprised by it, and he believes it harms his interests. Humans naturally seek to give voice to their emotions; not expressing emotion requires effort. An obvious means of expressing resentment is by employing one's capacity for strongly normative judgements, as in 'you ought not to have acted that way'. Just as I apply my reasoned criteria of assessment to disapprove of your behaviour *despite its advancing your own interests*, the emotion of resentment drives me to apply my capacity for normative censure against your unexpected and (to me) harmful behaviour despite its advancing your own interests.

Now for the second point. Subject to a caveat explained in the next paragraph, it is difficult to resist applying one's normative beliefs concerning the behaviour of others to one's own behaviour. Simple consistency exerts a strong influence on self-representation. If one withholds esteem from others for dishonesty or littering, then it will be difficult to avoid disapproving of oneself for the same behaviours. One might like to grant oneself an exception, but the esteem-judgement is not an intentional act. The psychology of esteem plus the power of consistency creates the conditions in which it is likely that one judges oneself negatively for failing to live up to the standards on which one grants approval or disapproval to others. One will understand and accept the resentment others feel towards oneself and that will make it likely that one internalises the norm and feels something like guilt or anxiety at one's violation. Internalisation is not the same as a strong normative allegiance to the norm, but my argument here is parallel to that above: When one's behaviour violates one's own criteria of assessment and causes (not resentment but) guilt or anxiety, a person with the capacity to make non-prudential ought judgements will likely exercise that capacity by forming such judgements. Again, the emotion sparks the strongly normative judgement.

A strong egoism would block this last step. Perhaps one's sole criterion of assessment is whether another individual's actions benefit oneself. If and only if your behaviour serves my interests, I esteem you. Your lying to me harms my interests and so induces me to disapprove of you. My lying to you, however, might serve my interests, and so I do not disapprove of myself. Such a person might also easily resist ever internalising the norm. If one's behaviour conforms to one's criteria of assessment and fails to trigger guilt or anxiety, it is unlikely to trigger the capacity for censure of one's own behaviour. Because of this possibility, I do not claim that there is anything inevitable about the transition from strongly normative beliefs about others to strongly normative beliefs about oneself. But the nakedly egoistic way of thinking is, I think, sufficiently rare (unlike more subtle rationalisations) that the transition is a common one.

This resentment theory predicts that social norms will command a non-prudential allegiance whenever they forbid behaviour with primarily negative externalities or require behaviour with primarily positive externalities. Because a great many norms have just this structure (eg norms against violence and theft; norms requiring contributions to public goods) the resentment theory predicts that a great many norms will be normative in this strong sense.

Yet the resentment theory has the virtue of being consistent with the non-normative basis of certain rules. It predicts that norms will remain merely prudential if the violation of the norm fails to harm others. The rules of etiquette present an example in favour of the theory: 'mere' failures of etiquette do not obviously cause harm to others and thus do not elicit resentment. Or perhaps it would be better to say, given the difficulty of defining harm, that people do not usually perceive themselves as being harmed by another person's etiquette violation (although I consider an exception below). Of course, the theory will only be as good as the empirical evidence allows; perhaps an investigation will show the existence of merely prudential norms against behaviour with primarily negative externalities or the existence of strongly normative norms against essentially harmless behaviour.[11]

My intuition is that a great many norms, including most legal norms, do prohibit externally harmful behaviour or require externally beneficial behaviour, so that the theory correctly predicts that most people feel a non-prudential allegiance to most norms. Even the contrary etiquette example requires a qualification: 'mere' rules of etiquette are not strongly normative, but they might appear to be so in contexts where breaches of etiquette fail to show respect and are insulting. An insulting breach of a norm of etiquette may breach a norm of respect for which there is a strong normative allegiance (for the reasons given above: the breach is unexpected and harmful to an individual). So even though

[11] Presumably, one could survey individuals to determine whether they conceptualise the 'ought' behind a norm in a prudential or non-prudential way. For example, one could ask a respondent about a particular norm he supports whether he agrees (merely) that conformity is (a) the best way to avoid disapproval or guilt, or also (b) that it is the right thing to do regardless of disapproval or guilt. One could then study whether, as I predict, the latter, non-prudential sense of ought tends to support (all but only) those norms that prevent harm to others.

etiquette norms lack strong normative commitment, adhering to etiquette will in some cases be necessary to show respect and to avoid eliciting resentment; thus, sometimes one feels obligated to adhere to a rule of etiquette. In the end, I think it is the rare case where a long-standing norm fails to attract a non-prudential normative commitment. I am therefore inclined to turn around the question Pettit poses: the puzzle is not how the norm–normative gap is bridged, but how we explain the exceptional cases where the gap persists, ie the few purely prudential norms against the ordinary background of norms that command a non-prudential, normative allegiance.

Pettit's Explanation of Norms of Honest Expression: Some Objections

Pettit offers to explain how the norm of honest communication becomes normative. Assuming the norm of honest communication first arises naturalistically, Pettit's key move is to introduce excuse for sincere but false expression. Pettit says that 'excuse may not be strictly definable on the basis of the naturalistic concepts',[12] yet 'the practice of invoking excuses . . . is bound to have a place under any norm of honesty'.[13] The appearance of excuse inevitably leads to the practice of commitment and censure that he associates with the internal perspective on norms. When one makes a statement that foregoes the possibility of excuse, 'it is natural to say that you commit to the belief'.[14] I take this to be a definitional claim: that what constitutes a commitment is tying oneself sufficiently to the belief one expresses, as by 'put[ting] evidential excuses . . . out of reach'.[15] I take no issue with this claim. But Pettit's further claim is that commitment inevitably brings with it strong normativity, a non-prudential allegiance to the norm of honest communication and censure of those who violate it. I question Pettit's optimism about the inevitability of this internal form of commitment and censure.

First, I do not believe that the concept of excuse necessarily emerges from a naturalistic norm of honest communication. Pettit imagines that the naturalistic norm of honesty arises in an iterated prisoners' dilemma from some kind of conditional co-operation, such as tit-for-tat strategies. Each party is honest in his communications only because he fears that dishonesty, at least when discovered, will induce retaliation (as by retaliatory dishonesty, a refusal to engage in exchange, or some other sanction). This is plausible; but let us pay greater attention to the set-up for conditional co-operation because I think it shows a

[12] Philip Pettit, Chapter 13 at 236.
[13] *Ibid.*
[14] *Ibid* 237.
[15] *Ibid.*

way that excuses are not necessary. One can dispense with the concept of excuse by redefining the behaviour the norm requires.

In a real world prisoners' dilemma, there is frequently more than one way to 'co-operate' (and because defection is any move besides co-operation, there is more than one way to 'defect').[16] This is an easy point to miss in the context of abstract prisoners' dilemmas, like the ones used in computer tournaments, because they simply define two possible moves, one being co-operation and the other defection. But frequently, there are many possible behavioural moves, and one might draw the line between co-operation and defection in more than one place. To sustain conditional co-operation, it will be necessary that the parties draw the line in the same place—that they co-ordinate on how to co-operate. Otherwise, there will eventually arise a case where one party plays what it thinks is a co-operative move, but which the other party views as defection. The latter party's retaliatory defection is one that the target will understand as an initial defection, requiring it to reciprocate with defection. The resulting spiral of defection is likely to cause co-operation to unravel.

Now let's apply this point to the context of communication. In an iterated prisoners' dilemma involving communication, there are at least two ways to define co-operation: (1) true communication or (2) sincere communication. Suppose the second definition forms the basis of a co-operative equilibrium in an iterated game. Under this equilibrium, if a party speaks sincerely, that counts as co-operation regardless of whether the content turns out to be false. The recipient responds to sincere (even if false) communication with co-operation and to insincere (even if true) communication with defection. Thus, the party who speaks sincerely but falsely *requires no excuse.* There is, of course, a need for evidence to determine whether the false statement was sincere, and that evidence may be hard to come by in some cases. But the naturalistic explanation of the norm does not logically entail excuse, and Pettit's claim does not inevitably follow.

Now suppose instead the first definition, true communication, serves as the basis for a co-operative equilibrium. Why would the parties choose true communication as the definition of co-operation when they could instead have chosen sincere communication? The only sensible reason is that the parties *are not interested in excuse.* Choosing the true communication definition implies a situation where the parties benefit most from demanding truth of each other and retaliating against falsity, regardless of whether the person who speaks falsely is at fault. We see this sort of 'strict liability' rule in some areas of the law and there is no reason it may not occur in informal norms.[17] In sum, it would be odd that the

[16] *See* Richard H McAdams and Janice Nadler, 'Coordinating in the Shadow of the Law: Two Contextualized Tests of the Focal Point Theory of Legal Compliance' (2008) 42 *Law and Society Review* 865, 871.

[17] I thank Jim Staihar for this point.

parties would select as the basis of co-operation the complex rule 'true communication subject to an excuse for unintended falsehoods' when they could have initially selected the simple rule 'sincere communication' discussed above. In either case, there is no role for excuse.

In any event, assume Pettit is correct and we arrive at a norm in which, when one speaks falsely, sincerity operates as an excuse. Assume also that a speaker sometimes will forego the excuse and commit to true communication. I also don't see how this commitment entails non-prudential normativity. This is my second objection: the decision to make oneself vulnerable to sanctions for speaking falsely, even though one could avoid such sanctions, can be given a naturalistic explanation. For purely instrumental reasons, an individual may seek to 'commit' himself to the truth of his assertions.

In the commercial context, this kind of commitment is a 'warranty'. A new seller wants to convince a potential buyer to buy the seller's goods. The seller claims that the goods have high quality, but the buyer is not persuaded. The seller's claim might not be sincere but, even if it is, a seller of goods is likely to be biased about their quality, so the sincerity of his belief is not especially informative. For this reason, the seller offers something stronger that he is not obligated to provide: a warranty. As in: 'I warrant that the goods are of high quality and, if they are not, you (the buyer) are hereby given special remedies against me'. By giving these additional remedies, beyond what would be provided in the absence of a warranty, the warranty induces a sale where mere sincerity would not.

The choice to bind oneself with a warranty is a commitment but it does entail the judgement that one ought, in a non-prudential sense, to speak sincerely. In this case, the seller sees the instrumental value of making the commitment: it increases sales. The seller need harbour no internal perspective that he 'ought' to make or honour the commitment. If he could get the sale without the commitment or maximise his profits by making but dishonouring the commitment, he would see no reason not to.

Thus, while I think Pettit traces out a plausible scenario whereby a particular naturalistic norm becomes strongly normative, I do not see it as an inevitable result. There is no necessity for excuses and no necessity that the commitment of foregoing excuses involves a non-prudential allegiance to the norm of honest expression.

Conclusion

Pettit identifies an important problem—the norm–normative gap. I believe, however, that there are more general solutions than the one he proposes and that his solution is not as inevitable as he claims.

15

Positivism and the Separation of Realists from their Scepticism

Normative Guidance, the Rule of Law and Legal Reasoning

GERALD J POSTEMA

Opening section 3 of his Holmes lecture,[1] Hart announced that his aim was to answer 'a distinctively American' challenge to the positivist doctrine of the separation of law and morals. He mainly had in mind the Realists, who had made a significant impact on American law schools by mid-century, but he also included Lon Fuller amongst the challengers. However, although he addressed some of his comments to this challenge, the main line of argument in this section actually used the separation doctrine to answer a different Realist challenge rooted, as Hart saw it, in a deep misunderstanding of the rule-guided character of legal reasoning. He did not seek to offer a theory of legal reasoning in this short section or in his somewhat more elaborated discussion in chapter 7 of *The Concept of Law*.[2] He sought, rather, to draw resources from what he took to be fundamental and widely recognised features of the concept of law to correct the misunderstandings of the process of legal reasoning that had tempted some members of the American camp to a deep scepticism about the integrity and rationality of that process.

Lon Fuller, in his response to the Holmes lecture,[3] detected in Hart's discussion an undercurrent of concern for the ideal of the rule of law ('fidelity to law') and what he took to be a characteristically positivist understanding of this ideal. Many commentators on the Hart–Fuller debate find Fuller's attribution of such a concern to Hart incredible, but if one looks carefully at Hart's arguments and

[1] HLA Hart, 'Positivism and the Separation of Law and Morals' in *Essays in Jurisprudence and Philosophy* (Oxford, Clarendon Press, 1983) 49–87.

[2] HLA Hart, *The Concept of Law*, 2nd edn (Oxford, Clarendon Press, 1994).

[3] Lon L Fuller, 'Positivism and Fidelity to Law' (1958) 71 *Harvard Law Review* 630.

tries to locate the sources of their plausibility, Fuller's claim takes on more credibility. Assumptions, some of them expressed, some implicit, about law's fundamental mode of operation and about why we look to law to aid in social ordering, are essential to Hart's argument. I shall argue here that these assumptions, when fully understood, lead to a view of law and of legal reasoning that has more in common with the perspective of Hart's challengers (at least its moderate wing) than with that of Hart's positivists, both his intellectual ancestors and some of his descendents. This should not surprise, since Hart's lecture was inspired by Bentham's positivism, whose jurisprudence was shaped in reaction to Blackstone's awkward version of classical common-law jurisprudence, while the views of Fuller and the (moderate) Realists reflected, again sometimes awkwardly and sometimes flamboyantly, their common-law heritage. The view to which Hart's assumptions lead, I will argue, shares much with that common-law tradition.

I propose to explore Hart's attempt to counter the American challenge and to argue that Hart's fundamental jurisprudential assumptions lead us away from what I will call his 'settled-meaning positivism' to a view of law as a disciplined practice of public practical reasoning. This story begins with Hart's attempt to characterise the 'American challenge' in terms of his distinction between the core and penumbra of rules. In the second section below, I set out Hart's critique of the Realists' flirtation with scepticism. In the third section we explore Hart's reasons for refusing the Realists' invitation to extend to the domain of the core the account of reasoning they and Hart accept for the domain of the penumbra. It is here that the assumptions underlying Hart's arguments are exposed by looking briefly at two directions in which his incomplete statements of these arguments have been elaborated. The fourth and fifth sections argue, first from widely accepted assumptions about the ideal of the rule of law and then from the assumption of law's essential normative-guidance technique, that rather than 'settled-meaning positivism', and subsequent elaborations of it, something closer to the common-law view of law as a disciplined practice of public practical reasoning is to be preferred.

Characterising the Challenge: Rules, Judgement and Indeterminacy

Hart's approach to the Realists' challenge was irenic. Acknowledging a core of good sense in the Realists' criticism of 'formalist' judges and jurisprudence, he offered a more measured formulation of the criticism, identifying a plausible source of the concerns that motivated the criticism, in hopes of domesticating them and preventing the slide into the scepticism they invited. To this end he offered an articulation of certain features of practical reasoning in general and judicial reasoning in particular, taking conditions of linguistic communication as a point of departure, and a diagnosis of the concerns underlying the Realists' criticisms.

To begin, Hart observed that, like successful linguistic communication, successful regulation of human behaviour by law depends on a generalised capacity of members of a linguistic or legal community to grasp rules and recognise instances in which they apply. Realists, he acknowledged, forcefully called to attention 'one cardinal feature of human language and thought' and hence of this capacity to grasp and apply rules.[4] Around a core of settled meaning, there is a penumbra of uncertainty or 'open texture,' as he put it in *The Concept of Law*. In their core, rules apply clearly to cases, but in their penumbra doubts and disputes can arise; application is not strictly dictated by the rule. The facts to which we fit the rule are dumb, Hart wrote, and 'logic is silent on how to classify particulars'.[5] When operating in the penumbra of rules, those charged with making decisions must take responsibility for *deciding* whether *to apply* the rules *to* situations facing them or not. Because the deciding is not dictated by logical deduction,[6] an ineliminable element of choice is involved—or, rather, 'something in the nature of choice'.[7] However, he hastened to add, this choice need not be bare or arbitrary choice. There is an important role for the exercise of practical reason in the penumbra, albeit not that of tracing the logical relations of premises to conclusions.[8] Thus, there is room for disagreement in the penumbra, but disagreement that invites argument, and the arguments offered can be assessed with respect to their soundness, even if they are not conclusive, and the decisions judged as correct insofar as they are based on sound arguments. If in some case this is not possible, at least we can say that some arguments offered are better or stronger than others and the decisions based on them more reasonable.[9] We judge the reasoned decision to be correct or at least better than alternatives according to some criterion or standard, and this standard typically involves some notion of what the rule ought to be.[10] In this way, Hart articulated the insight of Realist jurisprudence, an insight he fully embraced.

We can distinguish four moments in Hart's analysis of the Realists' insight. First, he offers an analytic frame for the problems to which the Realists called

[4] Hart, 'Positivism and the Separation of Law and Morals', n 1 above, at 63.

[5] *Ibid* 63, 67.

[6] *Ibid* 63–4.

[7] Hart, *The Concept of Law*, n 2 above, at 127. Hart does not say explicitly that reasoning in the domain of the core is a matter of logical deduction, but he does say that reasoning in the penumbra 'cannot be a matter of logical deduction', that the rationality of decisions in this domain 'must lie in something other that a logical relation to premises' ('Positivism and the Separation of Law and Morals', n 1 above, at 64). Since the exclusive contrast of this characterisation is with reasoning in the core, the necessary implication is that the positive correlate of his characterisation applies to the latter.

[8] Hart, 'Positivism and the Separation of Law and Morals', n 1 above, at 64.

[9] *Ibid* 64.

[10] *Ibid* 64.

attention: the problems are traced to a feature intrinsic to rules or norms,[11] namely, the fact that the core of settled meaning is surrounded by a penumbra of open texture. The modes of application are taken to be sharply different: the element of choice and decision characteristic of the penumbral domain is absent in the domain of the core. Secondly, Hart offers a diagnosis of the need for decision and choice in the penumbra: it lies in the logical gap between general propositions and particular instances. Thirdly, he observes that the gap can (often) be closed by reasoned argument, which guides, but does not eliminate, choice in the penumbra. Fourthly, he recognises that this presupposes a criterion by which it is possible to assess reasoning as sound even if not conclusive. He associates this criterion with considerations regarding 'what the rule ought to be', ie how it ought to be settled.

With this articulation of the Realists' insight in hand, Hart sought to separate Realists from the sceptical conclusions about judicial reasoning they were tempted to draw. However, before we look at his efforts to this end, we should note one problematic feature of this analysis. Hart's diagnosis of the problem of uncertainty in the penumbra relies on the fact that 'logic is silent about how to classify particulars' which is supposed to explain the existence and profile of choice and discretion in judicial decision-making which the Realists called to attention. However, this diagnosis is ill-suited to the categories of core and penumbra in which Hart framed his analysis. Hart points here to the familiar Kantian problem of judgement,[12] but that problem is entirely pervasive in thought; the gap between general and particular arises as much in the settled core as in the penumbra of rules, whether they are practical or theoretical. Logic cannot bridge this gap. It takes an act of judgement to take *any* empirical particular as an instance of a concept or *any* particular action as an instance of a rule. *Every* instance escapes in some respects the bounds of a concept or rule. Moreover, the gap is not bridged by making the rules more detailed and determinate, nor is it solved by appeal to other rules, policies, purposes, standards, or the like. (Thus, the problem is not that of the over- or under-inclusiveness of rules relative to their aims or purposes.) All these proposed solutions share the same problem-causing feature of generality relative to particular facts, situations or actions. For every intermediary another intermediary is needed, for every interpretation another interpretation. Thus, judgement bridging this gap is needed as much in the settled core of rules as in their penumbra. Of course, where matters appear settled, this also does not appear to us as a problem, but it is a very important question for philosophical jurisprudence how this is possible. Hart was right to insist that, despite the element of 'choice', it

[11] Hart frames the discussion in linguistic terms but the point is more general. The rules he considers could be linguistic, conceptual or practical, arising from example as well as expressed in an articulated proposition (see Hart, *The Concept of Law*, n 2 above, at 125–7).

[12] Immanuel Kant, *Critique of Pure Reason* (Norman Kemp Smith (trans), New York, St Martin's, 1929) 177–9 (A 132–6; B 171–5).

would be a mistake to conclude that application of rules, whether in the core or penumbra, is arbitrary or unguided by reason, for this conclusion would have the radical consequence of removing reason from the entire domain of thought and practice. But, similarly, Hart cannot explain the role of choice in judicial reasoning in the penumbra by appeal to the problem of judgement.

In *The Concept of Law*, Hart offered an alternative diagnosis of the problems in the penumbra. He claimed that they arise from the inevitable and ineliminable vagueness or indeterminacy of rules and rule-like phenomena, including customs, precedents and examples of all kinds. The indeterminacy of rules in law lies not in inherent deficiencies of language, but in 'our relative ignorance of fact' and 'our relative indeterminacy of aim'.[13] Hart's response to this problem is exactly his response to the problems of the penumbra: (1) there cannot be indeterminacy of rules if there is not also, first of all, a zone of determinacy, a core of settled application, and (2) choice in the zone of indeterminacy, when exercised responsibly, is often guided by a kind of reasoning that builds on the settled core and perhaps other things as well.[14] This diagnosis provides Hart with a more plausible analysis of the Realists' insight and a more promising basis for his response to their challenge. We turn to the first phase of that response now.

Containing the Challenge: Rules, Reasoning and Choice

To contain the Realists' challenge, Hart first sought to block their inference from recognition of problems in the penumbra to the broadly sceptical conclusion that judicial reasoning is irremediably arbitrary, or at least not within the control of judicial reason. Against this version Hart offered two objections. First, he insisted on the necessity for law of the core of settled application. If there is no core of settled meaning, he argued, legal regulation of human behaviour is impossible; for legal regulation of behaviour in a community depends on the effective communication of rules to, and a general grasp of the rules in, that community, and laws could not function as rules if people could not count on some substantial range of settled application. To this the rule-sceptic might reply that legal regulation is possible, but just not regulation *by* or *with* rules *functioning as* normative guides. To this, Hart has several possible responses, but one is central to our purposes. Hart argued that, if regulation by means of rules functioning as normative guides is not possible, then *law* is not possible, for law *just is* a specific form of social control, namely, control through the instrumentality of rules. This premise, shared with Fuller, is fundamental to Hart's argument in 'Positivism and

[13] Hart, *The Concept of Law*, n 2 above, at 128.
[14] *Ibid* 127.

the Separation of Law and Morals' (and *The Concept of Law*, chapter 7). From this premise it follows that to deny law the instrumentality of rules is to usher law out of existence.

More generally, Hart argued that broad scepticism is unwarranted; for, even when an element of choice is involved, as in the penumbra, the choice is reason-guided. Reasoning is not absent from the penumbra, he argued; it just takes a different form from reasoning in the domain of the core. With approval, he noted that Austin regarded legal reasoning in the penumbra to be in part a matter of tracing the influence of competing analogies drawn from past judicial decisions.[15] Moreover, when responsible judges choose 'to add to a line of cases a new case' they take care to proceed by analogy 'so as to ensure that the new law they make is in accordance with principles or under-pinning reasons which can be recognized as already having a footing in existing law'.[16] Of course, such arguments depend on judgements of resemblances which themselves are 'defended as both legally relevant and sufficiently close . . . [where] the criteria of relevance and closeness of resemblance depend on many complex factors running through the legal system and the aims and purposes that may be attributed to the rule'.[17] Because 'cases do not arise in a vacuum but in the course of the operation of a working body of rules', judges often have available to them 'a multiplicity of diverse considerations' which are widely 'recognized as good reasons for a decision'.[18] Thus, deciding to apply a rule to an instance outside its settled core is often a matter of reasoned elaboration of the rule, drawing on diverse considerations running through the law. At times, when reasoning in the penumbra, decision-makers may even feel as if they have no choice at all.[19] That feeling is illusory, Hart insisted, since choice is unavoidable, but the process and its rationality are not.

This is a modest and measured response to the Realists' challenge, but in one respect it concedes more to the Realists' rhetoric than is warranted, I believe. Hart found the language of 'choice' helpful because it enabled him to mark clearly the fact that the penumbral domain is characterised by a degree of uncertainty and contestation in which 'there jostle too many alternatives too nearly equal in attraction between which judge and lawyer must uncertainly pick their way'. Thus, language that disguises choice and presents the decision as a matter of 'recognizing something awaiting recognition' is neither clear nor candid.[20] Hart argued that in the penumbra, reasons and arguments drawn from the body of law limit judicial choice, but they do not determine the choice itself.[21] I understand this to mean that reasons and arguments can rule out certain options as *ineligible*,

15 Hart, 'Positivism and the Separation of Law and Morals', n 1 above, at 65.
16 HLA Hart, *Essays in Jurisprudence and Philosophy* (Oxford, Clarendon Press, 1983) 7.
17 Hart, *The Concept of Law*, n 2 above, at 127.
18 *Ibid* 107.
19 Hart, 'Positivism and the Separation of Law and Morals', n 1 above, at 84–5.
20 *Ibid* 87.
21 *Ibid* 87.

and select and support others that are *eligible*; and that choice must be made among the eligible, reasons-supported options. But the language of choice can be equally misleading, I believe.

Viewed from outside, penumbral issues are occasions of doubt or uncertainty, but judges faced with them must engage in reasoned deliberation regarding them. At some point, perhaps, a judge may responsibly conclude that all the reasons and arguments drawn from settled law evenly balance out such that among a range of eligible options none is better supported than any of the others; but sometimes a judge might also responsibly conclude from consideration of the relevant arguments that one of the eligible options is better supported than any other and, on that basis, decide as they direct. Notice, however, that both conclusions are based on assessments of the strength of the arguments; neither follows from the fact that other competent judges came to different conclusions. Moreover, disagreement is possible not only with respect to the latter conclusion, but also with respect to the former. Disagreements about both kinds are disagreements about the strength of arguments and judgements based on them, and these disagreements are resolved only by further argument.

If this is true, then the language of choice obscures reasons-guided decision-making. In the penumbra, as Hart characterised it, there is likely to be uncertainty going into consideration of an issue and often disagreement after consideration about how that uncertainty is best resolved. However, in the face of the latter disagreement, where reasonable colleagues draw different conclusions from the arguments, the proper characterisation is not 'I chose option X but she chose option Y'; but rather 'I decided X and she judged Y'. The former fails to capture the logic of the situation. From *the fact* of disagreement it concludes that the disagreement is due to the balance of *the reasons*, but this misdescribes the normative status of the conflicting judgements and it obscures key implications of this conflict. Officials are accountable for their judgements and their reasoning to them. They can be challenged with respect to both and both can be redeemed only by further argument. Thus, at the point that different reasonable judges come to different conclusions after deliberation, it is always legitimate in principle (although often pragmatically difficult or inappropriate) to press for further reasons, to explore arguments not yet considered, or return to explored arguments for a closer look.

Of course, we may reach a point at which *all* relevant reasons and arguments are exhausted and the disagreement remains, but, in view of the vast network of reasons and arguments that the settled law offers for responsible deliberation, it would be a mistake to think we have reached that point just because sincere and competent decision-makers find themselves in disagreement. Even if we reach this point, the best characterisation would be that, after conscientious and exhaustive exploration, the parties have come to conflicting judgements based on the arguments, judgements for which they are accountable. This characterisation of the process and practice of legal reasoning in the penumbra does full justice to the uncertainty and openness that Hart was so keen to stress, but it also keeps fully in view the limits and the demands of responsible judgement and decision-making.

Answering the Challenge

Hart thought moderate Realists would accept his characterisation of judicial reasoning in the penumbra, but he worried that they were inclined to extend it to all of judicial reasoning, thereby jeopardising the integrity of the core. Realists, he observed, invite us to 'include in the "rule" the various aims and policies in the light of which its penumbral cases are decided on the ground that these aims have, because of their importance, as much right to be called law as the core of legal rules whose meaning is settled'.[22] Hart urged us to decline the invitation. What exactly was that the invitation and what evils did Hart seek to avoid by refusing?

Understood in one way, Hart sought to prevent lawyers and judges, urged on by Realist rhetoric, from reasoning in the penumbra under colour of law, pretending that their contestable claims and arguments, and even worse their personal ideological commitments, are sound conclusions and solid arguments of law.[23] Understood in another way, Hart sought to insulate reasoning in the core from the context- and purpose-sensitive argumentation characteristic of reasoning in the penumbra, where the proper understanding of a rule can only be settled by putting it in the context of the whole body of law (or some substantial part of it) and tracing its content-determined relations with other rules, decisions, and the like.[24] It is not clear which of these concerns was most prominent in his mind, but two things about his critique of moderate Realists are clear: he insisted (1) that the kind of reasoning in the area of the core is sharply distinct from that available in the penumbra, and (2) that *law* is restricted to the core of settled meaning and so *legal* reasoning is restricted to reasoning within the domain of the core.

The reasons Hart offered for these conclusions were: clarity and the separation thesis. Clarity favours the classical positivists' position which sharply distinguishes reasoning to and with legal rules alone from reasoning that appeals beyond them. The positivists' conception enables us to say everything true that the Realists sought to say, Hart insisted, in a less mysterious and misleading way. Secondly, he argued that the separation thesis—the positivists' sharp distinction between law as it is and law as it ought to be—implies that 'the hard core of

[22] *Ibid* 71.

[23] See Benjamin Zipursky, 'Practical Positivism Versus Practical Perfectionism: The Hart-Fuller Debate at Fifty' (2008) 83 *New York University Law Review* 1170.

[24] Frederick Schauer, 'A Critical Guide to Vehicles in the Park' (2008) 83 *New York University Law Review* 1109.

settled meaning is law in some centrally important sense', for without a settled core of meaning 'the notion of rules controlling courts' decisions would be senseless'.[25] I will call this 'settled-meaning positivism'.

These reasons are unpersuasive. Clarity demands that we not confuse reasoning using the settled core of meaning with reasoning in the penumbra of legal rules, and insists that the law is restricted to the settled meaning of rules, *only if* (1) and (2) are true. Similarly, it is surely a mistake to confuse law as it is with law as it ought to be; to do that would be a species of wishful thinking. However, until we have an account of what makes law what it is, we will not be able to determine whether considerations of value of any kind play a role in determining (metaphysically) whether something is law (ie a law, a legal system, or a matter of law) and so whether we should limit attention to the settled meaning. The separation thesis, without a substantive theory of the nature of law that enables us to distinguish law from that which is other than law, cannot help us decide whether law is a matter of settled rules or includes disputed considerations; and when the separation thesis is supplemented with an account of law, that is, when it is given its distinctively positivist understanding, it is no longer needed for that job. The *positivist version* of the separation thesis does not *support* the identification of law with settled meaning, it just is the proposal to do so.

The larger framework of Hart's critique of Realism suggests a rather different argument for settled-meaning positivism.[26] This argument rests on the premise that the law's basic task is to control human behaviour by general rules.[27] We can express this point more cautiously and accurately as the claim that law's fundamental mode of operating is through guidance of self-directing agents by norms. Operating in the mode of law requires, inter alia, that power be exercised through communication of clear and public norms and that activities of courts be limited to administering the norms meant to guide the behaviour of those subject to the law. And such norms or general rules cannot be communicated and cannot do their necessary guiding work unless there is a settled core of meaning that all can recognise, even if there is also some penumbra of uncertainty surrounding it. We cannot allow the uncertainty of the penumbra to penetrate the core of rules without crippling the law's essential technique of social control. Thus, law must be clearly identified with that settled core of meaning and legal reasoning must be restricted to reasoning to and from the settled core of rules.

However, this argument is a non sequitur. Settled meaning may well be necessary for law to do its essential norm-guiding work, but it does not follow

[25] Hart, 'Positivism and the Separation of Law and Morals', n 1 above, at 71.

[26] Later in *ibid* 75–8, Hart offers normative reasons for the separation thesis, and a fortiori for settled-meaning positivism, arguing that it underwrites and encourages the salutary habit in citizens of looking critically at law's claims to authority. It is much debated whether these are central to his case for positivism. I will not enter the lists on this issue here.

[27] Hart, *The Concept of Law*, n 2 above, at 124; 'Positivism and the Separation of Law and Morals', n 1 above, at 63.

that law embraces only that which is clearly included in the settled and undisputed core of law's norms. Hart's argument needs to be augmented or elaborated. Since the publication of *The Concept of Law*, Hart's position and argument has been developed in basically two directions. (I summarise here, unavoidably too roughly, over three decades of developments.)

First, appealing to law's alleged claim to authority, elaborated to embrace law's aim to offer normative guidance, it has been argued that law is limited to source-identified norms, and that reasoning to establish the content and requirements of law is limited to reasoning with source-based legal norms.[28] However, on this view, proper judicial reasoning is not limited to such considerations. Judges are authorised and sometimes duty-bound to appeal to considerations not included in the set of source-based norms, for example, considerations of substantive political morality. The adjudicative power of judges is often 'directed' to resolve uncertainties by appeal to extra-legal considerations. This 'exclusive positivism' is an extension or elaboration of Hart's simpler 'settled-meaning positivism', but it is in the spirit of Hart's view and is typically defended, especially in recent years, by appeal to arguments regarding law's normative guidance function. On this view, while law is restricted to source-based rules (or settled meaning), judicial reasoning is not and must not be so restricted.

The second direction in which Hart's argument has been developed is toward a more sophisticated formalism. On this view, not only is *law* restricted to something like settled meaning, but so too must be judicial reasoning, and the restriction of judicial reasoning to the core is interpreted as a restriction to rule-bound reasoning.[29] 'Rule-bound reasoning' recognises that there are strong reasons for judges to follow legal rules, even though the rules may be over- or under-inclusive relative to their underlying rationales and in consequence following the rule may 'get it wrong' relative to those considerations. Reasons of decision-making efficiency, predictability, control of official exercise of power, coordination of social interaction, and other such familiar considerations counsel (a strong presumption in favour of) adherence to the rule in the face of likely consequences contrary to their purposes and of other compelling considerations against doing so. Rule-bound decision-making regards the rules as opaque to their underlying rationales and the balance of competing considerations bearing on the actions governed by the rules. In this way, the core of settled meaning of rules is insulated from the influence of purposes and competing considerations that stir up uncertainty in the penumbra. The case for holding courts to this more sophisticated formalism rests on considerations of effective guidance of behaviour, of effective control of the exercise of political power wielded by law-applying institutions, and of related rule of law values.

[28] Joseph Raz, *The Authority of Law* (Oxford, Clarendon Press, 1979) 37–52; *Ethics in the Public Domain* (Oxford, Clarendon Press, 1995) 238–53, 326–40.

[29] Frederick Schauer, *Playing by the Rules* (Oxford, Clarendon Press, 1991); Larry Alexander and Emily Sherwin, *The Rule of Rules* (Durham, NC, Duke University Press, 2001).

These two ways of elaborating Hart's suggestion stand in a curious relationship. Both appear to be unstable and reasons against one view incline one strongly to the other only to be upset by considerations that incline one back to the first. The circle does not appear to be virtuous. The first view faces the following problem. Since the exclusivist account accepts that judicial reasoning typically and properly (that is, as a matter of judicial duty or responsibility) involves appealing to considerations that are not encompassed within 'settled meaning' or the range of approved sources, it is hard to see what is gained by restricting 'law' and 'legal reasoning' to the core of settled meaning or source-based rules. Perhaps the appearance of arbitrariness of this restriction can be dispelled if we take seriously law's fundamental aim to guide the behaviour of citizens and hold courts to decision-making that serves that task. However, this argument is puzzling. If norm-guidance of law-subjects is materially affected by the activities of law-applying institutions, as this view assumes, will not prudent law-subjects focus their attention on the activity of the institution as a whole, and thus judicial reasoning in general, and not merely the settled-meaning or source-based rules? If they seek guidance from the courts, why would they restrict their attention to law narrowly construed? If effective guidance is the aim, then labelling certain parts of the practice 'law' without binding the courts to those parts is unlikely to restrict the focus of guidance to those parts of the practice. To put the point another way: if the aim of law is to offer directives that settle matters for citizens, how can it do so effectively without constraining judicial reasoning to a substantial degree to those directives?

Something like this line of thought, I believe, moved Lon Fuller to attribute to Hart a conception of 'fidelity to law' (or rule of law) despite the fact that Hart never mentioned the idea in his Holmes lecture. Since Hart had to have *some* reason for restricting 'law' to settled meaning of legal rules, Fuller attributed to him the most plausible reason he could think of consistent with Hart's general sympathy with the broad direction, if not the particular details, of classical positivism. And that reason, in Fuller's view, arose from the classical positivist answer to the question why we find valuable law's specific mode of exercising political power. That answer, he thought (with Hobbes and Bentham in mind), was that we hold control of the exercise of power by holding those who wield it to rules that are public and undisputed. It is, he thought, a particular conception of the value and importance of law that underlay Hart's commitment to settled-meaning positivism. That conception puts a premium on certainty, predictability and control of the exercise of public power. Considerations like these lead us to some version of sophisticated formalism, which holds judges to rule-bound reasoning.

Yet, Hart himself offered persuasive reasons for resisting formalism,[30] which apply also to the more sophisticated version. Certainty, he argued, can be bought

[30] Hart, *The Concept of Law*, n 2 above, at 128–30.

at a price too high. We must leave significant room in legal reasoning for adjustment to future circumstances which call for refined formulation of existing rules and standards and even more for refined grasp of the reasons, aims and goals, and their relative importance, that inform the rules. We need some core of settled meaning, he insists, but we must not 'freeze the meaning of the rule' thereby 'settling in advance, but also in the dark, issues which can only reasonably be settled when they arise and are identified'.[31] Moreover, a degree of openness to the future is not just useful, it is essential to law's doing its work. We look to law for predictability as a hedge against arbitrary exercise of power, but that predictability must itself avoid arbitrariness. As Bentham argued long ago, when we permit inflexibility to dominate, predictability and control of arbitrariness are undermined,[32] for the need to avoid arbitrariness of the rules generates public pressure towards greater judicial flexibility, the exercise of which, however, is able to hide behind the appearance of adherence to rules, thereby loosening the reins of control. It is difficult to block judicial appeal to purposes and considerations behind the law, considerations that are in play in the penumbra, without undermining its ability to guide action and control political decision-making, because these are effective only if there is a significant degree of confidence in the non-arbitrary, reasons-intelligible character of the constraints. If this is, in broad strokes, correct, then we seem to be pushed back in the direction of the exclusivist understanding of settled-meaning positivism, a position which, we have seen, is unstable precisely in ways that push us back to the formalist understanding.

There is not time here or space properly to develop this dialectic fully. I present this suggestion of antinomy only to motivate a deeper exploration of the considerations on which Hart's initial argument, and these two competing elaborations of it, seem to rest. This exploration can proceed from two directions, one put on the agenda by Hart in his Holmes lecture, the other put there by Fuller's response. The former looks more carefully at what is involved in law's distinctive technique of normative guidance; the latter looks at the implications of certain widely accepted features of the ideal of the rule of law for our understanding of law and legal reasoning.[33] In the next two sections, I argue that these explorations will lead us away from Hart's settled-meaning positivism and

[31] *Ibid* 129, 130.

[32] I called this Bentham's 'paradox of inflexibility' in *Bentham and the Common Law Tradition* (Oxford, Clarendon Press, 1986, 1989) ch 8.

[33] No great distance separates these points of departure, since it is widely agreed that we must defend the central components of a plausible conception of the rule of law by appeal to law's essential and distinctive mode of operation. This is the direction Fuller takes in his defence of the 'inner morality of law' (*The Morality of Law*, 2nd edn (New Haven, CT, Yale University Press, 1969); it is also the starting point of Raz's classic analysis and defence of the ideal of the rule of law ('The Rule of Law and its Virtues' in Raz, *The Authority of Law*, n 28 above, at 210–29).

its elaborations in the direction of a conception of law and of the rule of law with affinities to classical common-law jurisprudence.[34]

Normative Guidance

According to common-law jurisprudence, law is best conceived not as a set of discrete rules, but as a discipline of public practical reasoning that provides a framework and forum for critical exploration as well as authoritative determination of public norms. This conception is favoured by Hart's own orienting assumption regarding law's distinctive task or mode of operation; or so I shall argue. This basic and widely shared understanding of law's distinctive modus operandi locates at the centre of the concept of law the notions of norm and authority. On this view, law-subjects typically take legal norms as guides for their action; as self-directing agents, they regard them as norms, having authority for them, and they direct their own actions by their understanding of these norms. This is a good start, I believe, but Hart and many who have followed his lead work with a conception of the normative guidance offered by law that, in my view, is too limited. They take guidance by authoritative directives as a model, but this model obscures important features of the way in which law typically provides normative guidance. At least three such features are worthy of mention here.

Publicity. To do their distinctive work, legal norms must be 'communicated' and such communication is not a matter of issuing general directives to each law-subject individually, but rather of addressing general norms to the public at large. Law does its work only when it is in force in a community, when it is the law of the community and used by its members.[35] The guidance it offers is addressed to individuals engaged in complex networks of social interaction. Among these agents it is common knowledge that they are rational, self-directing agents. So, effective guidance is possible only if their understanding of the norms and of the authority of the norms is common. Law's directives must be publicly recognisable and interpretable. The reasons they give must be reasons that law-subjects generally appreciate and readily understand that others appreciate. This need for public understanding and appreciation puts law-subjects and law-maintaining officials into a complex network of interdependence and, as Fuller often argued, imposes on them a discipline of reciprocity. Each law-subject and each official must engage in a kind of triangulation to arrive at his or her understanding of legal norms. Law-subjects must test their individual understandings against what they expect from other law-subjects with whom they are

[34] I have tried to capture central features of this view of law and legal reasoning in 'Classical Common Law Jurisprudence' (2002) 2 *Oxford University Commonwealth Law Journal* 155 and (2003) 3 *Oxford University Commonwealth Law Journal* 1.

[35] Gerald J Postema, 'Conformity, Custom and Congruence: Rethinking the Efficacy of Law' in Matthew Kramer (ed), *The Legacy of Hart* (Oxford University Press, 2008) 45–65.

likely to interact and from officials in whose jurisdiction they find themselves. Officials, likewise, must approach their understanding of legal norms, and their fixing of them where they are empowered to do so, guided by the understanding held by other officials and by the public generally. For this reason, debate over and determination of the meaning of legal norms must be institutionalised and made public.

The Constitutive and Evaluative Dimensions of Guidance. The second enrichment of our understanding of the way law offers normative guidance requires that we recognise that, in addition to the *directing* component, law's normative guidance has *constitutive* and *evaluative* or *vindicative* components. Unlike a regime of commands, law is fundamentally a mode of social ordering, *constituting* a network of relationships, normative conditions and statuses which reinforces and underwrites the normative infrastructure of the community. No philosopher has been more sensitive to this dimension of law than Bentham; indeed, it was his awareness of its importance which prevented him from publishing his initial thoughts about morals and legislation, shaped around a command model of law, until he could offer a consistent and plausible conceptualisation of law in its constitutive dimension. The fact that his attempt failed does not diminish the importance of the task. The failure (as Hart helped us to see clearly) was due in part to the fact that such legal relationship-establishing norms are more like maps than directives, providing resources for successful navigation of social interaction rather than defining specific tasks to perform, giving indirect guidance.[36]

The model of authoritative direction obscures this constitutive dimension of law. It also obscures the law's evaluative or vindicative dimension. Law provides the standards by which individuals evaluate their own behaviour, and evaluate the behaviour of others, in its public dimension, and vindicate that behaviour in response to its evaluation by others. Most importantly, it provides the framework within which we hold others accountable for their public behaviour. As we shall see below, this calls for a framework and a forum for challenging claims of officials and of citizens to act under colour of law, for assessing arguments made in response to demands for warrant for their actions.

The constitutive and vindicative dimensions of law are essential to its distinctive form of normative guidance. The essential role of the constitutive dimension in law's normative guidance is clear if we consider what is necessary for public understanding of legal norms.[37] If legal norms are to guide social interaction they must be practically intelligible to those whom they guide. For this purpose, an agent's determination of *what* a norm requires cannot be entirely divorced from her assessment of *why* it should be followed, what complying with it is meant to accomplish. It is too much, of course, to insist that the norm meet strict

[36] *cf* Raz's notion of 'indeterminate guidance' in his 'On the Functions of Law' in AWB Simpson (ed), *Oxford Essays in Jurisprudence*, Second Series (Oxford, Clarendon Press, 1973) 282–3.

[37] Postema, n 35 above, at 58 *et seq.*

conditions of moral justification, but it is necessary for the agent to attribute some practical point to the norm. Moreover, because law seeks to guide action through public norms, those norms must be intelligible to law-subjects in common. What is practically intelligible in common is never merely a function of the promulgation of norms in the common language of the community, but always also a function of the practices that structure the community's public life and relatively stable public relationships. Authoritative directives will be able to guide in the fashion distinctive of law (ie as norms, rather than as triggers for ritualised or fear-motivated behaviour) only when they can draw on the infrastructure of social relations provided by such norms and practices. Law in its constitutive dimension underwrites, reinforces and more or less subtly shapes these norms and practices. In political communities with mature legal systems there is likely to be a great deal of interdependency between informal social norms and the more formal constitutive norms of law, so much so that there is likely to be a grey area in which it is not possible sharply to distinguish them. Thus, law cannot authoritatively direct or regulate social behaviour in the manner of law without the continued assistance of its constitutive norms.

Likewise, law depends on its vindicative dimension for effective normative guidance. The reason for this is that guidance of social behaviour by public norms of law is possible only if conditions of congruence and continuity are met. The requirement of *congruence* is familiar to readers of Fuller. Official promulgation and public profession of legal norms are not sufficient to secure their effectiveness as guides of public behaviour if those whom law seeks to guide are not sufficiently confident that the law promulgated and professed is the law invoked and executed. Absent a sufficient degree of congruence between official profession and practice, law-subjects will, with good reason, ignore the professed norms (what the Realists liked to call 'law on the books') and look to the actions of officials for their clues to legal requirements on their behaviour. In that case, the game of social control changes from one in the mode of law to something in the mode of the arbitrary exercise of power. This, of course, is the lesson well-taught by Hart's vivid example of 'scorer's discretion'.[38] Similarly, *continuity* over time is essential to the normative guidance distinctively provided by law. Law provides the necessary bridge from the law-subjects' public past to their present legal-social constitution and commitments. Law can offer effective normative guidance only if it is congruent with their lives as these lives are structured over time. Law gives them that structure.

Law's vindicative dimension is critical for both its congruence and its continuity. Only by making available a framework and forum for accountability can law-subjects hold official practice to its profession, thereby enhancing congruence by incorporating within law's ordinary practice institutional resources for law-subjects to demand such congruence. In the same way, public articulation of

[38] Hart, *The Concept of Law*, n 2 above, at 142–6.

legal norms in the course of challenging and exploring alleged warrants of official action brings to public awareness the relationships between formal and informal constitutive norms, and between them and directive norms, and enables law-subjects and officials to shape the content of these norms and enhance their practical intelligibility.

Equally, making available a framework and forum for accountability promotes law's continuity over time. Law's persistence over time and the demands of a community's past as reflected in its law are not empirically given facts; they are, rather, matters to be determined, publicly and by argument in a framework and forum dedicated to deliberative assessment in public of competing understandings of them.[39] The forensic, discursive and argumentative dimensions of law are not merely a welcome accessory of law; they play an essential role in law's distinctive mode of normative guidance.

The Systematic Dimension of Law's Mode of Normative Guidance. Finally, the model of authoritative directives obscures the discursive and systemic character of law and its mode of normative guidance. Law offers those it seeks to guide not an aggregate of discrete rules or directives, but a system of interconnected norms related by content. The meaning of particular legal rules is typically conditioned by their interaction with many other rules and provisions. Moreover, these rules function in deliberation by providing reasons for action that implicate (commit their agents to) other actions or judgements and which themselves are grounded in further reasons and norms. Deliberation in law involves locating particular rules or reasons in a network of mutually conditioned norms. Reasons or norms offered by law at any point are grasped and understood not by intuition but by use, locating them in the network of reasons and norms, applying them to other situations, testing them by hypothetical situations, looking to other reasons or norms to ground them or illuminate their underlying rationales. The normative guidance offered by law is *systemic* and *discursive.*

It is this systemic character of law that both demands and makes possible the extensive role of reasoning by analogy in law. It is surprising, then, that, although he recognised the critical role of reasoning by analogy in law,[40] Hart never explored why it is so important. The reason, I suggest, lies in part in the kind of normative guidance law seeks to provide, namely, that which involves presenting itself as an intelligible and coherent network of constitutive and directive norms, rather than an aggregate of discrete directives.[41]

On this richer understanding of normative guidance in the manner of law, it is a mistake to identify law merely with settled rules. In order to offer even minimally effective normative guidance, law must be public, systemic, discursive and argumentative. It must not seek 'to cut off all occasion of discord', as Hume

[39] See Gerald J Postema, 'Melody and Law's Mindfulness of Time' (2004) 17 *Ratio Juris* 203, 225.

[40] Hart, 'Positivism and the Separation of Law and Morals', n 1 above, at 65; *The Concept of Law*, n 2 above, at 127.

[41] I am indebted to Jeremy Waldron for this point.

thought, but rather to subject it to a disciplined practice of public reasoning. It is a practice of *public* practical reasoning because it focuses on public matters: on matters of the political community, on the commitments of those in political power to its members and of members of the political community to each other. It is also public in the sense that it is the practice in and for the political community as a whole, not just some elite segment of it. Because it is practised in a distinctive institutionalised (forensic) context, and because it is only part of the daily work of a political community, a segment of that community (the legal profession) is much more actively involved in it than the general public; indeed, the participation of the legal profession tends to exemplify the practice. Nevertheless, the practice is not, and if law is to be effective in normatively guiding behaviour it cannot be, limited to this segment. Participation in the practice of a healthy legal system by members of the political community in general is typically mediated, but never supplanted, by the legal profession. It is a *disciplined* practice in the sense that it imposes structure, method and articulated responsibilities on the practical reasoning of participants. The fact that the practice, in its most manifest form, takes place in a public forum, with its distinctive institutionalised procedures and rules, decisively shapes the practice. As a discipline of practical reasoning, it involves skills and strategies that are learned over time and that may vary from one legal system to another. Common to them all, however, is the fact that public practical reasoning is anchored in a body of decisions, rules, codes and conventions widely acknowledged to be normative for deliberation because they represent commitments of the political community over time. This body of materials provides a rich context of relatively fixed points from which discursive argument on contested issues of law can proceed. This view of law has much more in common with common-law jurisprudence than with settled-meaning positivism or its more sophisticated contemporary elaborations.

Law, Reasons and Accountability

Similarly, a very widely shared understanding of the rule of law favours a common-law conception of law and legal reasoning over Hart's settled-meaning positivism and its more sophisticated elaborations. We look to law to subject the exercise of political power to public accountability and public accountability adequate to this task requires an institutionalised discipline of practical reason as conceived broadly along lines of common-law jurisprudence rather than conformity to determinate public rules. Let us see why this is so.

The notion of the rule of law builds on the core idea that law is a distinctive *mode* of exercising political power; put more generally, it is a distinctive mode of social ordering that includes the exercise of political power. We look to law for protection against the arbitrary exercise of power. Where rule of law is observed in a community, ie where law rules, it provides a substantial measure of protection in two dimensions: protection of the governed against the arbitrary power of those who govern (vertical) and protection of members of the society against the arbitrary exercise of power by their fellows (horizontal). We can highlight central features of this ideal of the rule of law by contrasting it with a mode of governance that stands just beyond the pale of (and masquerades as) the rule of law that I call 'rule with law'.

Rule with law obtains where political power is exercised by means of public rules and institutions to administer them just to the extent that social control is efficiently maintained and the goals of those in power are efficiently promoted. It is not something about these goals themselves that puts the exercise of power beyond the pale of the rule of law, but rather a particular feature of the attitude of those in power towards the law. For them, law is exclusively a tool of governance, not a constraint on their power. In a reversal of Plato's classic formulation in the *Laws*,[42] law does not rule, it is not master of, but rather slave to, those who govern. Thus, rule *with* law, lacks a key feature of the rule *of* law: *reflexivity*. Where political power can be more efficiently exercised without the law or outside its ordinary boundaries, those who govern recognise no reason to use it. Of course, the formalities of law prove useful to those in power precisely because it is widely believed by those subject to their governance that law constrains the exercise of power and can put obstacles in the path of the realisation of the goals of those who exercise it. That is, those who are inclined to rule with law realise that law is an effective tool of governing just insofar as it is possible to mask their use of it as a mere tool. Rule with law is always parasitic for its power on successfully masquerading as the rule of law.[43]

What is it for law to rule? This idea of the rule of law seems to ignore the commonplace of political thought since before Plato: laws do (can) not rule; only human beings exercising power can rule. Or, more precisely, laws rule through human beings exercising power. Augusto Pinochet was reported once to have said to lawyers who threatened to prosecute some of his henchmen: 'If someone touches one of my men, the rule of law is over'.[44] When law rules, political power is constrained, but only, it appears, by submission of those in power. Ironically, Pinochet's arrogant assertion illustrates a deep truth about the ideal of the rule of law: the rule of law depends on a *commitment* to exercise power only within the limits of law and its governing ideals. Governing in the mode of law is a fundamental political choice, a commitment, of a political community, a commitment manifest in the vertical and the horizontal dimensions of the rule of law. Law can function as the fundamental mode of governance in a community only

[42] At 715d.

[43] See Martin Krygier, 'The Rule of Law: An Abuser's Guide' in András Sajó (ed), *The Dark Side of Fundamental Rights* (Utrecht, Eleven International Publishing, 2006) 129–61.

[44] Quoted in Ignacio Sánchez-Cuenca, 'Power, Rules, and Compliance' in José María Maravall and Adam Przeworski, (eds), *Democracy and the Rule of Law* (Cambridge, Cambridge University Press, 2003) 62.

when there is wide commitment of the community and its government to this mode of governance, to *fidelity to law*, as Fuller liked to put it.

The commitment at the foundation of the ideal of the rule of law must be understood in public and normative, not personal and quasi-psychological, terms. It is not a matter of personal resolve or determination, of *holding oneself* to some course of action, but rather a matter of *being held* to some *standard* of behaviour. Commitment is normative in two respects: one can *mistake* what it is one is committed to, and one can *fail* to act on the commitment. In both respects, commitments involve according authority to others to judge one's performance.[45] Thus, accountability to others lies at the centre of the notion. This accountability can be understood in two different ways. On the hierarchical model, one is held to a commitment by someone who in virtue of a position of superiority is able to assess one's actions relative to the commitment and, where necessary, impose corrections. But since such assessments are also subject to assessment and correction, there must be someone superior to one's superior to assess and correct the latter's assessments. In contrast, on the reciprocal model, others hold one to a commitment on the condition that they acknowledge one's standing to hold them to their commitments as well. One is accountable to others on the condition that their assessments are subject to one's own assessment. This mode of holding to account describes a circle, of course, but it can be an entirely virtuous one.

The rule of law is seriously compromised if accountability is understood on the hierarchical model, because this model, familiar in modern political theory from Bodin and Hobbes to Austin, avoids a regress by putting one superior beyond the scope of accountability. However, accountability at the heart of the rule of law is given effective expression in the reciprocal model. Thus, the commitments on which the rule of law rests, commitments that make possible genuine reflexivity of law's rule in both of its dimensions, call for robust modes of reciprocal accountability. And where the commitments are public, ie commitments of members of a community and of those who exercise public power in that community, these modes of reciprocal accountability must be fully public.

We can approach this same conclusion from a different quarter. We observed that the rule of law at its heart is concerned with protecting against arbitrariness, not merely the arbitrariness manifest in unpredictable exercises of power, but the arbitrariness of power that is not bound to act on principled reasons. At the core of this concern is subjection to the arbitrary will of others, their *libero arbitrio*. One who must act at the discretion or pleasure of another is subject to the other party's arbitrary will, even if that other party acts for good or sound reasons. As Kant observed in his *Rechtslehre*, power is arbitrary and without sound reason, from the point of view of one subjected to it, if the other party cannot be held

[45] Robert Brandom, *Articulating Reasons* (Cambridge, MA, Harvard University Press, 2000).

accountable.[46] Even sincere claims to act with right or warrant, if there are no means available for assessing those claims, leave one no less subject to the arbitrary will of another. Effective protection against such arbitrariness, again, depends on the availability of robust public devices for reciprocal accountability.

Finally, if this accountability is to be robust, several things are necessary. First, there must be manifest and publicly accessible norms which can effectively guide behaviour of officials and citizens and function as public warrants for that behaviour. Secondly, there must be structures for reciprocal accountability of behaviour. Consider accountability of official actions under law. The rule of law demands not only that officials act with sufficient warrant in the law for their actions, but demands also that an official's claim to act or to have acted with that warrant be open to public challenge.[47] It requires a public forum in which claims can be assessed by marshalling arguments drawn from the body of law, arguments that proceed through 'the labour of the negative' (as Hegel put it), that is, by way of drawing contrasting or conflicting claims and testing their adequacy in the context of the law (or the relevant part of it) as a whole. *De legibus disputandum est.* Accountability will be ineffectual and will fail to be reciprocal if one party is able to dictate the terms of the assessment. So, any claim to warrant must be assessable not only with respect to whether the actions actually conform to the norm alleged to justify it, but also with respect to how the norm is to be understood and the force it has relative to other potentially competing norms, and with respect to claims made on the basis of the place of the alleged warranting norm in the body of law as a whole. And reciprocal accountability requires forums in which inevitably conflicting assessments can be tested and measured by the only appropriate measure of such assessments, namely, deliberative reasoning and discursive argument. Claims of warrant and justification can be discharged only through argument; public claims of warrant can only be discharged through public argument in public forums.

Thus, legal reasoning structured to reflect the demands of reciprocal accountability cannot be limited to matters already settled. The rule of law demands that law provide the focus, forums and resources for robust reciprocal accountability through fully public argument from and with respect to public norms. This mode of public reasoning is subject to a discipline shaped, in the first instance, by the practice of those entrusted to maintain the community's public norms; but not just them, for their exercise of this practice is also subject to accountability in the wider community. The rule of law calls for a discipline of public reasoning, shaped by its practice in a public forum and tethered to an interconnected body of rules, decisions, norms and examples that are normative for the community because they represent its past and precedent for its future.

[46] Immanuel Kant, *The Metaphysics of Morals* (Mary Gregor (trans), Cambridge, Cambridge University Press, 1991) 77, 84.

[47] Neil MacCormick, 'Rhetoric and the Rule of Law' in David Dyzenhaus (ed), *Recrafting the Rule of Law: The Limits of Legal Order* (Oxford, Hart, 1999) 163 at 172–4.

From this line of argument it appears that Hart had strong reasons to resist the sharp distinction between reasoning in the settled core of law and reasoning in conditions of uncertainty in the penumbral domain beyond it. I am inclined to conclude that core commitments of the idea of the rule of law call for law conceived more along lines of classical common-law jurisprudence than those suggested by classical or contemporary positivist jurisprudence. And, thus, if the arguments of this section and the previous section are sound, we may conclude that considerations that lie at the foundations of Hart's attempt to answer the challenge from the American camp actually lead to a view that many in that camp, Lon Fuller most prominent among them, might find entirely congenial.

16

Legal Reasoning, the Rule of Law and Legal Theory

BRIAN H BIX

Introduction

In his incisive chapter Gerald Postema uses ideas about American Legal Realism, statutory interpretation and the rule of law to construct (and justify) a common law view of the nature of law. Postema reflects on the debate between HLA Hart and Lon Fuller that appeared in the *Harvard Law Review* in 1958,[1] focusing on the response HLA Hart gave to the American Legal Realists, in which Hart tried both to respond to the Realists' scepticism, and to ground his own legal theory, which Postema labels 'settled-meaning legal positivism'.[2] Hart's strategy, as Postema observes, was to insist that legal (judicial) interpretation must be something different when dealing with core meanings of legal texts, where meaning and application are certain, in contrast to the penumbra, where the application is uncertain. Postema points out that Hart's analysis does not hold up, either on its own terms or as an attractive view of law's role (given Hart's own view of law's function in society).

Starting from Hart's view of law's role, that it is one of normative guidance, Postema constructs an intricate and nuanced overview of the various functions of legal rules and the role of reasoned argument and justification within the legal system. The result, Postema argues, is a vision of law modelled roughly on the operation of common law legal systems, some distance from the 'settled-meaning legal positivism' Hart himself advocated.

While Postema's critique of Hart on legal reasoning is persuasive, questions can be raised about whether or to what extent that critique can then ground a

[1] HLA Hart, 'Positivism and the Separation of Law and Morals' (1958) 71 *Harvard Law Review* 593; LL Fuller, 'Positivism and Fidelity to Law: A Reply to Professor Hart' (1958) 71 *Harvard Law Review* 630.

[2] Gerald Postema, Chapter 15 at 267.

theory of the nature of law, as Postema proposes. In the next section, I review Postema's analysis and critique of Hart's response to the Realists. In the following section, I evaluate Postema's efforts to ground a theory of law on an idea, or ideal, of the rule of law, before concluding.

Postema's Analysis

Postema argues that Hart's response to the American Legal Realists was built on certain assumptions about law's role, and the reasons we ask law to take up this role, and that *taking those assumptions seriously* would lead to a different view of the nature of law than the one Hart advocates. In particular, Postema claims that focusing on assumptions underlying the ideal of the rule of law and law's essential normative guidance technique leads to a view of law as 'a disciplined practice of public practical reasoning', a view that is closer to the common law view of law[3] than to Hart's ('settled-meaning') legal positivism.

Postema offers a number of criticisms of Hart's response to the American Legal Realists. In Hart's distinction between the core and the penumbra, he had asserted that a legal norm's core was where there was a single and settled right answer, while in its penumbra application would respond to contextual reasoning and reference to extra-legal standards.[4] Hart conceded that the penumbra was not devoid of reasoning of a legal sort, as judges tried to make their decisions in the penumbra coherent with other legal standards and with the objective of justice.

Postema offers a series of criticisms of Hart's analysis of the difference between reasoning in the core and in the penumbra. First, for Hart, core reasoning is clear, and penumbral reasoning comes down to choice. As Postema points out, 'choice' in Hart's sense (that the text does not state how it is to be applied) is a minimalist, Kantian sense of judgement that applies in the core as well.[5]

Secondly, while Hart noted that reasoning in the penumbra is not limitless, but is usually guided by some sense of justice or coherence with other legal standards, he did not sufficiently take into account the implication that penumbral reasoning is thus not mere (arbitrary) choice, but rather reasoned argument, subject to demands of justification and tests of adequacy.[6]

Hart had wanted to separate the way reasoning is done in the core from the way it is done in the penumbra (urging judges dealing with core matters to avoid the contextual reasoning needed for the penumbra), and appeared to argue that 'law' or '*legal* reasoning' is confined to reasoning in the core. While Hart defended

[3] Gerald Postema, Ch 15 at 275. One might wonder if in celebrating the common law conception of (the rule of) law, Postema's view indicates that civil law systems may be lesser forms of legal systems (if they are legal systems at all).

[4] Hart, 'Positivism and the Separation of Law and Morals', above n 1, at 607–15.

[5] Gerald Postema, Ch15 at 262.

[6] *Ibid* 262–3.

these assertions on the grounds of clarity and the separation thesis, Postema observes that such arguments beg the question.[7]

Postema offers an alternative justification for Hart's position, based on Hart's view that law's basic task is guiding human behaviour through rules. This would show the value of rules—at least the core of rules, where meaning is clear and application predictable. However, it is insufficient to show that law encompasses only clear meaning.[8]

One point of Postema's critique is to indicate that law best fulfils its function of guidance through rules, while protecting against arbitrary exercise of power, when it has certain characteristics. For example, its norms must be manifest and publicly accessible, and officials' claims to have warrants for their actions must be subject to challenge by public argument in a public forum.[9] For Postema, the rule of law means that government is accountable to citizens in a way that requires public, reasoned justification for its actions, and this need for justification is not limited to when matters are settled. This all points, Postema argues, to a common law conception of law, in contrast with Hart's 'settled-meaning legal positivism'.

Legal Reasoning, The Rule of Law and Theories of Law

One way of understanding Postema's chapter is as an effort to derive a theory of law from an analysis of legal reasoning. Certainly, much of Chapter 15 is given over to a careful critique of Hart's response to the American Legal Realists regarding how judges should reason, and how we should characterise judicial reasoning; and Postema's own views about law build from the discussions of how judges should decide cases.

This might lead one to wonder: What is the relationship between a theory of legal reasoning and a theory of law? Can one ascertain how to interpret legal texts from one's theory about the nature of law, or at least exclude certain approaches one might otherwise consider? And could it work in the other direction (as, at times, it seems to in Postema's chapter), such that one might be able to work towards a theory of the nature of law from a theory of legal interpretation? This, in turn, raises a different question: is a theory of legal reasoning a theory of *the best* approach to legal reasoning, or the determination of some form of reasoning that is universal, distinctive or essential for or among legal systems? Elsewhere in the literature, one can find what appear to be general theories of legal interpretation: eg Larry Alexander's intentionalist theory of legal interpretation,[10] or the

[7] *Ibid* 266–7.

[8] *Ibid* 267–8.

[9] *Ibid* 271–8.

[10] eg L Alexander and S Prakash 'Is that English You're Speaking? Why Intention Free Interpretation is an Impossibility' (2004) 41 *San Diego Law Review* 967.

general theories of (all) interpretation one finds in Ronald Dworkin's writings[11] and in the recent work of Stanley Fish.[12] A claim that some approach to legal reasoning was *necessary* might easily be connected to assertions about the necessary features of law.[13]

Hart devoted only a small portion of his jurisprudential writing to discussing the proper interpretation of statutes and other legal texts. He clearly did not see legal interpretation as central to his theory of the nature of law. The topic appears to come up in the exchange with Fuller only because Hart perceived a challenge in the American Legal Realists' discussion of legal interpretation, a possible basis for arguing against a separation of 'law as it is' from 'law as it ought to be'.[14] Those who have followed Hart (eg Joseph Raz[15] and Jules Coleman[16]), elaborating Hart's form of legal positivism in different ways, have, if anything, had even less to say about statutory interpretation. Within legal positivism generally, one might say, the unstated assumption is that a (legal positivist) theory of law has few if any implications for legal interpretation, and that there is little reason to consult one's theory of legal interpretation before constructing a theory of law.

There is one (non-legal positivist) theorist who takes a different view. Ronald Dworkin famously argues that there is no sharp line between one's theory of law and one's theory of how to decide particular legal disputes.[17] However, in this assertion he is taking a position that seems counter-intuitive to many theorists (and not just legal positivists), most of whom would urge a sharper separation between one's general (or conceptual) theory of (all) law, and a theory regarding the best forms of legal process of or within a particular legal system.

In any event, the question about connecting theories of legal reasoning and theories of law may, in the end, not be apt for evaluating Postema's argument. It might be more accurate (as well as more charitable) to read Postema's chapter not as grounding his view of the nature of law merely on a theory of legal

[11] eg R Dworkin, *Law's Empire* (Cambridge, MA, Harvard University Press, 1986) 49–68.

[12] eg S Fish, 'Intention is All There Is: A Critical Analysis of Aharon Barak's Purposive Interpretation in Law' (2008) 29 *Cardozo Law Review* 1109. Fish, famously, once advocated a quite different approach to interpretation. See S Fish, *Is There a Text in This Class? The Authority of Interpretive Communities* (Cambridge, MA, Harvard University Press, 1982).

[13] One more complication: the exchange between Hart and Fuller on which Postema bases his argument deals primarily with *statutory* interpretation: how to apply legal rules like 'no vehicles in the park'. Hart does elsewhere assert both that the problem of core and penumbra is like the direction from example one finds in precedential reasoning (HLA Hart, *The Concept of Law*, 2nd edn (Oxford University Press, 1994) 124–6), and that the 'penumbra of uncertainty must surround all legal rules' ('Positivism and the Separation of Law and Morals', n 1 above, at 607). Still, it is not hard to imagine that the issues of common law reasoning and constitutional interpretation might differ in significant ways from those involved in applying simple statutes.

[14] Hart, 'Positivism and the Separation of Law and Morals', above n 1, at 606, 612–13.

[15] While Raz has written on the topic of legal interpretation (see J Raz, *Between Authority and Interpretation* (Oxford, Oxford University Press, 2009) 223–370), he has not argued that his views on legal interpretation are entailed by or closely tied to his theory about the nature of law.

[16] eg J Coleman, *The Practice of Principle: In Defence of a Pragmatist Approach to Legal Theory* (Oxford, Oxford University Press, 2001).

[17] eg Dworkin, above n 11, at 90.

interpretation. Rather, perhaps one should see the discussion of interpretation as being used only as a path to a discussion of (an ideal of) the rule of law: that law should function as a constraint on arbitrary official power, requiring reasoned justification by government officials, and emphasising reciprocity in the relationship of government and citizens. (As a proper honour to the Hart–Fuller debate, Postema throughout the article echoes many themes raised by Fuller, both from the debate with Hart and from Fuller's later work,[18] and the references to reciprocity between government and citizens is a prime example.)

Postema is by no means alone in building a legal theory on the ideal to which law does or should strive; he mentions the parallels between his work and Fuller's, and one could also list the more recent work by theorists like Nigel Simmonds, Robert Alexy and perhaps also Neil MacCormick.[19] These approaches have their own problems;[20] additionally, in these other cases (Fuller prominently excepted), the ideal in question is the moral-political ideal of justice or moral correctness. Postema's ideal seems to be more of the sort of dialogical ideal one finds in Jürgen Habermas's work.[21] Postema focuses on the rule of law, maximally understood,[22] with the hope that sufficient procedural safeguards, publicity, transparency, justification, etc will collectively lead to fair rules and just outcomes.

Yet, at other times Postema's argument for his approach to legal theory is not couched in terms of ideals. For example, he argues against both Hart and some who have followed Hart (most prominently, Joseph Raz)[23] that if we focus on law's guidance function, it makes no sense to attach the name 'law' to what judges do in deciding cases within the core and the name 'not law' or 'extra-legal' to judges' decisions in the penumbra. For citizens seeking guidance will focus on

[18] Fuller, above n 1; L Fuller, *The Morality of Law*, revised edn (New Haven, CT, Yale University Press, 1969).

[19] N Simmonds, *Law as a Moral Idea* (Oxford, Oxford University Press, 2007); R Alexy, *The Argument from Injustice: A Reply to Legal Positivism* (SL Paulson and BL Paulson (trans), Oxford, Clarendon Press, 2002); N MacCormick, *Institutions of Law: An Essay in Legal Theory* (Oxford, Oxford University Press, 2007).

[20] eg M Kramer, 'Scrupulousness Without Scruples: A Critique of Lon Fuller and His Defenders' (1998) 18 *OJLS* 235; J Raz, 'The Argument from Justice, or How Not to Reply to Legal Positivism' in G Pavlakos (ed), *Law, Rights and Discourse: The Legal Philosophy of Robert Alexy* (Oxford, Hart Publishing, 2007) 17–36.

[21] J Habermas, *Between Facts and Norms* (Cambridge, MA, MIT Press, 1996).

[22] In the history of the concept of 'the rule of law', there have been quite minimal/procedural conceptions and, in competition, more substantial and substantive versions. BZ Tamanaha, *On the Rule of Law: History, Politics, Theory* (Cambridge, Cambridge University Press, 2004). Friedrich Hayek's writings exemplify the latter. Postema's conception of the rule of law is clearly substantial, if not especially substantive.

[23] eg J Raz, *The Authority of Law: Essays on Morality and Law* (Oxford, Clarendon Press, 1979); J Raz, *Ethics in the Public Domain: Essays in the Morality of Law and Politics* (Oxford University Press, 1994).

judicial decisions, and will not make (even if they were competent to make) distinctions between decisions in the core and those in the penumbra.[24]

Further, Postema insists that his argument is not based on any sort of ideal view of law, but rather on showing what is required for even 'minimally effective normative guidance'.[25] However, earlier, when Postema distinguishes 'rule of law' from 'rule with law'[26] (the latter referring to cases of tyrants using legal rules, and their veneer of legitimacy, to express their power, rather than to constrain it), the implication is that such 'rule with law' is still a kind of 'law' and does guide behaviour, however sub-optimally.

If Postema's approach *is* based on some ideal of the rule of law, is there anything wrong with building one's theory of law around an ideal? Teleological theories (theories equating essence with that to which an entity aspires) go back at least to Aristotle. And if it is based on some view of the function of law, functional theories are no stranger to philosophy generally, or to jurisprudence in particular.[27]

There is certainly no a priori reason for rejecting such approaches, but one should certainly have some justification for choosing one methodological alternative over others.[28] To consider the merits of Postema's conclusions regarding theories of law, one should consider, at least briefly, foundational methodological questions, regarding what theories about the nature of law *are*, and what they are meant *to do*.

One might reflect on an alternative approach: Hart's great work is called *The Concept of Law*,[29] and those who have later explored the methodological aspects of legal positivism have affirmed that what is going on in this part of analytical legal theory is an analysis of 'the concept of law' – or '*our* concept of law'.[30] Under this approach, theories of the nature of law are explorations of the necessary and sufficient conditions for the application of the concept 'law' (and the related concept, 'legal'). This approach raised its own set of concerns,[31] but it fits fairly

[24] Gerald Postema, Chapter 15 at 269. This critique is reminiscent of an exchange between Raz and Dworkin, where Raz wanted to distinguish legal standards judges have an obligation to apply in deciding disputes and extra-legal standards that judges might nonetheless be obligated to apply, while Dworkin saw no reason not to equate 'law' with whatever norms judges were obligated to apply. J Raz, 'Legal Principles and the Limits of Law' in M Cohen (ed), *Ronald Dworkin and Contemporary Jurisprudence* (Totowa, NJ, Rowan and Allanheld, 1984) 73–87; R Dworkin, 'A Reply by Ronald Dworkin' in *ibid* 247–300.

[25] Gerald Postema, Chapter 15 at 274.

[26] *Ibid* 276.

[27] See MS Moore, 'Law as a Functional Kind' in RP George (ed), *Natural Law Theory: Contemporary Essays* (Oxford, Oxford University Press, 1992) 188–242.

[28] One cannot blame Postema for not considering all the methodological issues in Chapter 15, given the limitations of space, and the fact that his chapter was properly focused on Hart's critique of the American Legal Realists.

[29] Hart, *The Concept of Law*, n 13 above.

[30] See J Raz, 'On the Nature of Law' (1996) 82 *Archiv für Rechts- und Sozialphilosophie* 1; Raz, *Between Authority and Interpretation*, n 15 above, at 17–46; Coleman, n 16 above, at 173–4.

[31] B Bix, 'Joseph Raz and Conceptual Analysis' (2007) 6(2) *American Philosophical Association Newsletter on Philosophy and Law* 1.

comfortably with what philosophy and philosophical theories normally do. Here is an approach to theorising about law (whatever its other strengths and weaknesses) that seems neither to depend on a theory of legal reasoning nor to entail one.

Conclusion

Postema has pointed out, through characteristically clear and sharp analysis, that legal interpretation is not as Hart portrayed it during the *Harvard Law Review* debate with Fuller: it is not a division between unreflective application and arbitrary choice. Hart's picture is neither a good description of what actually occurs, nor an attractive prescription for what should occur.

Postema offers a richer and more attractive picture of both interpretation and law generally: one in which there is reciprocity between the government and the governed, arbitrary governmental action is avoided through the requirement of reasoned justification and the availability of judicial (and political) review, and legal norms and social norms interact in intricate and mutually supportive ways. Postema characterises all of these as aspects of the rule of law, and argues that they point to a common law theory of law, far distant from Hart's sparer settled-meaning legal positivism.

A harder question regards the appropriateness of moving from a prescription for law to a theory of law. While there is precedent for building a theory of law on an ideal to which law aspires or on assertions about the law's function(s), these are controversial methodological approaches that require justification, more justification than Postema was able to offer in Chapter 15, concerned as he was with other, perhaps more important, topics.

Index

www.ingramcontent.com/pod-product-compliance
Ingram Content Group UK Ltd.
Pitfield, Milton Keynes, MK11 3LW, UK
UKHW020259051026
15470UKWH00024B/1852/J

9 781841 138947